AF478052

Navigating the West

GEORGE CALEB **BINGHAM**

& the River

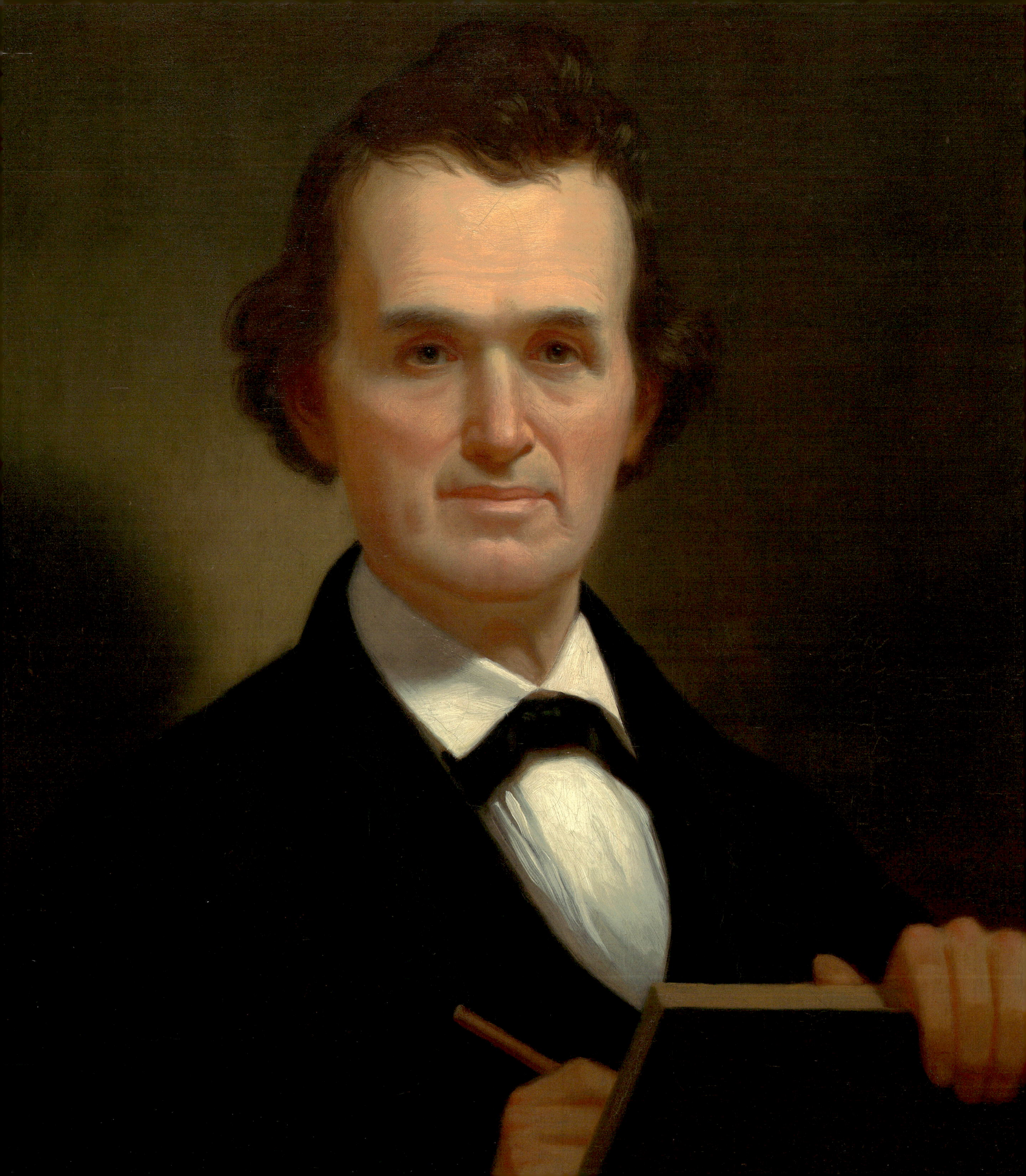

Navigating the West

GEORGE CALEB BINGHAM

& the River

Nenette Luarca-Shoaf, Claire Barry, Nancy Heugh,
Elizabeth Mankin Kornhauser, Dorothy Mahon,
Andrew J. Walker, and Janeen Turk

with contributions by
Margaret C. Conrads,
Brent R. Benjamin, and Andrew J. Walker

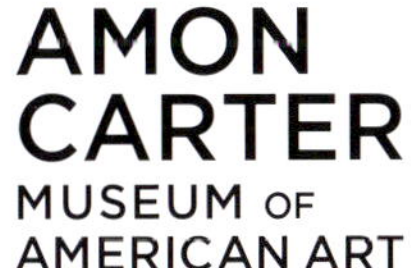

SAINT LOUIS
ART MUSEUM

Distributed by Yale University Press, New Haven and London

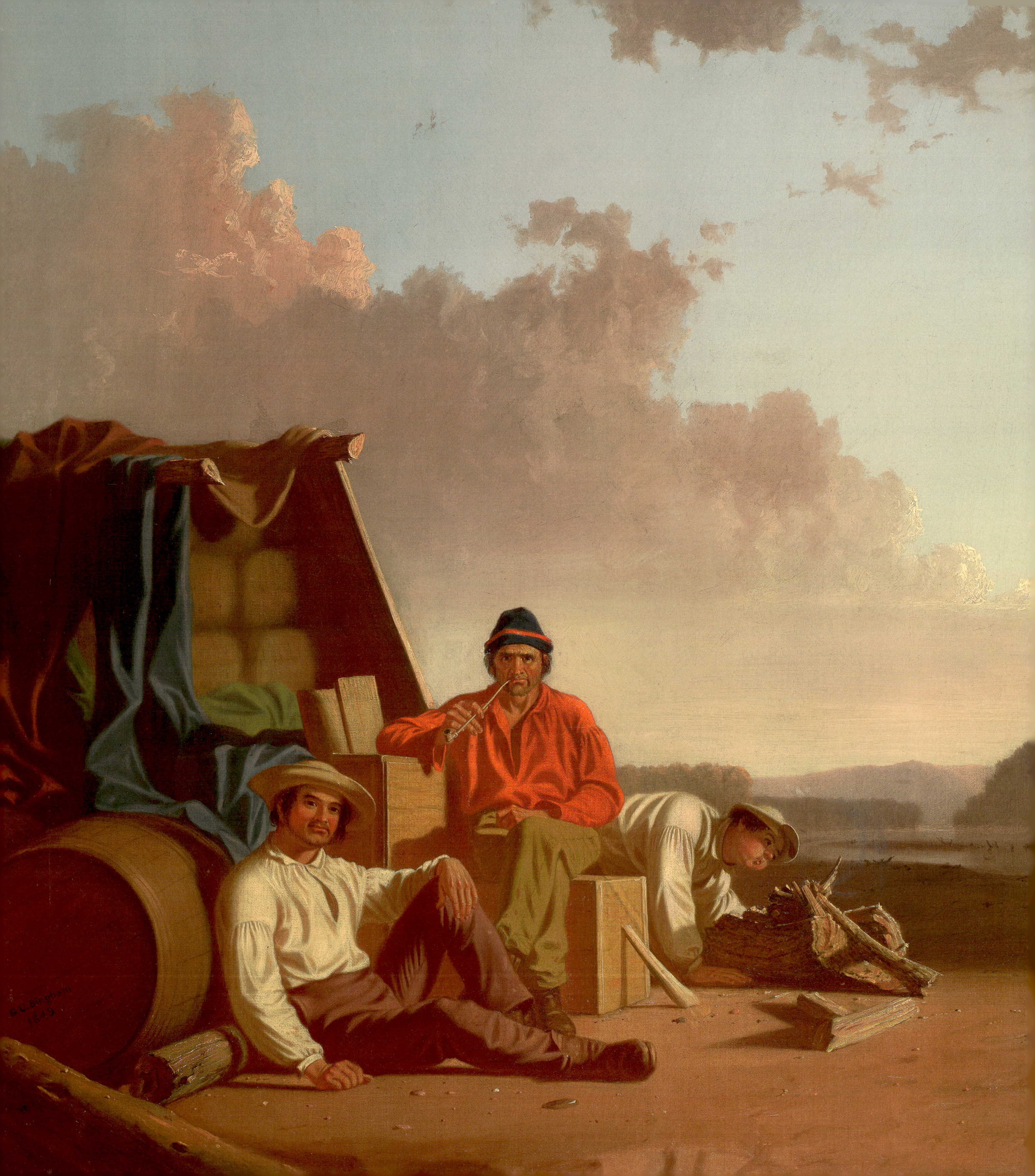
G.C. Bingham
1849

CONTENTS

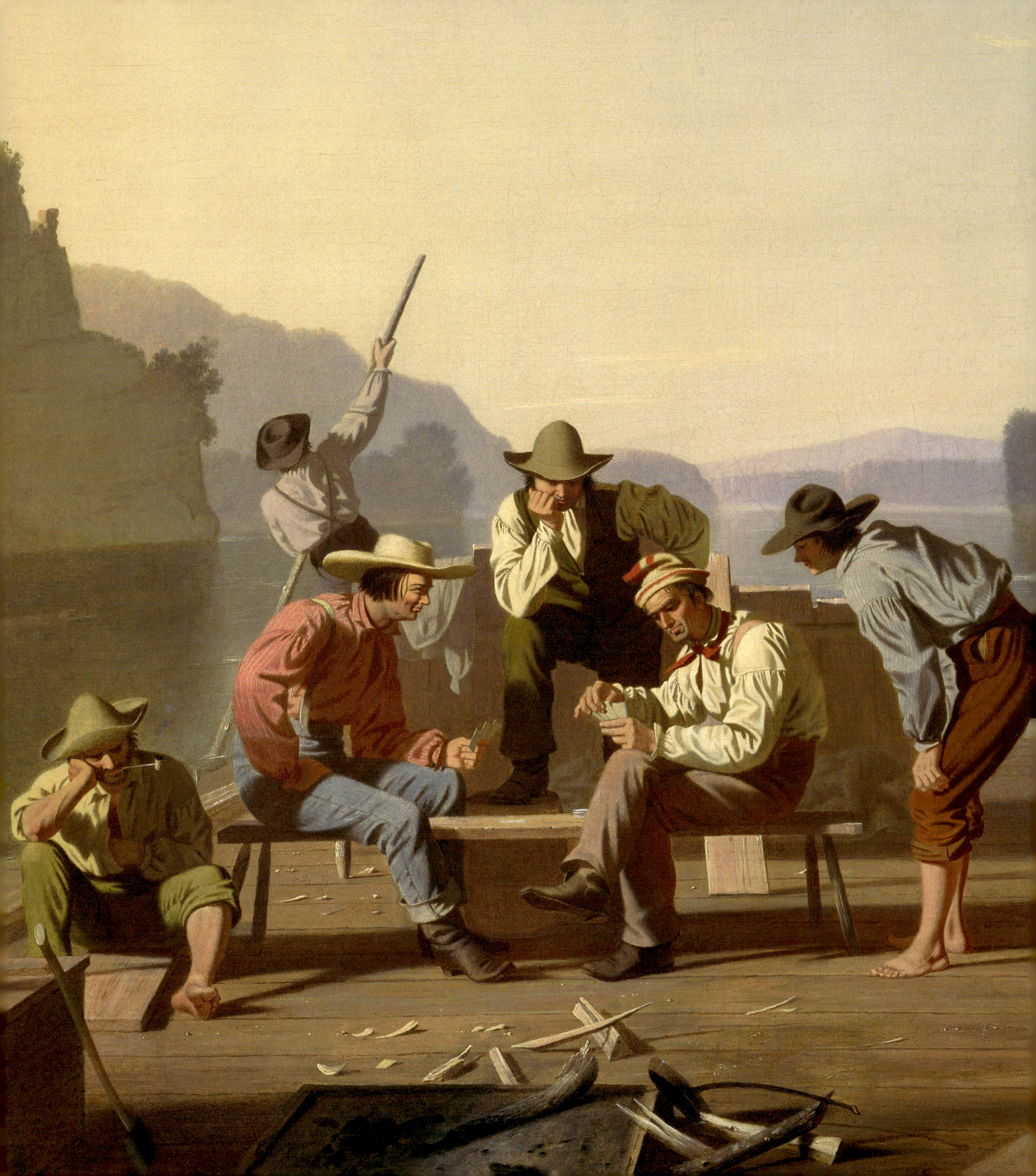

FOREWORD

In 1990, the Saint Louis Art Museum partnered with the National Gallery of Art to mount the exhibition *George Caleb Bingham*, which brought together more than one hundred of the artist's drawings and paintings and gave rise to a pioneering catalogue by the same title. The monographic display followed by more than fifty years the first major twentieth-century showing of Bingham's art, organized by Saint Louis in 1934. That exhibition constituted a rediscovery of Bingham's work and reintroduced him to the national stage. These landmark efforts, which showed the luminous breadth of Bingham's production in portraiture, landscape, and beyond, confirmed his place in the canon of American art. Now, on the heels of Bingham's bicentennial celebration in 2011, the Saint Louis Art Museum has again turned its attention to the Missouri Artist, this time partnering with the Amon Carter Museum of American Art to organize *Navigating the West: George Caleb Bingham and the River*, a project that sheds new light on the artist's strongest and most iconic work—his river paintings.

In Bingham's oeuvre, there is a deep aesthetic strength to the series of paintings he began in the mid-1840s when he took as his subjects the Missouri and Mississippi rivers, along with the men who plied them. His appreciation for the great rivers as the engines of cultural and commercial significance, and for the boatmen who worked them as unheralded frontiersmen of the western waterways, manifests itself with subtlety and power. Then, as now, they are genre paintings. But Bingham reached for a weightier cultural significance in these pictures, an effort that resonated with the concurrent interests of his day. As a serious artist striving to hone his process and perfect his output, he created with this series a defining body of work of both artistic and social importance in the years before the Civil War.

Alongside his river pictures, the present study also considers the numerous preparatory drawings—works of art in their own right—that informed much of Bingham's production during these years, providing a fascinating comparative examination overlooked in previous surveys. Bingham's working method, from graphite study to underdrawing to finished oil, is explored in these pages as never before. Bingham applied himself intensely to draftsmanship, producing drawings he then transferred to his canvases as singular statements within the broader visual narratives of his finished works. In this catalogue lies the opportunity to appreciate anew not only the important commentary of Bingham's work but *how* he worked.

The partnership between Saint Louis and the Amon Carter has proved ideal for the subject at hand: Saint Louis owns three of Bingham's seminal river pictures, houses half the related drawings, and has been a committed champion of the artist for more than eighty years. Since its inception in 1961, the Amon Carter has been known for its historical interests in exploring and publishing the art of the American West, an important, if

Raftsmen Playing Cards (detail), 1847, Plate 26

complicated, narrative that fundamentally draws a perimeter around the nation's westering growth. Bingham has always been an artist moving from West to East, and it is fitting that the Metropolitan Museum of Art is the third venue for the exhibition. Once again, Bingham is going to New York to tell his story.

We extend our deep gratitude to the Federal Council on the Arts and the Humanities, which granted an indemnity for this exhibition, and to both the Henry Luce Foundation and the National Endowment for the Arts, which provided financial support. The exhibition is complete only because of the lenders who agreed to participate, and we are indebted to them for their generosity: Colin B. Bailey and Michele Gutierrez-Canepa, Fine Arts Museums of San Francisco; Graham W. J. Beal, Detroit Institute of Arts; Jack Becker, Joslyn Art Museum; Sarah E. Boehme, Stark Museum of Art; Thomas P. Campbell, Metropolitan Museum of Art; Marcee Craighill, Diplomatic Reception Rooms, U.S. Department of State; Stuart Feld, Hirschl & Adler Galleries; Marshall A. Field; Elizabeth Glassman, Terra Foundation for American Art; Howard Godel, Godel & Co., Inc.; R. Crosby Kemper III, Kansas City Public Library; Gary R. Kremer, State Historical Society of Missouri; Richard A. Manoogian; Earl A. Powell III, National Gallery of Art; Malcolm Rogers, Museum of Fine Arts, Boston; Kevin Salatino, Huntington Library, Art Collections, and Botanical Gardens; Charles E. Valier, Bingham Trust; and Elizabeth Westfall and Julián Zugazagoitia, Nelson-Atkins Museum of Art.

The project would have been impossible to organize were it not for the efforts, begun in the 1970s, of Missouri Governor Christopher S. "Kit" Bond and his counsel, Charles E. Valier, both of whom serve today as trustee and chairman, respectively, of the Bingham Trust. In 1974, upon realizing that a group of more than one hundred drawings by Bingham—including those reproduced in this catalogue—were slated for auction, Bond engaged Valier to negotiate the purchase agreement for the objects and to launch a campaign to raise funds for their acquisition. The two then spent more than a year and a half leveraging the generosity of state businesses and citizens to acquire the sketches and thus keep them assembled in Missouri. Had Bond and Valier not pursued this initiative, the drawings would likely have been divided and scattered—and this current project much diminished as a result. The account of these Bingham champions, as set down by Valier, follows:

> *In 1868, former Saint Louis Mayor John How donated his collection of 112 preparatory drawings by George Caleb Bingham to the Mercantile Library, a public subscription library and the only semipublic repository for art then in existence in the city. There they remained, stored first in the pedestal of a partner's desk in a back office, and then packed in two crates in a public warehouse, until the summer of 1974. That is when George McCue, the arts editor of the* St. Louis Post-Dispatch, *revealed that the drawings were to be dispersed at auction to pay for air conditioning for the library, which had gradually fallen on hard times with the advent of a free public library system in Saint Louis in 1901.*
>
> *Governor Christopher S. "Kit" Bond, a collector of Bingham engravings, took up the challenge of keeping this valuable collection of detailed figure studies of Bingham's paintings of fur traders, fishermen, ruffians, rivermen, and stump-speaking politicians together. He delegated the task of organizing a campaign to raise the necessary funds to purchase the drawings to his counsel, Charles E. Valier. Two appraisals were ordered, and negotiations under the leadership of Judge William H. Webster, later director of the FBI and CIA, were successfully concluded with the Mercantile Library to purchase the drawings for $1,800,000. The governor had three years to complete the purchase, with fund-raising to be successfully concluded within eighteen months, by June 30, 1976.*

Initially, the campaign focused on public awareness of the importance of Bingham as "Missouri's Artist" and his role in state politics encompassing the crucial period of the Civil War. The Saint Louis department store Famous-Barr held its own exhibition of the drawings as the campaign opened. The principal method used toward this goal was the development of a comprehensive educational project designed and organized by a group of volunteers, led by Mary Cordonnier, at schools throughout Missouri. Nancy Edelman Work then curated a nine-month, seven-city traveling exhibition of Bingham's genre paintings and drawings, followed by a special exhibition at what is today the Smithsonian American Art Museum.

Governor Bond traveled statewide encouraging support for the campaign, which included an event at the home of Thomas Hart Benton, the honorary chairman of the campaign, who died shortly thereafter. As a challenge to their elders, Missouri schoolchildren donated nickels and quarters in their classrooms until $40,000 was raised to purchase a study of Bingham's son, Horace. Following this success, a generous contribution by the May Company foundation launched the fund-raising portion of the campaign. Funds were raised from disparate sources: admission fees to the exhibitions, sales of the exhibition catalogue Bingham's Missouri, *a grant from the Missouri Legislature, corporate largesse, and a flood of individual contributions. Two months shy of the June 30 deadline, the campaign was $250,000 short of its goal. A mass appeal by mail to 300,000 Missouri residents not only met the shortfall but established a fund of $140,000 to maintain the drawings.*

After all the pledges were satisfied and the 112 drawings conveyed by the Mercantile Library, the Bingham Trust was established for the benefit of "The People of Missouri," and the drawings were loaned to the Saint Louis Art Museum and Nelson-Atkins Museum of Art in Kansas City for preservation, study, and exhibition.

As Bingham himself had foreseen: "The absence of art in any nation will ever be a mark of its ignorance and degradation. . . . It is the chief agent securing national immortality."

Thanks to this initiative, along with the early collecting activities of the Saint Louis Art Museum and the Nelson-Atkins Museum of Art, Missouri is today rich with the creative output of its native son George Caleb Bingham. His paintings and drawings are a common denominator across these holdings, and these institutions appreciate their shared history in stewarding the work of an artist who, dedicated to his local scene, transcended the regionalist mantle to assume his place among America's great artists.

Brent R. Benjamin
Director, Saint Louis Art Museum

Andrew J. Walker
Director, Amon Carter Museum of American Art

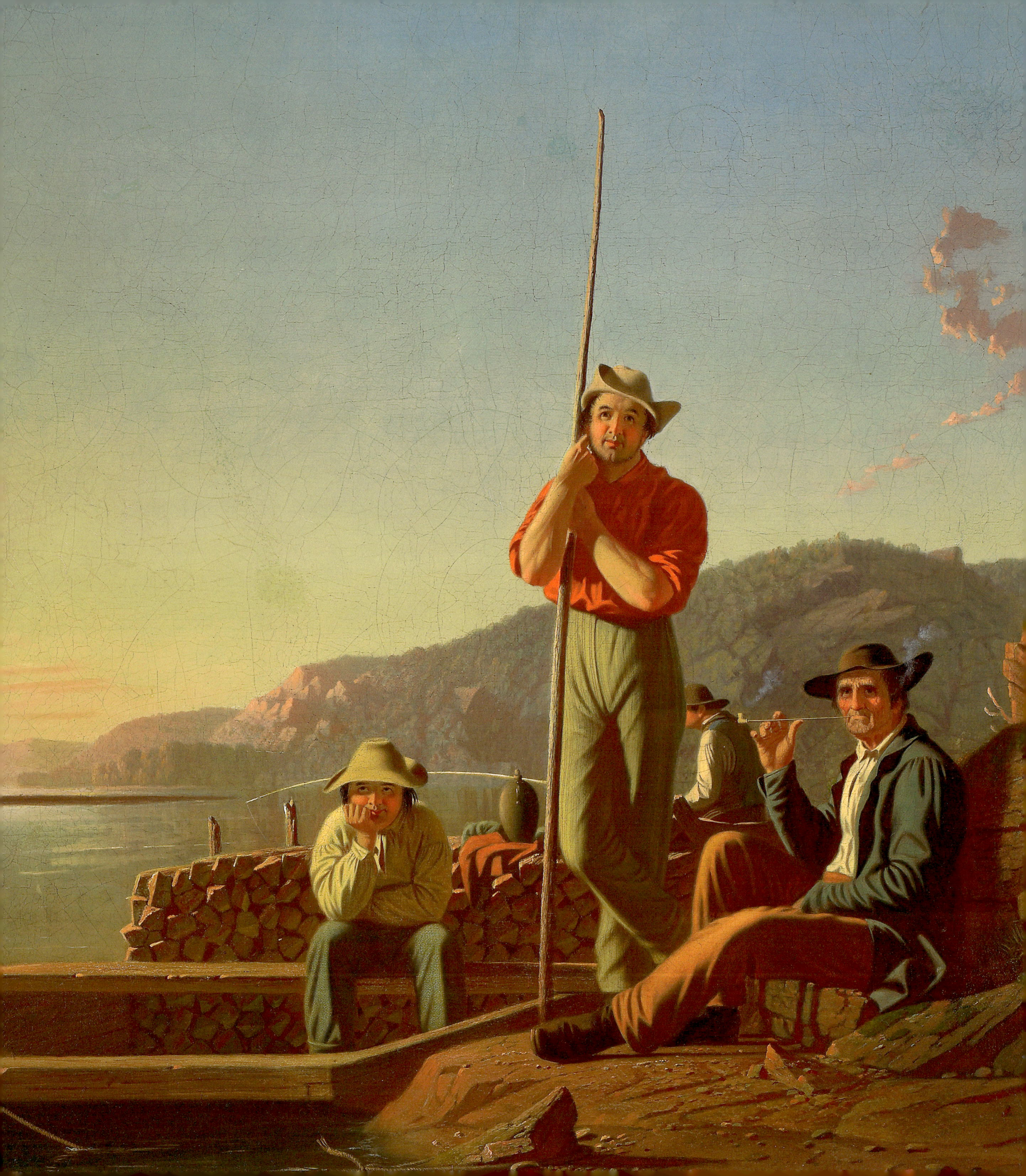

INTRODUCTION

For more than 150 years, George Caleb Bingham (1811–1879) has remained a source of great pride in his home state of Missouri. But the artist and his work, particularly his beloved river paintings, have also remained important touchstones in the ongoing conversation on American art. *Navigating the West: George Caleb Bingham and the River* considers how Bingham employed images inspired by the Mississippi and Missouri rivers—and those who worked them—to establish a unique visual language of the frontier that shaped contemporaneous understanding of the mid-nineteenth-century American West. The study also provides an unprecedented look into the process by which Bingham made his drawings and paintings, revealing new discoveries about his methods and particular canvases. Finally, it traces the artist's evolving legacy in the visual narrative of American art.

George Caleb Bingham was an ambitious man. Throughout his adult life, he applied that ambition to two careers—politics and painting—that he pursued simultaneously and with equal passion. Yet, first and foremost, Bingham considered himself a painter. Beginning as an itinerant portraitist, the young artist soon appropriated waterways as a useful device in shaping his more ambitious compositions, a convention that coincided with a lifelong belief that the great western rivers were vital to the success of American commerce and national unity. He found riparian subjects rich in possibilities as he sought greater national prominence and moved toward creating, from the early 1840s onward, a body of work that was stylistically distinct and contributed to the mythic historical record being shaped by the painters he admired most, key among them Thomas Cole, William Sidney Mount, and Thomas Sully. Although he drew, literally and figuratively, from a range of historical and contemporary European and American sources, Bingham created a particular aesthetic that conveyed his personal background and interests. He imbued his river paintings with enough ambiguity that they possessed a flexibility of meaning that appealed to a range of viewers, regardless of their geographical locale or urban or rural experience.

Nenette Luarca-Shoaf's leading essay explores how Bingham integrated the theme of these western rivers and boatmen into the larger fabric of American art and life. Weaving together the contexts of the region from which Bingham's painting sprang and the national art arena in which his work moved, Luarca-Shoaf reveals how the paintings were positioned, through their original motif and distinct aesthetic presentation, to especially contribute to the growing body of national visual culture. Understanding that he painted topics that were exotic to many viewers, Bingham represented as tamed what generally was considered wild—both the environment and the inhabitants. Using compositional designs that favor quietude and stasis and suggest flexible, rather than

The Wood-Boat (detail), 1850, Plate 28

proscribed, narratives, he presented the unknown and threatening as quotidian and ordinary. Picturing a working West, from the 1840s through the Civil War he offered viewers new ways to consider western identity that aligned more seamlessly with eastern practice and expectations, despite the frontier settings of his pictures. In this context, Luarca-Shoaf's review of the proliferation and effect of Bingham's imagery, especially that of his jolly flatboatmen canvases, sets the stage for understanding the impact of his river scenes in American art.

Bingham's drawings and their relationship to his river paintings are thoroughly examined by conservators Claire Barry and Nancy Heugh, whose essay significantly enhances our understanding of how Bingham created his paintings, from initial concept to final layer of varnish. Bingham's creative method was born of a blend of firsthand observations, exposure to popular drawing and painting manuals, and the study of American and European contemporary and historical art. His technique mirrors standard operating procedure for many artists from the Renaissance forward, yet, without formal training and with only intermittent opportunities for studying a broad spectrum of original art, Bingham formulated a methodology that, while based on tradition, was his own. The forceful outline drawings of men, who became the main characters in his river works, reflect his early experiences as a sign painter and portraitist as well as his likely study of drawing manuals. The consistency with which he applied his technique—in the use of his drawings, palette choices, and paint application—not only evinces a craftsman's approach to his trade but, taken together, ensured his art had a personal stamp. This way of working, cogently detailed by Barry and Heugh, provided the backbone of Bingham's creative process and speaks to a stability and practicality that aided him as he constantly sought to balance his dual careers, endured frequent separations from his family, pursued his entrepreneurial tendencies, worked through bursts of energy and fragile health, and struggled with a perennial lack of funds.

Bingham's *Fur Traders Descending the Missouri* (Pl. 3) has long been recognized as an icon of American art. The painting is all the more remarkable because of its early place in Bingham's career. Elizabeth Mankin Kornhauser and Dorothy Mahon of the Metropolitan Museum of Art, where the object resides, explore this canvas in a case study guided by state-of-the-art scientific analysis. They detail the artist's multilayered process, newly discovered changes to the composition, and sophisticated painting technique.

Andrew J. Walker and Janeen Turk present a blueprint of how Bingham's art functioned in twentieth-century America's uneasy relationship with its narrative art. The authors show that Bingham, beginning with his rediscovery by eastern audiences during the Great Depression and continuing through the height of Abstract Expressionism and related movements through the 1950s, provided twentieth-century Missourians with a meaningful link to the larger art world and gave art historians connective tissue in their quest to construct the story of American art.

In his own day, Bingham's river pictures enabled the artist to manipulate the balancing act he himself sought throughout much of his life—nationally recognized artist and politician—but from the position of a westerner whose deeply held beliefs included the necessity that the East recognize the critical importance of the West. Today, when water, transportation, commerce, and the art market are often headline news, it seems especially appropriate to reconsider the most important artist of life on our waterways. Through the study of George Caleb Bingham's river paintings, we have the opportunity to stand before a new window onto his complex world, which, in the end, contributes to a better understanding of our own.

Margaret C. Conrads
Deputy Director of Art and Research
Amon Carter Museum of American Art

PLATES 1–25

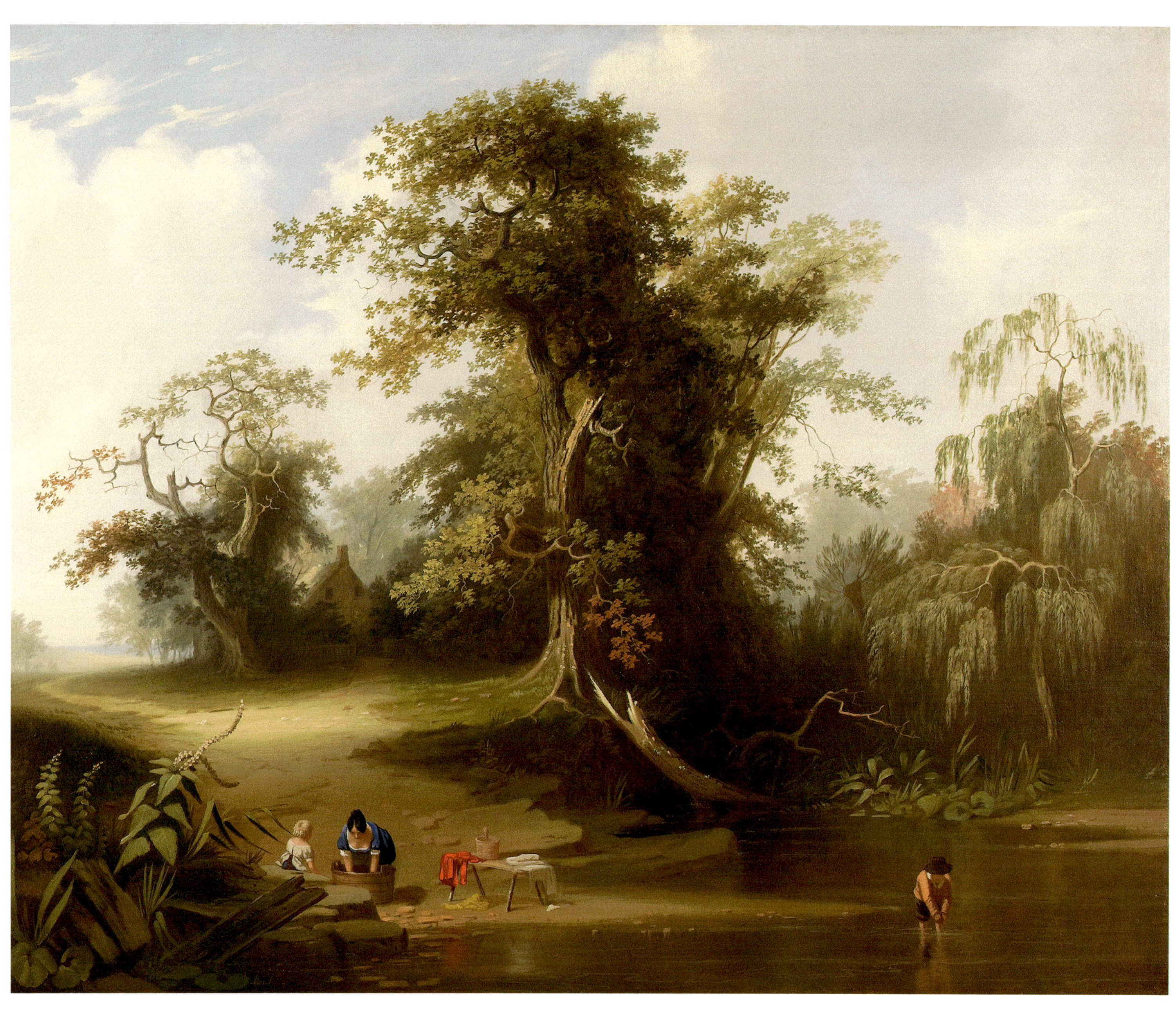

Plate 1: *Landscape: Rural Scenery*, 1845

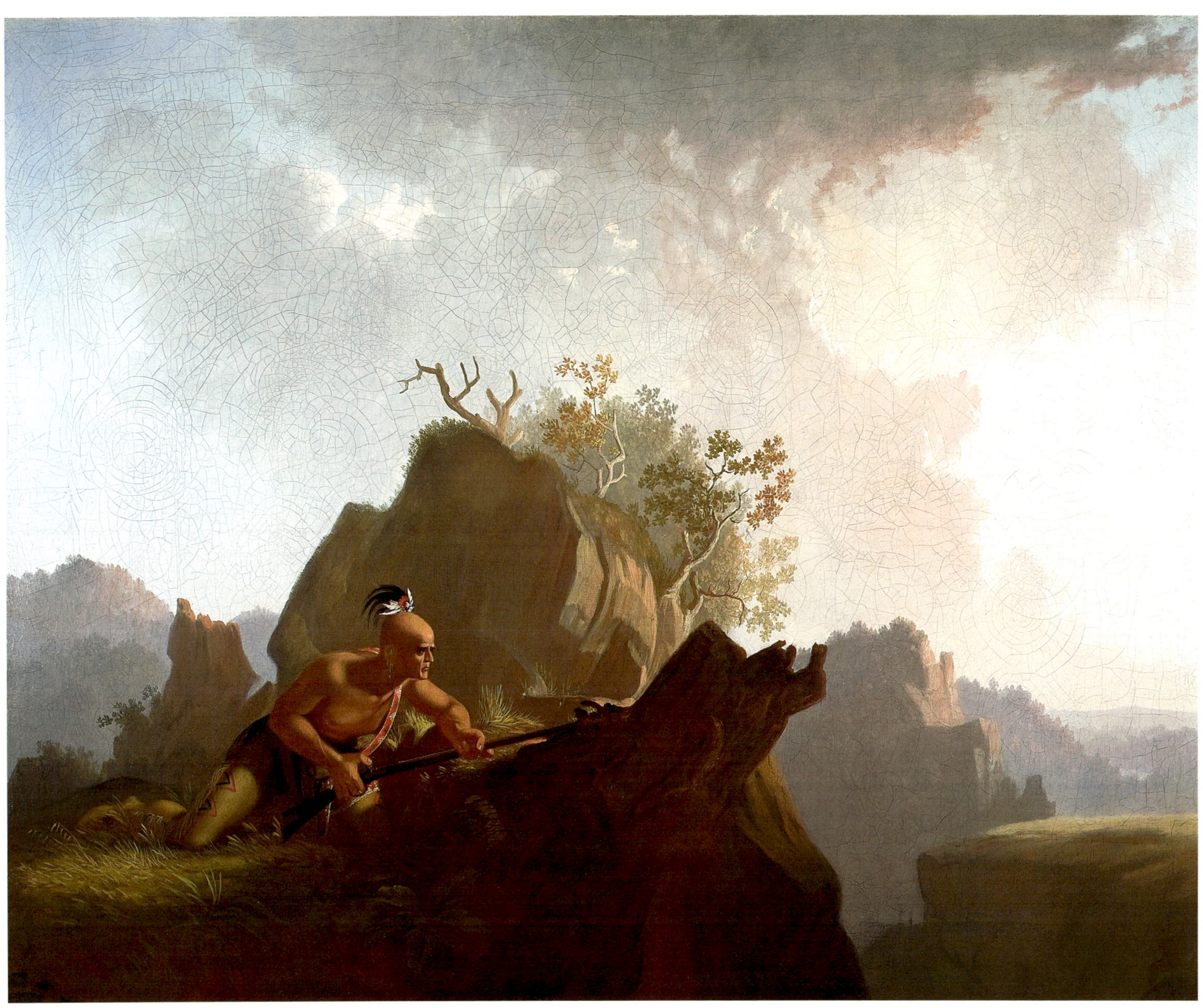

Plate 2: *The Concealed Enemy*, 1845

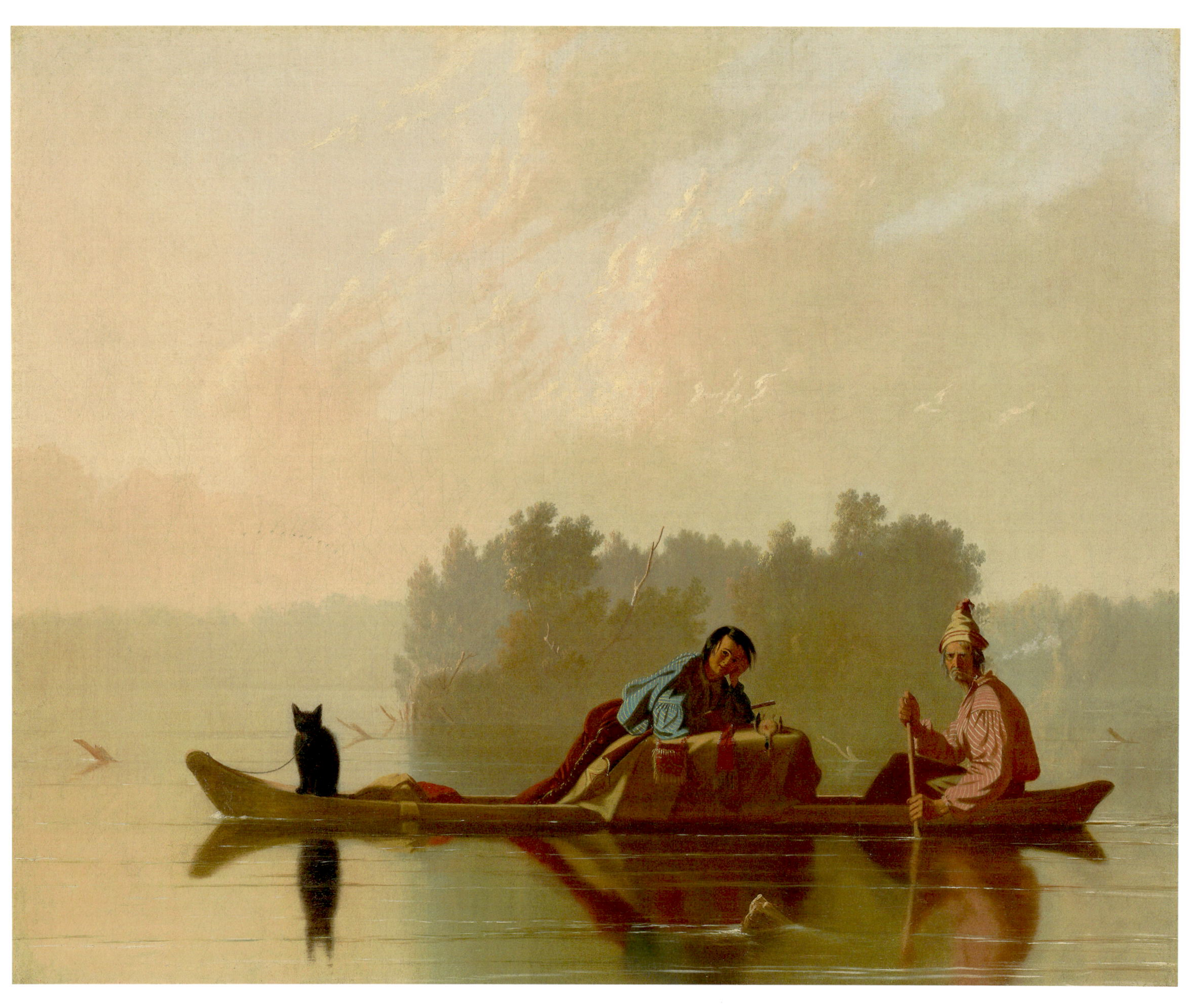

Plate 3: *Fur Traders Descending the Missouri*, 1845

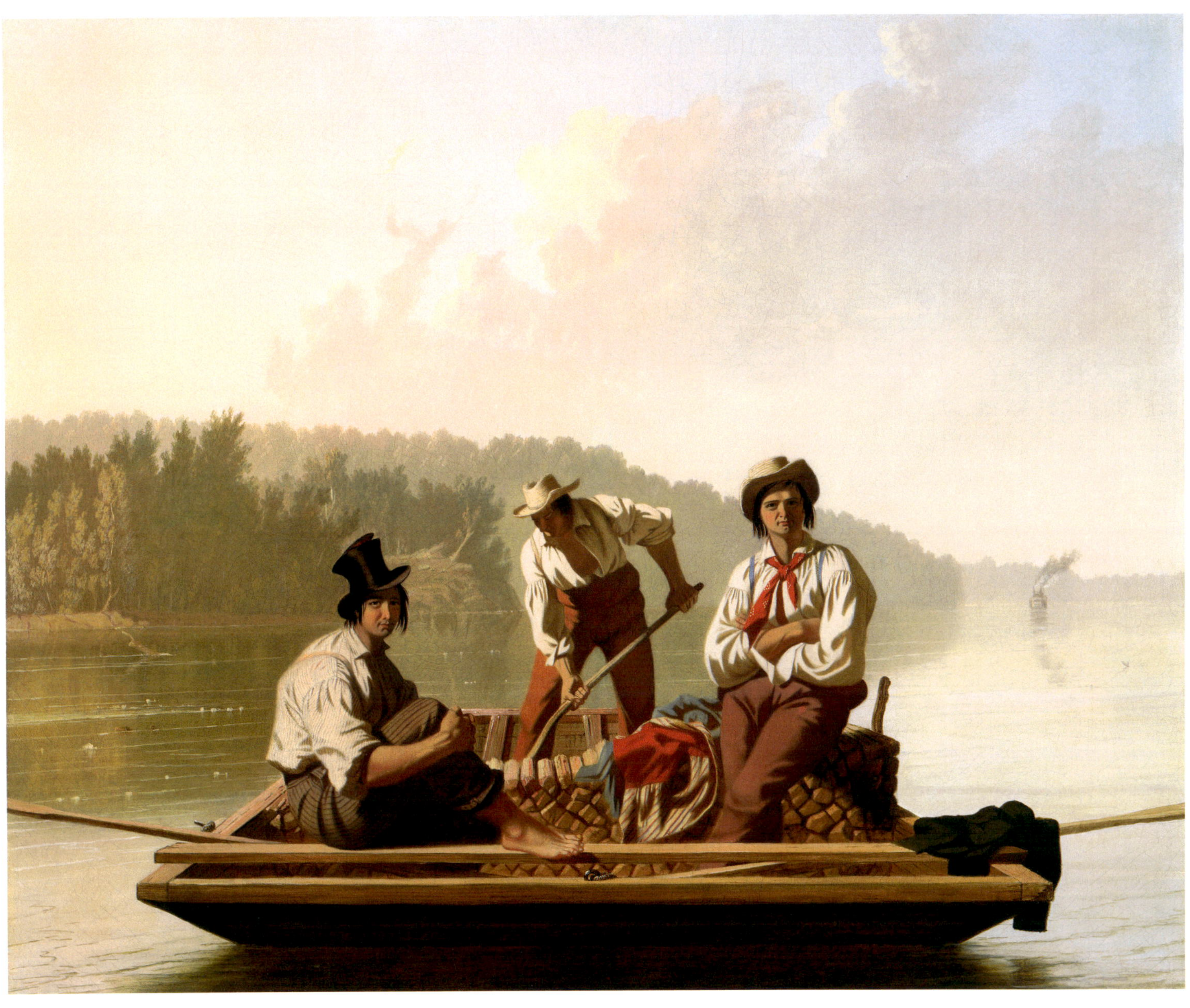

Plate 4: *Boatmen on the Missouri*, 1846

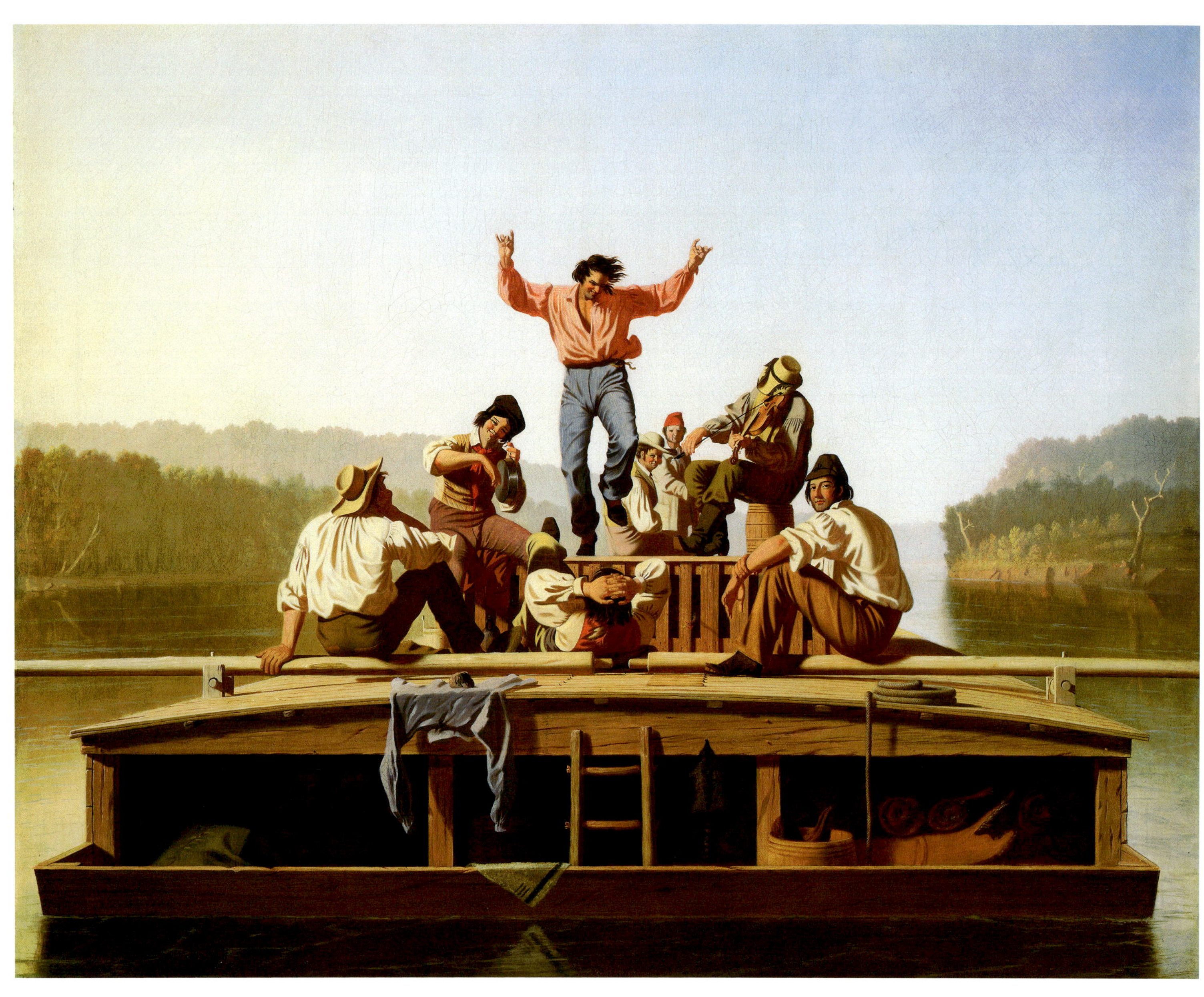

Plate 5: *The Jolly Flatboatmen*, 1846

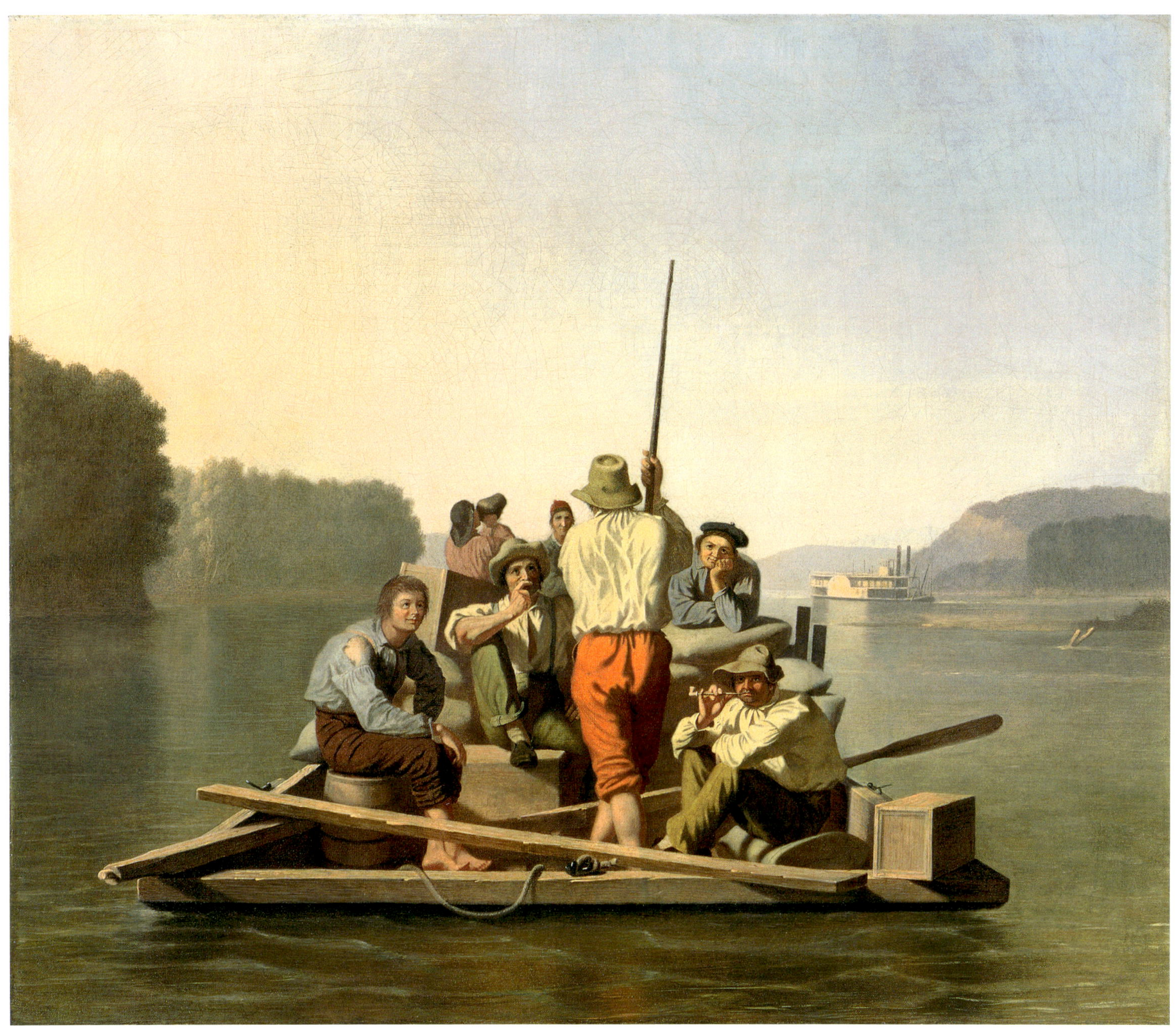

Plate 6: *Lighter Relieving a Steamboat Aground*, 1847

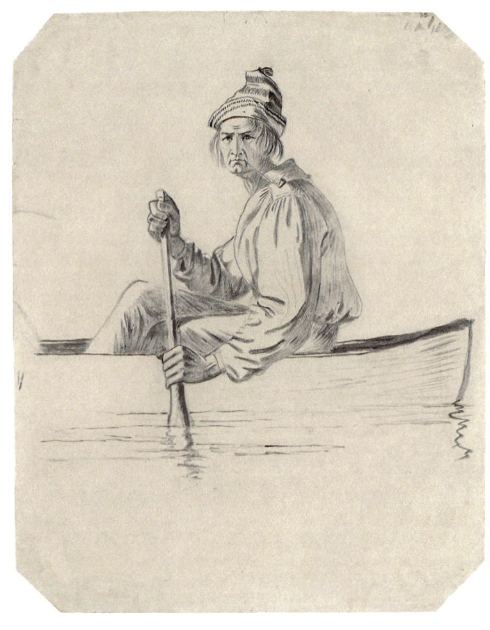

Plate 7: *Fur trader*, for *Fur Traders Descending the Missouri* (1845) and *Trappers' Return* (1851) with alterations

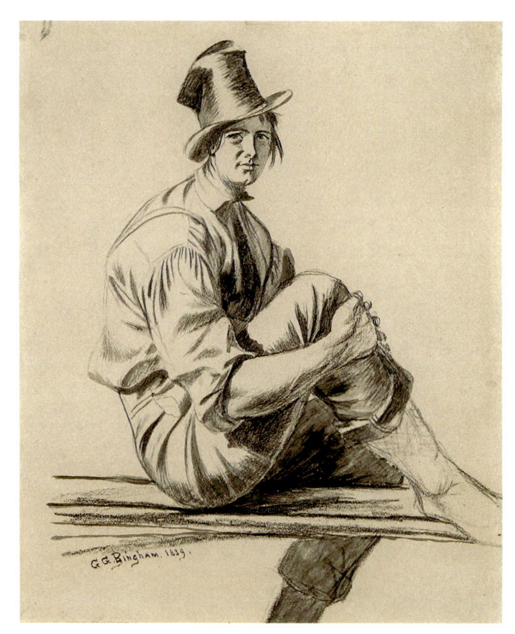

Plate 8: *Boatman*, for *Boatmen on the Missouri* (1846)

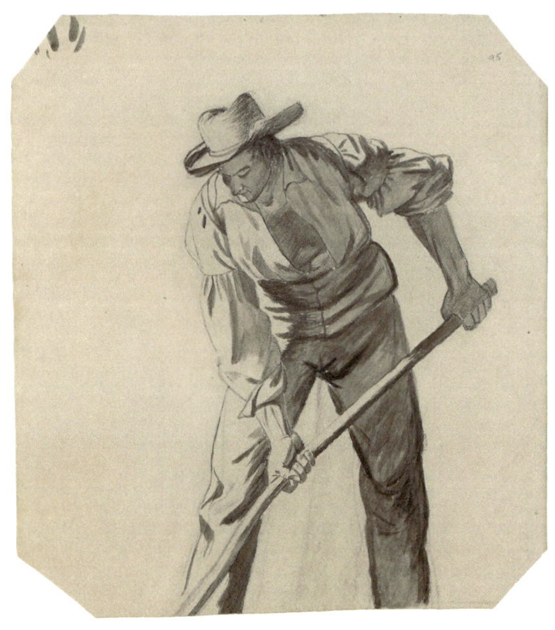

Plate 9: *Boatman*, for *Boatmen on the Missouri* (1846)

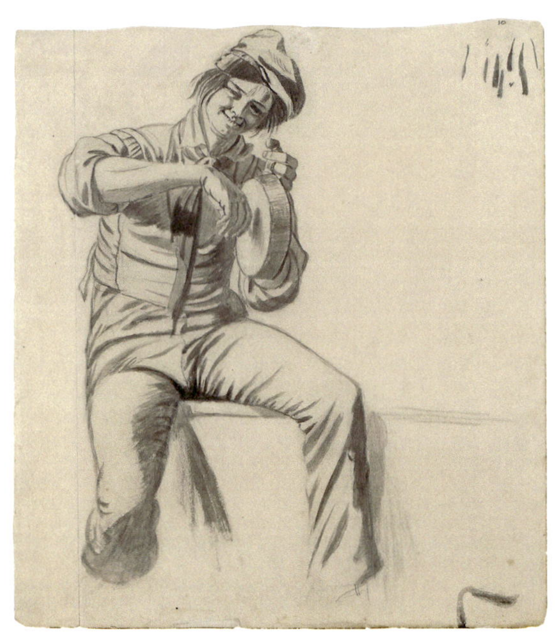

Plate 10: *Skillet-beater*, for *The Jolly Flatboatmen* (1846)

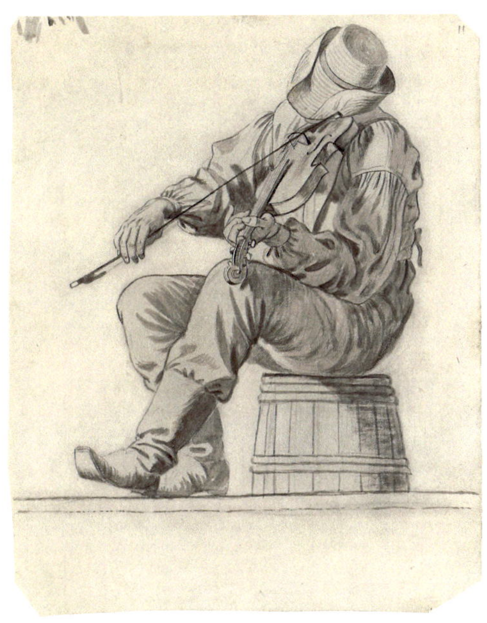

Plate 11: *Fiddler*, for *The Jolly Flatboatmen* (1846)

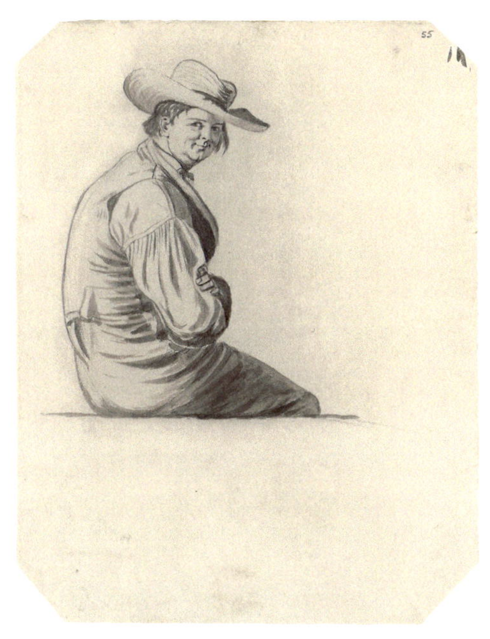

Plate 12: *Flatboatman*, for *The Jolly Flatboatmen* (1846)

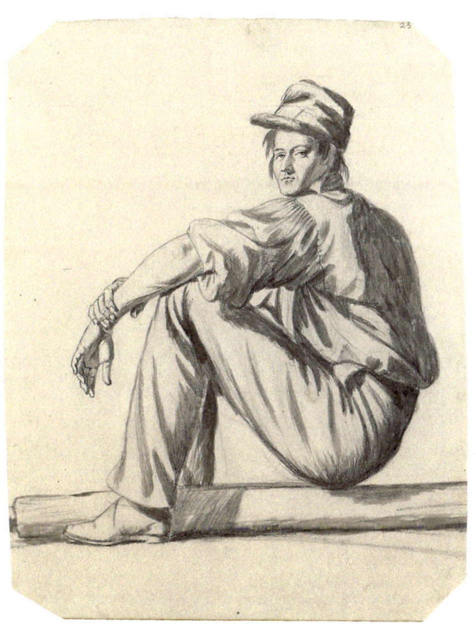

Plate 13: *Flatboatman*, for *The Jolly Flatboatmen* (1846) and *The Jolly Flatboatmen* (1877–78) with alterations

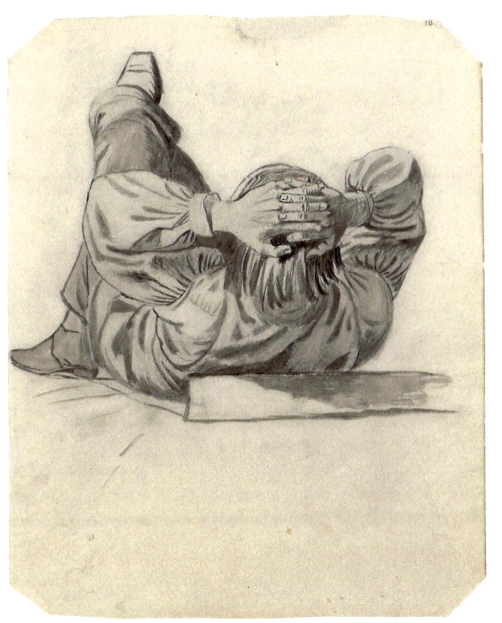

Plate 14: *Flatboatman*, for *The Jolly Flatboatmen* (1846) and *The Jolly Flatboatmen* (1877–78) with alterations

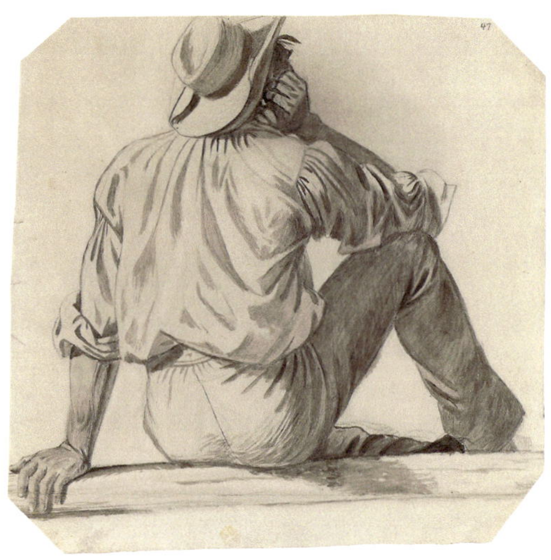

Plate 15: *Flatboatman*, for *The Jolly Flatboatmen* (1846) and *The Jolly Flatboatmen* (1877–78) with alterations

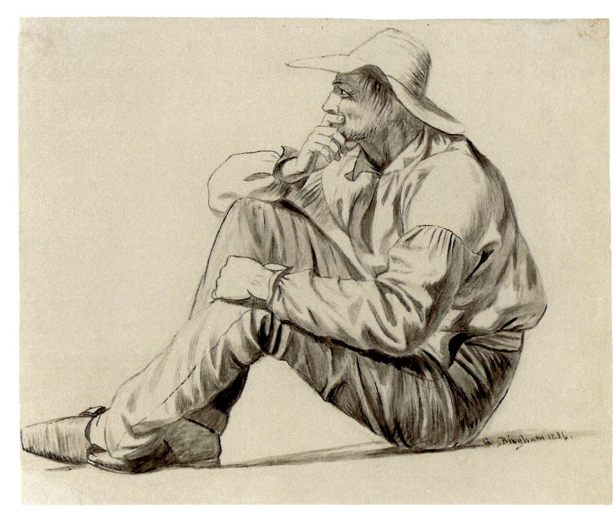

Plate 16: *Seated man in a broad-brimmed hat*, possible alternate study for *Lighter Relieving a Steamboat Aground* (1847)

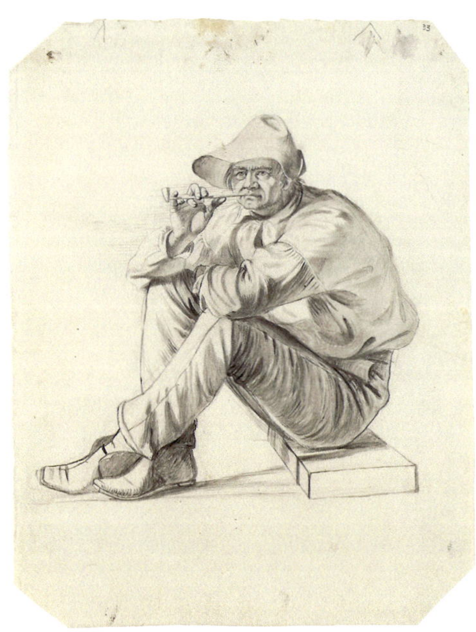

Plate 17: *Boatman*, for *Lighter Relieving a Steamboat Aground* (1847) and possible study for *Watching the Cargo by Night* (1854) with alterations

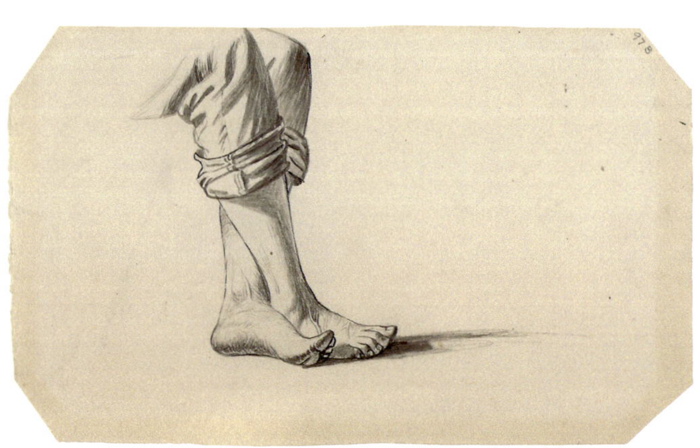

Plate 18: *Study of legs*, for *Lighter Relieving a Steamboat Aground* (1847)

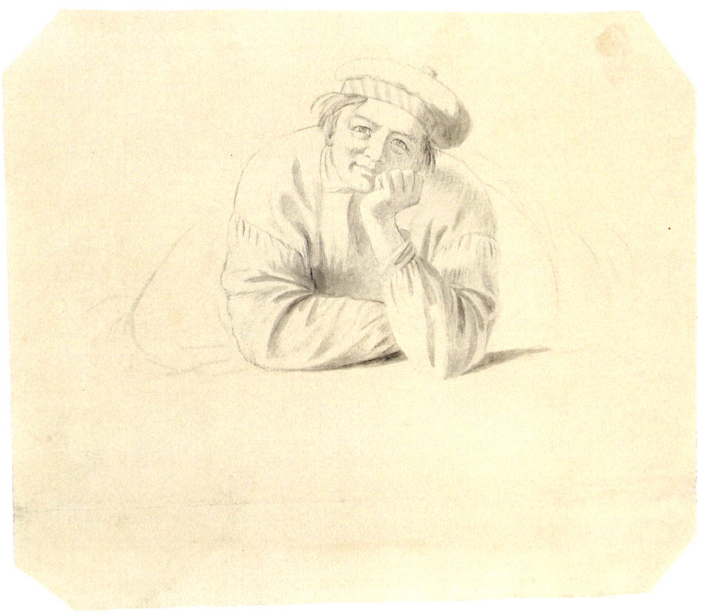

Plate 19: *Boatman*, (recto) for *Lighter Relieving a Steamboat Aground* (1847) and (verso) possible study for *Watching the Cargo by Night* (1854) with alterations

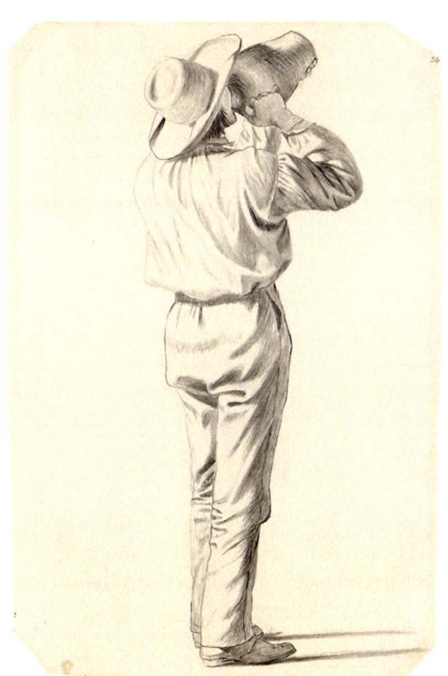

Plate 20: *Boatman drinking*, for *Lighter Relieving a Steamboat Aground* (1847)

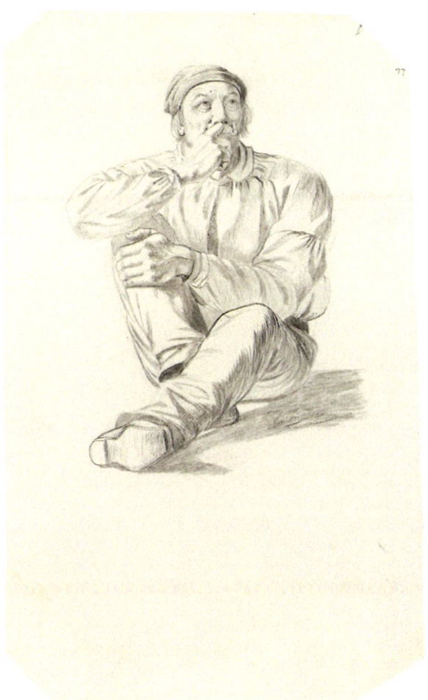

Plate 21: *Sceptic*, possible alternate study for *Lighter Relieving a Steamboat Aground* (1847)

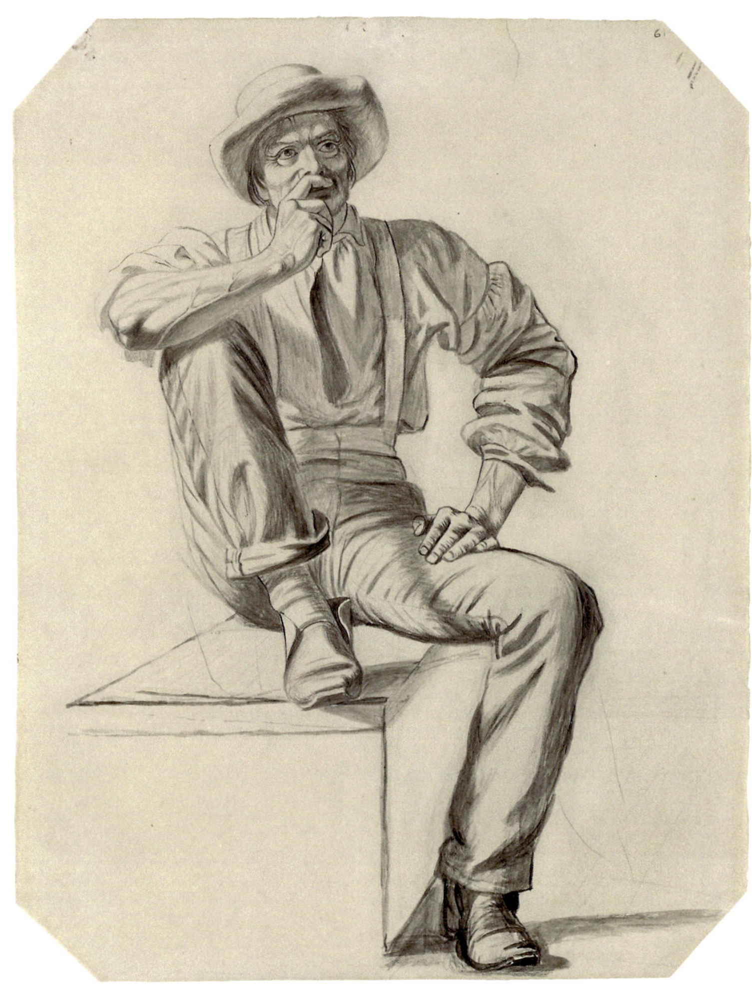

Plate 22: *Rapt listener*, for *Lighter Relieving a Steamboat Aground* (1847)

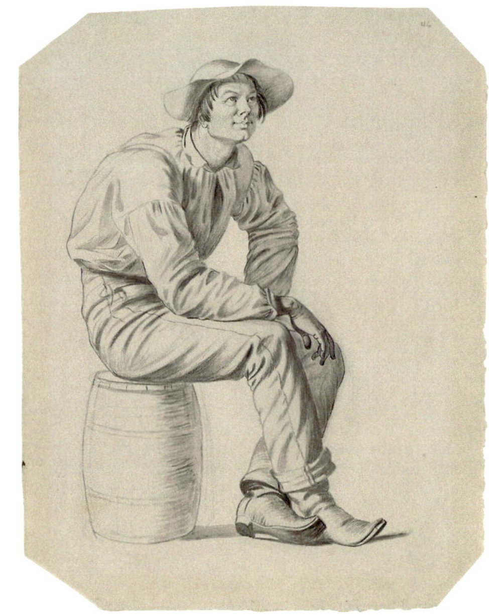

Plate 23: *Boatman*, for *Lighter Relieving a Steamboat Aground* (1847) with alterations

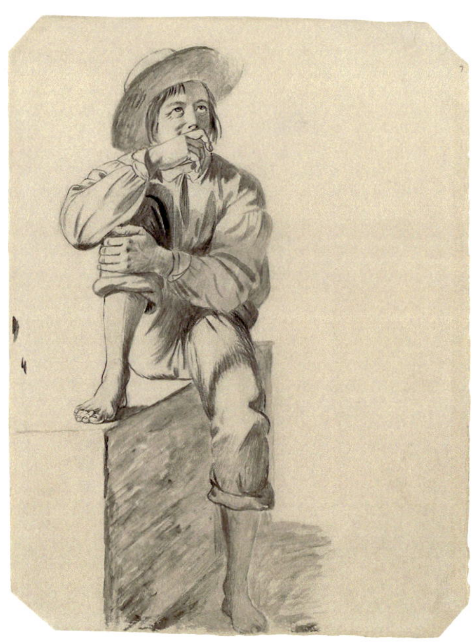

Plate 24: *Young boatman*, possible alternate study for *Lighter Relieving a Steamboat Aground* (1847)

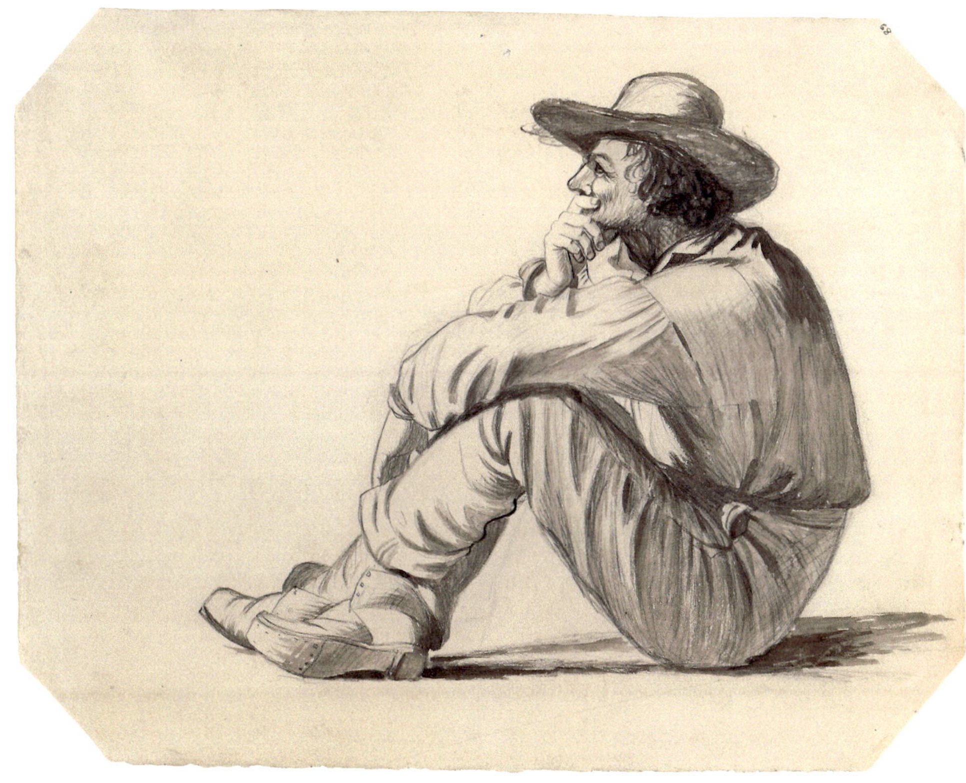

Plate 25: *Boatman*, possible alternate study for *Lighter Relieving a Steamboat Aground* (1847)

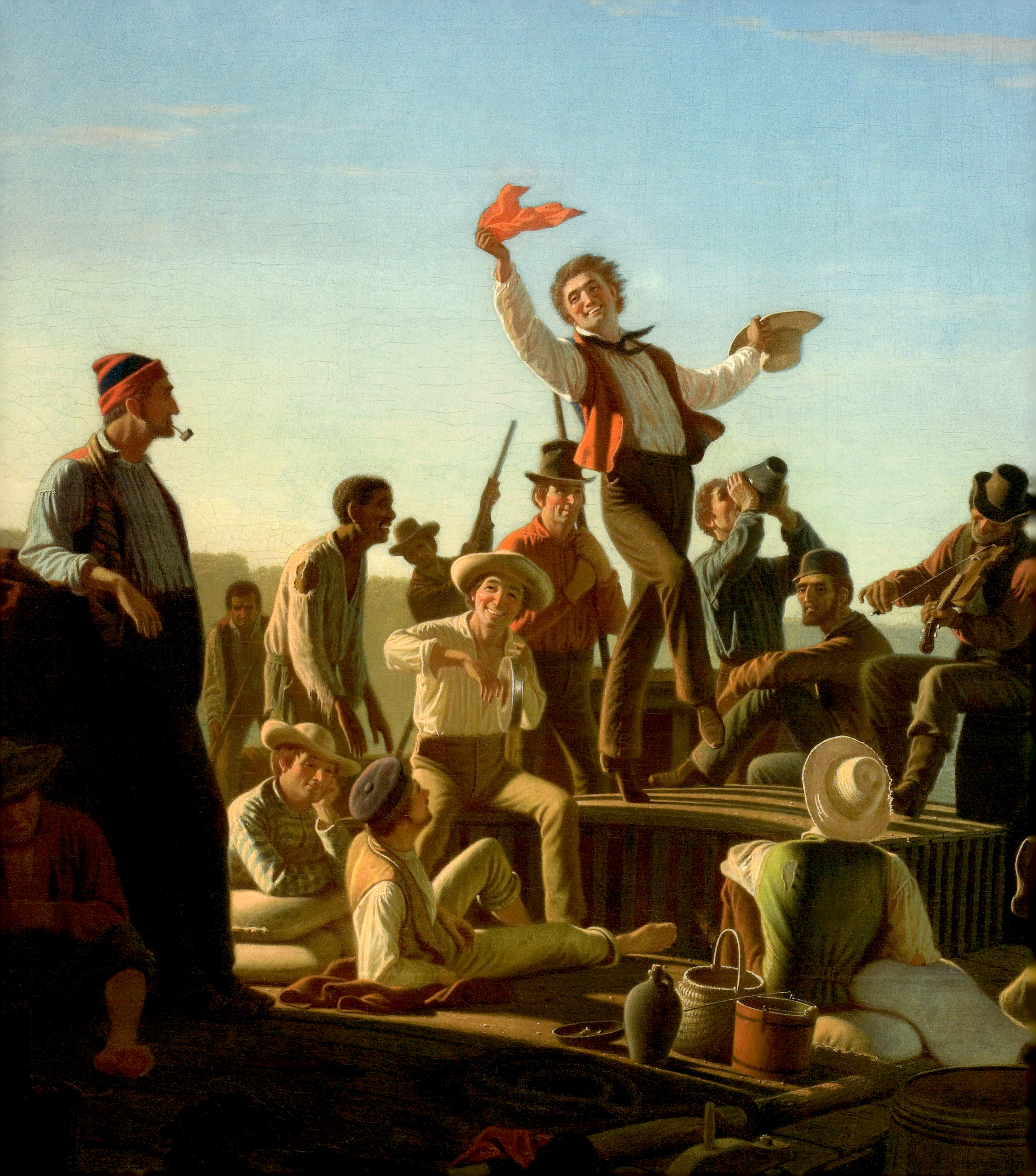

FLUID PRESENCE

George Caleb Bingham and the River

NENETTE LUARCA-SHOAF

In 1824 Missouri tobacco was gaining approval in markets all over the United States. The *Saint Louis Enquirer* reported:

> *Thirty-eight hogsheads of MISSOURI TOBACCO, with the stamp of* "Bingham & Lamme, Boon's Lick, Missouri," *were sold in the city of New York . . . at the highest price, being pronounced superior to any other description of Tobacco in market. Missouri Tobacco always [achieves] near the highest price in New Orleans, and has frequently had the preference in Philadelphia and Baltimore.*[1]

The success of Henry Vest Bingham (1784–1823), father of the artist George Caleb Bingham, and his partner William Lamme in exporting their goods was heralded as "important news to our state." But the *Missouri Intelligencer*, published in Franklin, Missouri, also claimed local patrimony for the products' appearance on the national stage: "The above mentioned Tobacco was raised in this County, and, together with a large quantity of manufactured tobacco, with the same stamp, was shipped from this town. We consider the character of our tobacco to be now fully established."[2]

More than two decades later, George Caleb Bingham found similar renown in both local and national contexts. Bingham had already built a career making portraits of aspiring and entrepreneurial Missourians, but once he embarked on a new endeavor—depicting men at work and play on the Missouri, Mississippi, and Ohio rivers—his artwork found a place in prominent New York exhibition venues, was included in collections around the country, and was disseminated in the form of engravings and lithographs. Like the stamp "Bingham & Lamme, Boon's Lick, Missouri" that marked his father's tobacco, Bingham had created a stylistic brand that could be identified wherever it was seen. In turn, the expanded exposure boosted his reputation at home in Missouri. Though Bingham painted a range of subject matter from the mid-1840s through the 1850s—portraits, western landscapes, and genre scenes of frontier life and political culture—it was by creating a sense of everyday life on the inland rivers that he developed an original approach that garnered recognition in art markets around the country. By submitting his paintings for sale and exhibition by the American Art-Union in New York, traveling between West and East throughout his career, and harnessing the mobility of reproductive print technologies, Bingham disseminated the milieu of the western rivers through different geographic and cultural terrains.

Most scholars have interpreted Bingham's work as celebrating the nineteenth-century doctrine of Manifest Destiny and the drive toward westward expansion. Though the Treaty of Paris of 1783 granted Americans the right to navigate the Mississippi River, the area remained contested space, since the

Jolly Flatboatmen in Port (detail), 1857, Plate 47

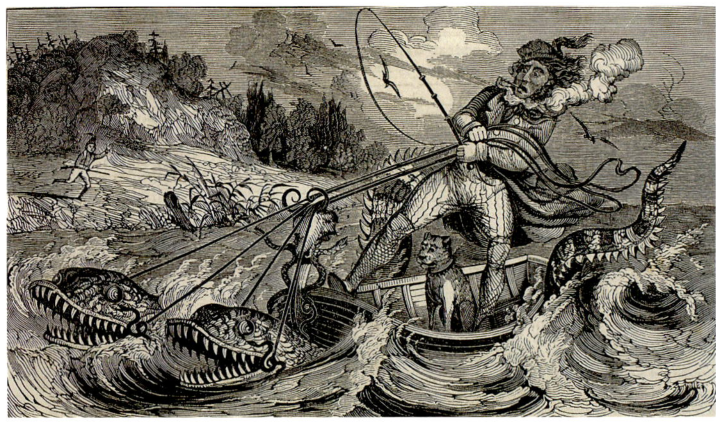

Fig. 1: *The Way they Travel in the West*, in *Davy Crockett's Almanac from 1840*, courtesy American Antiquarian Society

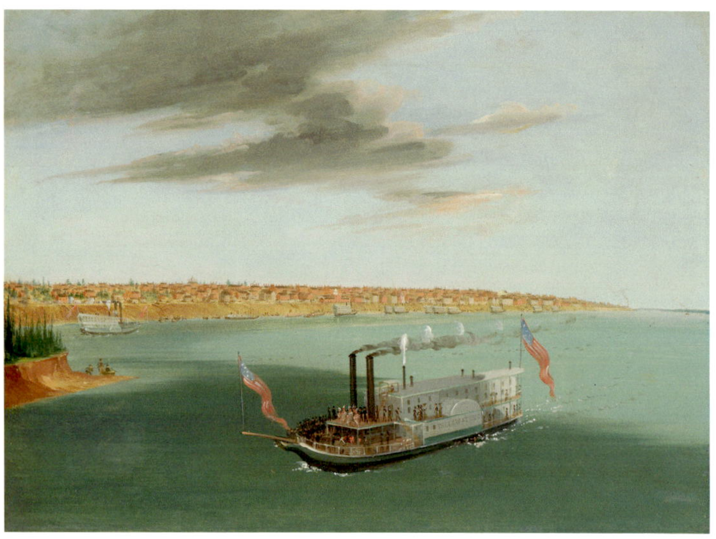

Fig. 2: George Catlin (1796–1872), *St. Louis from the River Below*, 1832–33, oil on canvas, 19⅜ × 26¾ in., Smithsonian American Art Museum, Gift of Mrs. Joseph Harrison, Jr., Art Resource, NY

Spanish and French retained control of the Lower Mississippi River and New Orleans. Once the Louisiana Purchase transferred governance of New Orleans and lands west of the Mississippi to the United States in 1803, flatboats played an important role in shipping raw agricultural goods down the Ohio and Mississippi to manufacturing centers in the eastern United States and western Europe. Thus, the river men and traffic depicted by Bingham were integral to incorporating what had been the frontier into the fabric of the broader United States.

Nevertheless, boatmen and the rivers on which they traveled had earned an ambiguous position within antebellum society. The men were simultaneously admired and disdained, valued for their free and unfettered movement through western spaces but feared for the corrupting influence their unruly and uncivilized manners might have on polite society. Bingham's figures have been interpreted as idealized, cleaned-up versions of the "half-horse, half-alligator" boatmen and unsavory rustics featured in popular publications and tall tales of the 1820s and 1830s, like the inexpensive, humorous *Davy Crockett's Almanac* (Fig. 1).[3] In contrast to these crudely rendered illustrations printed in heavy black ink, Bingham's works are distinguished by their orderly pyramidal arrangement, soft color, and lack of visible brushstrokes. Art historians have explained these qualities as Bingham's attempt to exert artistic control over the perceived chaos of the frontier in order to make his western scenes and, by extension, the activities of western men more acceptable to eastern viewers.[4] They have also noted that Bingham used old master prints and plaster casts of classical and Renaissance sculpture as his prototypes, in effect using aesthetic means to elevate these frontiersmen into river gods and national exemplars.[5] Angela Miller has further argued that Bingham's work offers a picture of regional integration in its display of unfettered transit. As she explained, it was important to make the West seem exotic so that it would appear compelling but at the same time safe enough for investment. Doing so conveyed the ability of regional people and commerce to become players in larger national interests.[6]

To claim a space for his vision and create work that was critically acceptable, Bingham had to contend with images of

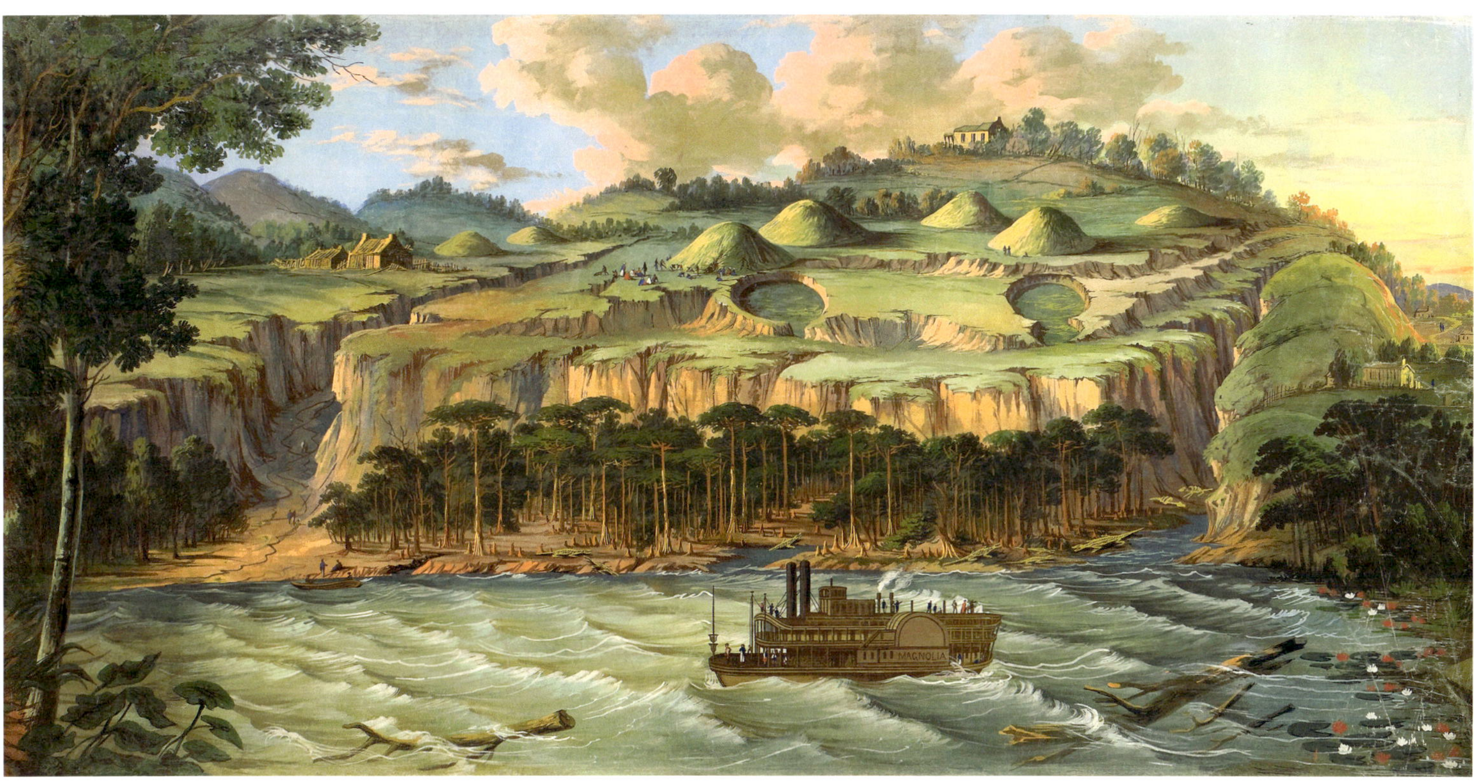

Fig. 3: John J. Egan (active mid-nineteenth century), "Ferguson Group; The Landing of Gen. Jackson," scene 18 from *Panorama of the Monumental Grandeur of the Mississippi Valley*, ca. 1850, distemper on cotton muslin, H: 90 in., Saint Louis Art Museum, Eliza McMillan Trust, 34:1953

the West that could be seen in works by both other fine artists and the outlets of popular culture. Starting in the 1830s, thanks to advances in transportation and printing technologies, images of the inland rivers were widely distributed throughout the United States, feeding the public's imagination about the territories to the west. Representations took the form of landscape and bird's-eye views (Fig. 2), theatrical productions, maps, book and magazine illustrations, and the most popular medium of them all, moving panoramas (Fig. 3). These giant scrolling paintings toured the United States and western Europe from the mid-1840s to the early 1850s, promising the experience of a steamboat trip on the broad expanse of the Mississippi in just a few hours and without the inconvenience of an actual journey. At the same time, an increasing number of people traveled to the rivers themselves, whether as tourists, migrants, missionaries, or businessmen, and the variety of pictures at their disposal informed and created expectations about what they would see. Bingham's work has a rare place in this crowded field of imagery because he intended his paintings and prints to function primarily within the realm of the fine arts. Yet by making western rivers the cornerstone of his artistic identity, he put his works in dialogue with other images of the West circulating in the burgeoning sphere of the mass media. By emphasizing a sense of the everyday over the sensational, Bingham's paintings counter existing stereotypes and assert a local's perspective, thereby bringing new facets of western identity to the fore.

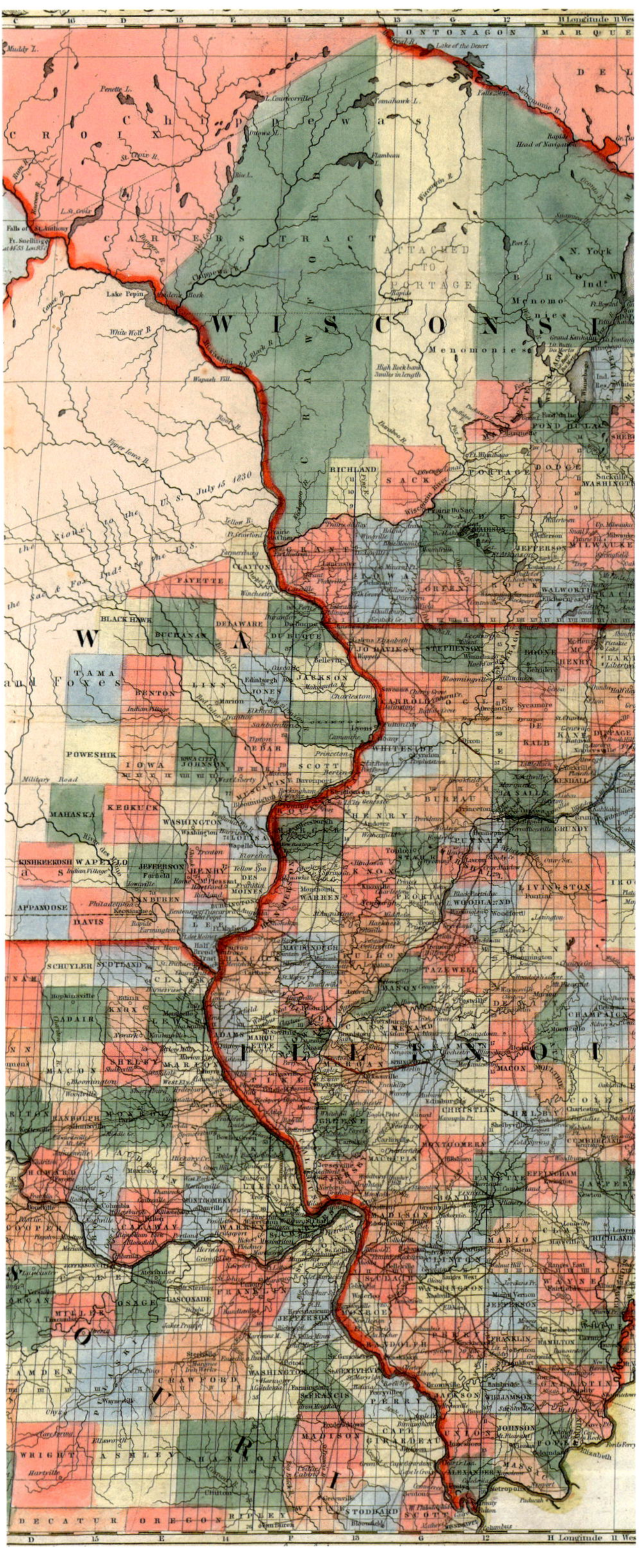

Fig. 4: J. H. Colton and J. Calvin Smith, *Guide Through Ohio . . .*, from *The Western Tourist Or Emigrant's Guide . . .* (detail), 1845, J. H. Colton, New York, David Rumsey Map Collection

The rivers functioned both locally and as connective entities. In the nineteenth century, they played a crucial role in determining the livelihoods and patterns of settlement for people living in the vast Mississippi watershed (Fig. 4). Additionally, in the words of the economic historian Timothy Mahoney, the local river "provided the context from which to understand the land as a place and perceive the region around one as an organized system in space."[7] The river connected people and places, but it also had a role in forging locals' sense of self in relation to others. For much of his life, Bingham lived in the vicinity of the Missouri and Mississippi rivers, leading some to dub him the "Missouri Artist."[8] Period commentators were quick to align his works with his point of origin, asserting that the pictures "could never have been painted by one who was not perfectly familiar with the scenes they represent."[9] Even twentieth-century scholars have described Bingham's works as "captur[ing] the essence" of the western frontier through direct and prolonged observation of its people.[10] Yet the expansion of steamboat travel also made it possible for Bingham and his work to move from the heart of Missouri to the bustling metropolis of Saint Louis and farther east to the cultural centers of New York and Philadelphia, just as they brought many easterners to the West for new opportunities.[11]

The choices that Bingham made in creating his western scenes paralleled the ability of the river to shift shape and direction. The artist knew that the rhythms of western life were often dictated by the unpredictable nature of the rivers. According to Mahoney, "observing the river and being aware of its changes played an important role in the lives of 'river people' and those who lived in towns along the rivers."[12] It was a malleable entity that required constant monitoring and vigilance because its water level had the potential to alter the surrounding topography, shortening or lengthening the relative distance between two places depending on fluctuating alluvial courses. Low or high water could inhibit the transport of people and goods and affect agricultural and town development. The enterprising men Bingham knew and painted in Missouri responded to the contingencies of their environment by cultivating adaptable professional lives. Bingham followed this pattern, pursuing diverse ventures in art and politics at various times of his life.

The fluid character of the river also offers a way to interpret the identity that Bingham created for himself and his subjects. He endowed his river paintings with a kind of flexibility by homing in on a repertoire of straightforward yet ambiguous narrative situations. For instance, despite the varied types of hats and behaviors displayed by the crew in *The Jolly Flatboatmen* (Pl. 5), none can be securely assigned to period stereotypes of race or ethnicity. Also, the landscape through which the boat travels is a hazy, unidentifiable place. For the most part, Bingham omitted the colorful variety of characters and roster of familiar landscape sights that fill many of the textual and visual accounts that describe travels on the rivers, nor did he include any indication of racial or sectional strife that marked the decades before the Civil War. Instead, he created the sense that he was depicting the quotidian western experience of Euro-American men by styling a gallery of relatively homogeneous men in generalized river environments that persist from one canvas to another. The uncanny familiarity of his paintings reinforces his stylistic brand, but it also allows his figures and their settings to remain elusive, unspecific, and thus amenable to different types of viewers.

Four decades before Mark Twain's tales of life on the Mississippi entranced readers, newspaper stories, travelers' reports, and sensational fiction all emphasized the fascinating mélange of people and languages that confronted passengers journeying by steamboats or disembarking at one of its ports. *The Big Bear of Arkansas* by T. B. Thorpe (first published in 1841) described a veritable parade of recognizable regional and social types that a sophisticated observer could discern and enjoy:

> *Here may be seen jostling together the wealthy Southern planter, and the pedler of tin-ware from New England—the Northern merchant, and the Southern jockey—a venerable bishop, and a desperate gambler—the land speculator, and the honest farmer—professional men of all creeds and characters—Wolvereens, Suckers, Hoosiers, Buckeyes, and Corncrackers, beside a "plentiful sprinkling" of the half-horse and half-alligator species of men, who are peculiar to "old Mississippi," and who appear to gain a livelihood simply by going up and down the river.*[13]

Bingham avoided these colorful characters in his work, even though Missouri had long been a "confluence region," where the Missouri, Mississippi, and Ohio rivers came together, along with many different nationalities and cultures.[14] The legacy of Native American dominance and French and Spanish colonialism during earlier centuries could still be seen in the names of places like Cape Giradeau or Saint Louis, and migration patterns created areas in which the descendants of French settlers, newly arrived German immigrants, Americans of Scotch-Irish descent, or slave-holding planters from Kentucky, Tennessee, and Virginia alternately dominated the local culture and economy.[15] Indeed, the area of the Missouri River where Bingham was raised, earned portrait commissions, and lived for much of his life was known as Little Dixie because of the prevalence of tobacco and hemp plantations that ran on slave labor.[16] The state was parceled up by demographic and political interests—between Yankee and Southern, urban and rural—and throughout the antebellum period, Missouri remained a border area precariously balanced between (as well as divided by) sectional interests and identities until the Civil War.[17]

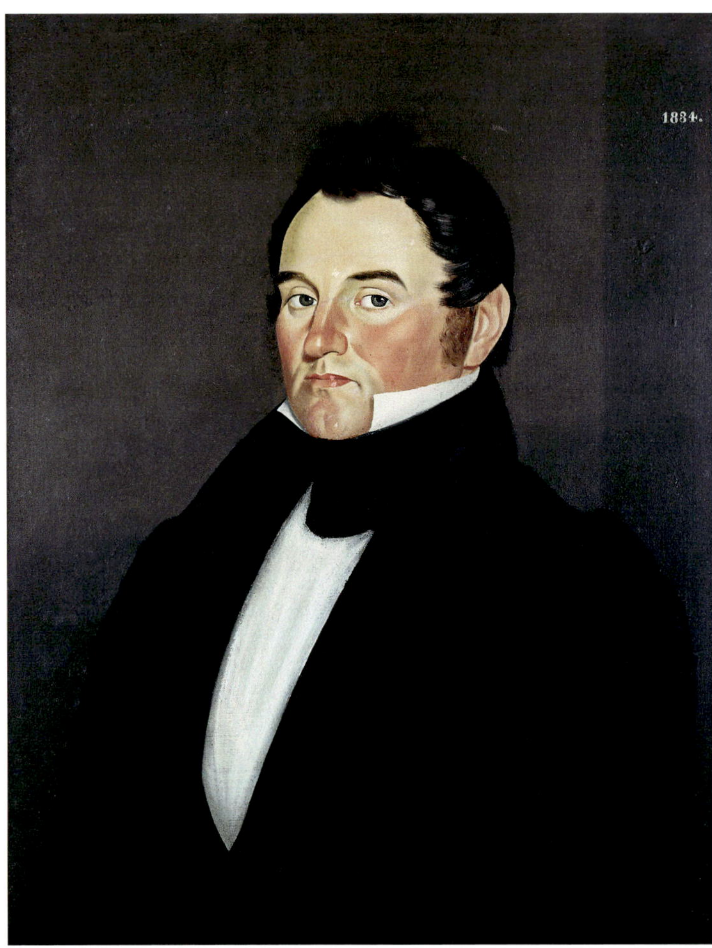

Fig. 5: George Caleb Bingham (1811–1879), *Portrait of Meredith Miles Marmaduke*, 1834, oil on canvas, 28 × 22½ in., Missouri History Museum, Saint Louis, Missouri

Working in central Missouri at the beginning of his career, Bingham focused on portraying entrepreneurial men who aspired to middle-class refinement, in effect creating a different type of image of the West that contrasted with depictions of an unruly frontier. Looking at Bingham's early self-training in art and a selection of his portraits from the 1830s reveals some of the ways in which he understood the West, a region defined by commerce, trade, and migration along the rivers, as well as his relationship to the men whom he painted.

One of Bingham's earliest recorded portraits depicts Meredith Miles Marmaduke in 1834 (Fig. 5). Marmaduke was typical of Bingham's sitters in that he made his money as a merchant, eventually becoming a large land and slave owner and participating in county and state politics.[18] Bingham renders him in three-quarter view, looking directly out toward the viewer with a serious expression. He wears a high-collared shirt with a black cravat. A simple but respectable dark suit jacket highlights his broad shoulders and upright posture. At the time this work was painted, Marmaduke was living in Columbia, Missouri, recently married into the locally respected Sappington family (members of which Bingham also painted), and had already earned a great deal of wealth by leading trading expeditions on the Santa Fe Trail.[19]

Marmaduke had emigrated at first from Virginia to the town of Franklin, Missouri. Established in 1817 and located on the northern bank of the Missouri River in Boon's Lick (or Boonslick) country, Franklin was for a time the most important settlement in Missouri Territory west of Saint Louis. The region, roughly defined as the land on either side of the Missouri River between the present-day cities of Jefferson City and Glasgow, earned its name about 1806 when sons of the famous pioneer Daniel Boone tried to establish a salt manufacturing facility nearby.[20] By the 1830s Boon's Lick had become the second most densely populated area in the state, after the burgeoning metropolis of Saint Louis, and attracted farmers, merchants, and land speculators who wanted to start anew, including Bingham's father. The loss of his father-in-law's tobacco plantation in Augusta County, Virginia, had spurred Henry to move to Franklin in 1819, around the same time Marmaduke arrived, and eventually purchase land across the Missouri River on which to establish a tobacco plantation.[21] Between its advantageous position as the originating supply depot for the trade to Santa Fe and its connections to major southern and eastern ports via the Missouri and Mississippi rivers, Boon's Lick was ideally situated to take advantage of the rapidly changing social, economic, and geographic landscape. Yet within the area, local fortunes constantly shifted. Bingham's father died in 1823 at thirty-eight, and the family was forced to move across the river to their farm near Arrow Rock. Not long after that, the town of Independence supplanted Franklin as outfitter for the Santa Fe Trail, and the latter was destroyed by the early 1830s after successive years of heavy flooding.[22]

In 1820, however, Franklin had a population of more than one thousand and its own post office, circuit court, U.S. land office, and county government, along with two blacksmith shops, thirteen merchandise stores, and four taverns, one of which, the Square and Compass, was owned by Henry Bingham.[23] A key moment in young Bingham's artistic development took place there, when he was just nine years old. He crossed paths with the portraitist Chester Harding in the summer of 1820, when Harding was on his way to paint the well-known frontiersman Daniel Boone, then ninety years old.[24] One art historian has described Harding's life as "a paradigm of the nineteenth-century American 'rags-to-riches' opportunity available then to a person of ability and charm."[25] In his autobiography, Harding emphasized his "backwoods origins" on the New York frontier and recounted his experiences as an itinerant peddler and cabinetmaker before he was inspired by a portrait painter he met passing through Pittsburgh on an Ohio River flatboat. After a brief period studying art in Philadelphia, Harding gained some success painting portraits in Kentucky, but once the commissions dried up there and in Cincinnati, Harding looked farther west. He stopped in Saint Louis first but then proceeded up the Missouri to Franklin. In the years that followed, Harding traveled to Washington to paint politicians and judges, and then to Philadelphia to garner more commissions and exhibit at the Pennsylvania Academy of the Fine Arts. Bingham's own career in the late 1830s and early 1840s would follow a very similar path, as he, too, studied in Philadelphia and painted politicians in Washington.

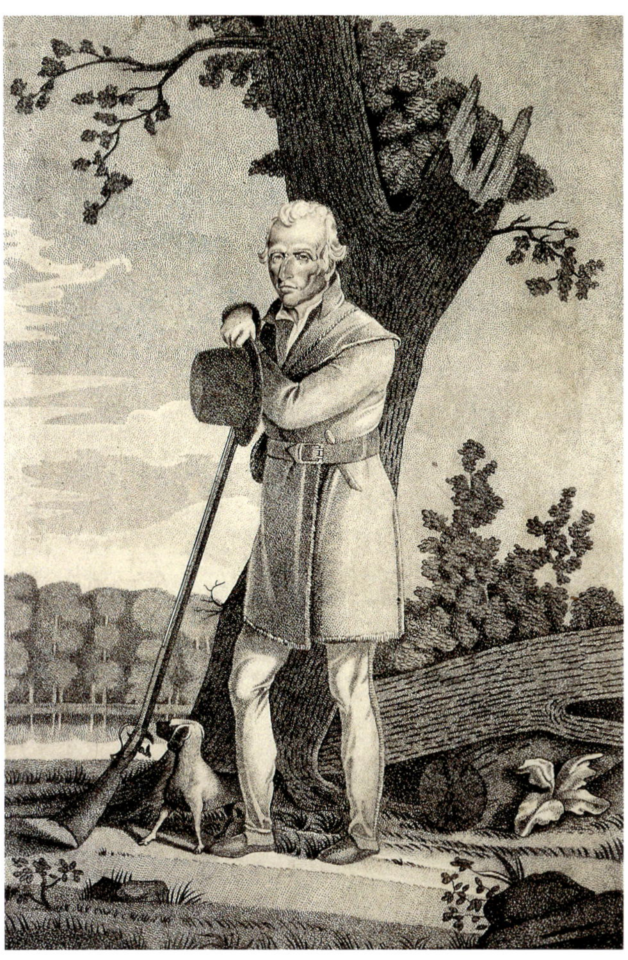

Fig. 6: James Otto Lewis (1799–1858), after Chester Harding (1792–1866), *Col. Daniel Boone*, 1820, stipple engraving, 13 9/16 × 8 3/16 in., Saint Louis Art Museum, museum purchase, 71:1943

The composition of Harding's now lost full-length portrait of Boone can be seen in a print that Harding and the engraver James Otto Lewis made in Saint Louis (Fig. 6). They charged three dollars per print and published an edition of two hundred engravings. Harding's reproduction and marketing of his work provided a precedent for Bingham's practice of making prints after his own paintings more than twenty-five years later. Though Bingham was quite young when he and Harding met, contact with the older artist may have planted the seed for

Bingham's artistic ambitions, or at least given him a framework for what an artistic career could look like. Bingham had the opportunity to observe Harding at work, recalling later in life that first the artist "made a pencil drawing and perhaps a study in oil from life, but the portrait was completed in his temporary studio in Franklin, and its completion witnessed by myself."[26] Drawing eventually played a key role in Bingham's formulation of genre paintings from the mid-1840s through the 1850s.

As a testament to his initiative and with the support of his mother, Mary, who valued both art and education, Bingham apprenticed himself to a cabinetmaker at age sixteen. Shortly afterward, he developed his portrait style by painting directly from his subjects rather than through formal study. Following Harding's lead, Bingham became an itinerant painter, traveling to nearby counties along the Missouri River and setting up a studio in the burgeoning metropolis of Saint Louis with easy access to the business district and levee, where he gained the patronage of upwardly mobile men, river travelers, and the attention of the city's press. He even journeyed as far down the Mississippi River as Natchez, Mississippi, to solicit that city's wealthy planter class.[27] He was prolific for a young artist, painting more than fifty portraits of sitters from six counties bordering the Missouri River, including the cities of Saint Louis and Natchez, before leaving to study art in Philadelphia in the spring of 1838.[28] Bingham considered his early portraits a crucial step in his artistic development, writing to his then fiancée from Saint Louis in 1835: "Nearly three years have elapsed and I have yet scarsely learned to paint the human face, after having accomplished which, I shall have ascended but one step toward the eminence to which the art of painting may be carried." Despite these self-doubts, Bingham affirmed his unflagging commitment to becoming a respected artist:

> *Though I am frequently under the influence of melancholy when my prospects appear dark and gloomy before me, yet I have never entirely despaired, and the determination to do my utmost to rise in my profession has ever remained strong in my mind. . . . Very few are aware of the mortifications and anxieties which attend the work of a painter; and of the toil and study which it requires to give him success and raise him to distinction.*[29]

Bingham's entrepreneurial moves, and those of Harding before him, should be considered within the context of developing conceptions about self-made manhood in the United States. Though the ideology is typically related to the growing merchant and professional classes striving to make their fortunes in urban settings, it was also important to the thousands of men who sought a fresh start in the West, such as Marmaduke and Henry Bingham. In his classic study of the self-made man, Irvin G. Wyllie points out that young, white, middle-class men and those who aspired to that status could have turned to a number of sources to learn about the ways in which one could better one's station and about the merits of acquiring wealth through hard work and self-motivation.[30] Wyllie cites a steep increase in the number of biographies of millionaire businessmen and other self-help books and magazines for aspiring merchants published from the 1830s to the latter part of the nineteenth century. These texts glorified the man who was not born into wealth or position but made his own way, earning it through limited public education, apprenticeship, and eventually affiliation with organizations of civic improvement.

Although period writers remarked on the primitive conditions in which Bingham began his career—"with such colors as a house-painter's shop could supply, and a half-dozen stumps of brushes left by a transient artist in a neighboring town"—and linked the "absolute life" in his western representations to the artist's frontier roots,[31] both Bingham and Harding before him were also evaluated on the aesthetic merit of their work and not just on the novelty of their origins. Writing to the theater critic and early American art historian William Dunlap, Harding credited his "being a backwoodsman, newly caught" as the reason for his meteoric success as a portraitist in Boston. At the same time, he pointed to a paradox for the self-trained artist: "There is no circumstance in the history of an artist that carries such charm with it as that of being self-taught—while to those competent of judging, it conveys no other virtue with it, other than perseverance."[32]

Bingham was deeply committed to improving his artistic skills, but it appears that he relied on the lessons provided by drawing manuals in lieu of any formal academic study. Scholars have not been able to determine which of the scores of drawing manuals published in the early nineteenth century he could have seen, yet the idea that an artist would begin his career by perfecting the rendering of faces before moving on to more complex compositions is at the heart of many of the lessons.[33] For instance, John Rubens Smith's *A Key to the Art of Drawing the Human Figure* (1831) explains that lessons would

> *[c]ommenc[e] with the Features, and progressing to Heads, Limbs and Trunks, with their principles of proportion, and their application to attitude . . . showing how to proceed on simple and correct Principles, well calculated for a Self-Instructor, an Amateur's Companion, or a Teacher's Assistant, and Guide to the Student's pursuits in an Antique or Model Academy.*[34]

Many manuals emphasized drawing as a useful pursuit for various occupations. John Gadsby Chapman proclaimed that drawing could be used "from the anvil of the smith and the workbench of the joiner, to the manufacturer of the most costly productions of ornamental art," for "strengthening invention and execution, and qualifying the mind and hand to design and produce whatever the wants or tastes of society may require."[35] Chapman underscored its association with a manual, artisan class but not at the expense of rational or aesthetic sensibilities.

In addition to accumulating artistic skills, during his early career as a portraitist, Bingham learned the social functions

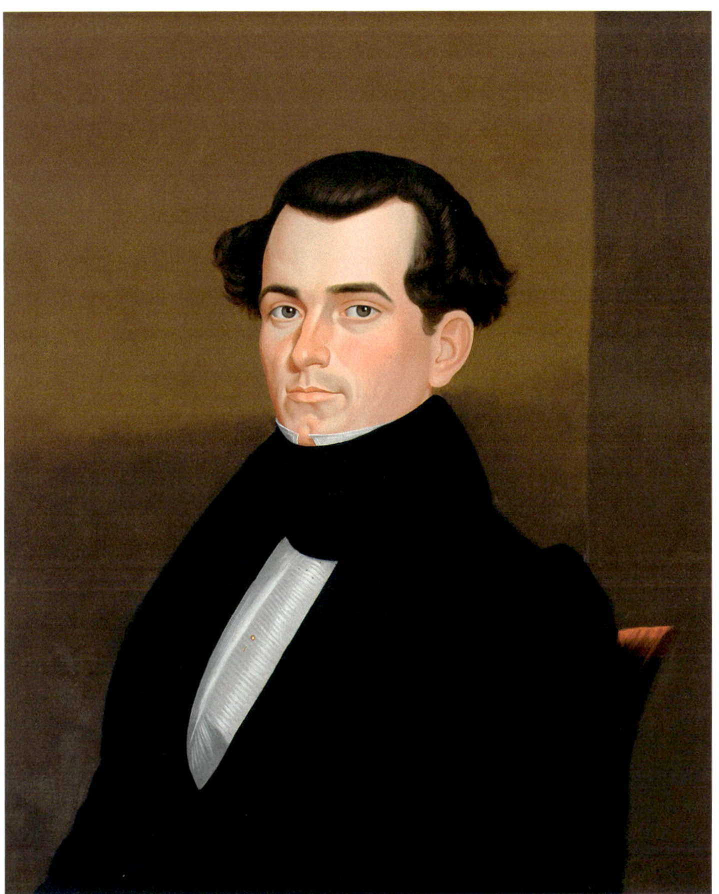

Fig. 7: George Caleb Bingham (1811–1879), *Portrait of James Sidney Rollins*, 1834, oil on canvas, 28 × 23 in., Private collection, photography by Wilson Graham

of portraiture. While painting prominent members of the local community, he came to understand their standards for what respectability looked like and learned the visual and professional traits that his sitters adopted in order to fashion their identities as upwardly mobile, self-made men. James Sidney Rollins, whom Bingham painted in 1834 (Fig. 7), was an important personal and professional connection he forged during a brief stint painting in Columbia, Missouri.[36] Rollins was an ambitious and newly practicing lawyer who had been schooled in eastern colleges. Soon after his portrait was made by Bingham, Rollins acquired the *Missouri Intelligencer* and *Boon's Lick Advertiser*, two newspapers published in Columbia, and embarked on a long political career that often intertwined with Bingham's own professional activities.

Unlike the commercial pursuits followed by Rollins and others, however, the artisanal path that Bingham followed for much of his life did not afford as much status in the hierarchy of nineteenth-century definitions of self-made manhood because it was not an arena in which one could acquire large amounts of wealth. Perhaps that is one reason that, in his youth, Bingham had numerous interests beyond forging an art career, dabbling in law, religion, and politics.[37] While a profession like politics was associated with "[a]ggression, . . . competition, and a spirit of self-interest," according to one cultural historian, the arts were "marked 'female.'"[38] Consequently, in his self-portrait of 1834–35 (Fig. 8), Bingham did not represent himself with the identifiable attributes of an artist. He does not hold a palette or show himself in the act of painting. Instead, he molds his persona in the pattern of his other sitters, in three-quarter view wearing a dark suit without any material goods save for the back of a chair. Here, the clarity of his features, the directness of his gaze, and the similarity of his likeness to those of other self-made men display his honorable status. In those portraits, too, visible attributes or details that might signal his sitters' professions rarely appear, perhaps because their absence acknowledged the fluidity of the ever-changing entrepreneurial and occupational pursuits of men in the West.

By the time Bingham depicted David Steele Lamme in 1837 (Fig. 9), not much has changed from the portraits of Marmaduke, Rollins, or himself. The background is lighter, making the contours of Lamme's body more apparent, and the handling of the facial features is softer, but the sitter's general pose and expression are the same. Another example of Bingham's many clients who pursued several business ventures during their lives, Lamme was involved in trading with the Southwest territories along the Santa Fe Trail, cultivating a large farm, and opening the first paper mill west of the Mississippi.[39]

Not long after painting Lamme, Bingham concluded that he needed to study in eastern cultural centers to achieve the artistic advancement he desired. Writing to Rollins, who by 1837 had become his closest friend and supporter, Bingham announced that he had resolved to take advantage of "[t]he greater facilities afforded [in the East], for improvement in my profession."[40] Bingham was based in Philadelphia in the spring of 1838, mostly copying and looking at artworks at the Pennsylvania Academy of the Fine Arts, but he also made trips to New York and Baltimore to copy plaster casts and acquire engravings and drawings to take back with him to Missouri for further study. A later biography reported that the time in Philadelphia allowed him to "[obtain] a little knowledge of color by looking at pictures, which before he had no opportunity of studying," casting Missouri as a cultural backwater.[41] Although he had hoped to work with the Philadelphia portraitist Thomas Sully at some point, that effort was thwarted by Sully's travel abroad. Still, the fact that Bingham continued to educate himself, rather than pursuing formal study in an art academy or with a master artist, speaks to his ongoing adherence to the ideology of the self-made man.

The eastern sojourn worked in the artist's favor, helping him to garner an important commission from a prominent Saint Louis family when he returned to Missouri. The art historian Kevin Muller suggests that Leonidas Wetmore and his family sought out Bingham for the portrait because the artist "presented himself as similar to the middle class Missouri men who were his patrons and . . . as capable of representing the latter according to the conventions that signified middle class manhood."[42] Wetmore, like Bingham, had arrived in the Missouri Territory with his family in the early 1820s after his father, an army paymaster, was stationed in Franklin (Fig. 10).[43] The portrait was done just before Wetmore left to fight the Seminoles in Florida with the U.S. Army's Sixth Infantry,

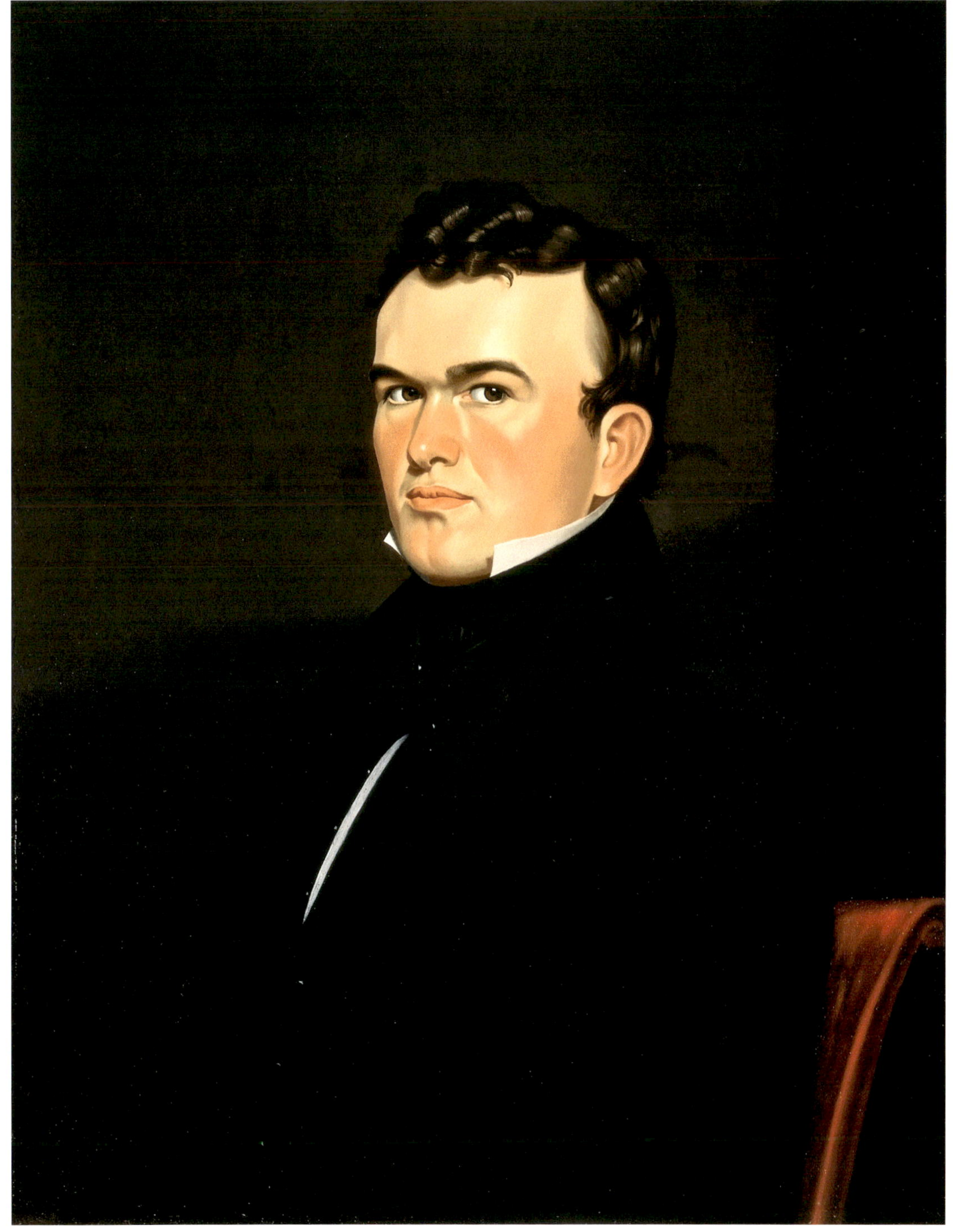

Fig. 8: George Caleb Bingham (1811–1879), *Self-Portrait*, 1834–35, oil on canvas, 28⅜ × 22 11/16 in., Saint Louis Art Museum, Eliza McMillan Trust, 57:1934

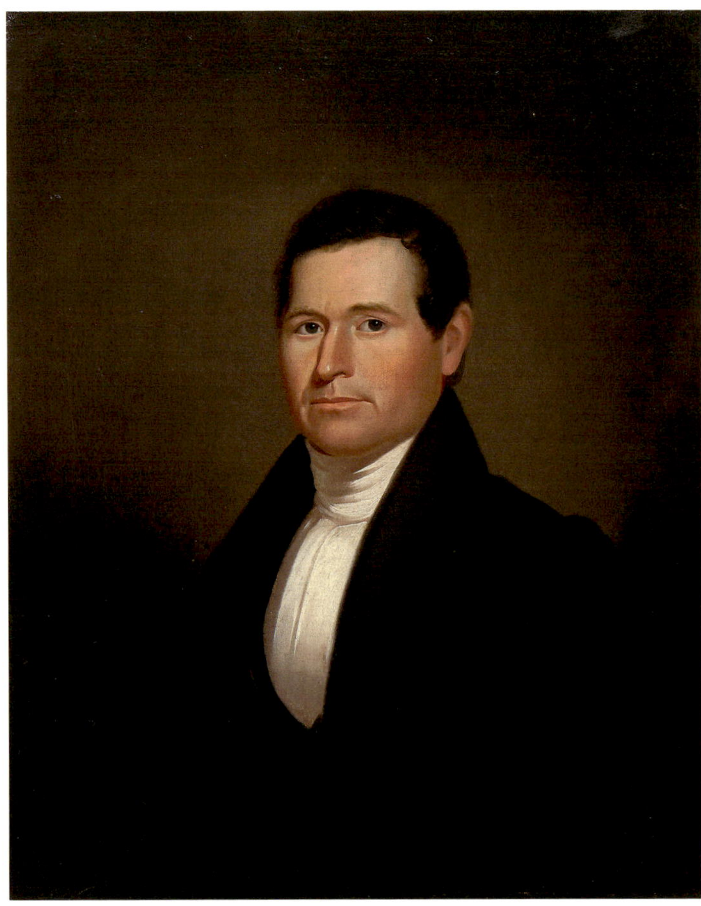

Fig. 9: George Caleb Bingham (1811–1879), *Portrait of David Steele Lamme*, 1837, oil on canvas, 28¼ × 22¾ in., Private collection, photography by Lee Ewing

distinguishing him from the merchants and politicians who made up most of Bingham's clientele. It is likely that Bingham took as a template two portraits of Daniel Boone, whom one historian has called "a new sort of 'American Native,' . . . no longer bound to the farm . . . his loyalties were rather to middle-class virtues as individual autonomy, enterprise, and mobility."[44] In Bingham's work, as in both the 1820 engraving after Harding's painting of the same year and another full-length image of Boone that appeared on a series of Missouri state bonds that circulated in 1837, the subject is shown within a landscape setting accompanied by distinctively western attributes, such as the Kentucky rifle.[45] He also wears a buckskin suit to reflect the influence of Plains Indian clothing and his life on the frontier, but Muller suggests that Boone's attire would "not [have] read as 'Indian'" and instead "denoted a distinctive western Anglo-American masculinity that was characterized by a pioneering spirit and superior hunting skills."[46] Bingham tempers these traits associated with stereotypical images of frontier lifestyles with more generally accepted middle-class expectations for decorum that would have been familiar to eastern viewers. The fitted tailoring of Wetmore's suit highlights his adherence to rules of respectable comportment, unlike the casually posed, reclining, or seated figures of Bingham's later genre paintings. At the same time, Bingham's forthright representation omits the violence inherent in Wetmore's civilizing project, relegating it to fashionable details like the gun and buckskin suit. Wetmore is already firmly ensconced in the landscape without having met any resistance.

The relative haziness of the river setting in Wetmore's portrait allows the gentility of the sitter to dominate his environment in clear, unambiguous terms. Bingham renders Wetmore as if he were outside, standing close to the river's edge. The clouds part just enough to illuminate a slice of the water's reflective surface. The river stands out amid the dark backdrop of trees more prominently than it ever had before in Bingham's work. Yet neither Native Americans nor any recognizable landmarks from the inland river valleys mark the setting as specifically western; instead, Wetmore's attire is the painting's sole geographic locator.

Comparing the representation of landscape in Wetmore's portrait to another work that Bingham completed about two or three years earlier is instructive for showing the gendered terms in which landscape is represented in the artist's oeuvre. At the same time he painted David Lamme, he also rendered an image of Lamme's new wife, Sophia Woodson Hickman, and her son from a previous marriage (Fig. 11).[47] Bingham

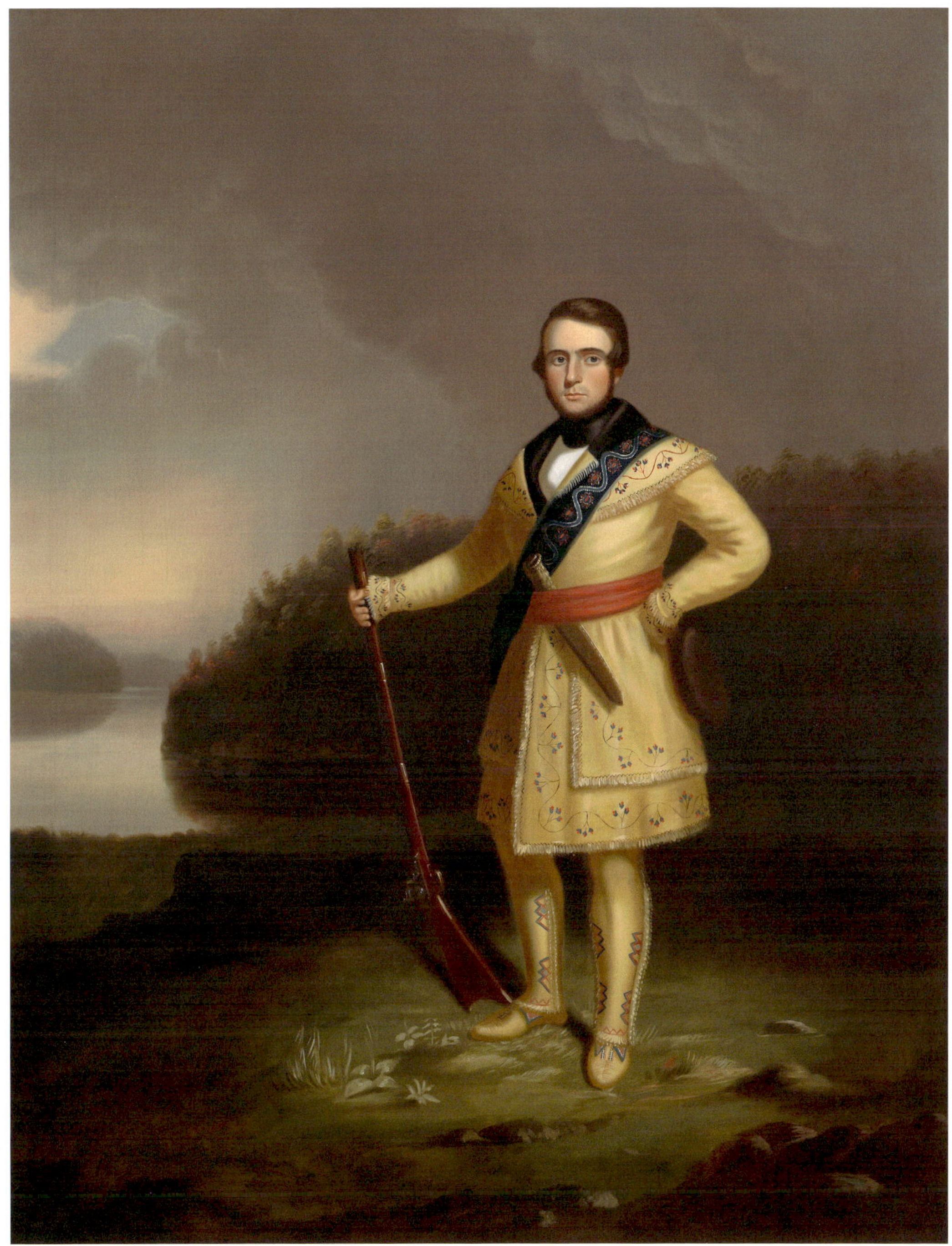

Fig. 10: George Caleb Bingham (1811–1879) *Portrait of Leonidas Wetmore*, 1839–40, oil on canvas, 60⅛ × 40⅛ in., Courtesy of The Diplomatic Reception Rooms, U.S. Department of State, Washington, D.C., 1993.0012

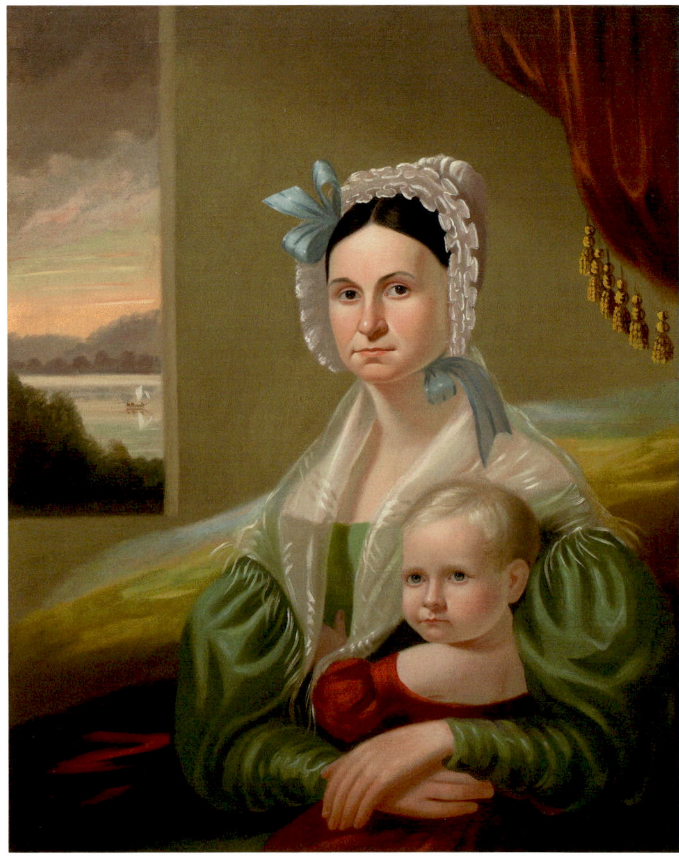

Fig. 11: George Caleb Bingham (1811–1879), *Mrs. David Steele Lamme (Sophia Woodson Hickman) and Son William Wirt*, 1837, oil on canvas, 35½ × 28½ in., Private collection, photography by Lee Ewing

often painted his portraits in pendants with nearly identical backgrounds, but in Sophia's portrait, he experimented with the composition by adding a tasseled curtain, upholstered sofa, and view of a sailboat on a body of water. The ostensibly local landscape may situate the Lammes geographically and socially within a river community, but it lacks features that might mark it as any one place in particular. In contrast to Wetmore's portrait, Sophia and her son are located securely within a comfortable interior, separated from the exterior by her seat, the window frame, and the dark shrubbery. Although her husband makes his money from commerce and investments related to inland river trade and commercial development, his wife retains her gentility by holding her son tightly, thereby emphasizing her maternal role, and remaining within a domestic setting. The landscape looks more like a representation than reality, perhaps allowing the portrait to comment on Sophia's ability—along with that of the portrait's viewer—to appreciate a picturesque landscape in the manner that a refined person would.[48]

If Wetmore's portrait conveys the sitter's pioneering spirit and military ambitions, the Lamme portrait commissions would have served David Lamme as emblems of his affiliation with fine art and the civilizing process occurring on the frontier. Later, he was active in his community as a founding trustee of Columbia College (now the University of Missouri). Using money gained through hard work and experience to cultivate their local educational, artistic, and civic culture was a key activity for self-made men who wanted to improve themselves with "self-culture."[49] The same could be said for Bingham. As early as 1836, the *Missouri Republican*, a newspaper published in Saint Louis, celebrated the artist's burgeoning reputation and the dedication he showed toward fulfilling his lofty ambitions: "He gives promise of attaining to an enviable celebrity in the profession which he has chosen, and to which he devotes himself with increasing industry."[50] The Columbia, Missouri, newspaper edited by his friend Rollins proclaimed that Bingham's "collection of well-finished portraits—each affording full evidence of a cultivated mimetic skill, and of an undoubted, high, creative genius," provided important evidence of "Trans-Mississippian progress towards a state of intellectual and social refinement." The author further boasted of the homegrown nature of Bingham's talent: "His boyhood was spent upon the banks of the Missouri; and never, since he reached the stature of manhood, has he been East of the Mississippi." Rather than looking solely to the East for cultural imports, he was glad to know that Bingham was working in Saint Louis, considered "the principal nursery of the fine arts, in 'the far west.'"[51] Thus, commissioning a portrait from a local artist like Bingham could be seen as an act of regional cultural development and civic responsibility.

Bingham's work was significant in the 1830s because, instead of adhering to eastern expectations, he was creating images of westerners as they wished to be seen. The historian Daniel J. Herman has discussed the "increasingly atomistic, commercial, mobile society" that characterized the antebellum West and provided the conditions for Bingham's formation as a man and as an artist.[52] Although waterways themselves do not appear in much of this early work, the geographic and economic presence of the inland rivers influenced and facilitated the social mobility and professional malleability that many of Bingham's sitters sought.

Despite the presence of a network of people in Missouri who supported Bingham's art through patronage and published reviews, as an itinerant portraitist he also actively sought patrons within a wide geographic area. From 1840 to 1844 he was again in the East, soliciting clients in Washington, D.C., Virginia, and Philadelphia. He also began working with new types of imagery, painting political banners for Whig party conventions in Missouri, as well as genre and landscape paintings for exhibition in New York. However, these efforts were largely unsuccessful in terms of gaining him mention in the press or expanding his list of clients outside Missouri.

It was not until he became involved with the American Art-Union, which provided support for him from 1845 to 1852, that Bingham emerged as a notable presence on the national art scene. The AA-U circulated and disseminated his imagery to audiences all over the country, from New Orleans to Pittsburgh and from Macon, Georgia, to Winsted, Connecticut. From its inception as an art union in 1840, the organization adopted the model established throughout Europe to promote the fine arts in the United States.[53] After paying an annual subscription fee of five dollars, each member was entered into a lottery at the end of the year with an original work of art by an American artist as the prize. But whether he or she garnered one of the hundreds of prizes awarded during the annual distribution at the group's headquarters in New York City, each subscriber was entitled to receive an engraving after one or more of the paintings the AA-U purchased that year. The organization sought to bind together the cultural tastes of the increasingly far-flung American citizenry through the purchase and dissemination of original artworks by American artists, on the one hand, and through the mechanisms of print culture—that is, newspapers, magazines, and reproductive print imagery—on the other.[54]

Though the leadership of the AA-U and its core activities were consolidated in New York City, the organization made sustained efforts to attract subscribers from a wider area. Early in its history, the management committee hired an agent to spend six months of the year traveling for the purpose of gathering subscriptions. The agent Wellington Solomons visited Philadelphia before heading south into Virginia and then up the Hudson River into New York State. The idea for him to venture west into the Ohio and Mississippi River valleys was broached in early 1843, and by that summer he had installed honorary secretaries in New Orleans; Natchez and Vicksburg, Mississippi; Louisville, Kentucky; Cincinnati; Pittsburgh; and smaller cities in between.

Despite the managers' ambitions for national cohesion, their efforts to attract memberships and distribute artworks were often met with challenges on the ground. Because he relied on the inland rivers as transportation and distribution networks, Solomons came face-to-face with the realities of voyaging on the Mississippi, evidenced by the marooned and broken-down steamboats in several of Bingham's river paintings from the later 1840s. In a letter to Robert Fraser, the corresponding secretary of the AA-U, from Vicksburg, Solomons describes the difficulties he encountered on one leg of his journey:

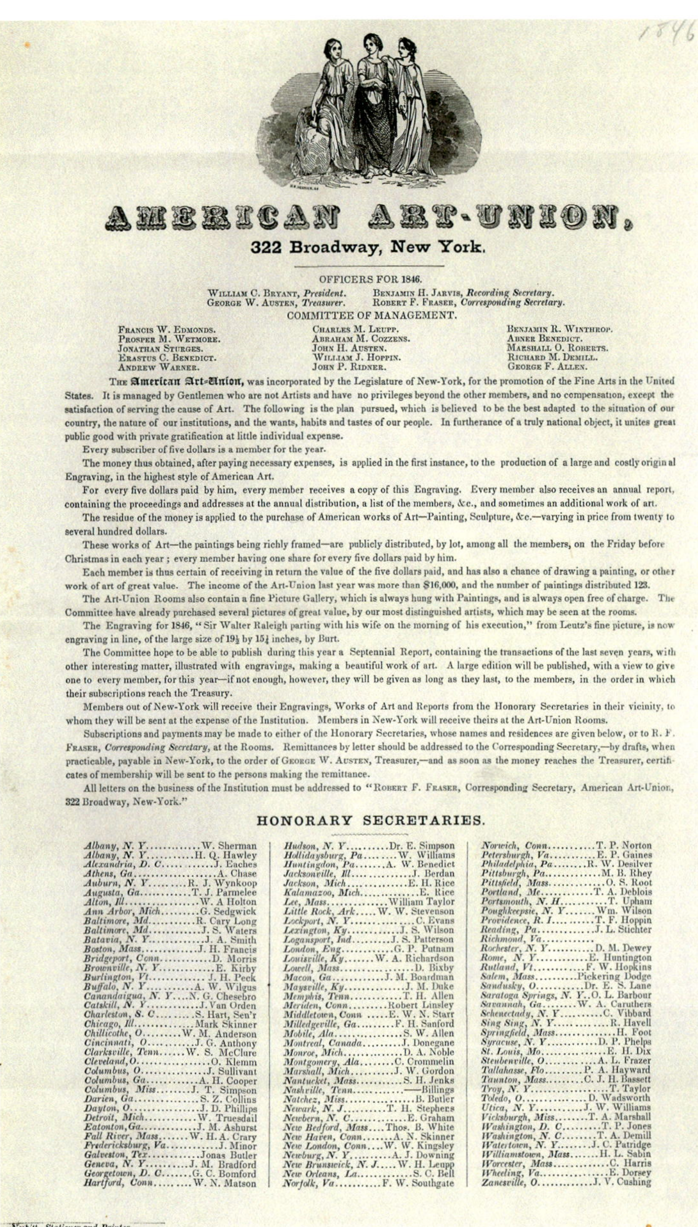

1846

AMERICAN ART-UNION,

322 Broadway, New York.

OFFICERS FOR 1846.

WILLIAM C. BRYANT, *President.* BENJAMIN H. JARVIS, *Recording Secretary.*
GEORGE W. AUSTEN, *Treasurer.* ROBERT F. FRASER, *Corresponding Secretary.*

COMMITTEE OF MANAGEMENT.

FRANCIS W. EDMONDS.
PROSPER M. WETMORE.
JONATHAN STURGES.
ERASTUS C. BENEDICT.
ANDREW WARNER.
CHARLES M. LEUPP.
ABRAHAM M. COZZENS.
JOHN H. AUSTEN.
WILLIAM J. HOPPIN.
JOHN P. RIDNER.
BENJAMIN R. WINTHROP.
ABNER BENEDICT.
MARSHALL O. ROBERTS.
RICHARD M. DEMILL.
GEORGE F. ALLEN.

THE **American Art-Union,** was incorporated by the Legislature of New-York, for the promotion of the Fine Arts in the United States. It is managed by Gentlemen who are not Artists and have no privileges beyond the other members, and no compensation, except the satisfaction of serving the cause of Art. The following is the plan pursued, which is believed to be the best adapted to the situation of our country, the nature of our institutions, and the wants, habits and tastes of our people. In furtherance of a truly national object, it unites great public good with private gratification at little individual expense.

Every subscriber of five dollars is a member for the year.

The money thus obtained, after paying necessary expenses, is applied in the first instance, to the production of a large and costly original Engraving, in the highest style of American Art.

For every five dollars paid by him, every member receives a copy of this Engraving. Every member also receives an annual report, containing the proceedings and addresses at the annual distribution, a list of the members, &c., and sometimes an additional work of art.

The residue of the money is applied to the purchase of American works of Art—Painting, Sculpture, &c.—varying in price from twenty to several hundred dollars.

These works of Art—the paintings being richly framed—are publicly distributed, by lot, among all the members, on the Friday before Christmas in each year; every member having one share for every five dollars paid by him.

Each member is thus certain of receiving in return the value of the five dollars paid, and has also a chance of drawing a painting, or other work of art of great value. The income of the Art-Union last year was more than $16,000, and the number of paintings distributed 123.

The Art-Union Rooms also contain a fine Picture Gallery, which is always hung with Paintings, and is always open free of charge. The Committee have already purchased several pictures of great value, by our most distinguished artists, which may be seen at the rooms.

The Engraving for 1846, "Sir Walter Raleigh parting with his wife on the morning of his execution," from Leutz's fine picture, is now engraving in line, of the large size of 19½ by 15¼ inches, by Burt.

The Committee hope to be able to publish during this year a Septennial Report, containing the transactions of the last seven years, with other interesting matter, illustrated with engravings, making a beautiful work of art. A large edition will be published, with a view to give one to every member, for this year—if not enough, however, they will be given as long as they last, to the members, in the order in which their subscriptions reach the Treasury.

Members out of New-York will receive their Engravings, Works of Art and Reports from the Honorary Secretaries in their vicinity, to whom they will be sent at the expense of the Institution. Members in New-York will receive theirs at the Art-Union Rooms.

Subscriptions and payments may be made to either of the Honorary Secretaries, whose names and residences are given below, or to R. F. FRASER, *Corresponding Secretary,* at the Rooms. Remittances by letter should be addressed to the Corresponding Secretary,—by drafts, when practicable, payable in New-York, to the order of GEORGE W. AUSTEN, Treasurer,—and as soon as the money reaches the Treasurer, certificates of membership will be sent to the persons making the remittance.

All letters on the business of the Institution must be addressed to "ROBERT F. FRASER, Corresponding Secretary, American Art-Union, 322 Broadway, New-York."

HONORARY SECRETARIES.

Albany, N. Y.............W. Sherman
Albany, N. Y.............H. Q. Hawley
Alexandria, D. C.............J. Eaches
Athens, Ga............A. Chase
Auburn, N. Y.............R. J. Wynkoop
Augusta, Ga............T. J. Parmelee
Alton, Ill............W. A Holton
Ann Arbor, Mich............G. Sedgwick
Baltimore, Md............R. Cary Long
Baltimore, Md............J. S. Waters
Batavia, N. Y.............J. A. Smith
Boston, Mass............J. H. Francis
Bridgeport, Conn............D. Morris
Brownville, N. Y.............E. Kirby
Burlington, Vt............J. H. Peck
Buffalo, N. Y............A. W. Wilgus
Canandaigua, N. Y....N. G. Chesebro
Catskill, N. Y............J. Van Orden
Charleston, S. C............S. Hart, Sen'r
Chicago, Ill............Mark Skinner
Chillicothe, O............W. M. Anderson
Cincinnati, O............J. G. Anthony
Clarksville, Tenn......W. S. McClure
Cleveland, O............O. Klemm
Columbus, O............J. Sullivant
Columbus, Ga............A. H. Cooper
Columbus, Miss............J. T. Simpson
Darien, Ga............S. Z. Collins
Dayton, O............J. D. Phillips
Detroit, Mich............W. Truesdail
Eatonton, Ga............J. M. Ashurst
Fall River, Mass.......W. H. A. Crary
Fredericksburg, Va............J. Minor
Galveston, Tex............Jonas Butler
Geneva, N. Y............J. M. Bradford
Georgetown, D. C.......G. C. Bomford
Hartford, Conn............W. N. Matson
Hudson, N. Y............Dr. E. Simpson
Hollidaysburg, Pa............W. Williams
Huntingdon, Pa.......A. W. Benedict
Jacksonville, Ill............J. Berdan
Jackson, Mich............E. H. Rice
Kalamazoo, Mich............E. Rice
Lee, Mass............William Taylor
Little Rock, Ark.....W. W. Stevenson
Lockport, N. Y............C. Evans
Lexington, Ky............J. S. Wilson
Logansport, Ind............J. S. Patterson
London, Eng............G. P. Putnam
Louisville, Ky.......W. A. Richardson
Lowell, Mass............D. Bixby
Macon, Ga............J. M. Boardman
Maysville, Ky............J. M. Duke
Memphis, Tenn............T. H. Allen
Meriden, Conn............Robert Linsley
Middletown, Conn .....E. W. N. Starr
Milledgeville, Ga............F. H. Sanford
Mobile, Ala............S. W. Allen
Montreal, Canada............J. Donegane
Monroe, Mich............D. A. Noble
Montgomery, Ala............C. Crommelin
Marshall, Mich............J. W. Gordon
Nantucket, Mass............S. H. Jenks
Nashville, Tenn............——Billings
Natchez, Miss............B. Butler
Newark, N. J............T. H. Stephens
Newbern, N. C............E. Graham
New Bedford, Mass....Thos. B. White
New Haven, Conn.......A. N. Skinner
New London, Conn....W. W. Kingsley
Newburg, N. Y............A. J. Downing
New Brunswick, N. J.....W. H. Leupp
New Orleans, La............S. C. Bell
Norfolk, Va............F. W. Southgate
Norwich, Conn............T. P. Norton
Petersburgh, Va............E. P. Gaines
Philadelphia, Pa........R. W. Desilver
Pittsburgh, Pa............M. B. Rhey
Pittsfield, Mass............O. S. Root
Portland, Me............T. A. Deblois
Portsmouth, N. H............T. Upham
Poughkeepsie, N. Y.......Wm. Wilson
Providence, R. I............T. F. Hoppin
Reading, Pa............J. L. Stichter
Richmond, Va............
Rochester, N. Y............D. M. Dewey
Rome, N. Y............E. Huntington
Rutland, Vt............F. W. Hopkins
Salem, Mass..........Pickering Dodge
Sandusky, O............Dr. E. S. Lane
Saratoga Springs, N. Y..O. L. Barbour
Savannah, Ga........W. A. Caruthers
Schenectady, N. Y............C. Vibbard
Sing Sing, N. Y............R. Havell
Springfield, Mass............H. Foot
Syracuse, N. Y............D. P. Phelps
St. Louis, Mo............E. H. Dix
Steubenville, O............A. L. Frazer
Tallahasse, Flo..........P. A. Hayward
Taunton, Mass.........C. J. H. Bassett
Troy, N. Y............T. Taylor
Toledo, O............D. Wadsworth
Utica, N. Y............J. W. Williams
Vicksburgh, Miss........T. A. Marshall
Washington, D. C.........T. P. Jones
Washington, N. C........T. A. Demill
Watertown, N. Y........J. C. Patridge
Williamstown, Mass.......H. L. Sabin
Worcester, Mass............C. Harris
Wheeling, Va............E. Dorsey
Zanesville, O............J. V. Cushing

Nesbitt, Stationer and Printer.

Fig. 12: American Art-Union broadside from 1846 showing a list of honorary secretaries to whom membership subscriptions and payments could be made.

Since I last wrote I have continued to do well, better than last year, although people complain much of hard times in these parts. I have been waiting for a boat, my business I finished 2 days ago here. The river is low but I Hope to get one some time this evening. . . . On the River I experienced the severest hurricane I ever felt in my life. The Boat I was on, half capsized. Shipped so much water, that it come very near washing me with some others in the River. I was completely drenched, took cold, and am now . . . unwell, have a fever on me, but hope when I get a boat and have more rest I may recover, if you should wish to answer thy direct to Chicago, Ills.[55]

In late 1845, when Solomons resigned his post, the AA-U managers decided to shift the burden of finding subscribers to the honorary secretaries based in each locale (Fig. 12). They also increased the organization's advertising by targeting national magazines and local newspapers.[56] AA-U publications continued to boast of the union's efforts to reach "every state in the Union, from the extreme north to the distant south, and from the Atlantic to the remote west, [each of which] contains choice specimens of American art, forming a nucleus for budding genius in every quarter."[57] The annual reports always listed the names of the honorary secretaries and the cities in which they lived. Moreover, the roster of distributed artworks included not only the artist's place of residence but also those of the prizewinners. Subscribers could see their names among a vast network of men and feel part of a larger community, and for the organization as a whole, that geographic reach was a point of pride.

In the West, the rivers played a key role in redrawing traditional lines of locale and region because they fostered the socioeconomic and geographic mobility of the types of men whom the AA-U sought as subscribers. In his economic history of antebellum Saint Louis, Jeffrey Adler emphasizes the fortuitous position of the city as a contact point for both the southern and western markets, particularly as its growth was fueled by "Yankee merchants and capitalists" from New York and Boston in particular.[58] These professional men traveled regularly for their business dealings, forming circuits between regional nodes such as Saint Louis, New Orleans, and commercial centers on the Ohio River such as Cincinnati and Louisville. Therefore, when the American Art-Union's national corresponding secretary Robert Fraser placed an advertisement in the *New Orleans Picayune* in 1846 soliciting subscribers, he gave not only the name of the honorary secretary for New Orleans (Samuel C. Bell) but also those for the whole Lower Mississippi valley up to Saint Louis, as well as others in Mississippi, Alabama, and Florida.[59]

The visibility of Bingham's work and the prominence of the AA-U (all told, it purchased twenty of Bingham's works, eleven of which depicted scenes taking place on the inland rivers or near their banks) gave him the opportunity to alter existing perceptions about the West, to shift from previous characterizations of the region as wild, wondrous, and unknown to more prosaic, everyday depictions of its people and places. To compete with the other types of western pictures, or at least to establish the viability of his particular perspective, Bingham still had to make his images compelling and convincing to the AA-U management and newspaper writers around the country. Featuring typical riparian settings such as wharfs, flatboats, and woodyards was key to this endeavor, as was his keen delineation of the men who populated those settings.

In describing an 1849 painting of a woodyard that Bingham submitted to the Cincinnati-based Western Art Union, one Cincinnati critic observed:

> *In this picture a broad stretch of the Missouri is seen, over which hangs a hazy atmosphere peculiar to it. In the foreground is a woodyard. Two men have discovered a boat in the distance, and are watching for the signal that wood is wanted; a third lounges on the bank with his feet hanging over the water, smoking his pipe. The accessories of the wood piles, axes, whisky jug, &c., go to make up a scene that cannot be mistaken by any one who has travelled on the Western Waters.*[60]

Bingham used a combination of environmental conditions, figures' postures and activities, and material details to enliven the scene and make it believable. He conveyed veracity by harnessing the familiar, enabling his work to stand out from other depictions of western places and people that were being made at the same time.

Though the painting cited above is now lost, one can imagine what it might have looked like by considering two others that also depict "woodhawks," men who sold wood to passing steamboats for fuel.[61] *Boatmen on the Missouri* (Pl. 4), on view in 1846 at the AA-U galleries, and *The Wood-Boat* (Pl. 28), purchased by the AA-U in 1851, each include diffusely lit riverscapes and a trio of men at center. In *Boatmen on the Missouri*, a departing steamboat—which may have just patronized the "wood boat"—can be seen in the distance. Two of the men have casually tossed their jackets onto the woodpile and gunwale of the boat. Rather than showing the men in the midst of loading wood on a steamboat, Bingham represents a quiet moment in which two of them pause to look directly at the viewer. Their expressions, however, remain inscrutable because so little action undergirds the scene.

Three men strike comfortably relaxed poses and look out from *The Wood-Boat*, seemingly even further removed from selling their wares, since their boat is moored on the riverbank rather than in the middle of the stream. A fourth man has cast his fishing line, indicating that the group will probably remain in place for some time. Bingham described this group as one that "the traveller daily sees upon the navigable waters of the west. The wood for sale is conveniently placed in a flat boat, while the hardy *choppers* await a purchase in some approaching steamer."[62] Yet the point of view is not that from an upper deck

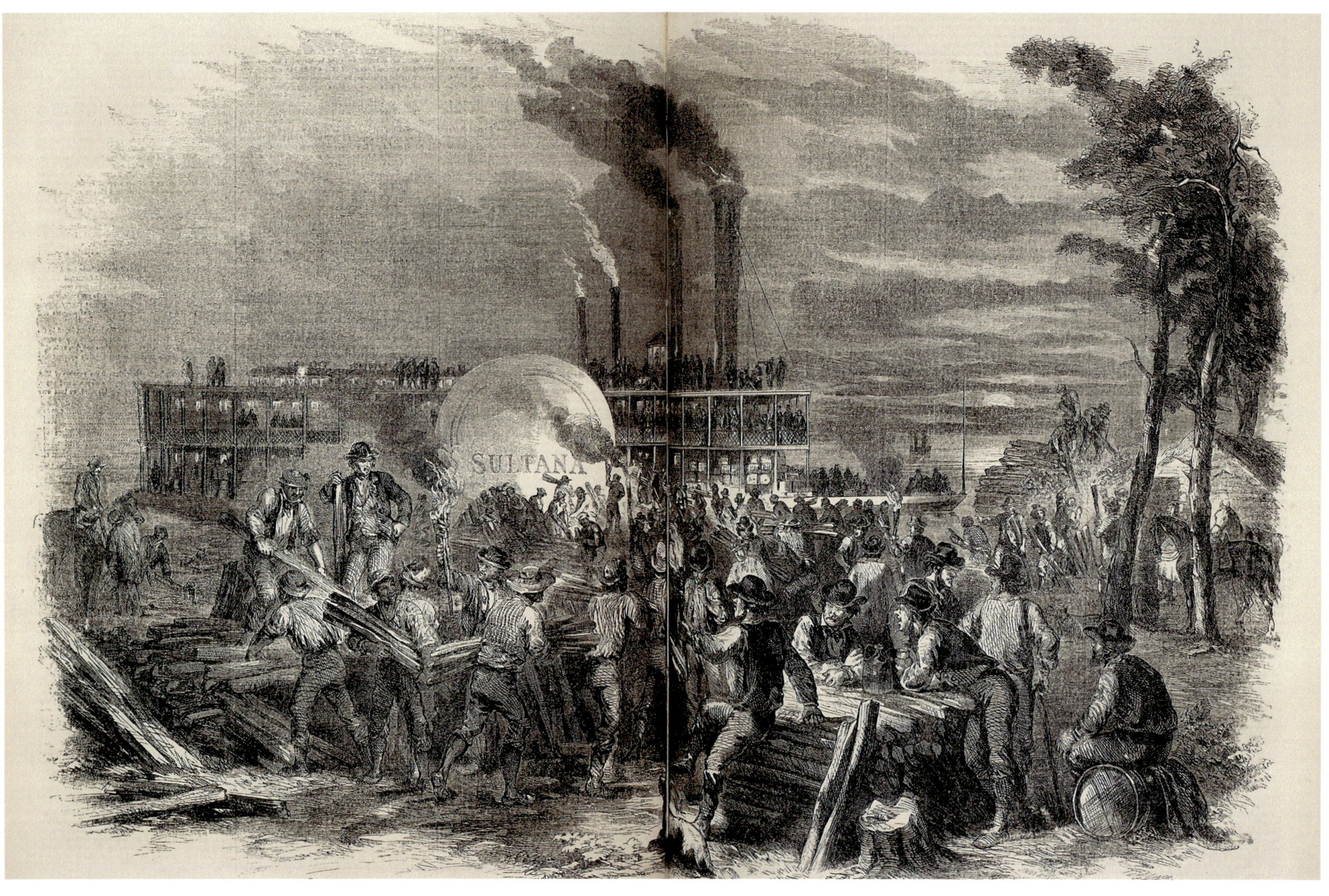

Fig. 13: *Wooding Up on the Mississippi*, in *Ballou's Pictorial Drawing Room Companion* 10, no. 23, 1856, 365, courtesy American Antiquarian Society

of a steamboat that most middle-class travelers would have had as they encountered the woodhawks.[63] Instead, the figures in *Boatmen on the Missouri* and *The Wood-Boat* are placed close to the picture plane, and viewers of the paintings are able to study their features, comportment, and clothing without becoming distracted by the frantic labor that "wooding up" often entailed, as evidenced by a later engraving in *Ballou's Pictorial Drawing Room Companion* (Fig. 13). The accompanying article describes "steam . . . rushing from the escape pipes, and the red light of fires and lanterns screaming athwart the volumed vapor, the lurid sky, the rushing waters, the impatient spectators, the busy hands, tramping round in a circle from shore to deck and back again."[64] By contrast, Bingham's scenes are nearly still, rendered in daylight rather than the more sensationally illuminated night. The figures have real presence, but the narrative of the scene remains fluid and open to interpretation. For a writer for a Saint Louis newspaper, it was precisely the abundance of small, ordinary details and the lack of drama in

The Wood-Boat that made Bingham's painting authentic and therefore special:

> *Here, again, the painter has combined, with the accuracy of scenery, boat, loading, &c., the distinctive peculiarity of dress, position, countenance, and expression of the men engaged in this important branch of commerce. The master, leisurely smoking his pipe, is a fac simile of men of that pursuit who are frequently met with.*[65]

Bingham makes the case for the authenticity of this scene by emphasizing its routine quality. As he noted, travelers through the area would see this daily. It is the repetitive and unremarkable character of the scene that makes it so convincing, but also so novel. He portrayed, in the words of one contemporary, "the simplest, most frequent and common occurrences on our rivers," resulting in "an entire new field of historic painting."[66]

Bingham's paintings stand in contrast with the earliest representations of the trans-Mississippi West that circulated widely in the United States. These resulted from federally funded expeditions such as the 1803 Corps of Discovery, better known as the Lewis and Clark Expedition; those led between 1805 and 1807 by Lieutenant Zebulon Pike, who was tasked with locating the source of the Mississippi River and exploring the edges of Spanish territory in the Southwest; and the journeys of Major Stephen H. Long, who led one of the first steamboat trips up the Missouri in 1819 with the artists Titian Ramsay Peale and Samuel Seymour. These excursions were to investigate lands that had previously been unknown to the U.S. government and most of its citizens, as well as to document and collect flora and fauna and encounter and locate native peoples. They sent back or collected artifacts and natural history specimens and produced primarily cartographic, ethnographic, botanical, and zoological images (Fig. 14).[67]

Artists who followed these early expeditions by traveling to the Upper Mississippi and Upper Missouri River valleys in the early 1830s, such as George Catlin and Karl Bodmer, focused on the West as an exotic place rife with possibility, but the trips required complex logistics and contact with Native Americans in order to traverse it.[68] Bingham displayed his awareness of other artists' regional representations as early as 1835, when he wrote to his future wife from Saint Louis that he had painted, for a patron to take to Louisville, landscapes depicting "bufaloe hunts of our western praris—they are thought by those who see them to be superior to the original paintings from which I coppied them."[69] He may well have been referring to contemporaneous works by Catlin or Peter Rindisbacher. These artists, both of whom had recently been working in Saint Louis, were known for painting buffalo hunts (Fig. 15). Rindisbacher's depictions of Native Americans as hunters and warriors that emphasized the West as a place for the sporting life were important for creating what Kathryn Hight has called an "iconography of adventure on the Plains."[70] Catlin, for his part, was greatly affected by traveling on the western rivers. For him, the Missouri was an especially wild place, and the change in the character of its waters from those

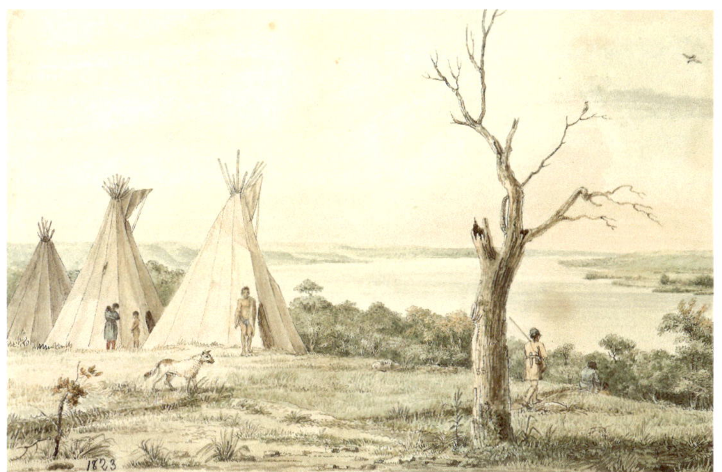

Fig. 14: Samuel Seymour (1775?–after 1823), *An American Indian Encampment on Big Stone Lake, Head of the Saint Peter River*, 1823, ink and watercolor on paper, 6½ × 9 in., The Dietrich American Foundation, photography by Will Brown

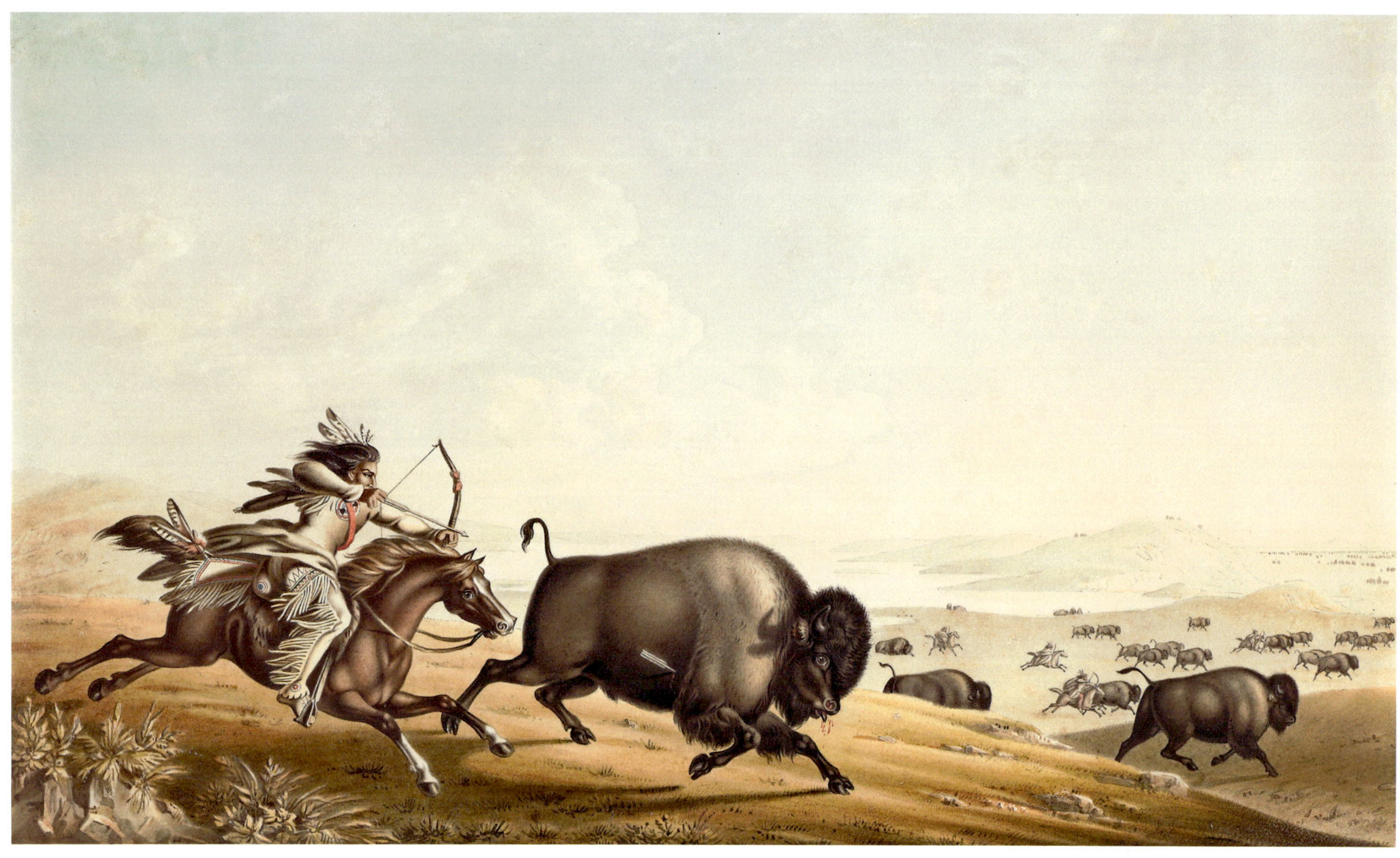

Fig. 15: Peter Rindisbacher (1806–1834), *Assiniboine Hunting on Horseback*, 1833, watercolor heightened with gum glaze over graphite on paper, 9¾ × 16⅛ in., Amon Carter Museum of American Art, Fort Worth, Texas, 1966.50

of the Mississippi signaled a departure from the known. He wrote in 1832: "There is a *terrour* in its waters which we sensibly feel the moment we enter it from the Mississippi. From the mouth of the Yellowstone to the mouth of the Missouri, it sweeps off in one unceasing current, and in the whole distance there is hardly a resting place."[71]

Catlin was particularly innovative in the way he brought the experience of being in the West to those in the East. To publicize and re-create his travels by steamboat and canoe on the Missouri and Mississippi rivers and by horseback along the Red River into Comanche and Wichita territory, he published letters from the field and exhibited paintings, objects he collected, and actual Native American people.[72] His words and images conveyed a feeling of movement to viewers of his Indian Gallery and readers of his published accounts. He describes setting up his easel on the deck of the steamboat to paint and, sometimes, just to look:

> *the upper part of the river, was, to my eye, like fairy-land; and during our transit through that part of the voyage,*

I was most of the time riveted to the deck of the boat, indulging my eyes in the boundless and tireless pleasure of roaming over the thousand hills, and bluffs, and dales, and ravines.[73]

The cadence of his list of landscape elements is similar to the visual rhythms he creates in his paintings. For instance, in *River Bluffs, 1320 Miles above St. Louis* (Fig. 16), the viewer can see a vista that would have been impossible to view from the river itself. One follows a continuous line from the left foreground that undulates across the gently rolling hills until it reaches the horizon. In the central third of the canvas, the Missouri River offers an additional channel for the viewer's gaze, as the long, horizontal strokes of pale blue color are set apart from parentheses of green plains. The momentum created by these receding lines prevents the eye from scrutinizing a Native American man—the only figure in the composition—and, instead, propels us in the ever-westward direction of Catlin's gaze.

In contrast to the unending and progressive impetus delivered by Catlin's paintings, Bingham represents unhurried, deliberate, and even disrupted motion. In *Raftsmen Playing Cards* (Pl. 26), six men drift downriver on a flatboat. At center, two cardplayers sit facing each other on a bench while two others lean in to watch the game. On the left side of the stern, one man successfully navigates the boat between a small sandbar at left and a snag on the right by pressing his weight on a steering pole. A barefoot man smoking a pipe sits by himself and reaches into the opening of his shirt; he neither pays attention to the card game nor looks out for potential hazards. As in *Boatmen on the Missouri* (Pl. 4) and *The Wood-Boat* (Pl. 28), Bingham de-emphasizes the exertions of labor. In *Raftsmen Playing Cards*, he does not even allude to the reason they are traveling the river: no cargo is in sight, as it is in *The Jolly Flatboatmen* (Pl. 5). Here, a group of men enjoy a moment of leisure during their journey downriver. Their craft floats along a serene and luminous passageway, burdened with the cargo—animal skins, barrels of tobacco or whiskey, a live turkey—that they are transporting to market, blissfully undeterred by natural or man-made obstructions to their route.

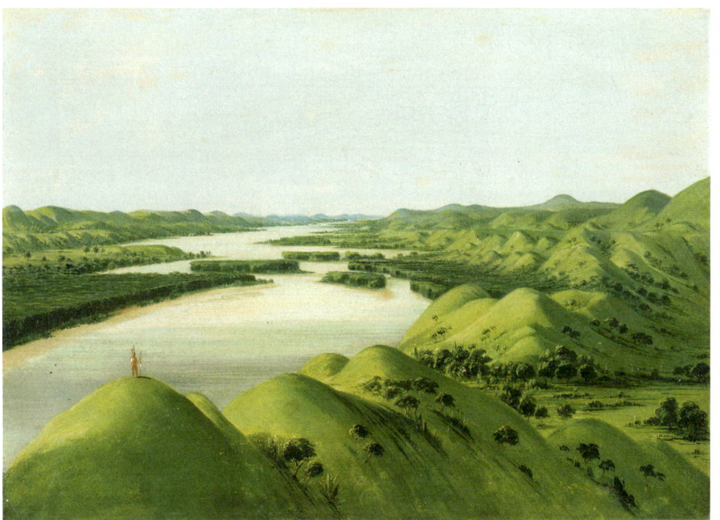

Fig. 16: George Catlin (1796–1872), *River Bluffs, 1320 Miles above St. Louis*, 1832, oil on canvas, 11¼ × 14½ in., Smithsonian American Art Museum, Gift of Mrs. Joseph Harrison, Jr., image courtesy Smithsonian American Art Museum, Washington, D.C., Art Resource, NY

Lighter Relieving a Steamboat Aground (Pl. 6), shown at the 1847 American Art-Union exhibition along with *The Jolly Flatboatmen* and *Raftsmen Playing Cards*, depicts transit interrupted. A small lighter has come to the aid of a steamboat that has run aground. Seven men have squeezed onto a crowded flatboat amid the boxes, barrels, and sacks of grain that they have unloaded from the defunct steamboat. At center, a man seems to command the attention of at least four others, but his back is turned to the viewer, obstructing not only a complete view of the boat but also what the group is doing. In this scene, the pole that the man leans on is not being used to steer a moving boat; it merely supports his weight as he tells a story.

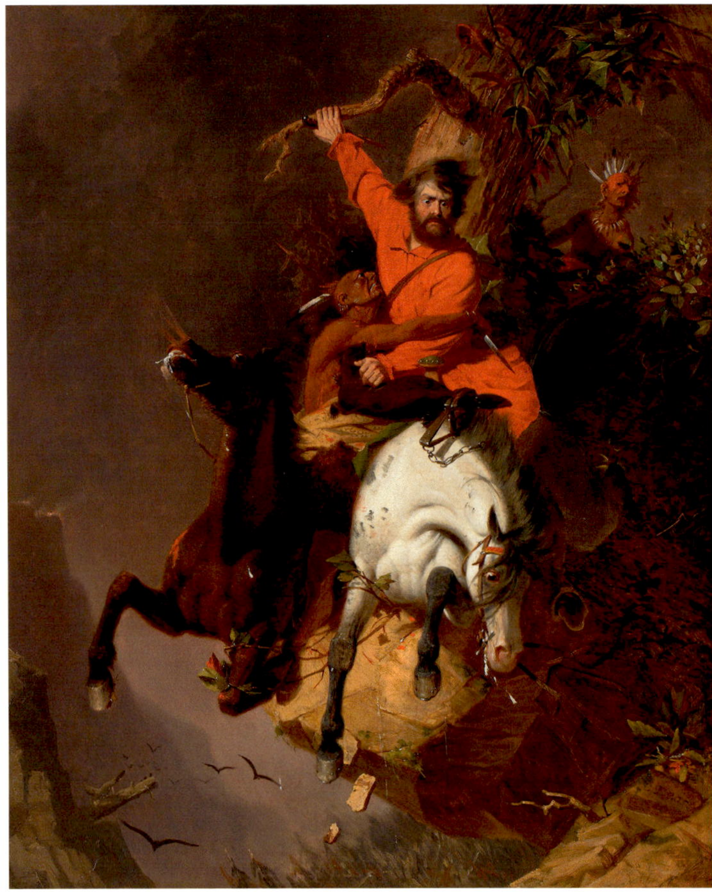

Fig. 17: Charles Deas (1818–1867), *The Death Struggle*, 1845, oil on canvas, 30 × 25 in., © The Shelburne Museum, Shelburne, Vermont

Watching the Cargo (Pl. 27), sold by Bingham to the American Art-Union in 1849, also depicts a state of travel interrupted. The silhouette of a steamboat marooned on a sandbar gives context to the large pile of cargo that has been offloaded and covered with rumpled tarps. The action of the man blowing at the base of a pile of wood to get a fire going insinuates that it will be a long time before the journey will resume.

Some visitors to the annual exhibition of the AA-U or their subscribers might have drawn on firsthand experience to relate to the stop-and-start motion that Bingham's work represents. The paintings recall the travails of the AA-U traveling agent as he navigated the Mississippi valley and, indeed, that of many other easterners who made steamboat journeys in the West. Frederick Gale, a lawyer from Massachusetts who practiced in Saint Louis between 1838 and 1843, wrote to his sister about "the dangers and uncertainties attendant upon travelling upon a Western Steamboat." Following delays in departure that he blamed on the captain's whims, he reports that the boat hit a snag only to have the steamer that came to rescue the passengers strike the same obstruction:

> *Do you know what a* snag *is? I presume not. It is an old tree with broken, projecting limbs wh. lies under water, and wh. is concealed, & when struck by the bottom of the boat, tears a hole. . . . The damage to our boat is considerable. . . . Prospects of staying here* several days *seemed pretty good!*[74]

Previous art historical studies have considered Bingham's river men in light of other western stereotypes exhibited at the American Art-Union at the same time. The work of Charles Deas and Alfred Jacob Miller, which features trappers, hunters, and fur traders, emphasizes horsemanship, adventure, and encounter and conflict with Native Americans as central to the western experience.[75] In *The Death Struggle* (Fig. 17), Deas conveys the danger of the frontier by showing the limbs of trapper, Indian, and beast intertwined.[76] The painting defines western masculinity as a life-and-death proposition in which Anglo-American civilization triumphs over the savagery of a Native American past.

Elizabeth Johns has argued that these "emblems of masculinity and vigor" held great appeal for viewers in New York, in part because western men seemed fundamentally different in that they were not subject to the same strictures of polite society.[77] In contrast, Bingham emphasized ideals the two regions may have held in common by neutralizing the threat of the frontier and focusing on the mundane. As Johns and

Angela Miller have pointed out, the river network was one way that the distance could be bridged because the space was not completely foreign to easterners' experiences or business interests.[78] Bingham's different tack—in not offering up familiar, unambiguous regional stereotypes—required viewers to adjust their expectations about the West.

Bingham's river paintings under discussion represent life in a broader region known collectively as the Mississippi River valley. The Mississippi forms the backbone of an expansive river network that includes numerous tributaries, and nineteenth-century commentators took national pride in the area's geographic breadth, describing it as a "valley, over which two thirds of the continent of Europe might be spread out, and hardly suffice to cover it."[79] Yet instead of trying to represent its entirety, Bingham's work focuses on an area defined by the burgeoning metropolis of Saint Louis that included the segment of the Missouri River that flows through the state of Missouri, the Middle Mississippi area between its confluences with the Missouri and the Ohio, and the portion of the Ohio that flows westward between Cincinnati and the Mississippi. The watery boundaries around Saint Louis took on the identity of a commercial space, as opposed to the Upper Mississippi or Upper Missouri rivers, images of which were typically populated by Native American peoples or by representations of the slave-supported plantation culture of the Lower Mississippi.[80]

Offering a different viewpoint in the same years that Bingham was making a name for himself, moving panoramas toured the country, attracting viewers in the thousands. While some promised views of the Holy Land, the Nile or Rhine rivers, or California and the far western United States, approximately seven featured the Mississippi River, the most popular subject of them all.[81] Painters such as John Banvard, John Egan, Henry Lewis, and Samuel Stockwell, who were better known for their work painting theatrical scenes than for creating fine-art easel paintings, crafted the gigantic scrolling paintings that were advanced by two upright rollers (Fig. 18). Audience members,

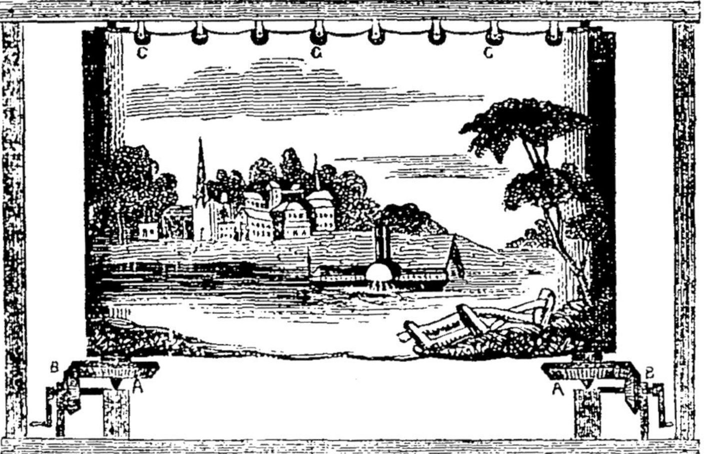

Fig. 18: The apparatus for John Banvard's *Panorama of the Mississippi* used two upright rollers to advance the scene. From *Scientific American* 4, issue 13, 1848

who typically paid a quarter to attend the two-hour show, sat in a darkened room while operators unrolled the scenic painting before their eyes. The shows were often multisensory, including music or special effects to simulate changes in weather, time of day, or environment.

Competition among panorama operators was fierce, particularly over whose painting portrayed the river with the greatest geographic breadth and fidelity. Some operators boasted that their works were three or four miles long, alluding to the wondrous length of the Mississippi River itself. Despite their claims of comprehensiveness, however, unremarkable portions of scenery were edited out in favor of conveying endlessly interesting views to a passive audience.[82] Supporting the claims of truthfulness were newspaper advertisements, reviews, and pamphlets that were sold to accompany the shows, which included testimonials from river captains and government officials who knew the region firsthand asserting the supremacy of one panorama over another. Moving panoramas relied on the same kind of hyperbolic rhetoric Catlin used and similarly conveyed the experience of a spectacular, ever-advancing

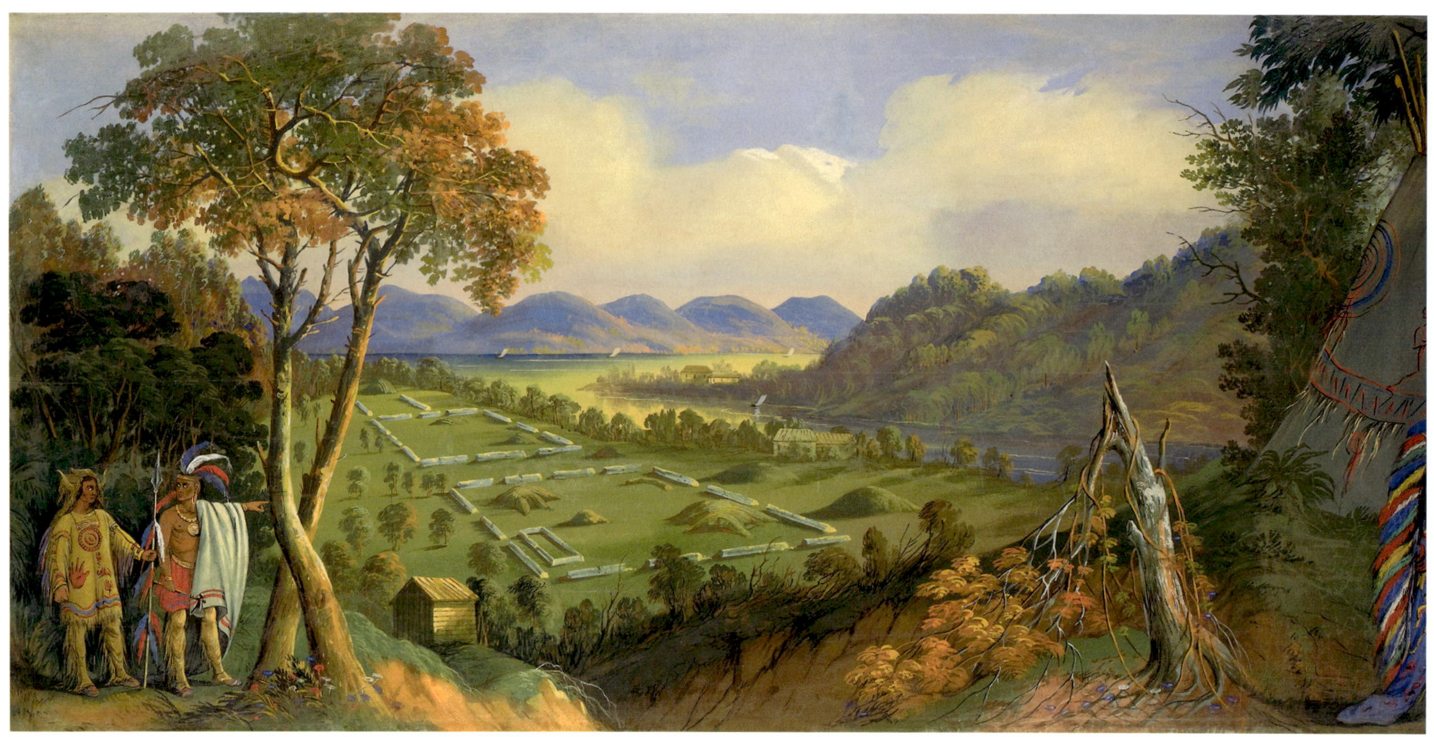

Fig. 19: John J. Egan (active mid-nineteenth century), "Marietta Ancient Fortification; A Grand View of Their Walls, Bastions, Ramparts, and Fossa, with the Relics Therein Found," scene 1 from *Panorama of the Monumental Grandeur of the Mississippi Valley*, ca. 1850, distemper on cotton muslin, H: 90 in., Saint Louis Art Museum, Eliza McMillan Trust, 34:1953

progression through the river valley rather than the sustained and everyday encounters with local people that Bingham's work provided.

Moving panoramas were typical of most representations of the river in that they were concerned with identifying specific locales so that a narrator could recount elements of historical, picturesque, or economic importance, as in a scene from Egan's panorama depicting Native American earthworks at Marietta, Ohio (Fig. 19). Panorama pamphlets read like a steamboat itinerary, and even Catlin's landscape paintings of the Missouri River include the number of miles between its subject and Saint Louis. In Bingham's case, painting titles rarely locate the scenes in a particular locale. He sometimes names the river, as in *Fur Traders Descending the Missouri* (Pl. 3), *Raftsmen on the Ohio* of 1849 (now lost), or *Fishing on the Mississippi* (Pl. 43), but, more often than not, the viewer is left to assign a locale to the settings, which is often what commentators did. Though Bingham does not include locating information for *Raftsmen Playing Cards* (Pl. 26) or *Lighter Relieving a Steamboat Aground* (Pl. 6), the *Saint Louis Weekly Reveille* placed them on the Upper Mississippi and the Missouri, respectively.[83]

This ambiguity contrasts with the specificity of numerous urban views that sometimes circulated in illustrated magazines and as lithographs or engravings, such as the lithograph of Saint Louis by John Caspar Wild that identifies not only the subject of the view but also the place from which it was taken (Fig. 20). They depict aspiring river towns and cities and either showcase the sweep of the river from a bird's-eye vantage

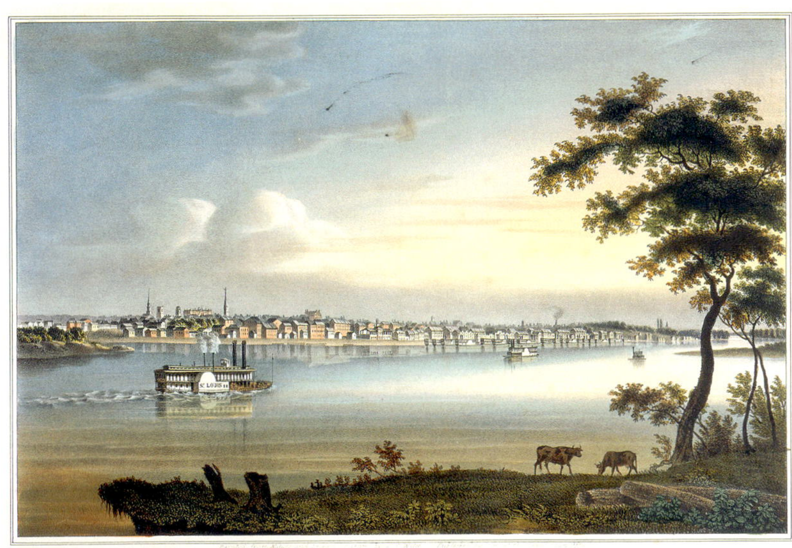

Fig. 20: John Caspar Wild (1804–1846), *South East View of St. Louis from the Illinois Shore*, ca. 1840, lithograph, Missouri History Museum, Saint Louis, Missouri

point or attempt a panoramic rendering of a city's shoreline according to what Michael Shapiro has called "a prevailing topographical orientation."[84] Bingham's paintings hint at but never display the broader spatial reach of the river. In *Boatmen on the Missouri* (Pl. 4), the distant steamboat rounds a bend, but the perspective from which Bingham paints the work puts the men at the center, denying more than a glimpse of the distant horizon. In *Fur Traders Descending the Missouri*, a small wooded island in the center of the painting and the figures themselves obscure any view of the expansive river beyond. To the left of the island, a bright light erodes any hint of a shoreline that might have offered a sense of the river's shape, and the horizon similarly disappears into the veiled boundary between land and water. In *The Jolly Flatboatmen* (Pl. 5) and *Lighter Relieving a Steamboat Aground*, the flatboat's width and the arrangement of boatmen block any view of the river beyond.

Instead of portraying a river of varied and notable landmarks, Bingham leaves it remarkably undifferentiated. In the majority of cases, Bingham repeats a small repertoire of landscape elements from one painting to the next, perhaps varying the heights of trees or the proximity of rounded, rocky bluffs in one or another. As Barry and Heugh show in their essay in this volume, Bingham summarily applied landscape backgrounds only after he had established—with painstaking attention—the foreground details of his paintings. He never represents an identifiable location, and even in the two instances when he does represent an urban port, he omits recognizable buildings such as the domed courthouse in Saint Louis, which Wild would have made sure to include.[85] The generalized nature of the paintings' settings allowed viewers to appreciate Bingham's work no matter where the paintings were seen, whether in Cincinnati at the Western Art Union, in Saint Louis at Wooll's Picture Store, or in the homes of the American Art-Union subscribers who were awarded his pictures.

One of the few works in Bingham's oeuvre to allude to specific racial and cultural dimensions of life along the Missouri River is *Fur Traders Descending the Missouri*. A gray-bearded fur trader paddles a canoe laden with goods and two passengers: his son and a black bear cub, tied to the boat with a leash around its neck. In their essay in these pages, Kornhauser and

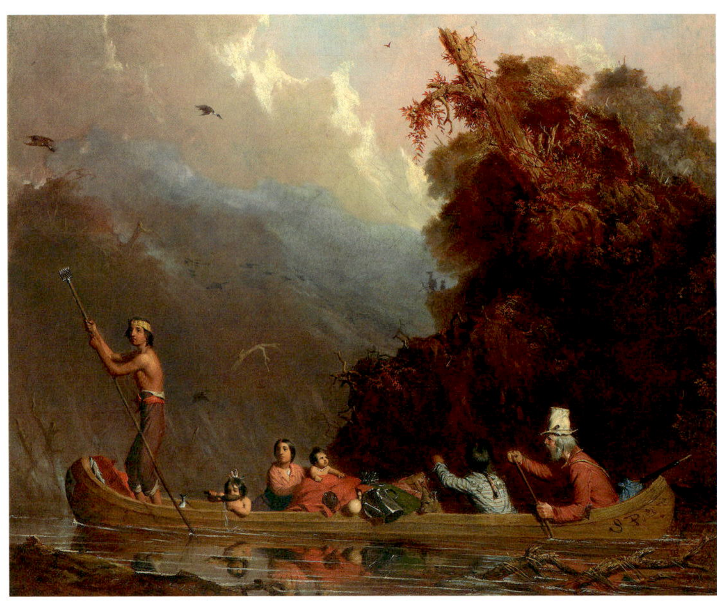

Fig. 21: Charles Deas (1818–1867), *The Voyageurs*, 1845, oil on canvas, 31½ × 36½ in., courtesy of American Museum of Western Art—The Anschutz Collection

Mahon discuss the substantial compositional changes that Bingham made to the painting, but records indicate that the title was also altered. When Bingham sold the painting to the American Art-Union in 1845, it bore the title *French Trader & Half Breed Son*. It is not known when the title was stripped of its racial and ethnic designations, but it happened sometime before the painting was awarded to Robert S. Bunker of Mobile, Alabama, at the annual prize distribution held on January 30, 1846. The new title no longer referenced the historical practices of accommodation and cooperation that took place between French and Native American peoples in the Upper Missouri River valley. Instead, it alluded to the trappers and other generic frontier stereotypes found in western imagery.

Fur Traders Descending the Missouri (Pl. 3) nonetheless still differs from *The Voyageurs* (Fig. 21), a painting by Charles Deas produced the previous year.[86] Bingham presents a simplified composition of figures arranged along a horizontal plane. He decreases the tension inherent in Deas's representation of a large family consisting of a French fur trader, his Indian wife, and their four children facing uncertain danger in an inhospitable wilderness. Whereas in Deas's canvas, the landscape threatens to engulf the dugout and the figures look vigilantly in various directions, in Bingham's, the few snags that peek out of the water's glassine surface do not obstruct the canoe's path.

Another painting that Bingham submitted to the AA-U in 1845 further demonstrates how he favored the tame over theatricality. Most recent scholarship has emphasized the binary relationship between *The Concealed Enemy* (Pl. 2) and *Fur Traders Descending the Missouri*, asserting that the artist might have intended them to be a pair illustrating different periods in a progressive history of Missouri.[87] *The Concealed Enemy* evokes the early decades of the nineteenth century, when white settlers increasingly encroached on lands previously designated by treaties as belonging to Shawnee, Delaware, and Osage Indians, while *Fur Traders Descending the Missouri* refers to previously accepted practices of cultural integration between Native Americans and whites, before "inclusion gave way to exclusion" around the time of Missouri statehood in 1821.[88] Yet it is possible that these paintings are connected in other ways. The triangular star pattern decorating the leggings of the Indian, who has been called an "Osage warrior" because of his hairstyle, is very similar to the pattern painted on the robe on which the younger fur trader is leaning.[89] Perhaps Bingham merely used the same generalized geometric pattern for both, but the parallel could allude to kin or tribal linkage between the "half-breed" and the warrior. The affinity could also indicate that the fur traders and the warrior had encountered one another through trade. In either of the latter two cases, the threat of this "concealed enemy" is rendered less acute.

A possible precedent for *The Concealed Enemy* is John Casper Wild's frontispiece for *The Valley of the Mississippi Illustrated* (see Fig. 51).[90] Here, the man draws back his arrow, clearly aiming at settlers chopping down a tree near their log cabin. Bingham separates the Plains Indian man from the fur traders whom some have interpreted as potential targets. He lies close to the ground, holding a gun but not aiming it. Furthermore, technical studies reveal that Bingham painted over another Native American figure, a man who was looking out toward the viewer. Thus, rather than inciting fear or sympathy for any potential victims, the viewer is encouraged to admire the sole figure's musculature and the golden light emanating from the valley below. Though the presence of Native Americans in Bingham's river paintings helped to position his works as western, his tendency to de-emphasize conflict with Indians promoted the idea that the Missouri River was a place of civilization, safe for settlement by white Americans.

The river in Bingham's paintings is a racially white world, even though the state's black population markedly increased from 1830 to 1860.[91] He refrains from depicting black people (enslaved or free) in the river paintings of the 1840s and early 1850s. In so doing, he does not address the explicitly political North–South axis on which the boatmen travel and, in particular, the contentious on-the-ground conditions one would have experienced in Missouri or on the inland rivers. Enslaved black people were often transported via steamboat to cotton and sugar plantations downriver as part of the domestic slave trade. According to an account from the mid-1830s, slaves were sometimes bought in Tennessee but most frequently came from Kentucky and Virginia, the same states from which many whites in the Missouri River valley had emigrated.[92] Black men may have been present on steamboats as laborers, either because they belonged to the captain or steamboat company or because they were leased by their owners to work on the boat.[93] Bingham, however, never depicts a steamboat up close, representing only the wood boats that supported their journeys, the laborers who aided them when they broke down, and small-scale commercial transport facilitated by flatboats with crews of fewer than eight.

Flatboat crews tended to be men of European ethnicity. In his study of nineteenth-century boatmen, Michael Allen notes that French Canadians, like the older man in *Fur Traders Descending the Missouri*, were commonly employed in river transport before the steamboat age began in the 1810s and 1820s. Later wharf records indicate that from the 1830s to 1861, most boatmen were "American-born, and of English, Scotch, Scotch-Irish, Irish, or German ancestry," and Irish and German surnames appeared frequently during the 1840s and 1850s.[94] Yet the faces of the white men in Bingham's work do not bear the stereotypical traits of any particular nationality. They do not have exaggerated physiognomic features, their skin is ruddy and tanned ostensibly from working outside (and thus not necessarily attributed to ethnic background), their hair is usually colored with a limited palette ranging from gray to black or brown, and they usually are clean-shaven or sport light stubble. They do not wear the buckskin suits that Leonidas Wetmore and George Catlin wore in the 1830s to proclaim their association with the West and their prerogative to appropriate Native American customs. Bingham's flatboatmen wear loose-fitting cotton shirts and trousers that mark them as farmers or working class. Their clothes allow them to move freely as their labor required but also suits their casual comportment.

Bingham's boatmen recline with hands folded behind their heads, sit atop barrels and woodpiles, and often bend their knees to prop their feet on the various wooden surfaces of the boat. The same outward characteristics recur so often from painting to painting that critics remarked that there must have been some kind of family relationship, or the artist was accused of "showing such want of earnestness in the repetitions of the same faces that they are hardly entitled to rank."[95] The homogeneity in Bingham's canvases observed by the critic is due in part to the artist's working method. As Barry and Heugh's and Kornhauser and Mahon's essays show, the more than one hundred extant drawings Bingham made between 1845 and 1857 were crucial in the making of his paintings. However, it seems that he did not go to the woodyards and docks of the Missouri or Mississippi to draw from life but instead posed a small number of men of his acquaintance according to the types of figures he imagined for his paintings. The early Bingham scholar Fern Rusk published an account by one of Bingham's models, Oscar F. Potter, who described "dressing according to directions and standing in one position without moving for half an hour at a time."[96]

The drawings recall his early portrait work: Bingham focuses on faces and bodies rather than assigning them a particular occupational identity. Though it is clear from the figures' attire and comportment that they are of the working class, flatboating was a temporary station for some men, a rite of passage for merchants and farmers with higher ambitions.[97] In Bingham's compositions, their straightforward gazes and affiliation with river trade connect them in some ways with the artist's depictions of entrepreneurial, upwardly mobile westerners.

A hint of landscape setting sometimes appears in his drawings, as in *Young woodboatman* (Pl. 41), which depicts a figure seated on a bench resting his chin in his hands. Traces of watercolor behind his right shoulder suggest the ephemeral quality of light reflecting off the surface of water. Yet in most cases, like the drawing *Boatman* (Pl. 17), one of a number of drawings that depict a grizzled man sitting on the ground with his legs bent and smoking a pipe, the backdrop is left blank; the man could be anywhere. The ambiguity of Bingham's drawn figures allowed him the flexibility to put them into different contexts and, in some cases, reuse them in other paintings.

Despite the posed nature of Bingham's figures, the American Art-Union commented on the animated spirit of his boatmen: "His figures have some *vitality* about them. They look out of their eyes. They stand upon their legs. They are shrewd or merry or grave or quizzical. They are not mere empty ghosts of figures—mere pictures of jackets, and trouser, with masks attached to them."[98] The *Bulletin of the American Art-Union*, distributed to all of the organization's subscribers, invited readers to see both the artist and his work firsthand: "Mr. Bingham is at present in the city of New York and intends to remain until the autumn. His studio is at No. 115½ Grand-street, where an inspection of his portfolio of sketches will greatly gratify those amateurs who may call upon him."[99] The drawings allowed Bingham to bring a piece of the West to the East, and the fidelity of his paintings to the drawings bolstered the notion that he actually witnessed the scenarios he represented. The drawings—especially those that portray men in casual, mundane poses such as bending over to watch a card game (Pl. 34), drinking from a jug (Pl. 20), or simply reclining (Pl. 14)—were integral to his construction of the everyday and to promoting himself as a western artist.

Popular texts depicting the western frontier and rivers—such as those that appeared in *Davy Crockett's Almanac*, Catlin's publications, and the widely quoted memoirs of the pioneer missionary and writer Timothy Flint—used mostly first-person narration.[100] Bingham's paintings typically lack visible brushstrokes, painted flourish or facture, or any other element that might indicate the presence of the artist. Even in *Watching the Cargo* (Pl. 27), in which roughly hewn logs are painted with a sheen and impasto, the technique communicates the physical, substantive quality of the wood as it contrasts with the thinly painted and ethereal sky. Therefore, when Bingham applies a tangible sense of paint to canvas, it is to reinforce the material reality of the scene instead of to highlight the painter's skill. Bingham plays down his interventions in the composition, increasing the sense that his paintings were objective slices of river life.

Writers believed that the river environment—"its incidents and obstacles—its wild and beautiful scenery—its banks of rocks, or its snags, sawyers and sand bars"—was a catalyst that made the boatmen's essential traits visible.[101] Place mattered for critics in Saint Louis, insofar as Bingham was a westerner himself who had the insight and observational skill to capture the "singular race" of boatmen, among whom could be found "often in the same crew . . . all the varieties of human character, from the amiable and the intelligent to the stern and reckless man."[102] Seeing the figures in the painting up close allowed the viewer to discern something in the men that one would not normally notice because of the very banality of the moment. By contrast, one New York–based journal accused the objects and figures in *Raftsmen Playing Cards* (Pl. 26) of suffering from "the same want of handling . . . [likely] produced by going over the colors when wet with a 'softener,' in order to avoid hardness." The author continued, asserting that he would "rather see the figures as hard as statues than see light, shade, color, and texture swept thus into a mass of soft confusion."[103] Even though Bingham was at the peak of his exposure on the national art scene, there was no consensus on his work. Still, the paintings and drawings that Bingham made between 1845 and 1850 established his trademark style, distinguishing his work whether it was seen in Missouri or New York. At the same time, though he was praised as a "close observer of human nature,"[104] Bingham's people and places nonetheless retained a lack of particularity that allowed viewers to assign to them their own interpretations and meaning.

Bingham's river paintings share with those of other mid-nineteenth-century artists their portrayal of the West as a particularly masculine place, in which white women appear only as Indian captives or settlers' wives. *Landscape: Rural Scenery* (Pl. 1), Bingham's only domestic scene set near a river, shows a small family washing clothes in a creek or pond.[105] The woman has rolled her sleeves above the elbows and plunges her arms into a large basin of laundry while tending to a golden-haired child. On the table behind her are some linens and shirts. The third figure could be the man of the house or an older child, resulting in an image either of a nuclear family or one in which the father is absent. A warm light illuminates a fork in the path: the right side leads to a modest home in the middle ground, while the curving path on the left continues toward the distant horizon and what is likely a river. The male figure is in line with this part of the trail, perhaps indicating that the head of household makes his living there. The woman, however, is paired with the cottage that is directly in line with her body, so that her head, square shoulders, and hips mirror the shape of the house.

Though an increasing number of women traveled on the inland rivers, it was mostly via steamboat. During the journey, women's virtue was subject to the same monitoring it received on land. Ann Archbold, a former missionary who traveled by steamboat on the Ohio, Mississippi, and Missouri rivers as well as overland through Iowa, Illinois, and Indiana, felt compelled to publish *A Book for the Married and Single, the Grave and the Gay* when she returned to Ohio in 1850. She intended it especially for "the entertainment of steamboat passengers" after seeing religious books being shunned in favor of "the veriest trash of some emissary of darkness."[106] Archbold recorded her impressions of the landscape—"O! how I rejoiced to view [the Mississippi River], like a blue streak in the distance"—and its people—"passengers of all descriptions and grades, both saint and sinister, minister and gambler; white, yellow and black men, and last, but not least, a red man."[107] In one instance, the low water level of the Missouri spurred her to liken steamboat travel to the journey of life: "But we were voyagers in another, and more emphatical sense, with exceedingly frail barks; subject to destruction, any and every moment, going at a rapid rate, night and day . . . we were making constant advances toward our eternal port."[108] In what was essentially a travel narrative and memoir, Archbold offered her own pious behavior as a model for others.

Like the morality of women, the comportment of boatmen was of particular interest during the antebellum period, and in highlighting the latter as subject matter, Bingham had to

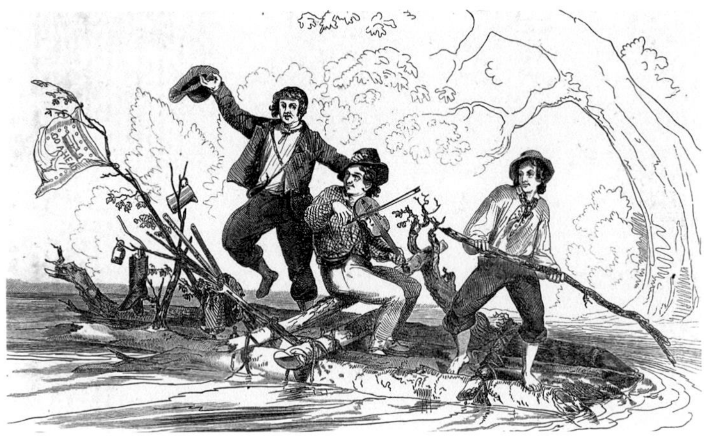

Fig. 22: J. G. Gordon (dates unknown), *Homeward Bound—Life in the West*, in *The Family Magazine*, 1840

contend with a range of cultural associations. Throughout the nineteenth century, the popular assessment of the boatman's status in society fluctuated. On the one hand, he was identified with youthfulness, freedom, and a pastoral ideal, as evidenced in this submission of "Original Rural Poetry" that appeared in a Doylestown, Pennsylvania, newspaper in 1805:

The jolly boatman down the ebbing stream,
By the clear moonlight, plying on his way,
With prosp'rous fortune to inspire the theme,
Sings a sweet farewell to the parting day.

His rustic music measures even time,
As in the chrystal wave he clips his oar,
And echo pleas'd returns the tuneful chim,
Mixt with soft murmurs from the rocky shore.[109]

In the poem, the boatman embodies the rustic and picturesque qualities of rural life. He is a buoyant, mobile figure whose movement is in harmony with the natural world, and the temporal aspect of his music is aligned with his passage through this realm on the river.

A story in the *Family Magazine* (1840) speaks to other lighthearted associations of boatmen and their exploits, seeing them as youngsters engaged in rites of passage. Three youths set out for adventures in the Wisconsin Territory, building a crude raft of four logs on which to float down the Kickapoo River home to Platteville, in present-day Wisconsin. After running out of food, "they tried the good effects of the fiddle," which distracted them from their troubles. An accompanying illustration by J. G. Gordon, *Homeward Bound—Life in the West*, depicts them at a blithesome moment on their ramshackle craft, flying a flag bearing Davy Crockett's motto, "Go Ahead" (Fig. 22). One of the barefoot explorers steers with a twisted branch, another plays the fiddle, while the third dances on one foot, waving his hat in the air. All is well, until they hit a snag in the river that upends their raft and causes them to lose their shoes. One of the resourceful boys makes moccasins from his fiddle case, leading the narrator to reason, "Hereafter, let no persons go to explore a new country without a fiddle, seeing the many useful purposes to which it may be applied." In the end, all is well, "caus[ing] a great deal of mirth in Platteville, and none seem to enjoy the laugh more than themselves."[110]

When Bingham turned his attention to the subject in earnest after 1845, the boatman's persona was also linked with popular entertainment and unrefined humor. Along with "Down the River" and "Jolly Raftsmen's Life for Me," "De Boatman's Dance" was among the songs most commonly performed by blackface minstrels throughout the decade. Written by Dan Emmett in 1843, it tells the story of a carousing crew, the chorus repeating: "De boatmen dance, de boatmen sing, / De boatmen up to eb'ry ting."[111] The lyrics originally referred to the Ohio River, but according to the historian Robert C. Toll, "black-faced riverboatmen sang, danced, and fought their way up and down rivers as far apart as the Susquehanna and the Mississippi," despite the fact that during this period western boatmen were typically not African-American.[112] A sheet music cover (Fig. 23) depicts various comical vignettes framed by snakes and catfish, corresponding to different performances by the "Ethiopian Quadrilles." The three central roundels show boatmen characters dancing and fighting with an alligator, activities often related to early nineteenth-century flatboatmen. The figure at top center throws his hands in the air and dances on one foot much like the carefree dancer in Bingham's *The Jolly Flatboatmen* (Pl. 5).

Minstrel songs, skits, and characters also carried regional associations and were appropriated by specific locales asserting civic pride and their link with river commerce. For instance, at an 1847 celebration of the founding of Saint Louis, white male attendees participated in a rousing sing-along of "Dance, Boatman, Dance."[113] Bingham had to tread carefully between these opposing readings. He did not always do so successfully, as evidenced by the eastern critic who called *The Jolly Flatboatmen* "a vulgar subject, vulgarly treated."[114]

Whereas the *Family Magazine* illustration emphasizes the youthfulness of the boys, Bingham's *The Jolly Flatboatmen* articulates a diversity of ages. The fresh-faced musicians, dancer, and spectators probably served as common hands, roles typically filled by unattached young men, relatives of the captain, or unemployed men who hung around the docks of Louisville, Saint Louis, or Cincinnati.[115] Two men observe the amusements of the crew without participating. However, the elder, perhaps the captain or owner of the boat, keeps a steady hand on the rudder; the portly middle-aged man is likely second pilot or steersman. The presence of these more experienced and serious boatmen undermined the idea that flatboating was a young man's occupation and a rite of passage. In later paintings such as *Watching the Cargo* (Pl. 27) and *The Wood-Boat* (Pl. 28), which feature a small number of figures—each having at least one older man with gray hair, a middle-aged man, and a young man—the men's roles are not quite clear. This ambiguity may have opened Bingham up to criticism by those sensitive to the negative aspects of the boatman stereotype encapsulated in bawdy minstrel songs or emblematized by characters like Mike Fink.[116]

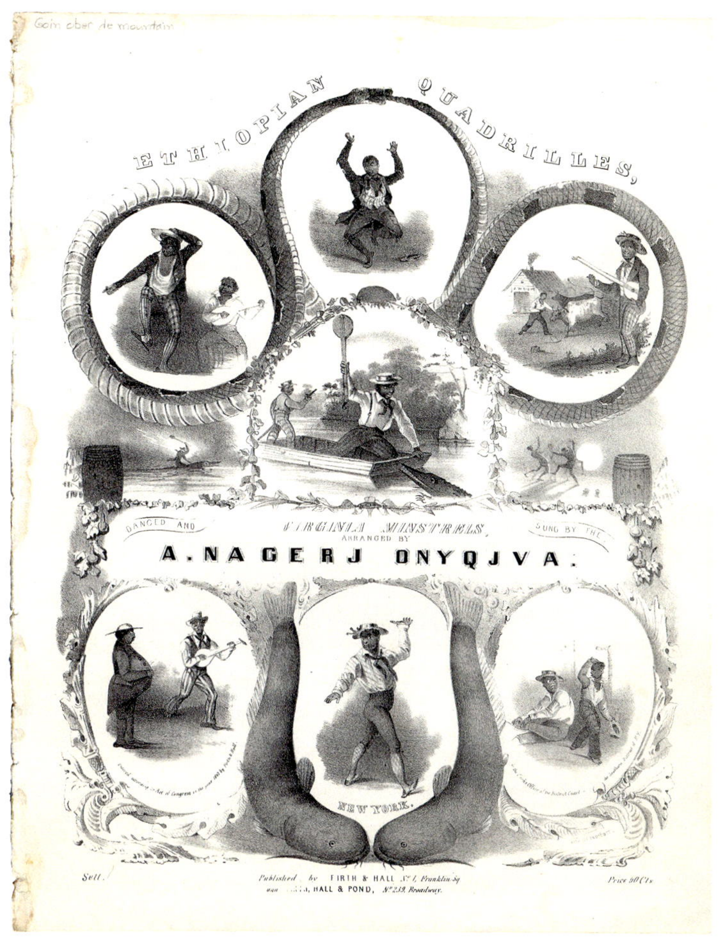

Fig. 23: Illustrated sheet music for the Ethiopian Quadrilles, 1843, lithographed sheet music, courtesy American Antiquarian Society

At best, these groups of unattached men were unruly and uncouth; at worst, they posed a danger to the social fabric. Religious commentators worried about the effects of "their long inland voyages," during which "they have been . . . removed from the means of grace."[117] The stakes in the battle over boatmen's morality were high on account of their mobility. In the words of one missionary, the character of boatmen mattered because of "the immense length of river coast along which, and the immense number of human beings over which, that influence will be exerted, either for good or evil."[118]

The mythic boatmen characters that easterners imagined and moralists feared differed from the men Bingham would have known and encountered in the West, men more like the businessmen David Lamme or Meredith Marmaduke. However, boatmen who plied the rivers in the 1840s and 1850s had more in common with these self-made men than they likely did with their rough-and-tumble predecessors on the early nineteenth-century river. Allen has shown that the profession had become safer and the transport more reliable owing to navigational improvements, and, "instead of fighting Indians and river pirates, the flatboatmen of the Steamboat Age fought 'the blues' and homesickness."[119] Yet he also asserts that there were still young men who turned to the job for adventure and to see the world outside their immediate locale. It was these more refined fellows who "discovered the mystique of the western boatmen and claimed it as their own."[120] They were attracted by the notion of being perceived as dangerous and free from the social constraints of adulthood.

The cultural historian Anthony Rotundo has argued that travel and the pursuit of mobile occupations such as sailor or river boatman allowed middle-class men to stave off the start of manhood, which often began with marriage, as well as the anxieties that accompanied the search for self.[121] Bingham's own early itinerancy can be seen the same way. Many of the men who would become the owners of Bingham's paintings through the American Art-Union had themselves traveled or moved across country to pursue professional ventures. For instance, Bingham's *Fur Traders Descending the Missouri* (Pl. 3) was awarded to Robert S. Bunker of Mobile, Alabama, in 1845. According to census records, Bunker was born in New York to parents from Massachusetts but eventually moved to the South and worked as an agent for the New England Mutual Life Insurance Company. Likewise, the following year *Boatmen on the Missouri* (Pl. 4) was awarded to the subscriber J. R. Macmurdo, a banker in New Orleans. Like Bingham, Macmurdo was born in Virginia but moved westward through the state of Ohio and eventually settled in New Orleans with his family. As was the case with Bingham's portrait sitters in Missouri, who were involved in commerce on the river, Bunker and Macmurdo were mobile, self-made men.[122]

While it is not known what Macmurdo or Bunker thought of Bingham's paintings, once they were awarded to a particular subscriber, they entered the closed worlds of private collections (and often remained in those families for generations and out of the public eye). Bingham's vision of the river gained its widest currency, therefore, through the dissemination of printed media. In December 1846 *The Jolly Flatboatmen* (Pl. 5) was chosen as the engraving to be distributed to all of the American Art-Union's subscribers the next year, and the commission for the engraving was awarded to the New York–based printmaker Thomas Doney.[123] Two prints were issued that year—the other being an engraving by John William Casilear after Daniel Huntington's *A Sybil* (Fig. 24)—the double distribution intended as compensation for the AA-U's inability to deliver a print the previous year.[124]

Subscribers got a glimpse of both prints when small-scale versions of them appeared in the annual report issued in early 1847. By that point, though, critical assessments signaled that it was not just Bingham's style that disturbed some reviewers. They believed his subject matter did not meet the criteria set out by critics and AA-U managers for choosing "productions of 'high art,'" that is, "to elevate and purify public taste."[125]

> *If every-day and unpoetical subjects are chosen, those that convey no graceful and refined images to the mind, however valuable the pictures may be as faithful delineations of real life, or as accurate and successful reproductions of nature, the highest object, the development, purification, and true cultivation of feeling, the element of which is innate in all minds, will not be attained.*[126]

Conceding that Bingham's work was "valuable . . . as faithful delineations of real life," this reviewer considered its "every-day" quality unsuitable. There was not the same debate over the worthiness of Huntington's more academic subject matter. His work featured an idealized bust of a classical prophetess gazing pensively into the distance. The most severe critic of Bingham's work reasoned that the choice to engrave Huntington's *A Sybil* could "amply atone for all that the other may lack."[127]

The stakes were high for determining which paintings would be chosen by the AA-U for engraving because of the large number of people the prints would reach and the potential for repeated encounters with the images. One writer cautioned that they would be "seen by young and old in every part of our land, the thoughts they suggest will dwell in millions of minds, and in addition to their moral effect, they exert an influence in relation to art. If the execution of the engravings is poor, the very frequency with which they are seen wearies and disgusts the mind."[128]

In the process of turning *The Jolly Flatboatmen* into a print, the AA-U may have taken steps to elevate the painting's aesthetic effect, compensating for what some interpreted as low or common subject matter by commissioning a mezzotint rather than an engraving. Mezzotints had been much less common in the United States than in England, especially before the master printmaker John Sartain immigrated to Philadelphia, and they had traditionally been used more often for portrait engravings.[129] In March 1848, about the time that AA-U subscribers were beginning to receive Doney's print of *The Jolly Flatboatmen*, *Godey's Lady's Book* carried an excerpt from *Scientific American* that explained that mezzotint, as opposed to other print processes, "has great softness of effect along with the strongest relief, and is peculiarly suited for pictures of females and young persons, as it gives the appearance of painting to all figures more than either etching or line engravings." Additionally, its making "requires much patience, skill and taste, and above all, a fine knowledge of light and shade."[130] The AA-U had commissioned mezzotints from Sartain in its first two years

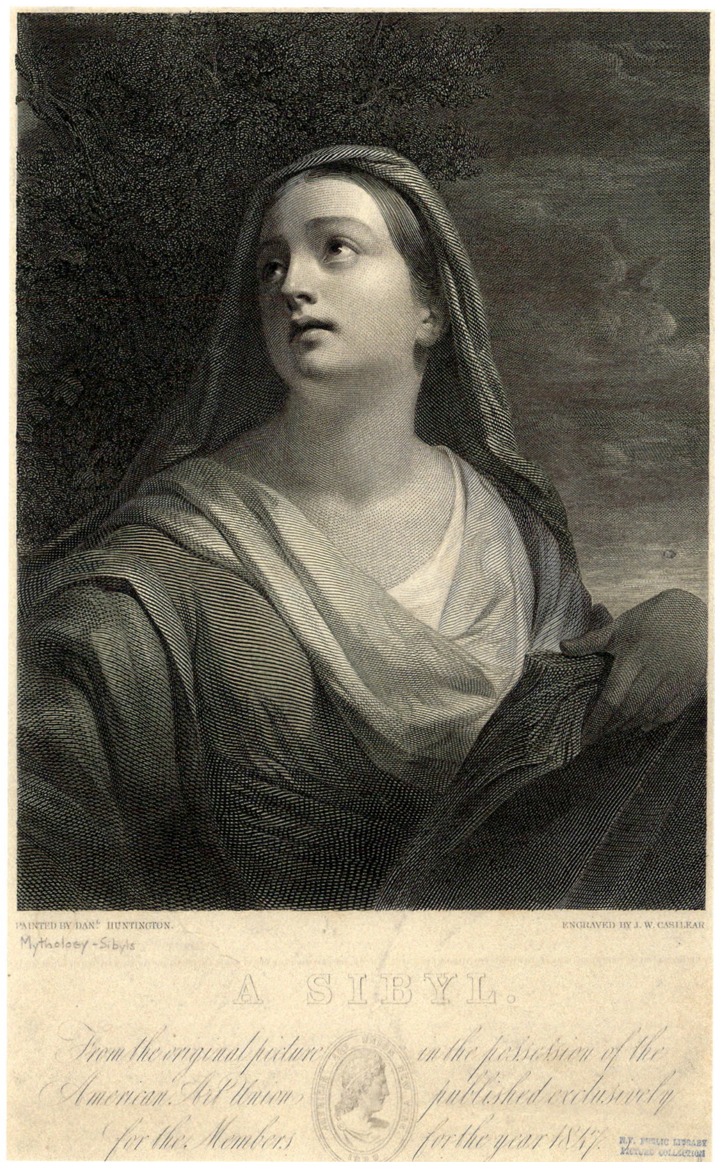

Fig. 24: John William Casilear (1811–1893) after Daniel Huntington (1816–1906), *A Sibyl*, 1847, engraving, 12⅛ × 8¼ in., Picture Collection, New York Public Library, Astor, Lenox, and Tilden Foundations

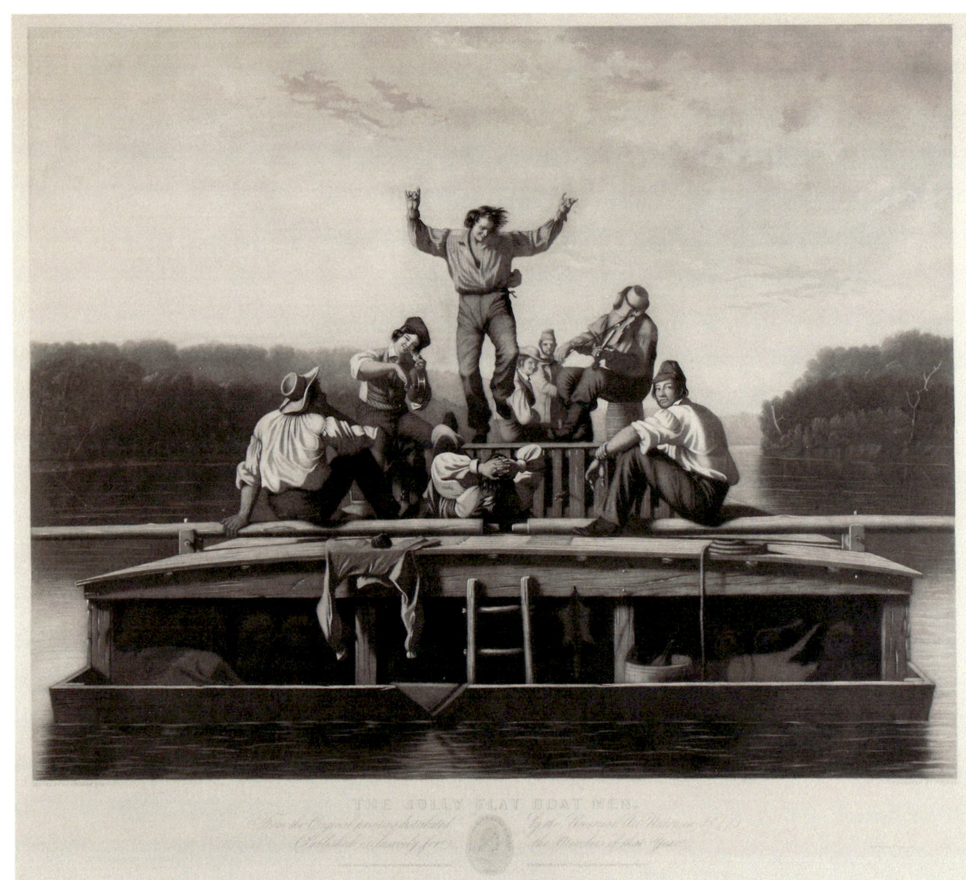

Fig. 25: Thomas Doney (active 1844–49) after George Caleb Bingham (1811–1879), *The Jolly Flat Boat Men*, 1847, printed by Powell & Co., published by the American Art-Union, New York, etching, aquatint, and mezzotint, 23 3/8 × 27 1/16 in., Philadelphia Museum of Art, Gift of Miss Harriet Sartain, 1947, 1947-59-19

of distributing prints, but the group had been favoring line engravings in recent years.[131] Hiring Doney to create a mezzotint signaled a shift in practice to some extent, but it would also have offered subscribers even more variety in the prints they were to receive that year, in both subject matter and medium.

Numerous delays plagued Doney's production of the print, and the plate had to be continually reworked. Extant examples of Doney's work, titled *The Jolly Flat Boat Men*, vary in quality and medium (Fig. 25). Some reveal techniques that look like mezzotint, while others show evidence of etching and steel engraving. The print was published in black and white, but many examples were eventually hand-colored (Fig. 26). In the black-and-white versions, etched patterns take the place of color and shading, lending a greater linearity and hardness to the print. The textured ground of a mezzotint would have approximated the subtle tonalities in Bingham's landscape more effectively than a line engraving, but Doney also had to add clouds to the sky so that it would not seem too bright in relation to the smoky blackness of the forest and cluster of figures below. At this point in the technological development of the medium, it was common for printmakers to etch their plates extensively before using a rocker to create the mezzotint.[132] As a result, etched lines make up the surface of the image, from the facial features of the men to the surface of the water and wood grain of the flatboat, endowing it with detail that the original painting lacked. For instance, in the painting, the two figures farthest away seem to fade into the haze of the horizon, but in the print, their features and those of the other

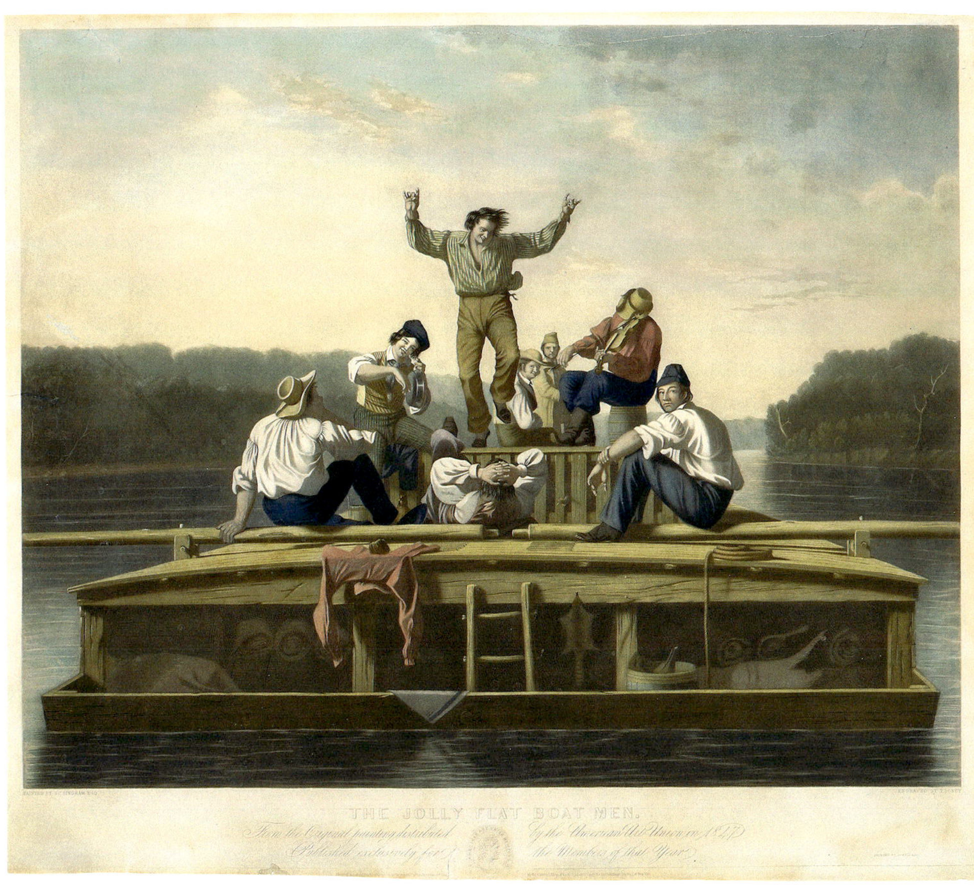

Fig. 26: Thomas Doney (active 1844–49) after George Caleb Bingham (1811–1879), *The Jolly Flat Boat Men*, 1847, aquatint, engraving, stipple, etching, and roulette with applied watercolor, 18 13/16 × 24 in., Amon Carter Museum of American Art, Fort Worth, Texas, 1971.44

boatmen come more starkly into focus. Some of the ambiguity in Bingham's painting – particularly in the faces and forms of the boatmen – crystallizes into etched pattern and line, though the haziness and softness of the landscape remain.

Whether or not the gambit swayed some viewers to believe that river boatmen were appropriate subjects for fine art, several newspapers highlighted the image's celebratory tone and its artistic merit when they finally received their copies of the mezzotint. The *Natchez Weekly Courier* proclaimed it "a splendid engraving" and "an exquisite work of art and more than worth the five dollars which enables a person to become a member of the society for one year."[133] Another newspaper, the *Atlas* of Lafayette, Indiana, asked its readers, "Who, that has seen the engraving of 'Jolly Flat-Boatmen,' but could desire to become its possessor?" It notes that the "scene, the attitudes, the life-like expression, the rich and softly blended shades of the mezzotint, all combine to give it interest, and render it worthy of extravagant admiration."[134] The *Maryland Free Press* validated the print not only for its aesthetic quality but also for its "historical interest":

> *The face of men which this engraving brings to our contemplation, best known on our Western waters, has gradually become, or is fast becoming extinct. Flatboatmen, Ferrymen, and Stage drivers, each class in its own way, exhibited an individuality, energy and raciness of character, which could only belong to a happy, careless, but bold and hardy life. Steamboats and Railroads have almost*

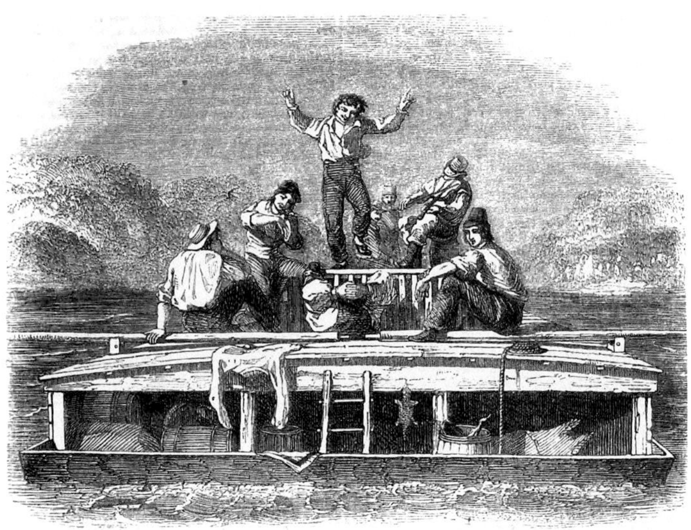

Fig. 27: H. Linton (dates unknown), "John Banvard's Great Picture: Life on the Mississippi," 1847, in *Howitt's Journal of Literature and Popular Progress*, September 4, 1847

> *exterminated them, and it is only here and there that we meet in our travels with a representative of either class; and when we do, his quirks, nodosities and quaintnesses remind us of an age that is past.*[135]

This account diffuses the threat of uncivilized boatmen by securing them in a past time, an immature phase of developing American civilization. Not everyone, however, thought that boatmen belonged to a previous era; assessments were often based on a writer's regional perspective. Two articles published the same week in 1846 expressed contrasting points of view: an article in *Scientific American* used the boatmen who lingered on the Mississippi in the face of their inevitable replacement by steamboats as metaphors for all those resistant to progress, while a merchants' magazine from Memphis cited statistics on the increasing number of boatmen – those working on steamboats *and* flatboats – as evidence of the robust commercial activity on the Mississippi.[136] Evidently, commentators in the West were more likely to consider flatboatmen an integral and continuing part of the operations and character of the river.

Thanks to a wide dissemination of Doney's prints that exceeded the wildest expectations of the American Art-Union, Europeans as well as Americans gauged the character of western men through Bingham's imagery. In addition to the nearly ten thousand engravings produced from Doney's large plate, several unauthorized adaptations of the dancing flatboatman motif circulated in the United States and abroad. On September 4, 1847, a wood engraving by H. Linton appeared in the London-based *Howitt's Journal of Literature and Popular Progress* to illustrate the article "John Banvard's Great Picture: Life on the Mississippi" (Fig. 27).[137] The text recounts Banvard's efforts to make his moving panorama and arrange for its impending exhibition in London, as well as the story of "his former life, which with its hardships, disappointments, and privations, had fitted him for the accomplishment of his great undertaking."[138] Banvard is represented as an ambitious, self-made man, as was Bingham in a brief biography of the artist published by the AA-U a few years later.[139] The article in *Howitt's* draws heavily from "a pamphlet before us," likely one of Banvard's own, and does not attribute the accompanying illustration to Bingham or Doney, saying only, "We have given at the head of this article an engraving of one of these peculiar boats, with its 'jolly flat-boat men,' for which we are indebted to a kind American friend, who has also furnished us with the material for the present article."[140] Several paragraphs explain the types of boats found on the river and the work and leisure pursuits of the men who operated them, text that Banvard himself quoted (without citing a source) from accounts published by Timothy Flint in the 1820s and 1830s.[141] Judging by the composition and the way that line has been used to build up the forms and landscape, Linton created his wood engraving from the etching Doney had made for the *Transactions of the American Art-Union* in 1846, which advertised the larger and more polished mezzotint that would not be finished until 1848.

Thus, the image in *Howitt's* is thrice removed from Bingham's original painting, and yet it remains virtually unaltered. The rounded edges of the vignette make it seem as if readers were glimpsing an everyday scene on the Mississippi as it was happening in the present day, or perhaps they were seeing something that Banvard had himself encountered while making sketches for his panorama a few years earlier. The article supports this impression at its outset: "In the year 1840, a young man hardly of age, took a small boat and, furnished with drawing materials, descended the river Mississippi."[142] As an illustration for text, Bingham's composition no longer stands alone as his creation. In using it, Banvard took his place among the men on Bingham's boat and authenticated his experience—and the one he would offer to ticket buyers—of the Mississippi.

Other appropriations of the jolly flatboatmen motif relocated Bingham's group from the Middle Mississippi farther south. For example, in *Das illustrirte Mississippithal* (1857), a book published by the panorama painter Henry Lewis after he emigrated from Saint Louis to Düsseldorf, Germany, Bingham's dancing boatman appears in a chromolithograph with the title "Bayon Sacra (Luisiana)" (Fig. 28), likely referring to Bayou Sara, a busy port on the Lower Mississippi a few miles north of Baton Rouge.[143] These colored lithographs were likely related to the moving panorama that Lewis toured throughout the United States and Europe beginning in 1849 and illustrated an expanded version of the pamphlet guides that were sold at the shows. In "Bayon Sacra," Lewis includes in the foreground a tall tree with Spanish moss hanging from its branches, the telltale signifier of a southern landscape, and a burgeoning town on the river's opposite bank. The flatboat is viewed from a more distant vantage point than in Bingham's composition, allowing the viewer to see the flatboat in its entirety instead of in a truncated, foreshortened view. As a result, the scene imparts more information about the boatmen's lifestyle. The men are slightly rearranged, and more laundry hangs on the back of the boat,

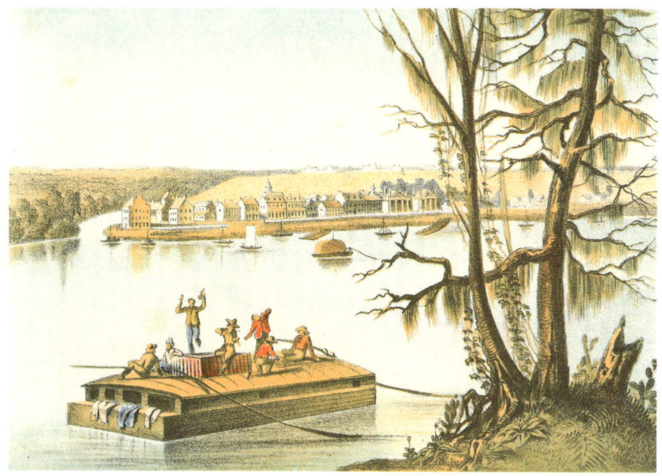

Fig. 28: Henry Lewis (1819–1904), *Bayon Sacra (Luisiana)*, in *Das illustrirte Mississippithal* . . . , 1857, chromolithograph with hand coloring, 5⅜ × 7¹¹⁄₁₆ in., Amon Carter Museum of American Art, Fort Worth, Texas, LIB.6.74

emphasizing the rustic living conditions on the frontier over the commercial aspects of flatboating. Yet the dancing figure is exactly the same. In this context and in the illustration for Banvard's article, *The Jolly Flatboatmen* (Pl. 5) stands in for the larger Mississippi and the broader frontier West; it no longer conveys the unidentifiable but still localized character it had in the context of Bingham's other river paintings.

Despite the efforts of Bingham and the American Art-Union to elevate his subject matter to the level of "high art," the image of the carefree, dancing boatman and his male cohort still resonated with such other aspects of American life as the frontier and blackface minstrelsy. For example, in *Flatboatmen on the Mississippi* by Carl Wimar, the central dancing figure is black instead of white (Fig. 29). Having immigrated to Saint Louis from Germany in 1844, Wimar was emblematic of the evolving racial and ethnic population in Missouri. He became acquainted with the work of some of the most important artists to depict the Mississippi, including Bingham, Deas, and Wild, through prints and local exhibitions. He may have

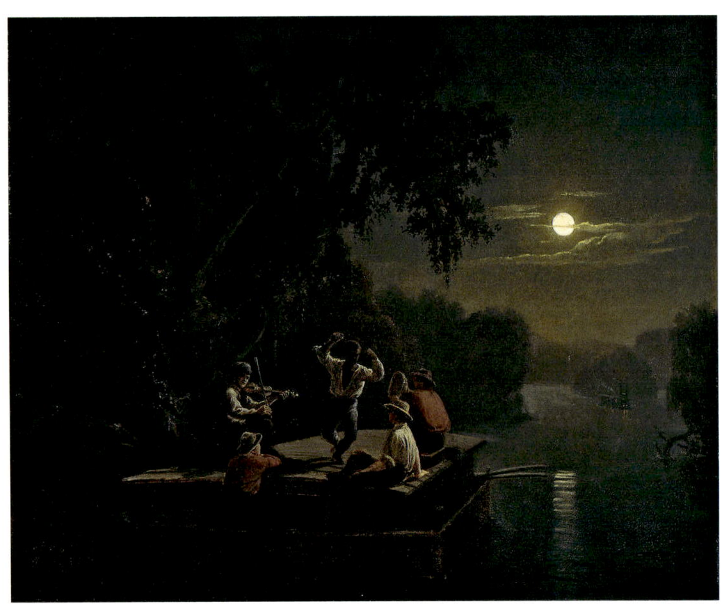

Fig. 29: Carl Wimar (1828–1862), *Flatboatmen on the Mississippi*, 1854, oil on canvas, 19⅛ × 23⅝ in., Private collection

accompanied the panorama painter Léon Pomarède on a sketching trip up the Mississippi to help him in the preparation of his moving panorama.[144] Like Bingham before him, Wimar traveled east for artistic training, following the history painter and German émigré Emanuel Leutze to Düsseldorf via New York City. He painted *Flatboatmen on the Mississippi* while in Germany, but it was on view in Saint Louis by 1859 and exhibited there twice more before the end of the century.[145]

A black man occupying the most prominent position in a well-known image might have proved controversial in a border state on the eve of the Civil War, but no public comment has been found. It is possible that the other alterations Wimar made to Bingham's motif defused any anxiety that may have existed. Unlike the steamboat that passes by in the background and could be illuminated with artificial light, safe travel for the flatboat was limited to daylight hours. In Wimar's painting, the boatmen have docked for the evening; no one mans the rudder, and the oars have been pulled down and placed in the boat. Thus, the men and their craft have been rendered immobile. Wimar used the full moon to reveal their leisure activities while keeping the men's features indistinct, and he also simplified the arrangement of figures by eliminating two of them. He turned the remaining men toward the dancer so that the painting's viewer could enjoy the picturesque scene without having any of the boatmen look back. The ease with which Bingham's *The Jolly Flatboatmen* (Pl. 5) was appropriated speaks to the mobility of reproductive prints during the mid-nineteenth century. But it also testifies to an undercurrent of ambiguity that exists in Bingham's river paintings, a result of the open-ended identities with which he endowed the people and places he depicted.

In the years that the jolly flatboatmen motif traveled between painting and prints, between the United States and Europe, Bingham, too, was on the move. After spending much of 1848 in Missouri, involved with state politics, he made a conspicuous return to art union exhibitions in 1849, at the American Art-Union, the newly formed Western Art Union in Cincinnati, and the Art Union of Philadelphia. He forged new professional relationships with patrons and printmakers through much of the 1850s while working in Missouri, Cincinnati, New York, Philadelphia, and Düsseldorf, among other places. Despite these peregrinations, he developed new ways of representing the river.

Bingham's portfolio of drawings—what E. Maurice Bloch dubbed a "pattern book of figures"—enabled him to continue setting his genre scenes along rivers while also experimenting with composition, even while traveling extensively.[146] As others have noted, several of the figures in the drawings appear in more than one of Bingham's paintings, and when there are variations between the drawings and paintings, they are often slight.[147] For instance, the standing figure in *The Wood-Boat* (Pl. 28), likely painted in Saint Louis in 1850, is very similar—he even wears clothing of the same color—to one of the men in *Fishing on the Mississippi* (Pl. 43), a work painted the following year in New York. From one painting to the other, there are slight differences: the fisherman's hat is altered, he stands with straight legs and looks down to bait his hook instead of grasping the pole with both hands, and the pole appears on the other side of his body. Such similarity shows that even as Bingham explored new subject matter such as fishing, he worked within a relatively narrow scope of postures and types.

At the same time, Bingham's drawings provided consistency during a peripatetic span in his life, allowing him to experiment with formal configurations and pictorial effects even after sending pictures for exhibition or sale. Though *The Wood-Boat* was sold to the American Art-Union in 1851, his retention of the detailed drawing of the standing man, *Woodboatman* (Pl. 40), enabled him to reuse the figure three years later in *Woodboatmen on a River (Western Boatmen Ashore by Night)* (Pl. 45), a nocturnal scene painted in Philadelphia. The configuration of boatmen is also familiar, harking back to the closed circle of men in *The Jolly Flatboatmen* or *Lighter Relieving a Steamboat Aground* (Pl. 6). Furthermore, the fisherman illuminated by the moon recalls other figures absorbed in various tasks and set apart from the central group, such as the poleman in *Raftsmen Playing Cards* (Pl. 26) or the drinker in *Lighter Relieving a Steamboat Aground*. What is new is Bingham's experimentation with chiaroscuro, created by the campfire in the lower left. The same year he also created the work called *Watching the Cargo by Night* (Pl. 46), perhaps a revision of his 1849 canvas that depicts the same occupation taking place during the day (Pl. 27).[148] The men's activities in Bingham's river paintings of the early 1850s recall those in his earlier canvases – storytelling, playing music, fishing by the riverside – doing anything but explicitly working or being located in an identifiable geographic setting.[149]

The somewhat formulaic quality of Bingham's river paintings during these years may have been due, as Bloch speculates, to the artist's need to "produce a steady run of paintings to submit to art unions."[150] In the same period, he was also experimenting with large-scale genre paintings that depict political subjects (Fig. 30). Thus, by working with a small number of compositional templates featuring well-worn boatmen types, Bingham could continue to create new river paintings while still refining his skills in rendering color and light, aspects that critics had long pointed out as weaknesses. For instance, Bingham revisited one of his most familiar compositions, *Fur Traders Descending the Missouri* (Pl. 3), making only a few alterations. In the 1851 version painted in New York and eventually called *Trappers' Return* (Pl. 31), the characters, though the same, are brought closer to the viewer as well as to the river's banks. One critic noted improvements compared with Bingham's previous work:

> *On the whole, this is the best picture we have seen from the pencil of this very clever artist. It is a lively representation of nature in her most becoming tints, the light and shade are ably managed; the perspective well understood, and the subordination of the tints, which are very delicately disposed of, impart a mellowness to the picture which we do not find in the earlier works of this artist.*[151]

In 1851 Bingham also returned to the 1847 painting *Raftsmen Playing Cards*, resulting in *In a Quandary* or *Mississippi Raftmen at Cards* (Pl. 44). This time, the reworking was prompted by his having entered into an agreement with Goupil and Company, a French publishing company that had started an art union and gallery of its own in New York, to produce three prints after his works.[152] There are significant formal differences between the earlier and later cardplayer paintings. The latter places more emphasis on the disheveled state of the flatboat and the locus of the cardplayers and onlookers than on the broader riverscape. There is also a stark contrast between the derelict boatmen in the foreground and the men who actively labor to move a flatboat in the distance, undermining the respectable qualities of boatmen that Bingham had tried to cultivate in earlier paintings.

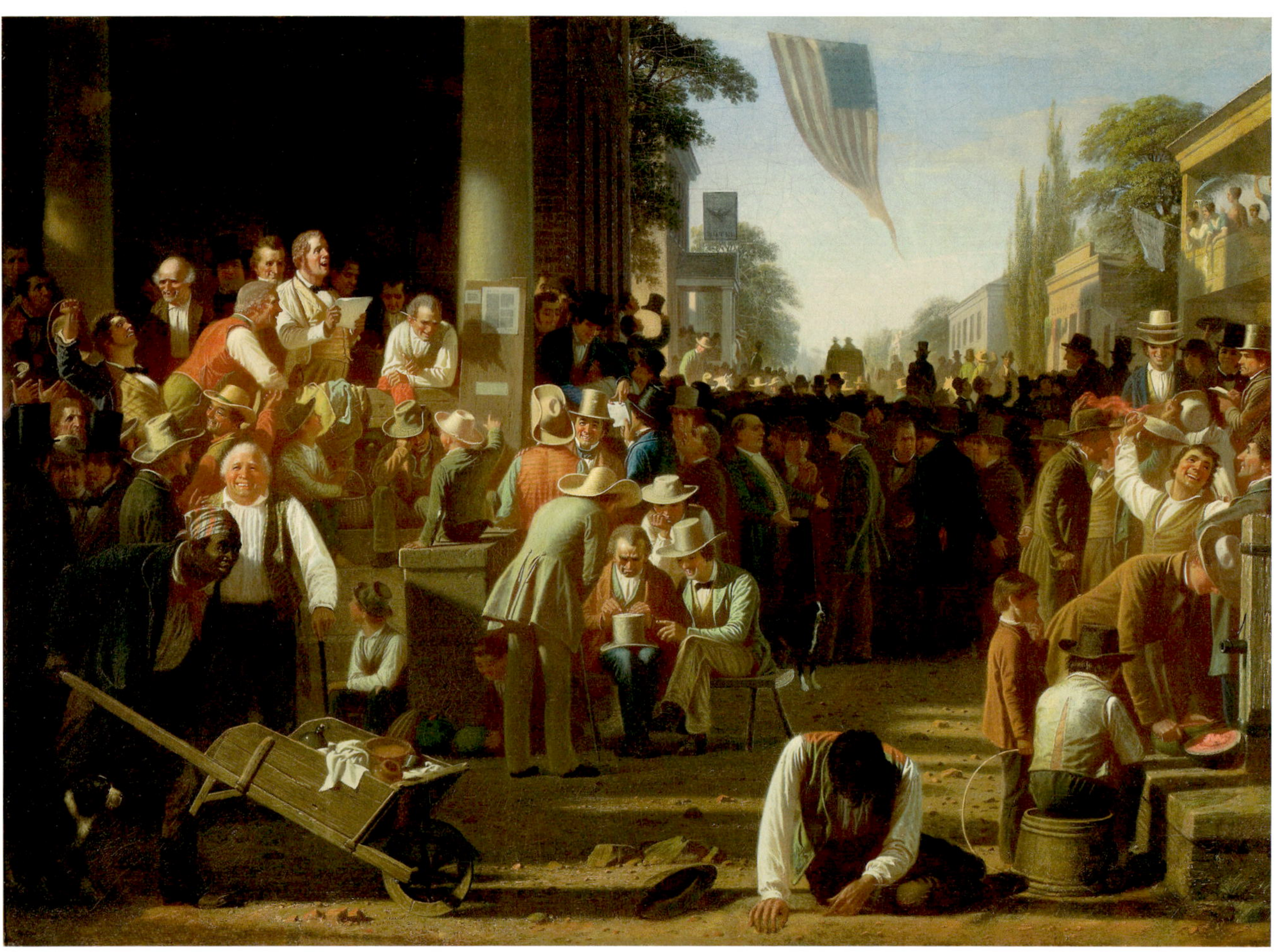

Fig. 30: George Caleb Bingham (1811–1879), *The Verdict of the People*, 1854–55, oil on canvas, 46 × 55 in., Saint Louis Art Museum, Gift of Bank of America, 45:2001

Bingham reported to his friend and supporter James Sidney Rollins that "publication by such a firm [as Goupil] was calculated to extend my reputation, and enhance the value of my future works."[153] The lithograph made after *In a Quandary—Mississippi Raftmen Playing Cards* (Fig. 31) was marketed by the company as one of a trio with lithographs after *The Power of Music* by William Sidney Mount (Fig. 32) and *Cornered! [Waiting for the Stage]* by Richard Caton Woodville (Fig. 33).[154] Rustic settings and themes of travel and the pursuit of masculine leisure link the three images. It is possible that playing up the roughness of the boatmen and their environment helped Bingham's scene seem more akin to genre paintings in the European tradition, often set in taverns or other nonurban settings. Since Goupil and Company's prints were also marketed in England, France, and Germany, Bingham may have adapted his imagery to conform to pictorial traditions more familiar to those markets.

Bingham's United States audience, by contrast, did not appreciate the artist's hardening of the features and temperament of his boatmen. *Mississippi Boatman* (Pl. 30), a painting

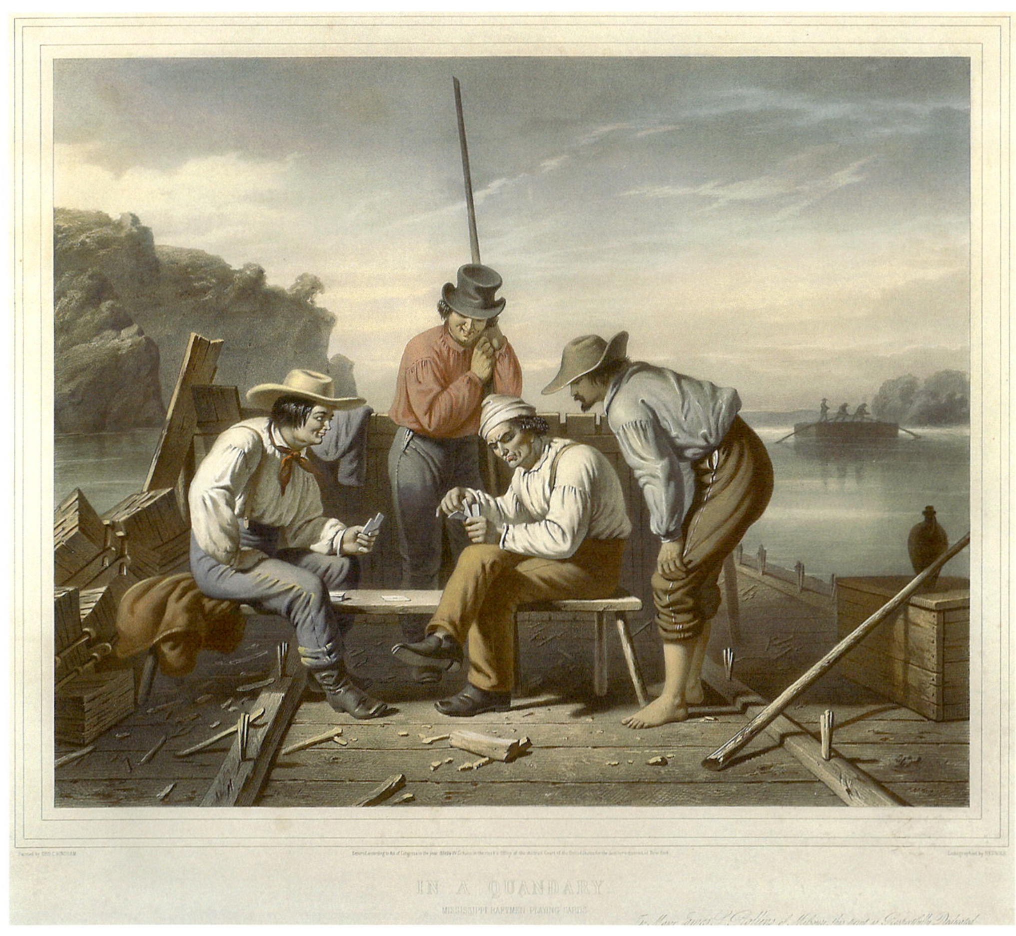

Fig. 31: Claude Régnier (active 1840–66) after George Caleb Bingham (1811–1879), *In a Quandary—Mississippi Raftmen Playing Cards*, 1852, lithograph with applied watercolor, published by Goupil & Co., New York, Amon Carter Museum of American Art, Fort Worth, Texas, 1971.45

whose sole figure is the central boatman in *Watching the Cargo* (Pl. 27), did not sell when exhibited at the Art-Union of Philadelphia in 1851. Bingham admitted to Rollins that it may not have been a "well-selected subject" compared to the two landscapes with farm scenes and cattle that he also submitted and that had been successful.[155] Franklin Kelly has speculated that the changes Bingham made to the main figure making him older and darkening his mood as well as bringing the viewer closer to him—"may have caused viewers to perceive a provocative, even confrontational scene."[156] This character study, along with *Mississippi Fisherman* (Pl. 29), a similar single-figure composition, lacks the qualities that made Bingham's paintings so attractive to self-made men in the previous decade: a sense of mobility, homosociality, and futurity. The space in both paintings is shallow and closed off, with barrels, crates, and a large tree limiting any movement toward the river or the horizon.

Despite the occasional misstep, Bingham remained prominent in the national press, and when he traveled to Europe for the first time in 1856, art journals reported on his activities. After spending about two months in Paris, Bingham went to Düsseldorf, a city set on another river—the Rhine—and the location of a thriving international art community, including many Americans.[157] By December he had begun working on portraits of George Washington and Thomas Jefferson commissioned by the state of Missouri and reported to Rollins that he

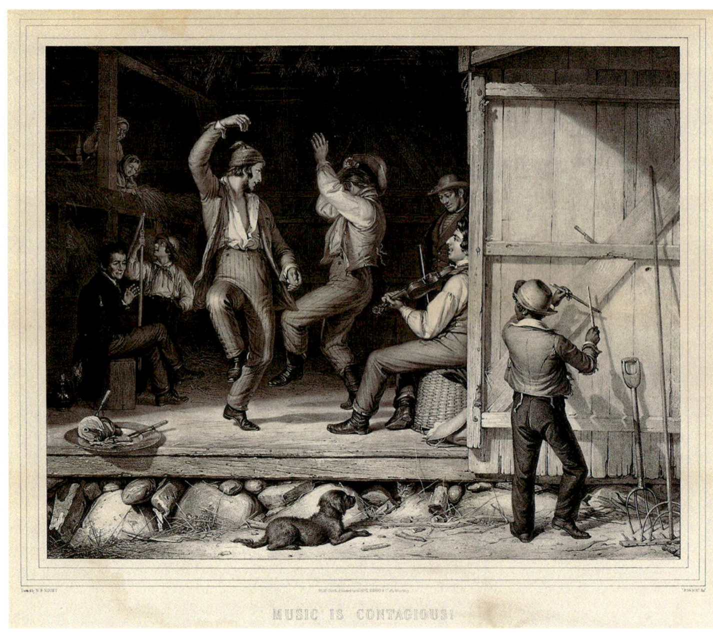

Fig. 32: Alphonse Léon Noël (1807–1884) after William Sidney Mount (1807–1868), *Music is Contagious!*, 1849, lithograph, Published by Goupil & Co., New York, courtesy American Antiquarian Society

was creating "a large picture of 'life on the Mississippi' which will not require a great while to complete and which promises to be far ahead of any work, of that class which I have yet undertaken."[158]

Despite its greater complexity and larger size, the painting probably did "not require a great while to complete" because Bingham had a host of existing drawings from which to formulate the work. *Jolly Flatboatmen in Port* (Pl. 47) reworks the 1846 version of *The Jolly Flatboatmen* (Pl. 5) but docks the central flatboat at an urban port, most likely Saint Louis but possibly New Orleans. As in earlier river paintings, it is impossible to identify the exact location because no landmarks can be seen. The river is wide but hazy, and just a few other boats are visible. All of the old characters are here, but their features are somewhat altered and their bodies enlarged, perhaps, as Barry and Heugh speculate, with the use of some means of projection. The exuberant central dancer now holds a hat and red scarf in his previously empty hands, but the fiddler and tin-pan player still flank him. Their audience has grown, but individual members are familiar from other canvases by Bingham: reclining figures, some of whom have their backs turned to the viewer; pipe smokers; a barefoot man reaching into his shirt; and, directly behind the dancer, a man wearing a red shirt who uses a tall pole to support his weight. Women are still absent, but any social threat potentially posed by this gathering of boatmen is softened by the presence of two children playing in the sunlight at the lower right. Two urban types wearing suits and hats, probably merchants or brokers who dealt with river commerce, are new to the composition, as is a black man. The latter stands in profile, stooped and wearing torn clothing in stark juxtaposition to the white dancer dressed well and light on his feet. Eleven years had passed since Bingham's first version of *The Jolly Flatboatmen*, and it is possible that increased sectional tension over slavery and associations with minstrelsy in his earlier work prompted the artist to make a clearer distinction between white boatmen and black labor, though it remains unclear if the black figure is enslaved.[159]

In the 1857 painting, Bingham grounds his figures temporally as well as socially by stilling the motion of the boat and removing them from the open territory of the river. By the time that he painted this work, flatboats were widely considered an emblem of the past even by those in the West. In "Address to the People of Missouri," the *Western Journal and Civilian* heralded the future and its possibilities by invoking the ambitious, go-ahead spirit of Americans:

> *Many are doing* well enough *with mule wagons and mudroads, but the steam horse with its iron sinews proclaims their thriftless folly. While the jolly flat-boatman was doing* almost too well, *the steam whistle startled*

him from his lazy jollity, and gave a tenfold energy to the commerce of our western rivers. . . . [L]ike true Anglo Saxons we repudiate the idea that anything is well enough *which can be bettered. We therefore unfurl the banners of our professions also inscribed with the glorious motto: PROGRESS.*[160]

That the jolly flatboatmen were "doing *almost too well*" while the rest were doing "*well enough*" indicates that they had overstayed their welcome. With this painting, Bingham situates the heyday of the boatmen squarely in the past. Painted in Germany under the guidance of Leutze, a scene that previously appeared as a glimpse of everyday life on the river, and thus suited for genre painting, now seemed inappropriate as the United States inched toward civil war. With *Jolly Flatboatmen in Port*, Bingham greatly enlarged the painting, bolstered its architectural setting, and increased the social complexity of its composition. In effect, he made a history painting at a time when the Mississippi River was becoming conceptualized as the center of the country, with the traits of a commercial center rather than the frontier.

In 1859, shortly after painting *Jolly Flatboatmen in Port*, Bingham returned to Missouri. Though he continued to travel—making a return trip to Germany that was cut short by the death of his father-in-law; going to Washington, D.C., for artistic and political meetings; and exhibiting in Philadelphia and Saint Louis—he never regained national prominence. Instead, he relied on commissions from Missouri patrons for the majority of his work. *Jolly Flatboatmen in Port* lived most of its "life" in Missouri as well. It was still in the artist's collection in 1860 and, after being exhibited in Washington and Philadelphia, was placed on indefinite loan to the Saint Louis Mercantile Library Association, where it could be seen for much of the 1860s and 1870s. In Saint Louis it could be incorporated into the writing of local history, and Bingham could once again be acclaimed as the "Missouri Artist."

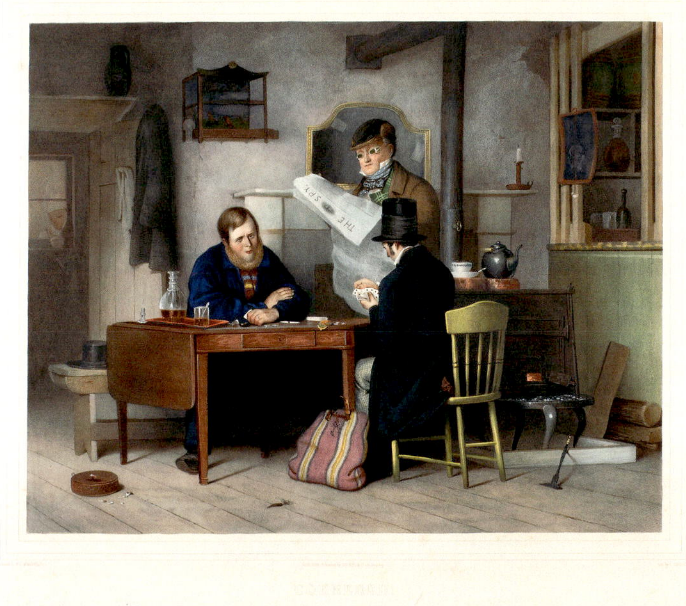

Fig. 33: Christian Schultz (dates unknown) after Richard Caton Woodville (1825–1855), *Cornered! [Waiting for the Stage]*, 1851, lithograph with hand coloring, Published by Goupil & Co., New York, courtesy American Antiquarian Society

Living in Jefferson City and serving as state treasurer, Bingham's experience of the Civil War years were focused on skirmishes at the Kansas-Missouri border that led to his painting *Order No. 11* (ca. 1869–70, State Historical Society of Missouri).[161] In fact, Bingham did not create any paintings set on the river—or any representations of the everyday—during the turbulent 1860s. Yet the national press headlines homed in on the Lower Mississippi as an important component of the war's western front. The stakes for its control were high, since the rivers cut at the heart of the western Confederacy and its supply lines.

Two watercolors by Frances "Fanny" Palmer that were eventually published as lithographs in 1865 by the New York–based firm Currier & Ives show how the river was used to represent the national fissure.[162] *The Mississippi in Time of Peace* (Fig. 34)

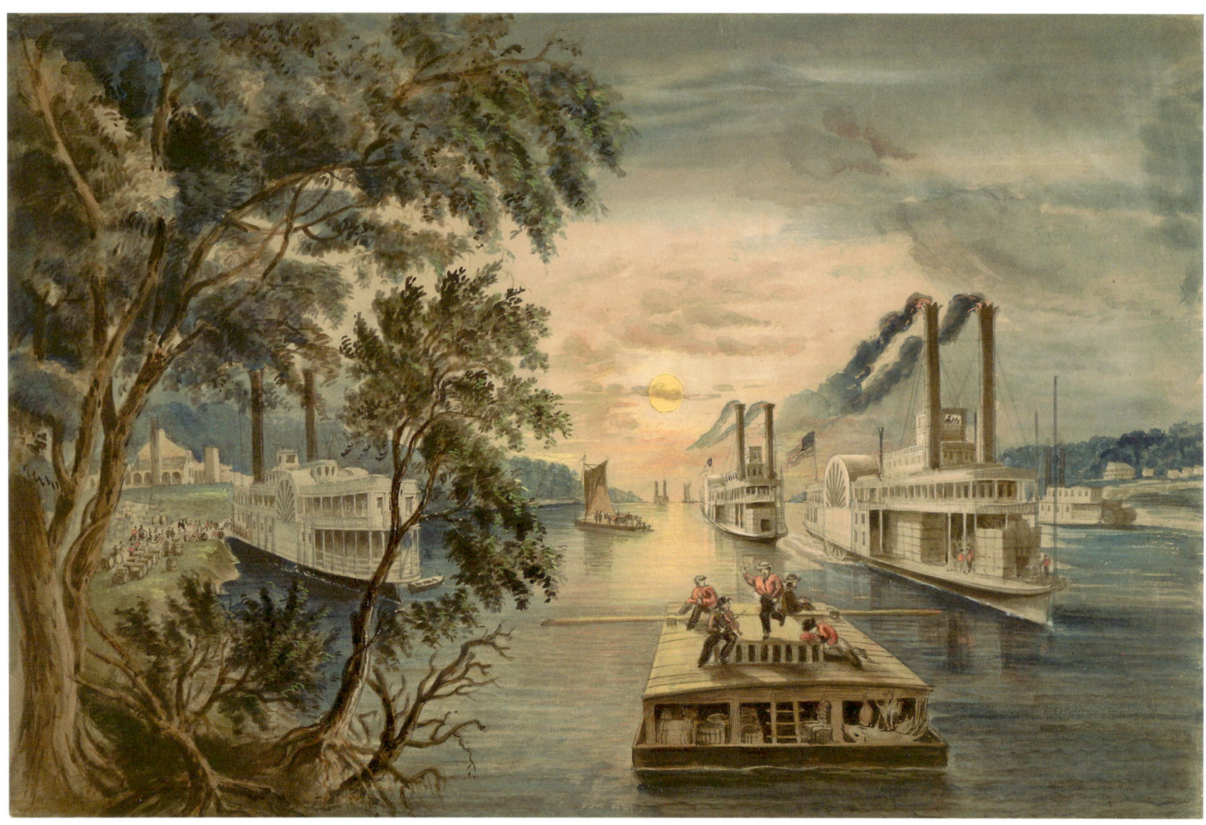

Fig. 34: Frances Palmer (1812–1876), *The Mississippi in Time of Peace*, 1865, produced for Currier & Ives, opaque and translucent watercolor and graphite on paper, 18 5/16 × 28 1/4 in., Museum of Fine Arts, Boston, Gift of Maxim Karolik for the M. and M. Karolik Collection of American Watercolors and Drawings, 1800–1875, 53.2451

appropriates several familiar motifs from antebellum imagery and consolidates them into one celebratory image: at left, a large number of black men load bales of cotton and hogsheads of sugar onto the deck of a steamboat; several types of watercraft, including a keelboat, a flatboat, and steamboats, glide downriver on the placid stream, their decks laden with cargo; and the group at center is recognizable from Bingham's painting *The Jolly Flatboatmen* (Pl. 5) in which a man dances atop a flatboat while his comrades watch and make music. Conversely, its pendant, *The Mississippi in Time of War* (Fig. 35), is a nightmarish scene in which Union gunboats fire on plantation houses, flames engulf steamboats, and the boatmen stand in disbelief or try to aid those who have been thrown into the water. The transition from sunset in *Peace* to the darkness of night in *War* indicates the passage of an idyllic, antebellum vision of river life to a bleak episode in the life of the country.

Though it seems that the river's golden days would be unrecoverable after such destruction, Currier & Ives issued at least eleven other lithographs in the next three decades that evoked the romance and thrill of the Mississippi River once again.[163] One of them, *Bound down the River* (Fig. 36), is another example of later works of art borrowing from *The Jolly Flatboatmen.* The completion of the transcontinental railroad in 1869 and an increased emphasis on the East–West commercial

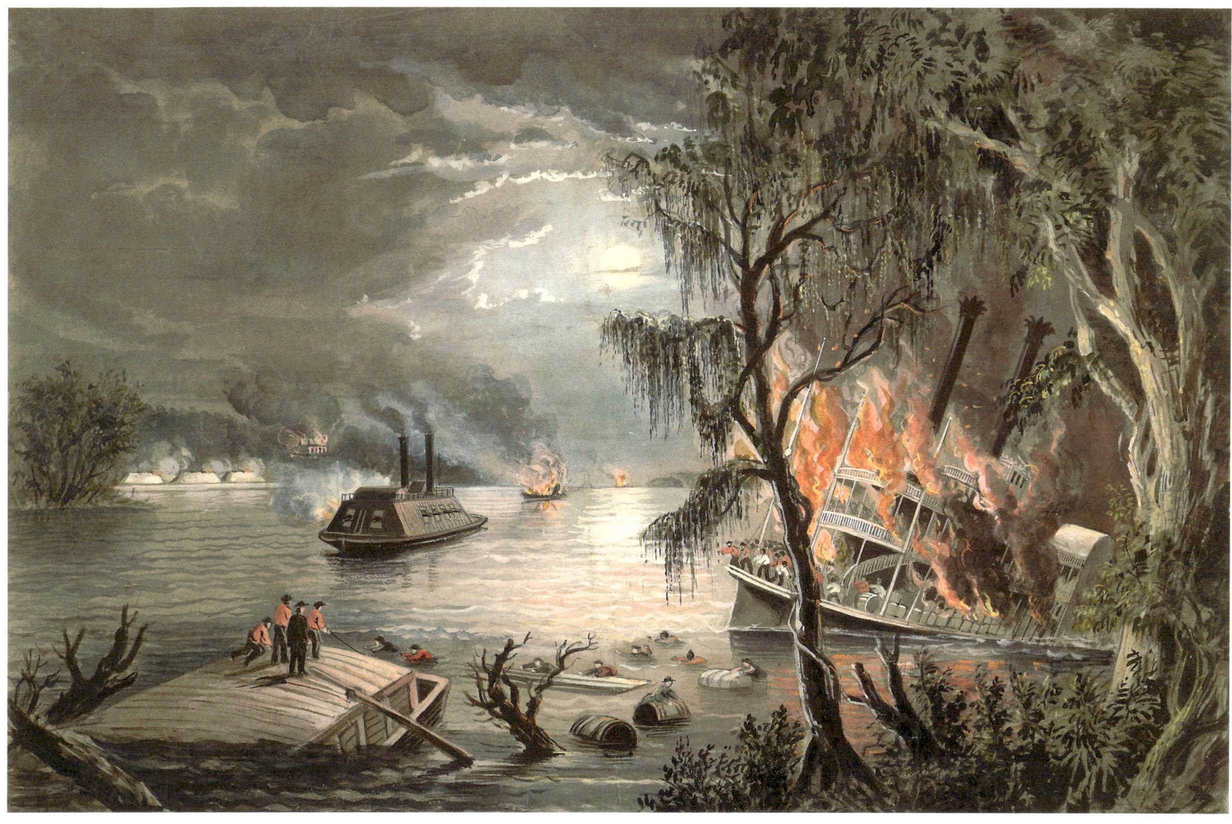

Fig. 35: Frances Palmer (1812–1876), *The Mississippi in Time of War*, 1862, produced for Currier & Ives, opaque watercolor and colored crayons over graphite on gray wove paper, 18 1/16 × 28 1/8 in., Museum of Fine Arts, Boston, Gift of Maxim Karolik for the M. and M. Karolik Collction of American Watercolors and Drawings, 1800–1875.53.2450

axis over that of the Mississippi valley, along with the wide dissemination of Currier & Ives prints and the publications of Mark Twain, made the river fertile ground for nostalgic reflection.[164]

Perhaps this is what spurred Bingham to revisit his jolly flatboatmen motif once more. Completed the year before his death, *The Jolly Flatboatmen* of 1877–78 (Pl. 48) exhibits an overall blue tonality that makes the sky and river a vibrant backdrop for the central group of figures. The painting is smaller than either of the two previous versions of the theme, as are the boat and the number of figures represented. Because there is no cargo under the deck, the flatboat becomes a stage rather than a vehicle transporting goods to market. The river is low and the boat has only one oar, calling further attention to the suspended forward motion of the group. Thus, instead of representing a slice of life during a trip down the river, the painting recalls a past era. Appropriately, then, the dancer faces the viewer more directly than before and appears to address his exuberant gestures toward the painting's viewer and not the other men on the boat. The execution of the painting may also have been prompted by Bingham's opening his studio for what would be his final exhibition. It took place at the recently

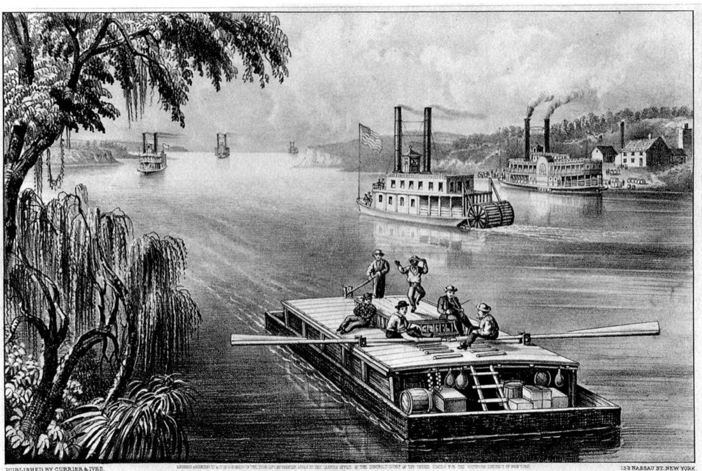

Fig. 36: Nathaniel Currier (1813–1888) and James M. Ives (1824–1895), *Bound down the River*, 1870, lithograph, 7⅞ × 12½ in., Library of Congress, Division of Prints and Photographs

established department of art at the University of Missouri, to which he had been appointed the first professor. Each facet of his diverse oeuvre was represented—portraits, landscapes, and election scenes—so it was only fitting that his most well-known and widely circulated artwork should have a presence, too.

At the end of his life, his ambitions were more localized than they had been in the 1830s and 1840s. Bingham focused his efforts on depicting historical events and figures of significance to Missouri, rather than designing works that engaged contemporary popular culture or economic currents. As a result, the inland rivers that had been central to defining the social and economic aspirations of his class and his career receded from view.

Bingham never withdrew from political life and remained interested in developing the commercial possibilities of his art by having prints made after his paintings. But, unlike the self-portrait he painted more than forty years earlier, his self-portrait of about 1877 puts his artistic profession and practice on display by portraying him in the act of drawing (Fig. 37). Reflecting on his position in the lineage of art history and the establishment and growth of an American tradition in particular, Bingham wrote to his longtime friend and supporter Rollins:

> *The humorous productions of Mount and others as seen in the "bargaining for a horse" "The jolly flat Boatmen" and "County Election," assure us that our social and political characteristics as daily and annually exhibited will not be lost in the lapse of time for want of an Art record rendering them full justice.*[165]

Using titles instead of his name to speak of himself, Bingham asserts that, along with the work of William Sidney Mount, the author of *Bargaining for a Horse*, his everyday scenes still had significance after more than two decades and a civil war. Indeed, he created "an Art record" that persists to the present day because of its capacity to sustain interpretation from multiple points of view. Though most of Bingham's art remains in Missouri—the number of portraits he painted of Missourians outpaced the rest of his oeuvre—his river paintings can be found in museums all over the United States. This distribution is partly the result of the routes that Bingham's paintings and prints took in the nineteenth century, spurred by his ambitions for wide acclaim. But as Walker and Turk show in their essay in this volume, the paintings' continued transit on the art market and in traveling exhibitions of the twentieth and twenty-first centuries also speaks to the ability of his works to operate within different historical contexts.

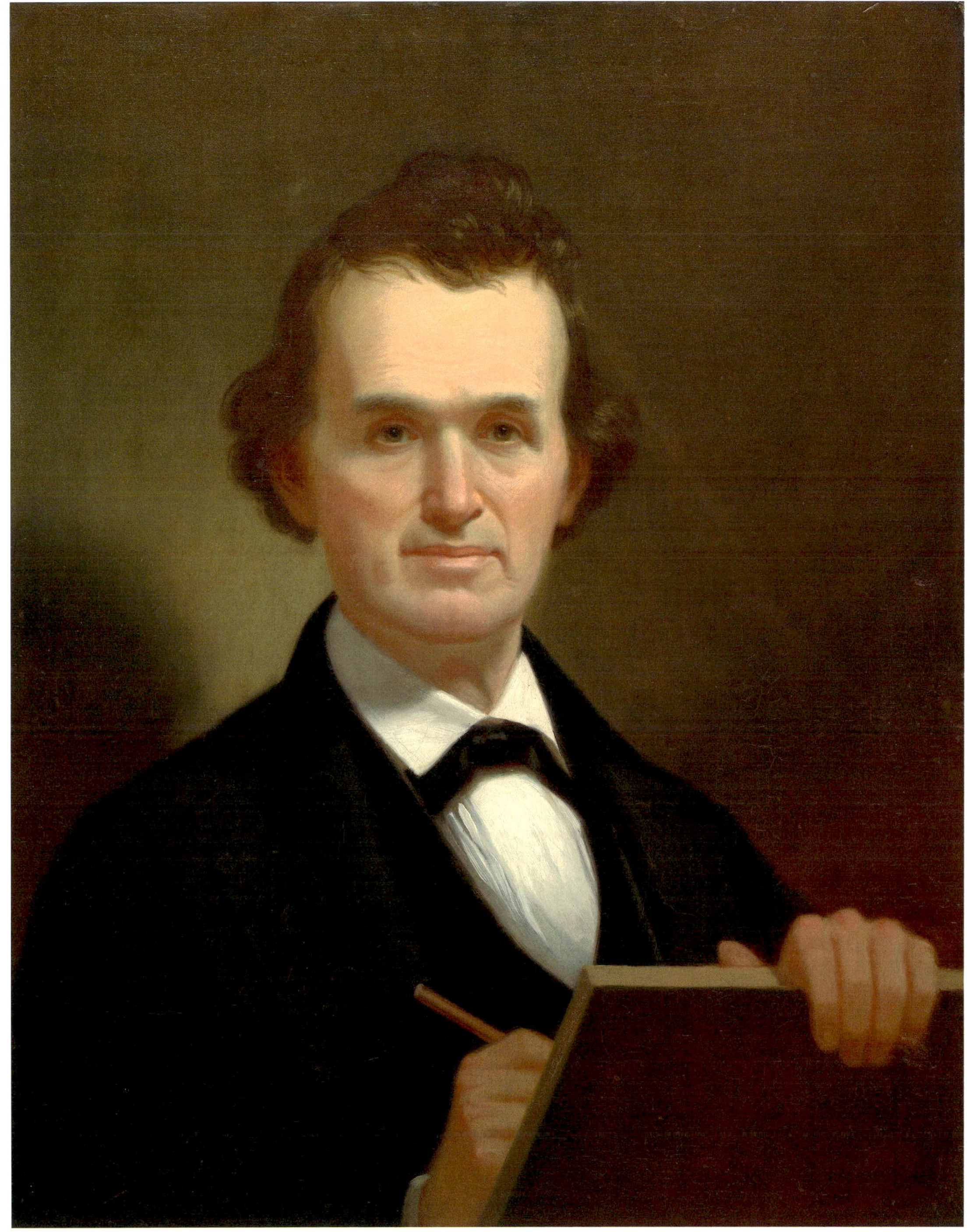

Fig. 37: George Caleb Bingham (1811–1879), *Self-Portrait*, ca. 1877, oil on canvas, 27 1/16 × 22 1/16 in., The Nelson-Atkins Museum of Art, Kansas City, Missouri, lent by the Kansas City Public Library, 1-1995

NOTES

1. *Saint Louis Enquirer*, quoted in *Franklin Missouri Intelligencer*, March 13, 1824.

2. *Franklin Missouri Intelligencer*, March 13, 1824.

3. The *Davy Crockett Almanacs* were published in several editions from 1835 to 1856, though the seed of the mythic boatman was planted in the 1820s and 1830s with stories about Mike Fink. Walter Blair and Franklin J. Meine, *Half Horse, Half Alligator: The Growth of the Mike Fink Legend* (Chicago: University of Chicago Press, 1956); Michael Allen, *Western Rivermen, 1763–1861: Ohio and Mississippi Boatmen and the Myth of the Alligator Horse* (Baton Rouge: Louisiana State University Press, 1990); David Tatham, "The Half Horse–Half Alligator and Other Members of the Jacksonian Bestiary: A Study in American Iconography," in *Graphic Arts & the South: Proceedings of the 1990 North American Print Conference*, ed. Judy L. Larson (Fayetteville: University of Arkansas Press, 1993), 3–30. See also Michael A. Lofaro, ed., *Davy Crockett: The Man, the Legend, the Legacy, 1786–1986* (Knoxville: University of Tennessee, 1985).

4. For Bingham's painting style, see John Wilmerding, "George Caleb Bingham's Geometries and the Shape of America," in *American Views: Essays on American Art* (Princeton: Princeton University Press, 1991), 178–94; Ron Tyler, "George Caleb Bingham: The Native Talent," in *American Frontier Life: Early Western Paintings and Prints* (Fort Worth: Amon Carter Museum, 1987), 25–49; Barbara Novak, *American Painting of the Nineteenth Century: Realism, Idealism, and the American Experience*, 2nd ed. (New York: Harper and Row, 1979), 152–64. Elizabeth Johns focuses on the role of eastern audiences in determining western subject matter in "Settlement and Development: Claiming the West," in *The West as America: Reintepreting Images of the Frontier*, ed. William H. Truettner (Washington, D.C.: Smithsonian Institution Press, 1991), 191–235. Elsewhere, Johns notes that Bingham approaches his construction of the western boatman type from "the perspective of an urban, traveled Westerner" who emphasized the positive contributions of Missourians to the nation. Johns, *American Genre Painting: The Politics of Everyday Life* (New Haven: Yale University Press, 1991), 82–87.

5. For instance, E. Maurice Bloch likens the pose of Bingham's dancing boatman figure in *The Jolly Flatboatmen* to a Dancing Satyr from Casa del Fauno, Pompeii, Museo Nazionale, Naples. Bloch also compares the card-playing motif in Bingham's painting *Raftsmen Playing Cards* to the cardplayers of Sir David Wilkie (1783–1841) and Louis-Léopold Boilly (1761–1845). Bloch, *George Caleb Bingham: The Evolution of an Artist* (Berkeley: University of California Press, 1967), 94–95, 97–99. Nancy Rash identifies Raphael's river god in an engraving by Marcantonio Raimondi of *The Judgment of Paris* and the Christ figure in Raphael's *Transfiguration* (Vatican Pinacoteca) as models for two figures in *The Jolly Flatboatmen*. Rash, *The Painting and Politics of George Caleb Bingham* (New Haven: Yale University Press, 1991), 82–85. Rash's book is also the source for an in-depth discussion of Bingham and politics, a topic that cannot be covered here.

6. Angela Miller, "The Mechanisms of the Market and the Invention of Western Regionalism: The Example of George Caleb Bingham," *Oxford Art Journal* 15, no. 1 (June 1992): 3–20.

7. Timothy R. Mahoney, *River Towns in the Great West: The Structure of Provincial Urbanization in the American Midwest, 1820–1860* (Cambridge: Cambridge University Press, 1990), 55.

8. According to John Francis McDermott, Bingham was first dubbed the "Missouri artist" in the *Jefferson City Inquirer*, June 26, 1845. McDermott, *George Caleb Bingham: River Portraitist* (Norman: University of Oklahoma Press, 1959), 49. Margaret C. Conrads notes that it was used even earlier, in "The Festival at Rocheport," *Boon's Lick Times* (Fayette, Mo.), July 4, 1840, quoted in Margaret C. Conrads et al., "Fishing on the Mississippi, 1851," in *The Collections of the Nelson-Atkins Museum of Art: American Paintings to 1945*, ed. Margaret C. Conrads (Kansas City, Mo.: Nelson-Atkins Museum of Art, 2007), 1:114. By 1849 the nickname (with the word "Artist" capitalized) was more widely known because it appeared in the artist's biography featured in the *Bulletin of the American Art-Union* 2, no. 5 (August 1849): 10, which had a national readership.

9. "The Gallery—No. 4," *Bulletin of the American Art-Union* 2, no. 5 (August 1849): 10.

10. McDermott, *River Portraitist*, 4.

11. William Lass, *Navigating the Missouri: Steamboating on Nature's Highway, 1819–1935* (Norman, Okla: Arthur H. Clark Company, 2008).

12. Mahoney, *River Towns*, 76.

13. T. B. Thorpe, "The Big Bear of Arkansas," in *The Big Bear of Arkansas and Other Sketches*, ed. William T. Porter (Philadelphia: T. B. Peterson and Brothers, 1846), 13. The story was first published in the May 1841 issue of the *American Turf Register and Sporting Magazine*.

14. Stephen Aron coined the term "confluence region" in relation to Missouri during its territorial phase in *American Confluence: The Missouri Frontier from Borderland to Border State* (Bloomington: Indiana University Press, 2006), xvii.

15. Mark Wyman, *Immigrants in the Valley: Irish, Germans, and Americans in the Upper Mississippi Country, 1830–1860* (Chicago: Nelson-Hall, 1984).

16. Unlike larger Lower Mississippi plantations and other areas of the Deep South, however, Little Dixie farmers were mostly small-scale slaveholders. See Diane Mutti Burke, *On Slavery's Border: Missouri's Small-Slaveholding Households, 1815–1865* (Athens: University of Georgia Press, 2010); Jeffrey Stone, *Slavery, Southern Culture, and Education in Little Dixie, Missouri, 1820–1860* (London: Routledge, 2006).

17. Besides the North–South axis, there were other ways to parse the region. For instance, local urban centers such as Saint Louis were alienated from the interior of the state by differing political ideologies as well as the character of evolving immigrant and emigrant populations. Aron, *American Confluence*, xxi, 233. For a discussion of the evolution from accommodation to exclusion on the frontier as Missouri inched toward statehood, see John Mack Faragher,

"'More Motley than Mackinaw': From Ethnic Mixing and Ethnic Cleansing on the Frontier of the Lower Missouri, 1783–1833," in *Contact Points: American Frontiers from the Mohawk Valley to the Mississippi, 1750–1830*, ed. Andrew R. L. Clayton and Fredrika J. Teute (Chapel Hill: University of North Carolina Press, published for the Omohundro Institute of Early American History and Culture, Williamsburg, Virginia, 1998), 304–26; Perry McCandless, *A History of Missouri*, vol. 2 (Columbia: University of Missouri Press, 2000).

18. E. Maurice Bloch, *The Paintings of George Caleb Bingham with a Catalogue Raisonné* (Columbia: University of Missouri Press, 1986), 132.

19. Mary Collins Barile, *The Santa Fe Trail in Missouri* (Columbia: University of Missouri Press, 2010), 22; Bloch, *Paintings of George Caleb Bingham*, 132–33.

20. Lass, *Navigating the Missouri*, 46.

21. For more details on Bingham's early life and that of his father, see Paul C. Nagel, *George Caleb Bingham: Missouri's Famed Painter and Forgotten Politician* (Columbia: University of Missouri Press, 2005).

22. Lass, *Navigating the Missouri*, 63–64.

23. Ibid., 47.

24. Though Bingham's meeting with Harding was subject to much debate in early scholarship, a letter Bingham wrote in 1872 that was discovered in 1984 has defused the controversy. See Leah Lipton, "George Caleb Bingham in the Studio of Chester Harding, Franklin, Missouri, 1820," *American Art Journal* 16, no. 3 (Summer 1984): 90–92. Nagel asserts that Bingham and Harding met twice more at crucial moments in Bingham's career, once in Boonville, Missouri, in 1830 or 1831, and once in Philadelphia in 1838. Nagel, *Missouri's Famed Painter and Forgotten Politician*, 14–15, 25.

25. Leah Lipton, *A Truthful Likeness: Chester Harding and His Portraits* (Washington, D.C.: National Portrait Gallery, 1985), 13. Also see Chester Harding, *My Egotistography* (Cambridge, Mass., 1866).

26. Lipton, "George Caleb Bingham in the Studio of Chester Harding," 92.

27. The location of Bingham's studio is indicated on a business card he published in the *Missouri Republican* in March 1834. See George McCue, *Bingham's Missouri* (Jefferson City, Mo.: Bingham Sketches, 1975), unpaginated. William H. Gerdts discusses the practices of a handful of other itinerant portraitists working in the Natchez area in *The South and Midwest: Art Across America: Two Centuries of Regional Painting, 1710–1920*, vol. 2, *The South and Midwest* (New York: Abbeville Press, 1990), 87–88.

28. Bloch, *Paintings of George Caleb Bingham*, 131–47.

29. Bingham to Sarah Elizabeth Hutchison, November 30, 1835, in *"But I Forget That I Am a Painter and Not a Politician": The Letters of George Caleb Bingham*, ed. Lynn Wolf Gentzler (Columbia: State Historical Society of Missouri, 2011), 36.

30. Irvin G. Wyllie notes that Henry Clay coined the term "self-made man" during a speech given on February 2, 1832: "In Kentucky, almost every manufactory known to me is in the hands of enterprising self-made men, who have whatever wealth they possess by patient and diligent labor." Quoted in Wyllie, *The Self-Made Man in America: The Myth of Rags to Riches* (New York: Free Press, 1954), 9–10.

31. *Saint Louis Reveille*, March 23, 1846.

32. Quoted in Lipton, *Truthful Likeness*, 17.

33. On Bingham's use of drawing books, see Nagel, *Missouri's Famed Painter and Forgotten Politician*, 9–16. Peter C. Marzio has determined that more than 145 different drawing books were published and sold in the United States between 1820 and 1860. Many of these manuals were published in Philadelphia, where Bingham continued his artistic education. Marzio, *The Art Crusade: An Analysis of American Drawing Manuals, 1820–1860* (Washington, D.C.: Smithsonian Institution Press, 1976), 1.

34. John Rubens Smith, *A Key to the Art of Drawing the Human Figure* (Philadelphia: Samuel Stewart, 1831), quoted in Carl W. Dreppard, *American Pioneer Arts and Artists* (Springfield, Mass.: Pond-Ekberg Company, 1942), 18.

35. John Gadsby Chapman, *The American Drawing Book* (New York: J. S. Redfield, 1847), 4, quoted in Marzio, *Art Crusade*, 12.

36. For more on the relationship between Rollins and Bingham, see Nagel, *Missouri's Famed Painter and Forgotten Politician*, 18–20; Bloch, *Paintings of George Caleb Bingham*, 133–34.

37. Nagel, *Missouri's Famed Painter and Forgotten Politician*, 9–16.

38. Anthony Rotundo, *American Manhood: Transformations in Masculinity from the Revolution to the Modern Era* (New York: Basic Books, 1993), 170; Wyllie, *Self-Made Man in America*, 9.

39. Bloch, *Paintings of George Caleb Bingham*, 140.

40. Bingham to James S. Rollins, May 6, 1837, in *Missouri Historical Review* 32 (1937): 7.

41. "Gallery—No. 4," 11.

42. Kevin Muller, "Cultural Costuming: Native Americans, Inversion and the Power of an Exceptional White Masculinity" (Ph.D. diss., University of California, Berkeley, 2003), 112.

43. Wetmore was born in Fort Jay, New York. His father, Alphonso, was the author of a successful play (*The Pedlar*, 1821) and other vignettes of frontier life that he published in the *Missouri Intelligencer*.

44. Daniel J. Herman, "The Other Daniel Boone: The Nascence of a Middle-Class Hunter Hero, 1784–1860," *Journal of the Early Republic* 18, no. 3 (Autumn 1998): 432.

45. Dawn Glanz, *How the West Was Drawn: American Art and the Settling of the Frontier* (Ann Arbor, Mich.: UMI Research Press, 1982), 6, 160n26.

46. Muller, "Cultural Costuming," 120.

47. Lamme was her second husband; her first died after they moved to Boone County from Kentucky. Bloch, *Paintings of George Caleb Bingham*, 141, notes that conservation treatment in 1978 "showed [that] considerable overpainting and alteration of color and detail" had occurred, in which the furnishings had been painted out, the background covered in dark colors, and the landscape completely covered by a curtain. He speculates that the changes were made to conform to a more conservative taste and outlook. It has been restored to its original state.

48. On the link between landscape appreciation and constructions of refinement and class, see Angela Miller, "Landscape Taste as an Indicator of Class Identity in Antebellum America," in *Art in Bourgeois Society, 1790–1850*, ed. Andrew Hemingway and William Vaughan (Cambridge: Cambridge University Press, 1998), 340–61; Kenneth John Myers, "On the Cultural Construction of Landscape Experience: Contact to 1830," in *American Iconology: New Approaches to Nineteenth-Century Art and Literature*, ed. David C. Miller (New Haven: Yale University Press, 1993), 58–79.

49. Wyllie, *Self-Made Man in America*, 100.

50. *Missouri Republican*, December 13, 1836.

51. *Columbia Missouri Intelligencer*, March 14, 1835.

52. Herman, "Other Daniel Boone," 432.

53. It began as the Apollo Association for the Advancement of the Fine Arts in the United States but was renamed the American Art-Union in 1844. Joy Sperling discusses the organization's roots in Europe in "'Art, Cheap and Good': The Art Union in England and the United States, 1840–60," *Nineteenth-Century Art Worldwide* 1, no. 1 (Spring 2002), www.19thc-artworldwide.org/index.php/spring02/196–qart-cheap-and-goodq-the-art-union-in-england-and-the-united-states-184060. Lillian B. Miller outlines the early history of the organization and its founding goals in *Patrons and Patriotism: The Encouragement of Fine Arts in the United States, 1790–1860* (Chicago: University of Chicago Press, 1966), 160–72. For overviews of the AA-U that also offer specific information about the works chosen by its management committees, see Maybelle Mann, *The American Art-Union* (Otisville, N.Y.: ALM Associates, 1977); Mary Bartlett Cowdrey, *American Academy of Fine Arts and American Art-Union: Introduction, 1816–1852* (New York: New-York Historical Society, 1953); Arlene Katz Nichols, "Merchants and Artists: The Apollo Association and the American Art-Union" (Ph.D. diss., City University of New York, 2003).

54. Patricia Hills, "The American Art-Union as Patron for Expansionist Ideology in the 1840s," in Hemingway and Vaughan, *Art in Bourgeois Society, 1790–1850*, 314–39.

55. Solomons to Robert F. Fraser, May 7, 1845, American Art-Union Papers, Letters Received, reel 10, New-York Historical Society.

56. Advertisements were placed in nationally circulated magazines such as those that would be "read in the parlor rather than the Counting rooms" such as the *Commercial Advertiser*, *Evening Post*, the *Home Journal*, and the *Democratic Review*, the first three being "emphatically family papers" with readers of "that class of persons who are most likely to subscribe to the Art-Union." The committee cites the *Democratic Review* as having "a large circulation among the prominent persons in the country" and able to garner "the attention of an important and influential class of individuals to the objects of the institution, and thus aid the agencies out of the City." American Art-Union Papers, Management Committee Meeting Minutes, December 8, 1847, and February 1, 1847, reel 1, New-York Historical Society.

57. *United States Magazine and Democratic Review* 23, no. 24 (October 1848): 374.

58. Jeffery S. Adler, *Yankee Merchants and the Making of the Urban West: The Rise and Fall of Antebellum St. Louis* (Cambridge: Cambridge University Press, 1991). Additionally, manuscripts and correspondence in the collection of the Missouri Historical Society in Saint Louis testify to the commercial connections between cities like Saint Louis and New Orleans and eastern businesses.

59. *New Orleans Picayune*, n.d., American Art-Union Papers, Newspaper Clippings, reel 3, New-York Historical Society. Another way that the AA-U dealt with the high frequency of travel was to place its year-end summary report, *Transactions of the American Art-Union*, in steamboats and hotels. Executive Committee, Minutes, July 20, 1848, reel 2, New-York Historical Society.

60. *Transactions of the Western Art-Union* 1, no. 5 (October 1849), quoted in McDermott, *River Portraitist*, 69. The location of this particular canvas is unknown.

61. David E. Schob, "Woodhawks and Cordwood," *Journal of Forest History* 21, no. 3 (July 1977): 124–32.

62. Bingham to American Art-Union, quoted in Bloch, *Paintings of George Caleb Bingham*, 188.

63. Schob, "Woodhawks and Cordwood," 127.

64. "Wooding Up on the Mississippi," *Ballou's Pictorial Drawing Room Companion* 10, no. 23 (June 7, 1856): 365.

65. *Missouri Republican*, n.d., quoted in McDermott, *River Portraitist*, 76.

66. *Saint Louis Republican*, April 21, 1847.

67. For the cultural influence and political implications of these projects, see Kenneth Haltman, "The Pictorial Legacy of Lewis and Clark," in *Knowing Nature: Art and Science in Philadelphia, 1740–1840*, ed. Amy R. W. Meyers (New Haven: Yale University Press, 2011), 330–55; Kenneth Haltman, *Looking Close and Seeing Far: Samuel Seymour, Titian Ramsey Peale, and the Art of the Long Expedition, 1818–1823* (University Park: Pennsylvania State University Press, 2008); William Goetzmann, *Army Exploration in the American West, 1803–1863* (Lincoln: University of Nebraska Press, 1979); Carolyn Gilman, ed., *Lewis and Clark: Across the Divide* (Washington, D.C.: Smithsonian Books, in association with the Missouri Historical Society, Saint Louis, 2003); Z. M. Pike, *An Account of Expeditions to the Sources of the Mississippi and through the Western Parts of Louisiana* (Philadelphia: C. & A. Conrad & Co., 1810).

68. For an extensive study of Catlin's career, see William H. Truettner, *The Natural Man Observed: A Study of Catlin's Indian Gallery* (Washington, D.C.: Smithsonian Institution Press, 1979). On Bodmer, see Brandon K. Ruud, ed., *Karl Bodmer's North American Prints* (Lincoln: University of Nebraska Press for the Joslyn Art Museum, 2004).

69. George Caleb Bingham to Sarah Elizabeth Hutchison, December 16, 1835, Bingham Family Papers, Manuscripts, 1814–1930, folder 4, State Historical Society of Missouri.

70. Kathryn Sweeney Hight, "The Frontier Indian in White Art, 1820–1876: The Development of a Myth" (Ph.D. diss., University of California at Los Angeles, 1987), 180.

71. George Catlin, *Christian Watchman*, November 9, 1832.

72. After his western sojourn, Catlin took his Indian Gallery of more than five hundred paintings on a highly publicized tour of eastern cities before continuing to London and Paris in late 1839. The exhibition featured hundreds of portraits of Native Americans, as well as scores of hunting, ballgame, village, and landscape scenes, and was accompanied by an extensive commentary by the artist about his adventures. His perspective, however, was always that of a traveler, an outsider who emphasized the wondrous otherness of the sights he depicted.

73. George Catlin, *Letters and Notes on the Manners, Customs, and Condition of the North American Indians Written during Eight Years' Travel amongst the Wildest Tribes of Indians in North America*, 2 vols. (London, 1841; repr., Minneapolis: Ross & Haines, 1965), 1:18. Also see Truettner, *Natural Man Observed*, 232–56.

74. Frederick W. Gale to Anna D. Gale, September 22, 1842, Frederick W. Gale Letters, Missouri Historical Society Library, originals, American Antiquarian Society, Worcester, Mass.

75. See, for example, Johns, *American Genre Painting*, 60–99; Glanz, *How the West Was Drawn*; Tyler et al., *American Frontier Life*.

76. Carol Clark, "Telling Tales in 1840s America," in Carol Clark et al., *Charles Deas and 1840s America* (Norman: University of Oklahoma Press in cooperation with the Denver Art Museum, 2009), 98–105.

77. Johns, *American Genre Painting*, 60, 76.

78. Ibid., 84–85; Miller, "The Mechanisms of the Market."

79. "Missouri River," *Pittsburgh Recorder*, March 28, 1823.

80. For examples, see Janet Whitmore, "A Panorama of Unequaled Yet Ever-Varying Beauty," in *Currents of Change: Art and Life along the Mississippi, 1850–1861* (Minneapolis: Minneapolis Institute of Arts, 2004), 12–61; *Mississippi Panorama* (Saint Louis: City Art Museum, 1949).

81. Sources that focus specifically on moving panoramas of the Mississippi River are John Francis McDermott, *The Lost Panoramas of the Mississippi* (Chicago: University of Chicago Press, 1958); Angela Miller, "'The Imperial Republic': Narratives of National Expansion in American Art, 1820–1860" (Ph.D. diss., Yale University, 1985), vol. 2; Joseph Earl Arrington, "The Story of Stockwell's Panorama," *Minnesota History* 33, no. 7 (Autumn 1953): 284–90.

82. Several scholars have characterized the viewing experience as passive and absorptive, leading them to suggest that the moving panorama can be considered a precursor to cinema. See Angela Miller, "The Panorama, the Cinema, and the Emergence of the Spectacular," *Wide Angle* 18, no. 2 (1996): 24–69; Alison Griffiths, *Shivers Down Your Spine: Cinema, Museums, and the Immersive View* (New York: Columbia Press, 2008), 37–78.

83. *Saint Louis Weekly Reveille*, April 20, 1847, quoted in McDermott, *River Portraitist*, 60. McDermott speculates that *Wood Yard on the Missouri* might have been the same painting as *Wood Station on the Mississippi*, shown at the Chicago Exhibition of Fine Arts in 1859, demonstrating how malleable the titles and settings of Bingham's works could be. McDermott, 69n6.

84. On Wild, see John W. Reps, *John Caspar Wild: Painter and Printmaker of Nineteenth-Century Urban America* (Saint Louis: Missouri Historical Society Press, 2006). Michael Shapiro, "The River Paintings," in *George Caleb Bingham* (Saint Louis: Saint Louis Art Museum in association with H. N. Abrams, 1990), 151.

85. The two paintings are *St. Louis Wharf* or *Saint Louis Landing*, exhibited in Cincinnati at the Western Art Union in 1849 before being sold to the American Art-Union, and *Jolly Flatboatmen in Port* of 1857. Although the former's whereabouts are unknown, a contemporaneous description indicates that the setting was probably much like the latter painting, focusing on the stacks of cargo, boatmen, and other people around the docks at the expense of any recognizable details about the city itself. See Bloch, *Paintings of George Caleb Bingham*, 180.

86. Clark, "Telling Tales," 106–13.

87. Henry Adams, "A New Interpretation of Bingham's Fur Traders Descending the Missouri," *Art Bulletin* 65, no. 4 (December 1983): 675–80. See also Bloch, *Paintings of George Caleb Bingham*, 172–73.

88. Faragher, "More Motley than Mackinaw," 305.

89. Barbara Groseclose discusses the two paintings as reflecting a progressive view of history and civilization and refers to the Indian figure as an "Osage warrior." Groseclose, "The 'Missouri Artist' as Historian," in *George Caleb Bingham*, 57. My thanks to Leah Bowe for pointing out this similarity in pattern.

90. Rash, *Painting and Politics*, 45–49.

91. Russel L. Gerlach, *Settlement Patterns in Missouri: A Study of Population Origins with a Wall Map* (Columbia: University of Missouri Press, 1986), 3, 15–29.

92. "Internal Slave Trade," *Liberator*, May 17, 1834. For a historical account of the domestic slave trade, see Steven Deyle, *Carry Me Back: The Domestic Slave Trade in American Life* (Oxford: Oxford University Press, 2005); Walter Johnson, *River of Dark Dreams: Slavery and Empire in the Cotton Kingdom* (Cambridge, Mass.: Harvard University Press, 2013).

93. Thomas C. Buchanan, *Black Life on the Mississippi: Slaves, Free Blacks, and the Western Steamboat World* (Chapel Hill: University of North Carolina Press, 2004).

94. Allen, *Western Rivermen*, 176.

95. "The Development of Nationality in American Art," *Bulletin of the American Art-Union* 9 (December 1, 1851): 137–39.

96. Fern Helen Rusk, *George Caleb Bingham: The Missouri Artist* (Jefferson City, Mo.: Hugh Stephens Co., 1917), 35.

97. Allen, *Western Rivermen*, 178.

98. "The Gallery—No. 4," 10.

99. Ibid.

100. For more on Flint's life, see John Ervin Kirkpatrick, *Timothy Flint, Pioneer, Missionary, Author, Editor, 1780–1840: The Story of His Life among the Pioneers and Frontiersmen in the Ohio and Mississippi Valley and in New England and the South* (Cleveland: Arthur H. Clark, 1911). A survey of the numerous travel guides and panorama pamphlets published in the 1830s and 1840s makes it clear that many authors took their cues from Flint's descriptions of the West, many quoting selections of his writings verbatim and only sometimes citing him as a source. The most commonly quoted was Timothy Flint, *Recollections of the Last Ten Years, Passed in Occasional Residences and Journeyings in the Valley of the Mississippi* (Boston: Cummings, Hillard, and Co., 1826). For a recent discussion of authenticity and authorial voice, see Nathaniel Lewis, "Truth of Consequences: Projecting Authenticity in the 1830s," in *True West: Authenticity and the American West*, ed. William R. Handley and Nathaniel Lewis (Lincoln: University of Nebraska Press, 2004), 9–33.

101. Edmund Flagg, *The Far West; or, A Tour beyond the Mountains*, vol. 1 (New York: Harper and Brothers, 1838), 30; *Daily Missouri Republican*, April 21, 1847.

102. Ibid., *Daily Missouri Republican*, April 21, 1847.

103. "The Art-Union Pictures," *Literary World* 2, no. 38 (October 23, 1847).

104. *Anglo American, a Journal of Literature, News, Politics, the Drama, Fine Arts* 9, no. 6 (May 29, 1847): 93.

105. The current owner of this painting is of the opinion that it was submitted to the AA-U in 1845. Bloch, *Paintings of George Caleb Bingham*, 173, notes that another, possibly identical, landscape may have been the one purchased by the AA-U.

106. Ann Archbold, *A Book for the Married and Single, the Grave and the Gay, and Especially Designed for Steamboat Passengers* (East Plainfield, Ohio: N. A. Baker, 1850), preface.

107. Ibid., 32, 52.

108. Ibid., 71.

109. "Original Rural Poetry," *Pennsylvania Correspondent, and Farmers' Advertiser* 1, no. 42 (April 23, 1805): 4.

110. "Homeward Bound," *Family Magazine: or, Monthly Abstract of General Knowledge* 8 (1840–41): 363–64, Google Books.

111. William J. Mahar, *Behind the Burnt Cork Mask: Early Blackface Minstrelsy and Antebellum Popular Culture* (Urbana: University of Illinois Press, 1999), 13, 15–16.

112. Robert C. Toll, *Blacking Up: The Minstrel Show in Nineteenth Century America* (New York: Oxford University Press, 1974), 41.

113. Rash, *Painting and Politics*, 75. See Eric Lott, *Love and Theft: Blackface Minstrelsy and the American Working Class* (New York: Oxford University Press, 1993) for a discussion of the complicated dynamic between white performers, audiences, the black roles they played, and African-Americans to whom those characters referred.

114. "The Art-Union Pictures," *Literary World* 2, no. 38 (October 23, 1847): 277.

115. Allen, *Western Rivermen*, 69–110, discusses the typical social and labor hierarchies on flat- and keelboats.

116. Blair and Meine, *Half Horse, Half Alligator*; Allen, *Western Rivermen*, 7–16.

117. "Western Boatmen," *Bellows Falls, Vermont, Chronicle*, July 2, 1830.

118. Ibid.

119. Allen, *Western Rivermen*, 188.

120. Ibid., 181.

121. Rotundo, *American Manhood*, 60. Related studies have focused on the emergence of white working-class identity, such as David R. Roediger, *The Wages of Whiteness: Race and the Making of the American Working Class* (London: Verso, 1991), and others on the middle class, as Stuart Blumin, *The Emergence of the Middle Class: Social Experience in the American City, 1760–1900* (New York: Cambridge University Press, 1989).

122. Robert S. Bunker was born about 1802 and died in 1895. 1860 Census, Mobile Ward 5, Mobile, Alabama, roll M653_17, page 405, image 405, Ancestry.com (accessed November 14, 2011); 1880 Census, Mobile, Alabama, roll 25, family history film 1254025, page 320C, image 0362, Ancestry.com (accessed November 14, 2011). John R. Macmurdo was born about 1813 and probably died in 1868. 1850 Census, New Orleans, Municipality 2, Ward 4, New Orleans, Louisiana, roll M432_237, page 268A, image 539, Ancestry.com (accessed November 14, 2011). Records of the Bureau of the Census, Record Group 29, National Archives, Washington, D.C.; *New Orleans Death Indices, 1804–1876*, vol. 43, 683, Ancestry.com (accessed November 14, 2011).

123. Thomas Doney was born in Tavistock, Devonshire, England, in 1809, though he received his artistic training in France. He died in Chicago in 1890. Michael Leja, "Fortified Images for the Masses," *Art Journal* 70, no. 4 (Winter 2011): 60–83. Doney's correspondence with the AA-U indicates that he was living in New York from 1847 to 1848 while working on the Bingham print.

124. Though Bingham's painting *The Jolly Flatboatmen* was first purchased in 1846, its selection for engraving later that year delayed the painting's debut in the annual exhibition until 1847, when it was awarded to Benjamin van Schaick, a New York City grocer, in the annual lottery. Daniel Huntington's painting *A Sibyl* had been given away earlier and had to be borrowed from that member to make the print.

125. "The Fine Arts," *Literary World* 9 (April 3, 1847): 208.

126. J., "Correspondence: To the Committee of Management of the American Art Union," *Literary World* 1, no. 15 (May 15, 1847): 347.

127. *Literary World* 1 (April 3, 1847): 209, quoted in Lillian B. Miller, "Painting, Sculpture, and the National Character, 1815–1860," *Journal of American History* 53, no. 4 (March 1967): 701.

128. R. C. W., "American Art and Art Unions," *Christian Examiner and Religious Miscellany* 48, no. 2 (March 1850): 15.

129. Relatively few engravers worked in mezzotint; preeminent among them was John Sartain. Ann Katharine Martinez, "The Life and Career of John Sartain (1808–1897): A Nineteenth Century Philadelphia Printmaker" (Ph.D. diss., George Washington University, 1986), 19.

130. "Notices of the Fine Arts—Bank Engraving," *Godey's Lady's Book*, March 1848.

131. The Apollo Association published a mezzotint by John Sartain after John Blake White's painting *General Marion in His Swamp Encampment Inviting a British Officer to Dinner* in 1840 and another after George Comegys's painting *The Artist's Dream*. Carol Wax points out that the London Art-Union often distributed mezzotints to subscribers not only because of their high prestige but also because of the inexpensive cost and relative speed with which they could be produced. Wax, *The Mezzotint: History and Technique* (New York: Harry N. Abrams, 1990), 108. On *Godey's* and other illustrated magazines published in Philadelphia, see Cynthia Lee Patterson, *Art for the Middle Classes: America's Illustrated Magazines of the 1840s* (Jackson: University Press of Mississippi, 2010), 88.

132. Wax, *Mezzotint*, 104, 108.

133. "American Art Union," *Natchez Weekly Courier*, October 24, 1848.

134. American Art-Union Papers, Newspaper Clippings, reel 3, New-York Historical Society.

135. *Maryland Free Press*, October 7, 1848.

136. "Female Labor," *Scientific American* 1, no. 42 (July 9, 1846): 3; "The Southwestern Convention, at Memphis," *Merchants' Magazine and Commercial Review* 15, no. 1 (July 1, 1846): 63. Some contemporary scholars have described Bingham as representing a fantasy, an Arcadian space that was not past or present but very much out of any real time. See Bryan J. Wolf, "History as Ideology: Or, 'What You Don't See Can't Hurt You, Mr. Bingham,'" in *Redefining American History Painting*, ed. Patricia M. Burnham and Lucretia Hoover Giese (Cambridge: Cambridge University Press, 1995), 243.

137. *Howitt's Journal of Literature and Popular Progress* 2, no. 36 (September 4, 1847): 145–48.

138. Ibid., 145.

139. See note 8 above.

140. *Howitt's Journal*, 148.

141. In *Recollections of the Last Ten Years*, Flint notes: "Almost every boat, while it lies in the harbour has one or more fiddles scraping continually aboard, to which you often see the boatmen dancing." Flint, *Recollections of the Last Ten Years Passed in Occasional Residences and Journeyings in the Valley of the Mississippi* (1826; repr., New York: Johnson Reprint Corporation, 1968), 15. In *The History and Geography of the Mississippi Valley* (Cincinnati, 1833), 1:151–53, he narrates a scene that seems to explicitly describe the conditions that produced the image of *The Jolly Flatboatmen*: "At this time there is no visible danger, or call for labor. The boat takes care of itself. . . . Meantime one of the hands scrapes a violin, and the others dance."

142. *Howitt's Journal*, 148.

143. For more on the complicated history of Lewis's panorama and subsequently published journal and images, see Henry Lewis, *The Valley of the Mississippi Illustrated*, trans. A. Hermina Poatgieter, ed. Bertha L. Heilbron (Saint Paul: Minnesota Historical Society, 1967); Bertha L. Heilbron, introduction to *Making a Motion Picture in 1848: Henry Lewis' Journal of a Canoe Voyage from the Falls of St. Anthony to St. Louis* (Saint Paul: Minnesota Historical Society, 1936).

144. Rick Stewart, Joseph D. Ketner II, and Angela L. Miller, *Carl Wimar: Chronicler of the Missouri River Frontier* (Fort Worth: Amon Carter Museum, 1991). For biographical information and Wimar's relationship to other artists, see esp. Ketner, "The Indian Painter in Düsseldorf," 30–79.

145. Wimar's painting was exhibited at the Fourth Annual Saint Louis Fair in 1859; at the Mississippi Valley Sanitary Fair in New Orleans in 1864 with the title *Moonlight on the Missouri*; and at the Seventh Annual Exhibition of the Saint Louis Exposition and Music Hall Association in 1890. In 1946 it was exhibited at the City Art Museum of Saint Louis as *Jolly Flatboatmen by Moonlight*. The painting was in the collection of the Amon Carter Museum from 1969 until it was deaccessioned in 2000. Curatorial files, Amon Carter Museum of American Art.

146. E. Maurice Bloch, *The Paintings of George Caleb Bingham with a Catalogue Raisonné* (Columbia: University of Missouri Press, 1986), 13.

147. McDermott, *River Portraitist*, 82; Bloch, *Drawings of George Caleb Bingham*, 184.

148. Bloch assigned the title by which this painting is known based on its similarity to the earlier work and did the same for *Western Boatmen Ashore by Night* of the same year. It is unknown what titles Bingham used. Bloch, *Paintings of George Caleb Bingham*, 204.

149. In these works, Bingham may have been inspired by *Fire at Night*, a painting by the seventeenth-century Dutch artist Egbert van der Poel, known for his firelight nocturnes, which was on view at the Pennsylvania Academy of the Fine Arts in the early 1850s. At the time, the academy collected artworks by European as well as American artists, though the painting has since been deaccessioned and no records of it exist. The American artist Walter M. Oddie also showed a nocturnal scene titled *Moonlight* in the same exhibition. *Catalogue of the Twenty-Ninth Annual Exhibition of the Pennsylvania Academy of the Fine Arts* (Philadelphia: T. K. and P. G. Collins, Printers, 1852), cat. nos. 249 and 158.

150. Bloch, *Drawings of George Caleb Bingham*, 98.

151. "Art and Artists," *Home Journal*, February 15, 1851. The article indicates that the painting was done for a Mr. George Austin, Esq.; however Bloch, *Paintings of George Caleb Bingham*, 196, identifies the painting as one submitted to the American Art-Union. It was eventually sold at the auction of its property in 1852 and purchased by H. Reed.

152. Bingham's relationship with Goupil and Company did not last long, as he decided to forego their publishing services for his print of *Verdict of the People*. Writing to James Sidney Rollins, Bingham indicated, "I have not the slightest fault to find with Goupil & co. in regard to any of the transactions, between us; but their interest is divided upon such a multitude of works that they cannot devote any special attention to the sale of one or two, and mine, like others, must, as a general thing, wait to be asked for before they can be sold." Bingham to James S. Rollins, June 3, 1857, in Gentzler, *Letters of George Caleb Bingham*, 184. Additionally, the Western Art Union also advertised that subscribers for 1852 would receive a copy of Bingham's *In a Quandary*, perhaps indicating a special arrangement with Goupil and Company. "Artists' Union of Cincinnati," *Plattsburgh (N.Y.) Republican*, December 18, 1852.

153. Bingham to James S. Rollins, March 30, 1851, in Gentzler, *Letters of George Caleb Bingham*, 90–91.

154. Marie-Stéphanie Delmaire, "American Prints in Paris or the House of Goupil in New York (1848–1857)," in *With a French Accent: American Lithography to 1860*, ed. Georgia B. Barnhill (Worcester, Mass.: American Antiquarian Society, 2012), 71.

155. Bingham to James S. Rollins, March 30, 1851.

156. Franklin Kelly, *American Masters from Bingham to Eakins: The John Wilmerding Collection* (Washington, D.C.: National Gallery of Art, 2004), 32.

157. Linda Joy Sperling, "Northern European Links to Nineteenth Century American Landscape Painting: The Study of American Artists in Dusseldorf" (Ph.D. diss., University of California, Santa Barbara, 1985); *American Artists in Dusseldorf: 1840–1865* (Framingham, Mass.: Danforth Museum, 1982); Donelson Hoopes, *The Düsseldorf Academy and the Americans* (Atlanta: High Museum of Art, 1972).

158. Bingham to James S. Rollins, June 3, 1857, 186.

159. Bingham was certainly very much against slavery, as is evident in a series of spirited letters he wrote to the *Columbia Missouri Statesman* protesting a recent proslavery tract. Bingham, "President Shannon and His Discourses upon the Subject of Slavery," *Columbia Missouri Statesman*, January 18, January 25, and February 8, 1856, in Gentzler, *The Letters of George Caleb Bingham*, 152–65. Adam Arenson speculates that the figure relates specifically to the Dred Scott case, recently decided in Saint Louis. See Arenson, *The Great Heart of the Republic: St. Louis and the Cultural Civil War* (Cambridge, Mass.: Harvard University Press, 2011), 98–99.

160. "Address to the People of Missouri," *Western Journal and Civilian*, from the *Missouri Statesman*, July 1852, 8.

161. For more on Bingham's activity during the war years, and particularly his history painting *Order No. 11*, see Rash, *Painting and Politics*, 174–215; Joan Stack, "The Fashioning of a Frontier Artist," in Gentzler, *Letters of George Caleb Bingham*, 12–15.

162. W. Fletcher Thompson Jr., *The Image of War: The Pictorial Reporting of the American Civil War* (New York: Thomas Yoseloff, 1959); Bryan F. Le Beau, *Currier & Ives: America Imagined* (Washington, D.C.: Smithsonian Institution Press, 2001), 72–81; Bryan F. Le Beau, "The Mind of the North in Pictures: Currier and Ives's Civil War," *Common-Place* 9, no. 2 (January 2009), http://www.common-place.org/vol-09/no-02/lebeau/. On Palmer's images of the Mississippi and plantation scenes, see Vlach, *Planter's Prospect*, 114–31.

163. The later prints include *Scenery of the Upper Mississippi* (date unknown), *Maiden's Rock—Mississippi River* (date unknown), *Floating Down to Market* (date unknown), *Bound down the River* (date unknown), *Wooding Up on the Mississippi* (1866), *Champions of the Mississippi* (1866), *Rounding a Bend on the Mississippi* (1866), *Low Water on the Mississippi* (1867), *High Water on the Mississippi* (1867 and 1868), *The Great Race on the Mississippi* (1870), and *A Midnight Race on the Mississippi* (1890). See *Currier & Ives: A Catalogue Raisonné*, comp. Gale Research Company (Detroit: Gale Research, 1983).

164. The mobility of the print medium has allowed for these antebellum river idylls to continue circulating, even today. Mark Twain's books *Life on the Mississippi* (1883) and *The Adventures of Huckleberry Finn* (1884) have had a great influence on how the Mississippi valley is perceived today, but recent nonfiction books perpetuate the river's cultural importance for popular audiences. For example, see Lee Sandlin, *Wicked River: The Mississippi When It Last Ran Wild* (New York: Pantheon, 2010).

165. Bingham to James S. Rollins, June 19, 1871, in Gentzler, *Letters of George Caleb Bingham*, 307.

PLATES 26–42

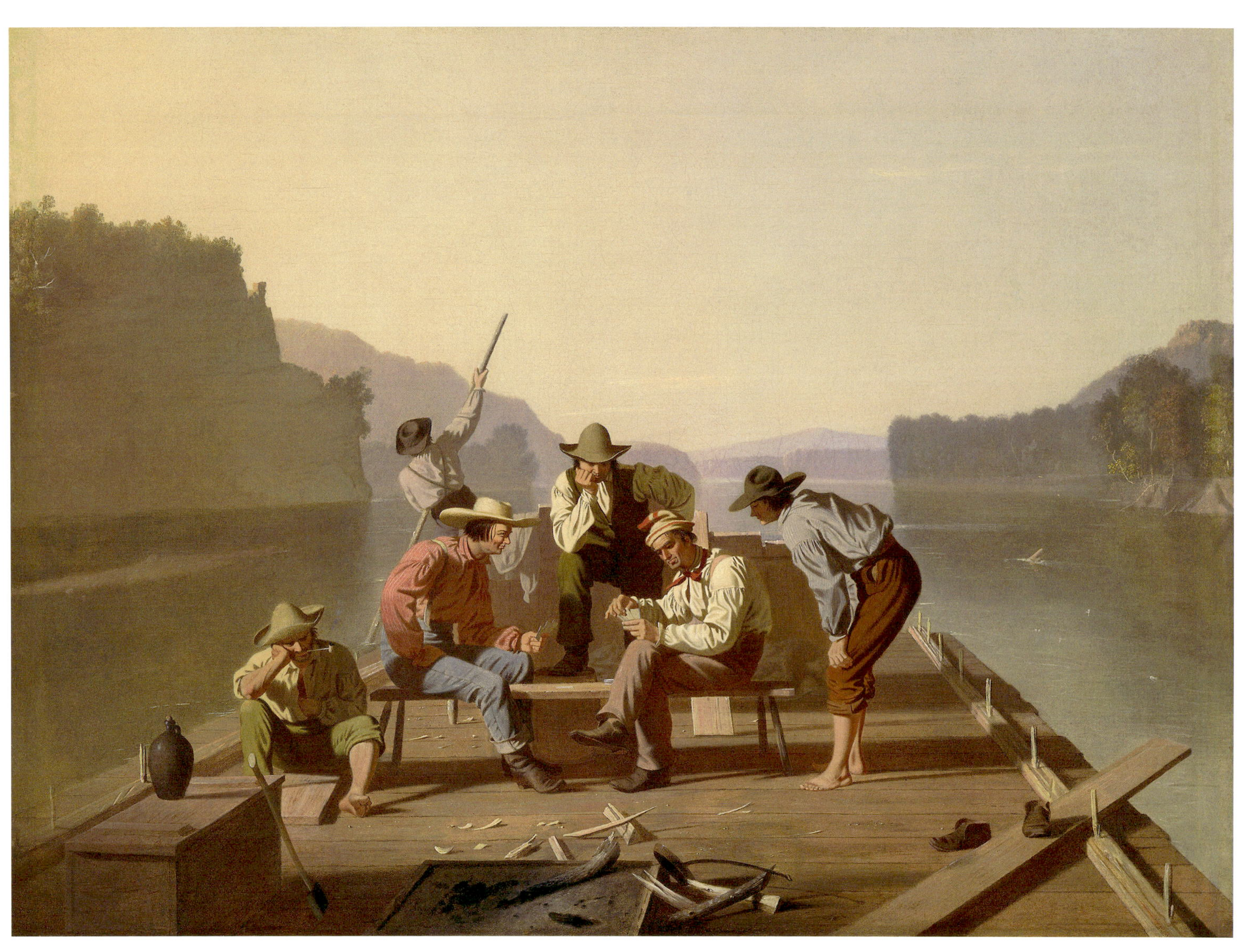

Plate 26: *Raftsmen Playing Cards*, 1847

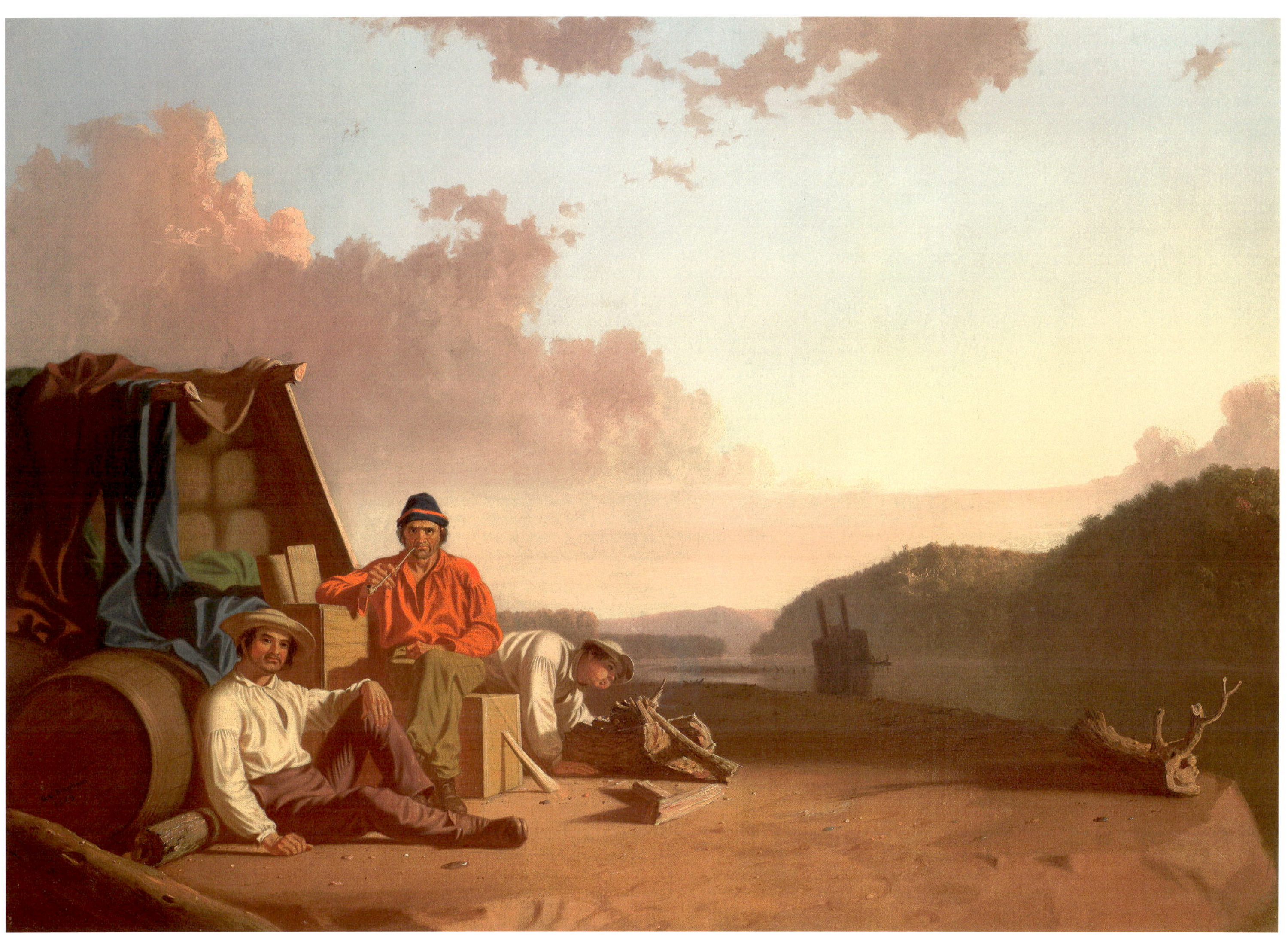

Plate 27: *Watching the Cargo*, 1849

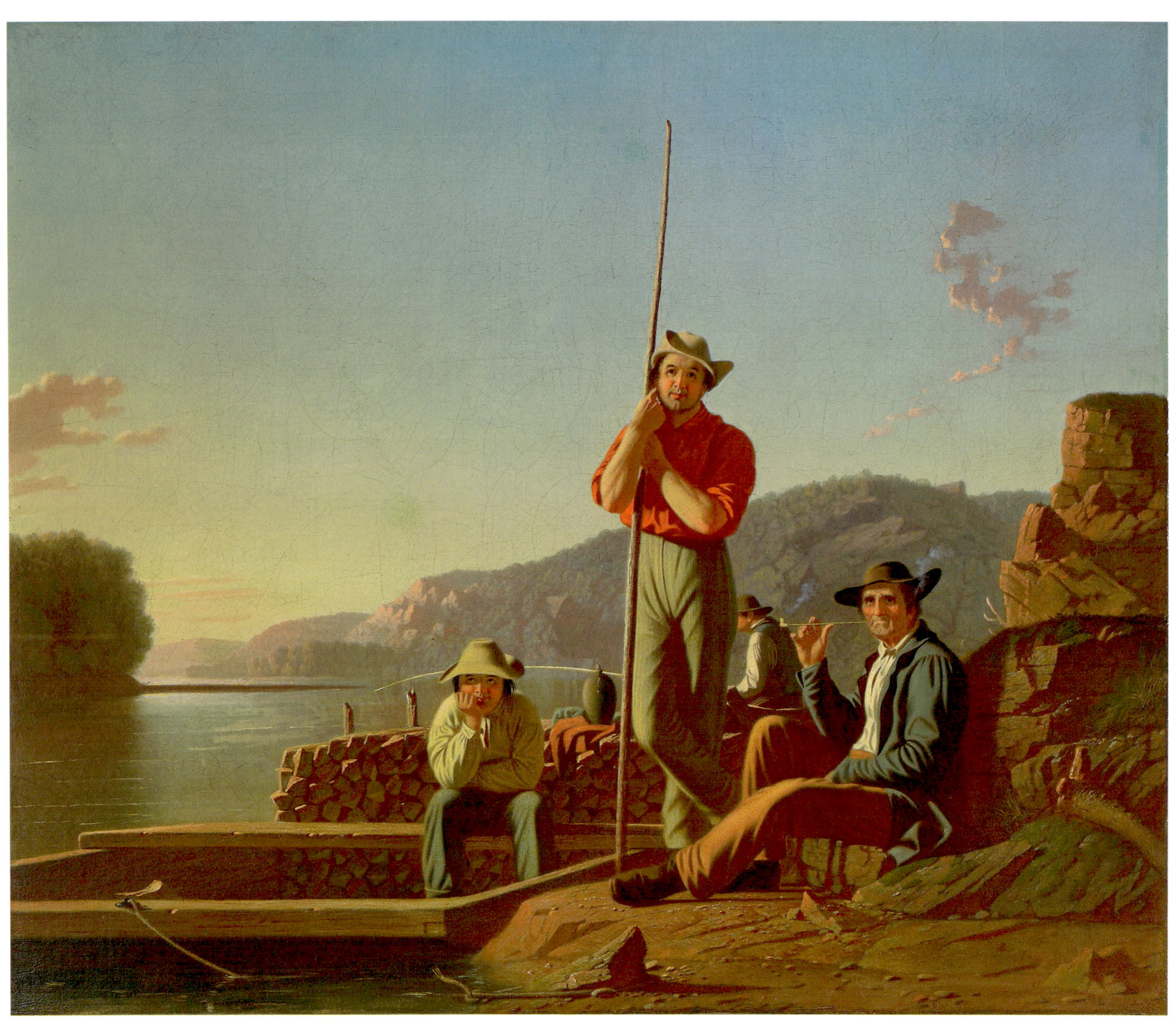

Plate 28: *The Wood-Boat*, 1850

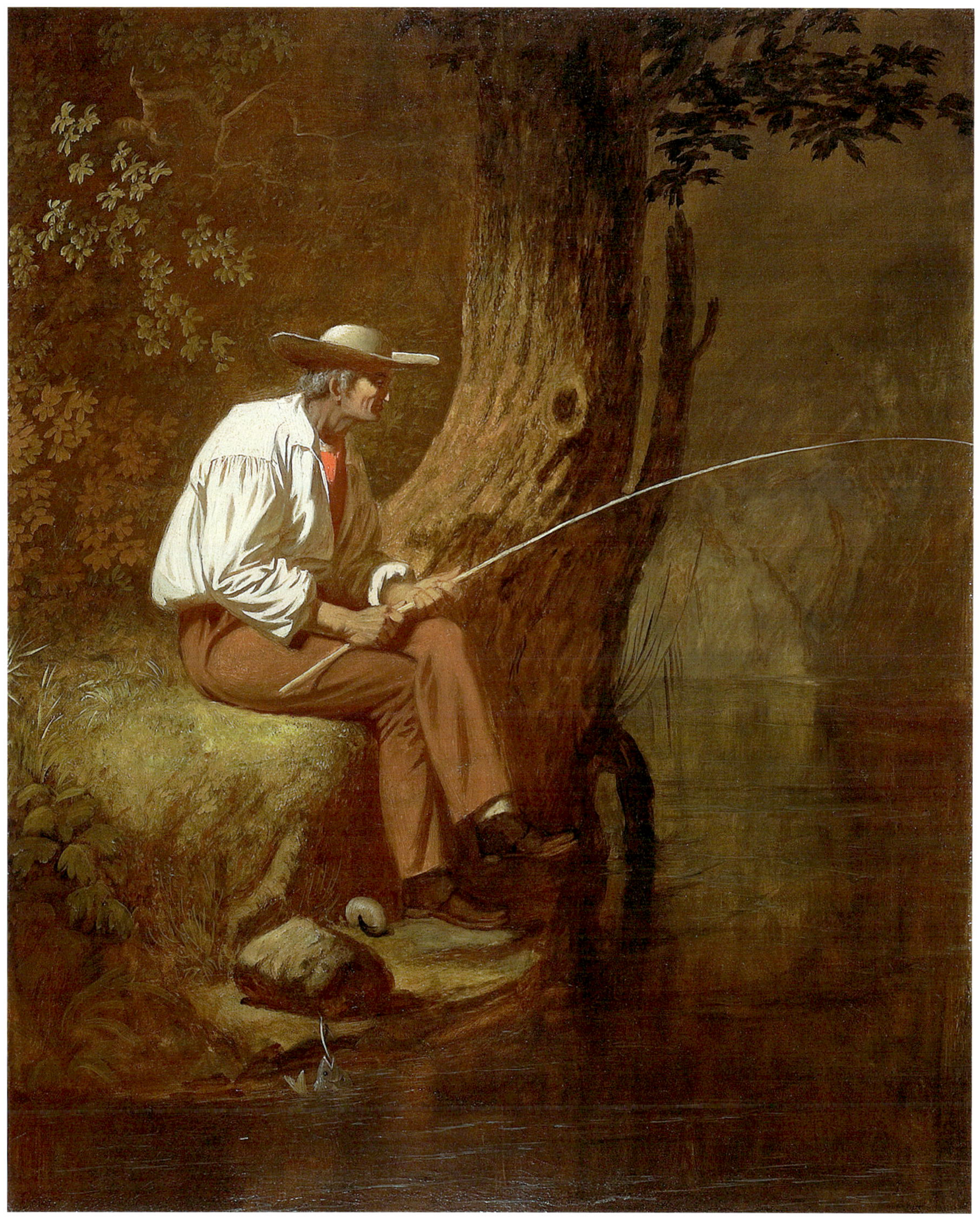

Plate 29: *Mississippi Fisherman*, ca. 1850

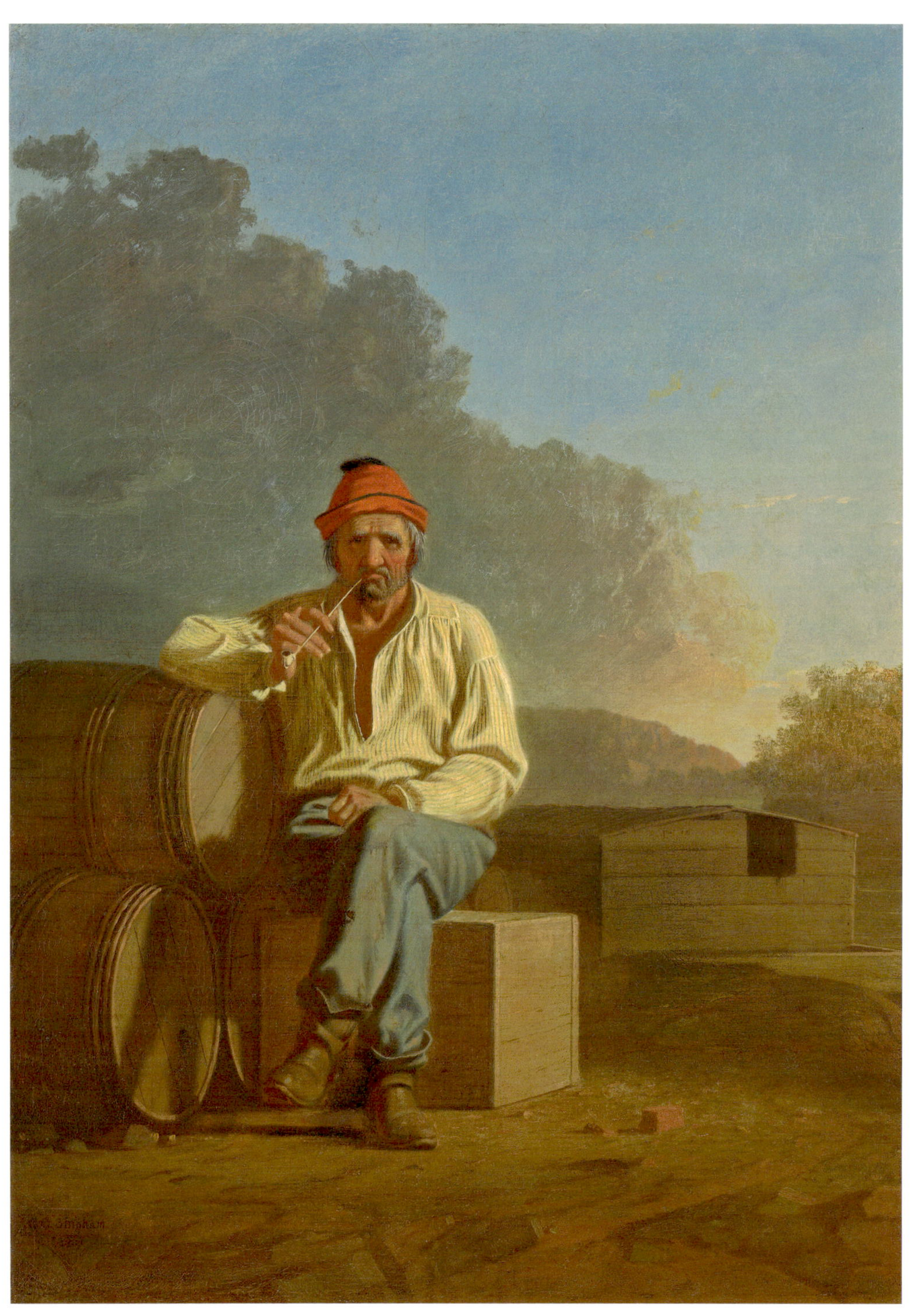

Plate 30: *Mississippi Boatman*, 1850

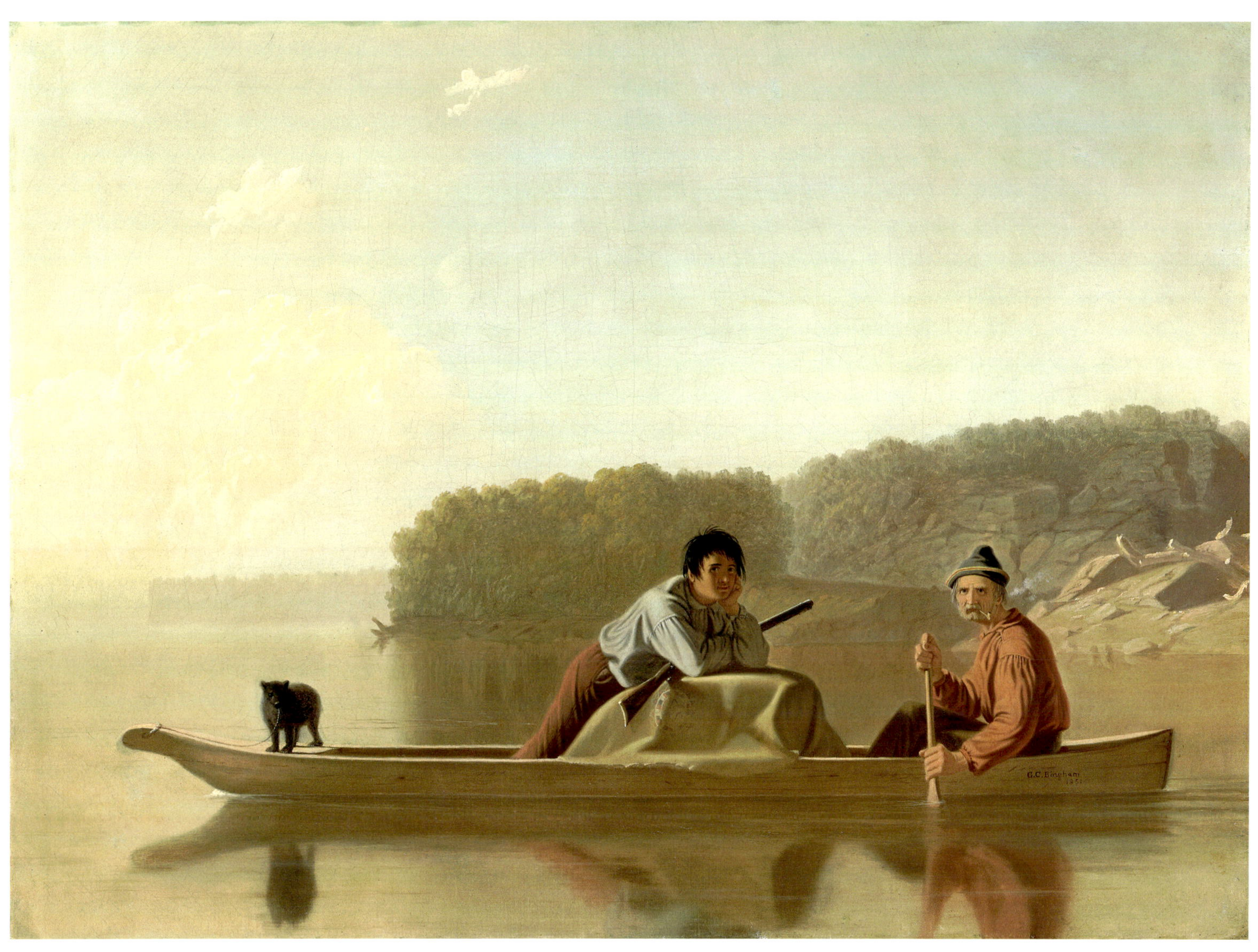

Plate 31: *Trappers' Return*, 1851

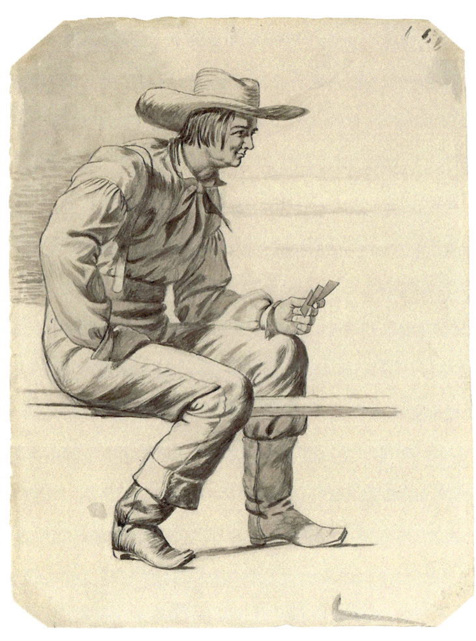

Plate 32: *Cardplayer*, for *Raftsmen Playing Cards* (1847) with alterations and for *In a Quandary* (1851) with alterations

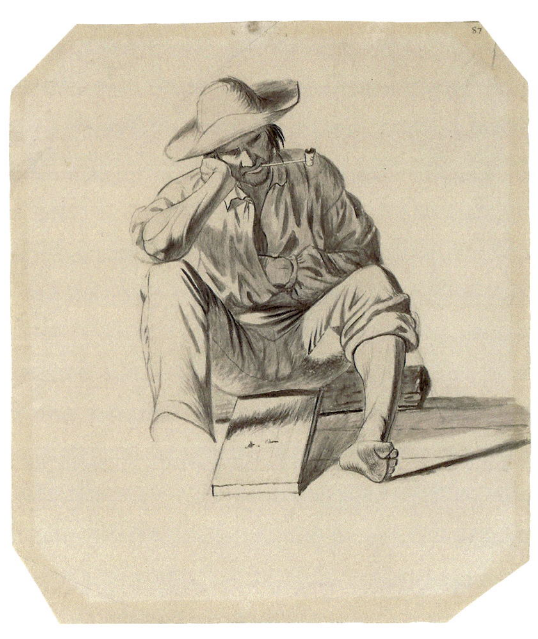

Plate 33: *Raftman dozing*, for *Raftsmen Playing Cards* (1847) and *Jolly Flatboatmen in Port* (1857)

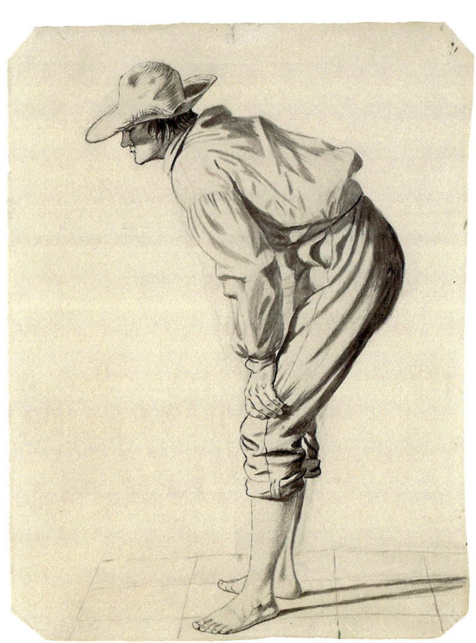

Plate 34: *Raftman*, for *Raftsmen Playing Cards* (1847) and *In a Quandary* (1851)

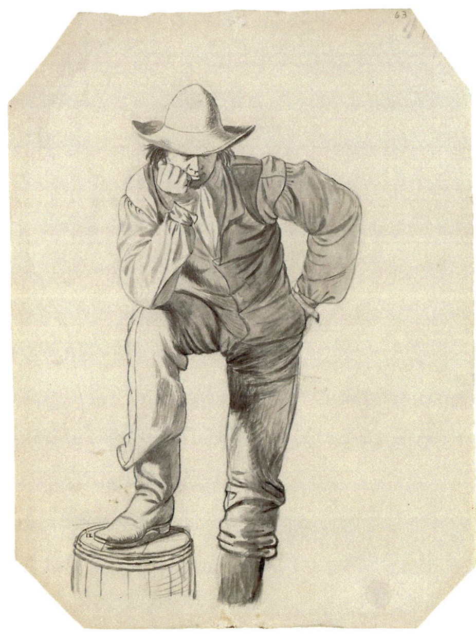

Plate 35: *Raftman*, for *Raftsmen Playing Cards* (1847) and *Jolly Flatboatmen in Port* (1857)

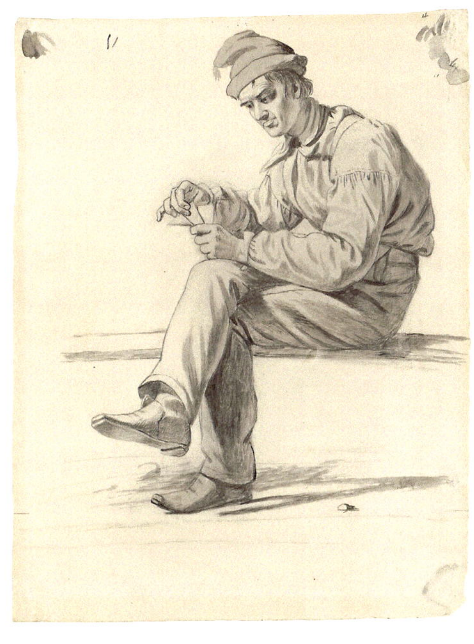

Plate 36: *Cardplayer*, for *Raftsmen Playing Cards* (1847) and *In a Quandary* (1851)

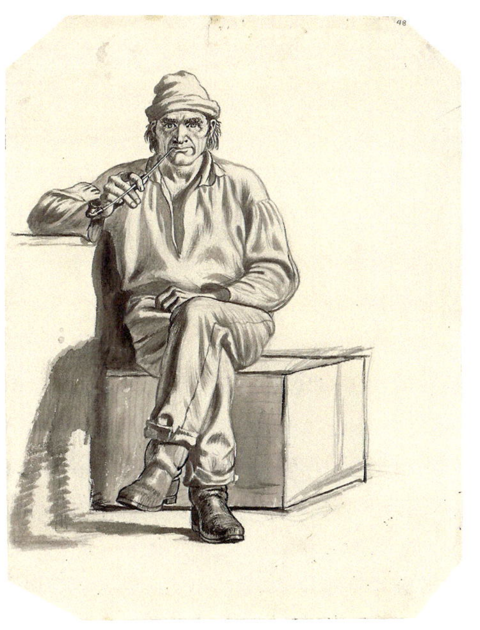

Plate 37: *Boatman*, for *Watching the Cargo* (1849) and *Mississippi Boatman* (1850)

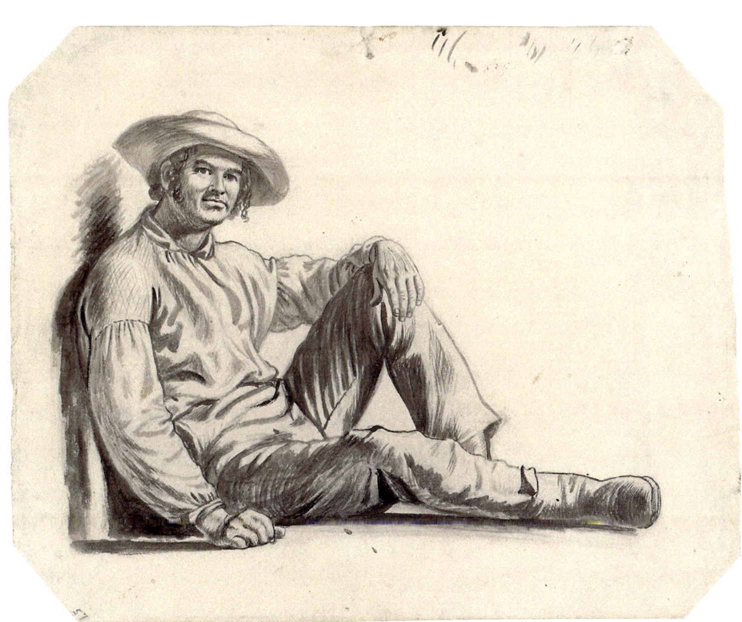

Plate 38: *Boatman*, for *Watching the Cargo* (1849)

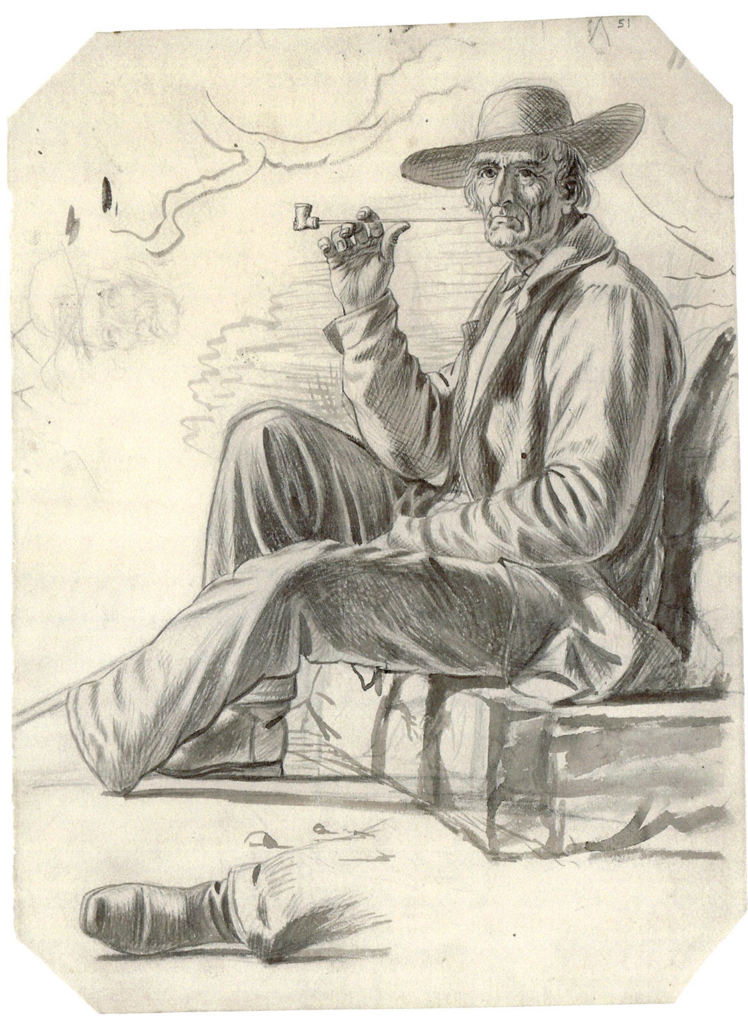

Plate 39: *Woodboatman*, for *The Wood-Boat* (1850)

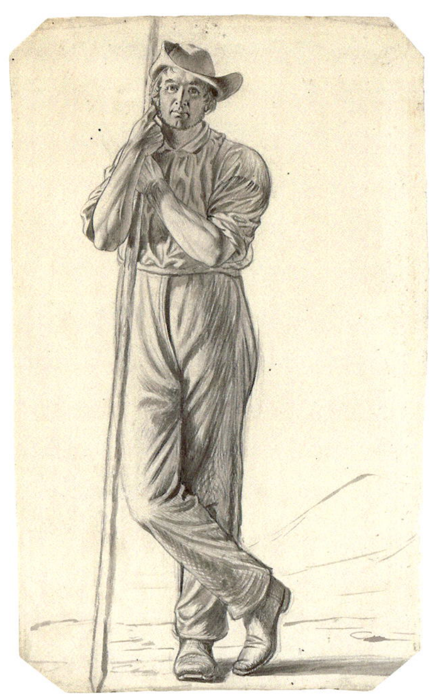

Plate 40: *Woodboatman*, for *The Wood-Boat* (1850)

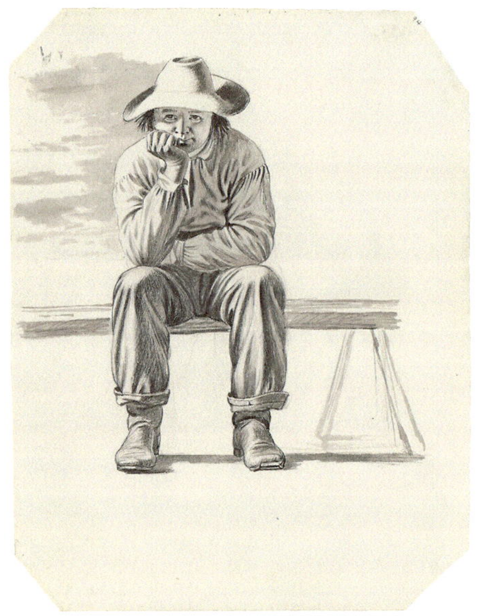

Plate 41: *Young woodboatman*, for *The Wood-Boat* (1850)

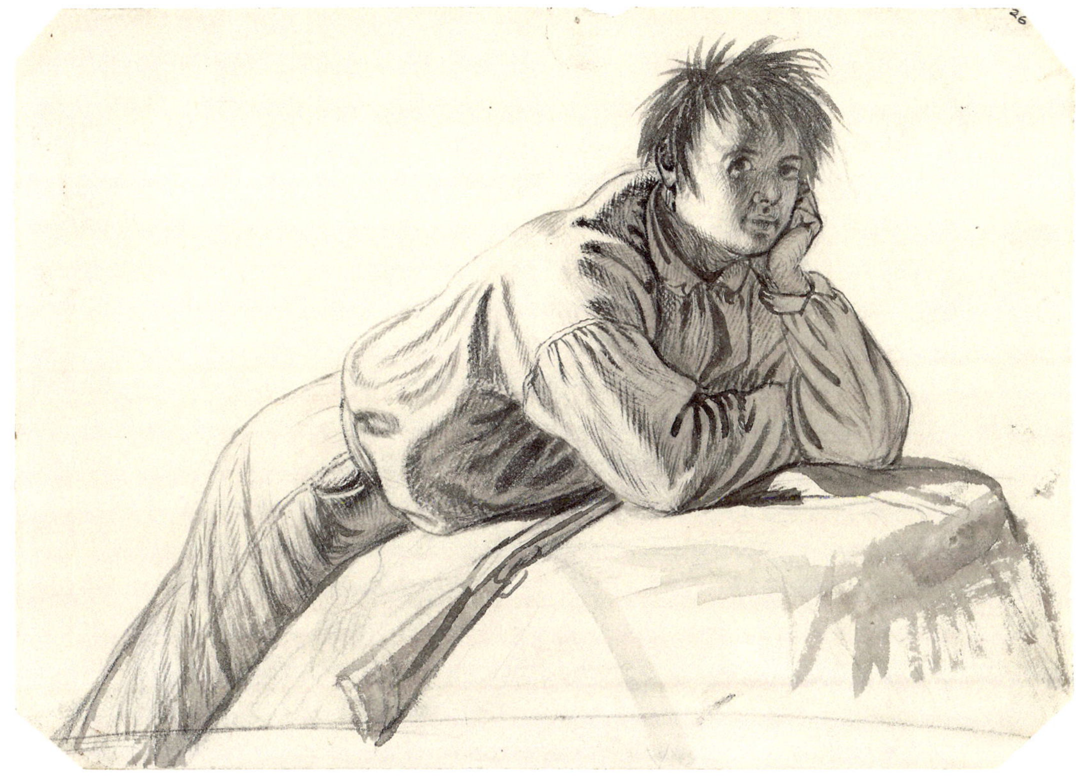

Plate 42: *Trapper's son*, for *Trappers' Return* (1851)

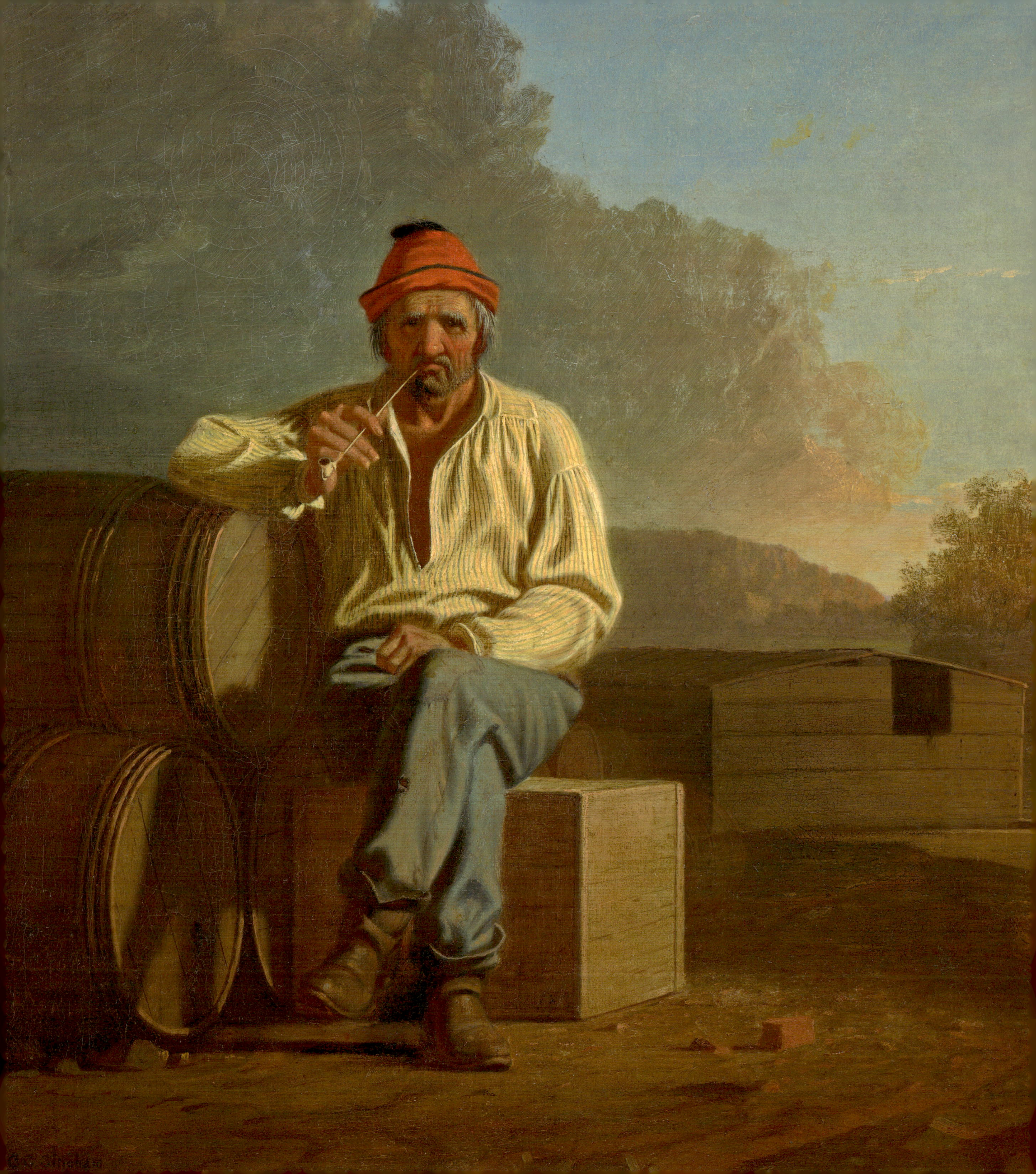

NAVIGATING THE PATH OF THE BRUSH

Exploring the Role of Drawing and Preparatory Layers in the Creation of the River Paintings

CLAIRE BARRY AND NANCY HEUGH

> *Sometimes we'd have the whole river all to ourselves for the longest time. Yonder was the banks and the islands, across the water; and maybe a spark—which was a candle in a cabin window; and sometimes on the water you could see a spark or two—on a raft or scow, you know; and maybe you could hear a fiddle or a song coming over from one of them crafts. It's lovely to live on a raft.* —Mark Twain, *Adventures of Huckleberry Finn* (1885)[1]

In the mid-1840s George Caleb Bingham, a self-taught Missouri artist, began creating a portfolio of drawings of boatmen, fishermen, gamblers, and traders that he used to depict the daily life of river flatboatmen.[2] The artist's meticulous graphite and India-ink studies were unprecedented in the detail with which they described the hardscrabble characters who populated the Mississippi and Missouri rivers. The figure studies, encompassing the men's unique physical characteristics, workaday clothes, expressions, and attitudes, are made with a precision that conveys an almost photographic realism. Although Bingham was recognized in his lifetime as a local artist who documented accurate, firsthand accounts of the riverboat experience, his models were often fellow Missourians and friends whom he posed as river people by dressing them in appropriate attire.[3]

Extending his artistic reach, Bingham created these drawings to launch a new type of genre painting that idealized the daily life of the Missouri flatboatman, hoping that these novel images would propel him into the ranks of America's foremost genre painters. He discovered what would become a critically important source of financial support in the American Art-Union in New York. This organization patronized artists by purchasing their works and distributing prints of their paintings among its membership. In 1845 Bingham's submission of two genre paintings of Missouri frontier life to the AA-U began a prolific, twelve-year period of collaboration during which the artist produced his greatest riverboat paintings in rapid progression. He offered *Fur Traders Descending the Missouri* (Pl. 3), considered the artist's masterpiece, to the AA-U in the spring of that year. Its subsequent purchase by the organization guaranteed Bingham the acknowledgment and affirmation that he sought. It also set the ever-practical artist on a new path as he strategically shifted his artistic efforts toward producing original genre paintings of Missouri river life for an eastern audience eager to learn about America's exotic western frontier. However, while Bingham claimed to portray authentic images of frontier river life, his paintings idealized the great Mississippi and Missouri rivers and visually suppressed the challenges inherent in navigating their waters. The flatboat, Bingham's chosen craft, was an ideal vessel for moving cargo through the

Mississippi Boatman (detail), 1850, Plate 30

rivers' varying depths, but it was already becoming obsolete by the 1820s when the Industrial Revolution ushered in larger, more powerful steamboats for hauling freight. Bingham's choice of the flatboat, however, provided the artist with both an appropriate setting and a convenient compositional device for organizing his riverboat scenes.

Bingham was highly selective in the characters he portrayed, focusing on everyday types engaged in fishing, card playing, fur trading, and even dancing on their flatboats, while generally avoiding images of the Native Americans and African-Americans who also inhabited the region. Bingham's flatboat paintings thus presented a nostalgic view of the western frontier, only occasionally hinting at the more negative activities associated with the Mississippi River, such as slave trading.

The artist intended these highly finished studies for practical use as individual cartoons, or preparatory drawings, in composing his paintings rather than for public display; the majority were executed on single sheets of fine-quality, handmade, wove rag paper. Although no cartoons of complete compositions have been found or documented, Bingham probably created individual studies with a specific composition already in mind. Many of the drawings are double-sided, with pencil studies and traced figures appearing in the exact but reverse pose on the verso. The numerous working marks left on the papers—pinholes, traced impressions, pencil registration marks, paint smudges, and fingerprints—show that Bingham worked directly from the sketches when preparing his paintings. The artist also reused many of the drawings for different riverboat canvases.

Bingham took these working drawings with him during his visits to New York, not only for help in composing his paintings but for sharing with his patrons, suggesting that the artist also used these studies on paper to help promote his Missouri riverboat paintings. The *Bulletin of the American Art-Union* of August 1849 stated: "[Bingham's] studio is at No. 115½ Grand-street, where an inspection of his portfolio of sketches will greatly gratify those amateurs who may call upon him."[4]

Bingham's images of flatboatmen now rank among the most iconic American paintings of the nineteenth century. The occasion of this exhibition offered the opportunity to explore the working methods of this highly individual artist who produced such lasting portraits of Missouri frontier life in the mid-nineteenth century, when the Mississippi River operated as the boundary between the more settled and industrialized East and the still sparsely populated and undeveloped West.

This study focuses primarily on the artist's technique as revealed by comparing forty-eight drawings to the underdrawings in seventeen of the river paintings made visible through infrared reflectography. The ink-and-graphite figure drawings were examined under various lighting conditions, including harsh raking light, transmitted light, and ultraviolet visible fluorescence. Embossed lines made with a stylus were examined under high magnification and compared to transferred lines in the underdrawings of related paintings. Thanks to recent advances in technology, specifically, newer infrared cameras with enhanced sensitivity that have the ability to capture clearer images of Bingham's underdrawings than ever before possible, the results from earlier investigations have been greatly augmented.[5] The current study represents the first systematic survey of the underdrawings, many of which were documented for the first time, in Bingham's western river paintings.[6] Comparative measurements and tracings were made of many of the drawings and their related figures on the canvases. Most of the paintings were also examined under the stereomicroscope, as well as through X-radiography. Some pigment analysis was also carried out using X-ray fluorescence analysis, and the current study also includes some observations about Bingham's grounds, paint layers, and use of color as well as the condition of his paintings.[7]

Bingham's lifelong interest in drawing began in his early childhood. His parents fostered his first attempts with this medium during his boyhood years in Virginia, when he practiced drawing on the walls of his grandfather's mill.[8] His father,

Henry Vest Bingham (1784–1823), also made pencil drawings as hobby, while his mother, Mary, encouraged Bingham through her love of books and learning.[9] After the family moved to the frontier town of Franklin, Missouri, in 1819, when he was eight, Bingham consulted the books in his mother's library, which likely provided his first exposure to engravings after Renaissance and Baroque paintings, nurturing his nascent curiosity and interest in composition and the visual arts.[10]

A major turning point in Bingham's early years took place when he first met the itinerant portraitist Chester Harding in 1820, an event that inspired the precocious youth to pursue painting as his life's work. In a letter written in 1872 to J. Colvin Randall of Philadelphia, the adult Bingham recalled that when Harding temporarily took up residence in Franklin in Henry Bingham's inn, the boy visited the artist in his studio on a daily basis, writing, "the wonder and delight with which his works filled my mind impressed them indelibly on my then unburdened memory."[11] Bingham's youthful enthusiasm and close observation of Harding in the act of painting established a recurring theme in his development as a painter. Almost entirely self-taught, he made a lifelong habit of studying the works of other artists and adapting their techniques to his own creative ends.[12]

Although Bingham wrote the 1872 letter to authenticate Harding's 1820 portrait of Daniel Boone (Fig. 38), the text is also significant for shedding light on Harding's working methods. Bingham wrote that before painting Boone's portrait in oil, Harding "made a pencil drawing and perhaps an oil study from life."[13] Harding's habit of making a preparatory pencil sketch before painting likely set an important example for the would-be painter, since in his artistic practice Bingham typically employed drawing in preparation for painting.

The significance of Bingham's early contact with Harding should not be underestimated. Before 1850, very few schools in frontier towns such as Franklin and Arrow Rock, Missouri, where Bingham spent his youth, devoted resources to art education.

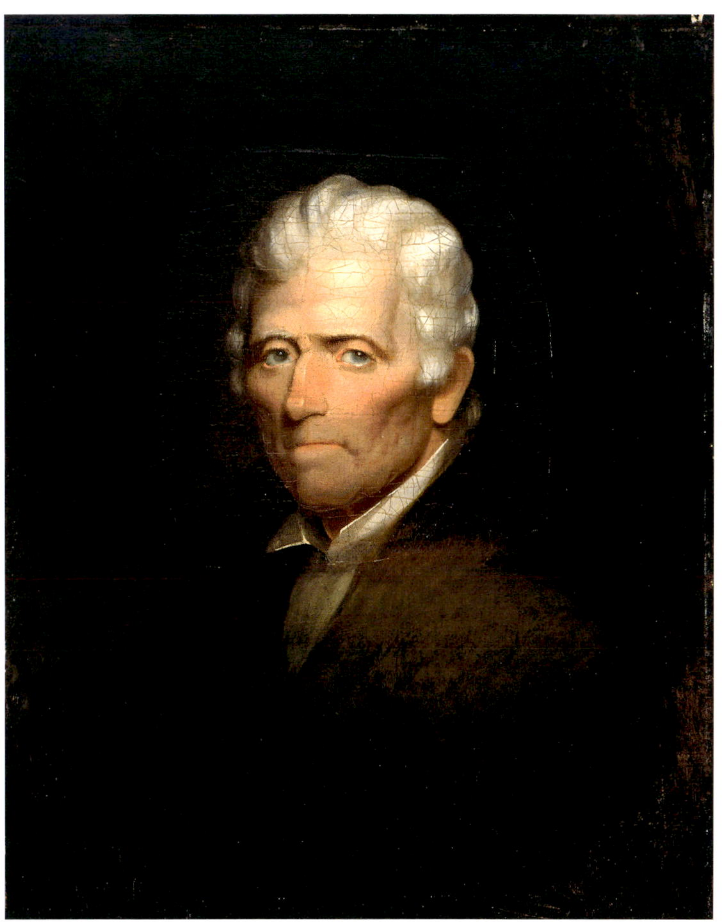

Fig. 38: Chester Harding (1792–1866), *Daniel Boone*, 1820, oil on oilcloth remounted on canvas, 22 × 17 in., Massachusetts Historical Society, Boston / The Bridgeman Art Library. Young Bingham visited Harding in his studio while the artist worked on this portrait from a preparatory pencil study of the sitter.

However, following his father's death in 1823, Bingham's mother opened a school for girls in Franklin and hired an art teacher named Mattie Wood. Bingham, who assisted his mother by working as the school's janitor, also took art instruction from Wood. According to tradition, he became her star pupil.[14] At age sixteen, Bingham apprenticed to Jesse Green, the first of two cabinetmakers (and Methodist ministers) who taught the

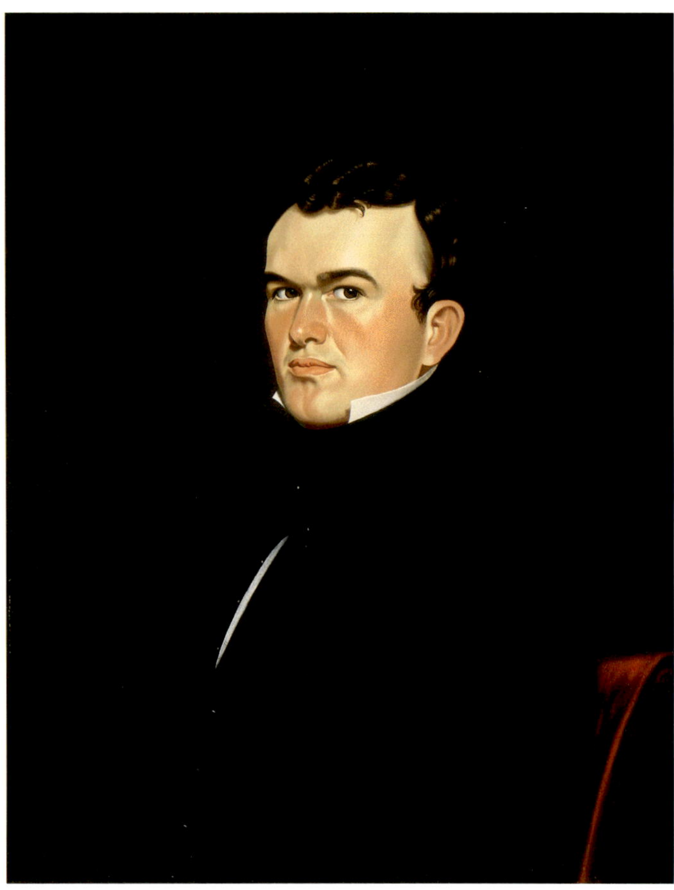

Fig. 39: George Caleb Bingham (1811–1879), *Self-Portrait*, 1834–35, oil on canvas, 28 3/8 × 22 11/16 in., Saint Louis Art Museum, Eliza McMillan Trust, 57:1934. With its polished surface, firm modeling, and chiseled features, Bingham's *Self-Portrait* recalls Harding's handling in his Boone portrait.

youth this craft, briefly kindling Bingham's desire to become a preacher.[15] Bingham also advanced his understanding of painting materials and techniques by helping local sign painters. By his early twenties, his resolve established, Bingham embarked on an independent career as an itinerant portrait painter.[16]

The fact that late in his life Bingham still owned a painting from Harding's early career reflects his enduring admiration and appreciation for the older portrait artist.[17] Bingham followed Harding's example by moving to Philadelphia in the spring of 1838 to study at the Pennsylvania Academy of the Fine Arts, one of the few professional organizations for aspiring artists then in operation in the United States.[18] In a letter to James Sidney Rollins dated May 6, 1837, Bingham wrote, "I am aware of the difficulties in my way, and am cheered by the thought that they are not greater [than] those which impeded the course of Harding, and Sully, and many others."[19]

Over the course of his long career, Bingham produced hundreds of portraits, which represent the vast majority of his artistic legacy. He began earning his living by painting likenesses, traveling through the small towns of Boonville, Columbia, and Liberty as well as to larger urban centers such as Natchez and Saint Louis along the Mississippi River. Throughout this period, Bingham's letters to his fiancée, Sarah Elizabeth Hutchison, underscore his dogged persistence at improving his painting skills: "the determination to do my utmost to rise in my profession has ever remained strong in my mind."[20]

Bingham's *Self-Portrait* demonstrates the young artist's developing talent in the art of portraiture (Fig. 39). With its polished surface, firm modeling, and chiseled features, it recalls Harding's handling in *Portrait of Daniel Boone*. Following Harding's approach, Bingham sometimes began his portraits by making a fairly complete preparatory sketch in graphite on canvas from the live model. However, the existence or degree of underdrawing in the artist's portraits varies considerably. In some cases, it reflects whether or not Bingham was painting from the live model or after a photograph of the sitter. Differences in the extent of Bingham's underdrawing were discovered during the infrared examination of the portrait pair *Dr. Benoist Troost* and *Mrs. Benoist Troost* (both ca. 1859, Nelson-Atkins Museum of Art, Kansas City, Missouri). For his portrait of Mrs. Troost, painted from life, the artist prepared a complete underdrawing in graphite with parallel hatching and cross-hatching for shading. By contrast, he worked from a photograph for his posthumous portrait of Dr. Troost and limited the underdrawing to just a few cursory lines to place the facial features.[21]

Bingham continued to work at improving his painting skills while simultaneously developing a successful career as an itinerant portraitist. He found a willing market for his portraits, and his correspondence often reveals the speed with which he rendered his subjects and the prices he charged, evidence of his entrepreneurial skill and concern for practical matters. By all accounts, there was a steady demand for his paintings. In a letter from Saint Louis dated September 19, 1836, Bingham wrote to Sarah that he had "four portraits commenced, which can be finished in four or five days."[22] Writing to Rollins from Natchez on May 6, 1837, the enterprising young painter attempted to procure commissions for a dozen portraits at twenty-five dollars each in order to finance a trip east to further his artistic education. As Bingham explained his motivation, "The greater facilities afforded there, for improvement in my profession, would be the principal inducement."[23]

In the spring of 1838, Bingham left for Philadelphia, the hometown of Thomas Sully, a painter whose portraits he had greatly admired and imitated. Three years earlier, Bingham had copied Sully's portrait of Frances Anne Kemble as Beatrice (Fig. 40), the role she portrayed in Shakespeare's *Much Ado About Nothing*, from an engraving by John Cheney.[24] Perhaps hoping to meet Sully and study his paintings firsthand to understand the artist's handling of color, Bingham must have been disappointed to learn that his hero had departed for England.[25] Bingham thus began a three-month period of study at the Pennsylvania Academy of the Fine Arts, where he pursued courses in anatomy and drawing after casts of antique sculpture. He wrote Sarah that he had purchased numerous drawings, engravings, and antique casts in order to continue his drawing studies when he returned home to Missouri.[26] His studies in Philadelphia also included his first prolonged exposure to examples of European painting that were on exhibit

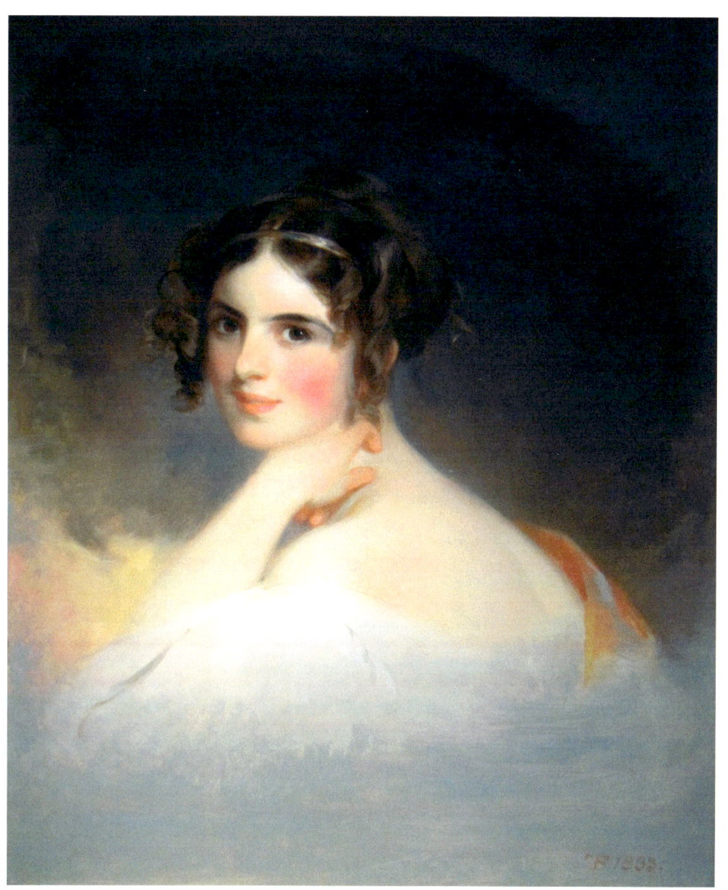

Fig. 40: Thomas Sully (1783–1872), *Frances Anne Kemble as Beatrice*, 1833, oil on canvas, 30 × 25 in., Pennsylvania Academy of the Fine Arts, Bequest of Henry C. Carey (The Carey Collection), 1879.8.24. Bingham greatly admired Sully's paintings and copied this portrait from an engraving.

in the galleries of the academy. Before returning to Missouri, Bingham visited New York City, where in 1838 he submitted a picture titled *Western Boatmen Ashore* (location unknown) to an exhibition at the gallery of the Apollo Association for the Promotion of the Fine Arts in the United States, the precursor to the American Art-Union. The title of the painting confirms Bingham's first known effort at expanding the subjects of his paintings to include genre paintings of frontier life. His choice

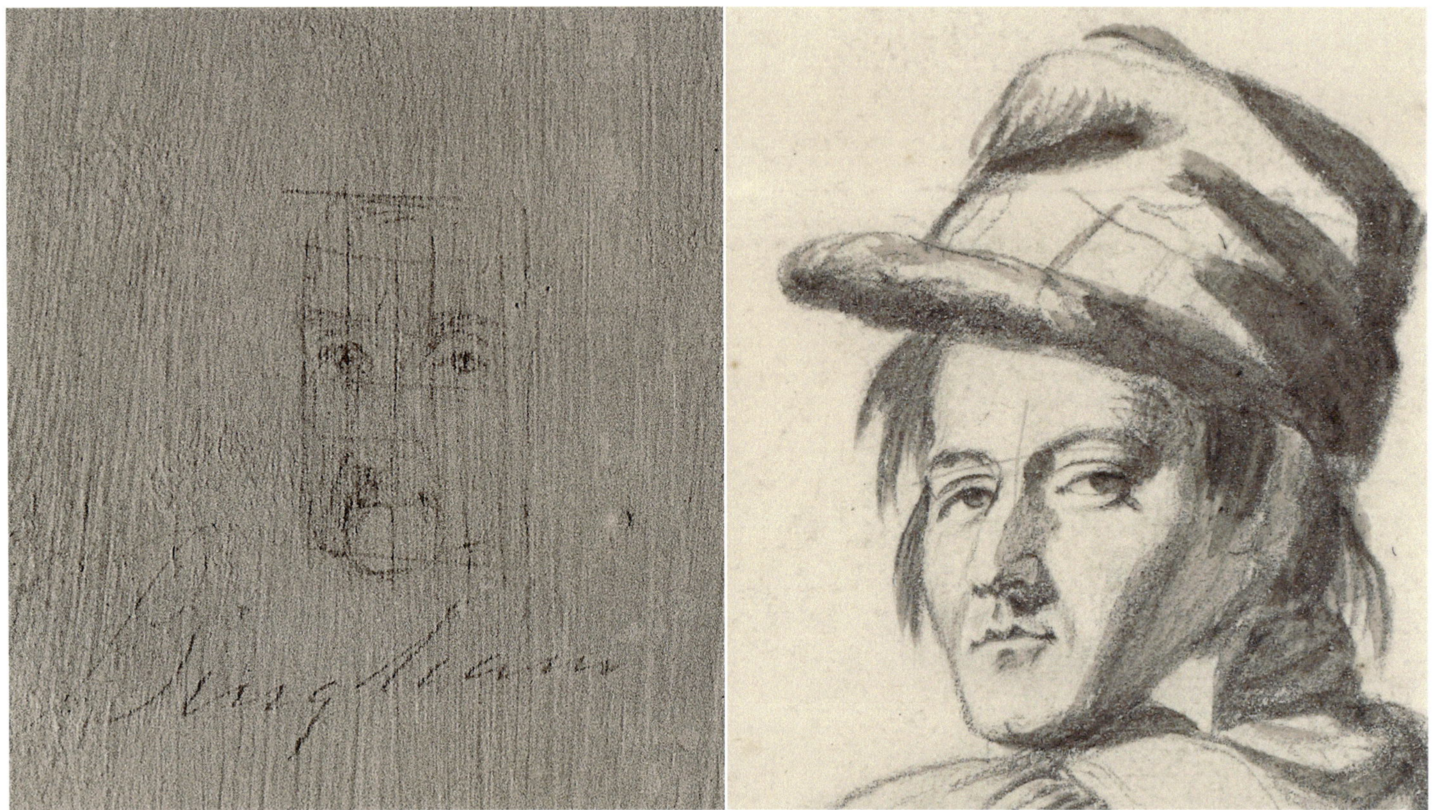

Fig. 41: These details from the verso of Bingham's *Portrait of Thomas Miller* (1837, left) and of the drawing *Flatboatman* (Pl. 13) show that Bingham followed an academic approach to drawing by beginning the faces of his figures with faint guidelines for positioning facial features.

of a western riverboat subject anticipated the future direction of his work.

At the onset of the 1840s, Bingham took up residence with his family in Washington, D.C., remaining there for nearly four years. In the summer of 1843, he and his wife traveled to Philadelphia, where the artist made a timely return visit to the Pennsylvania Academy of the Fine Arts. Seeing the recent genre paintings of some of America's leading artists on display there, such as those of Washington Allston, Asher B. Durand, William Sidney Mount, Thomas Sully, and Benjamin West,[27] motivated Bingham to continue to pursue genre painting of western riverboat life.[28]

Bingham's portfolio of studies of Missouri riverboatmen in the mid-1840s coincided with the publication of several American drawing manuals. In the mid-nineteenth century, American art education was becoming more democratic as these drawing manuals became widely available to aspiring artists across the country, providing step-by-step training that disseminated practical instruction in drawing beyond the walls of the few eastern academies. Given the importance Bingham placed on using carefully rendered drawings as the basis for his paintings, the relentless self-improver almost certainly studied these publications to better the quality of his draftsmanship. Among the drawing manuals that appeared in the country

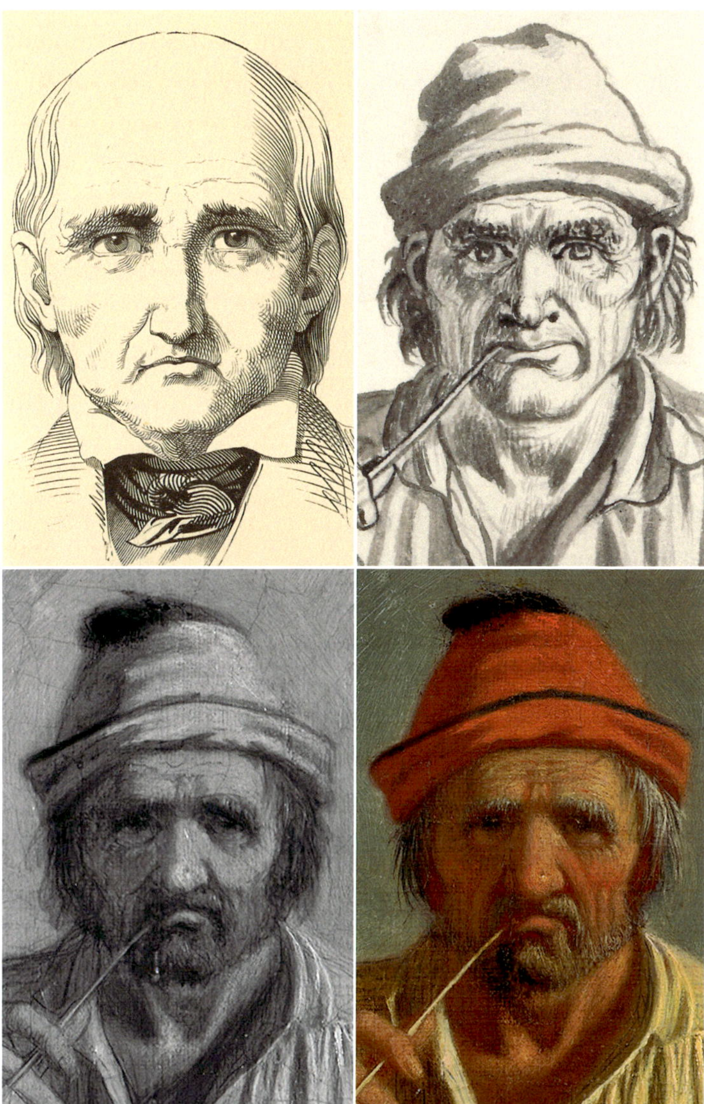

Fig. 42: Details left to right: J. G. Chapman's "Head Study" (1847), Bingham's drawing *Boatman* (Pl. 37), and head comparisons in infrared and normal light from *Mississippi Boatman* (Pl. 30). There is a remarkable similarity between Bingham's head and Chapman's illustration of the head of an older man in *The Rudiments of Drawing*, chapter 2, suggesting that Bingham consulted Chapman's popular manual. Bingham also likely borrowed this study for the head of the trapper in *Trappers' Return* (Pl. 31).

before the Civil War, John Gadsby Chapman's *American Drawing Book*, published in 1847, was the most highly regarded.[29] The publication date makes it possible that Bingham consulted Chapman's manual while executing many of his drawings. Traces of the artist beginning his head studies—with imaginary central lines through the faces and horizontal guidelines indicating the position of the eyes, nose, and mouth—can be seen on at least two drawings that predate the publication of the manual, as well as in a study of the seated *Flatboatman* (Fig. 41) from *The Jolly Flatboatmen* (Pl. 5).[30] Although the artist had undoubtedly acquired some academic drawing techniques before Chapman's manual was published, he almost certainly consulted this book while creating his paintings of Missouri flatboatmen. There is an uncanny similarity, for example, between the head of Bingham's ink-drawn *Boatman* and Chapman's illustration of the head of an older man in chapter 2 of his book titled "The Rudiments of Drawing the Human Head" (Fig. 42). Bingham's use of Chapman's illustration as the source for a key figure that would reappear in more than one of the flatboatmen paintings underscores his frequent practice of inventing his riverboat figures, whether from costumed studio models or prints, rather than creating portraits of actual boatmen.

BINGHAM'S WORKING PROCESS IN THE RIVER PAINTINGS

Bingham's composition process for the riverboat paintings began with lightly drawn, freehand sketches. Having spent much of his early career as a portraitist, he focused on accurately depicting facial features in both his drawings and paintings. Bingham chose quality papers that provided the ideal surface for detailed drawing with graphite pencil and for fluid ink washes. With few exceptions, his papers are medium weight and cream colored with a moderately smooth surface. There is some translucency to the sheets such that drawings on the recto could be easily traced on the verso when the sheet was

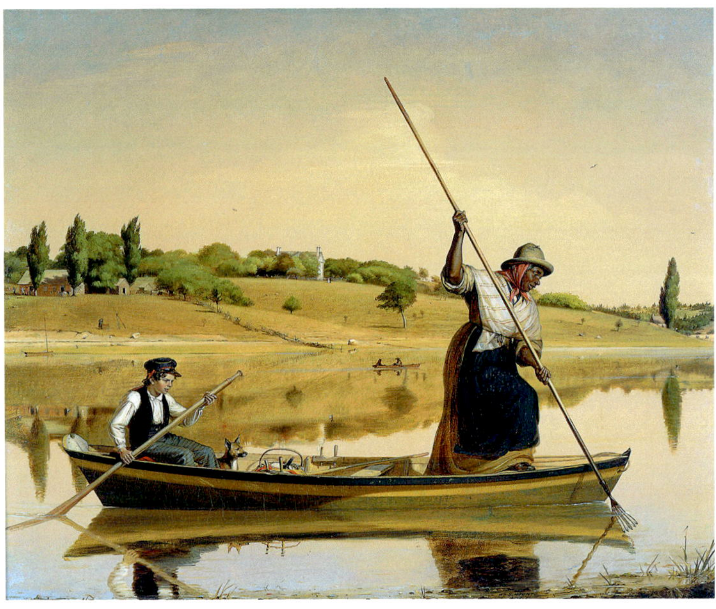

Fig. 43: William Sidney Mount (1807–1868), *Eel Spearing at Setauket*, 1845, oil on canvas, 28½ × 36 in., Gift of Stephen C. Clark, Fenimore Art Museum, Cooperstown, New York. Mount's iconic painting shares visual affinities with Bingham's *Fur Traders Descending the Missouri* (Pl. 3), including the use of a red imprimatura.

held against a window. The papers are compressible and sufficiently durable so that the stylus made only occasional tears when lines were repeatedly traced for transfer. Impressions are often visible on both the recto and the verso of the studies that Bingham employed as cartoons for the figures, and, when observed through infrared examination, these incised lines correspond to the underdrawings in the paintings.

In the paintings examined for this essay, Bingham used both plain-weave and twill-weave linen canvas commercially primed with white lead-based grounds. By adopting the more expensive twill weave for two later versions of *The Jolly Flatboatmen* (Pls. 47 and 48), he signaled the importance he placed on his most famous composition. The artist's use of a white lead-based ground provided a smooth, semiabsorbent surface that enhances the luminosity of his paintings, enabling him to unite portraits of hardscrabble boatmen in tranquil river settings with a crystalline light.[31]

In his iconic Missouri river scenes, Bingham emulated the idyllic, pastoral style of American landscape painting represented in the work of Thomas Cole and Asher B. Durand, two of the leading American artists in Bingham's time whose work was also purchased by the American Art-Union.[32] Bingham's use of a locally applied, red imprimatura (a thin, preliminary layer applied to the ground of a painting) in the foregrounds of several of the river paintings examined suggests that he also adopted specific painting techniques from Cole, whose practice of applying red underlayers that played a role in the appearance of the final image was well known at the time.[33]

William Sidney Mount also recommended the use of a red imprimatura.[34] His *Eel Spearing at Setauket* (Fig. 43) shares unmistakable affinities with Bingham's *Fur Traders Descending the Missouri* (Pl. 3) of the same year, especially in terms of the sharply delineated figures, the bright background sky, and the soft reflections in the water.[35] Bingham was surely aware that Mount was also among the leading American genre painters whose work was supported by the AA-U. In 1850 Mount recorded his idea for adapting the use of a red imprimatura to produce the most perfect ground for landscape painting. He recommended preparing the center third of the canvas or panel with gray, and the top and bottom thirds with a red imprimatura, so that the two colors "melt[ed] into each other."[36] We see Bingham adopting a variation of this approach in *Fishing on the Mississippi* (Pl. 43), in which he underpainted the sky with both light gray (right side) and warm light brown (left side) imprimaturas, while he underpainted the water with a light gray paint. This suggests that Bingham emulated Mount's working practice as well as his painting style.[37]

Bingham, who used a red imprimatura under the river landscapes as well as under their figures, was probably also aware of the use of this technique in the earlier European artworks he encountered during his travels to the East Coast and Europe. Paintings by El Greco (1541–1614), Nicolas Poussin (1594–1665), and Jacob van Ruisdael (ca. 1629–1682) are evidence of the long-established tradition among European artists of utilizing red-brown grounds, and Francisco Goya (1746–1828) employed red grounds that remain especially visible in his portraits.[38] Goya employed the red underlayer to create thinly painted half tones in the modeling of his figures, and where he left it exposed, the red imprimatura creates vivid red accents around the eyes, nose, and mouths of his figures, infusing them with a palpable sense of warmth and vitality.[39] Bingham's use of a hot red imprimatura in *Boatmen on the Missouri* (Pl. 4), which can be readily seen emanating from the boatman's arm and facial features, sets the stage for the artist's highly personal use of color in the painting (Fig. 44).

An unfinished *Portrait of a Young Woman*, 1877 (private collection),[40] which was discovered on a second primed canvas underlying Bingham's *Forest Hill*, 1877 (The Nelson Homestead, Boonville, Missouri),[41] reveals the artist's specific method for applying a red imprimatura. Working on top of a commercially primed white ground, Bingham established the portrait and overall composition in full monochromatic scale using a vibrant red underpainting.[42] Presumably, this toned imprimatura enabled him to paint the flesh tones more rapidly and efficiently, using the red underlayer as a half tone in the modeling of the face. This observation supports a key discovery of the riverboat painting study: Bingham's practice of painting on a red imprimatura is integral to his landscapes as well as his portraiture and political paintings. On the verso of many figure drawings, a residue of red paint often surrounds tack holes, presumably offset from the imprimatura during the transfer process.

Bingham's distinctive use of localized red underlayers imparts an intense luminosity to the riverboat paintings and creates the illusion of distance between the sharply focused foregrounds—where the figures and riverboats were executed over red undertones and appear to advance—and the tranquil, hazy backgrounds that provide a panoramic sense of space. By thinly executing the riverbanks and background foliage with cool green and mauve tints over the off-white ground, the artist evoked a tangible impression of light and atmosphere.

Examination of Bingham's riverboat paintings under infrared reflectography suggests that the artist's underdrawing style evolved as his career progressed and as his compositions grew more complex. One of the earliest paintings examined,

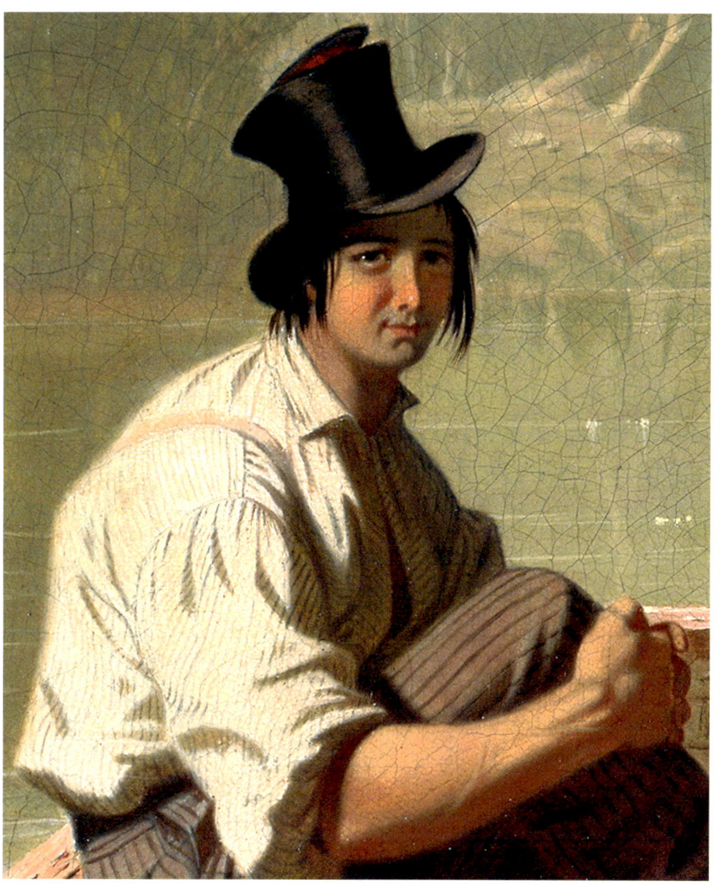

Fig. 44: This detail from *Boatmen on the Missouri* (Pl. 4) shows Bingham's use of a red ground, most notably in the boatman's arm and facial features. By modeling the flesh tones over a red imprimatura, the artist infused the figure with warmth and light.

Landscape: Rural Scenery (Pl. 1), shows no evidence of underdrawing; not surprisingly, none of Bingham's drawings relates to this painting of diminutive figures engaged in domestic activities. This composition was modeled after landscape prints, especially those by the English artist George Morland (1763–1804), which were printed in large editions and available in the United States.[43] Dated to the same year that Bingham painted and submitted *The Concealed Enemy* (Pl. 2) and *Fur Traders Descending the Missouri* (Pl. 3) to the American Art-Union, *Landscape: Rural Scenery* is a transitional work that immediately precedes the artist's more fully developed western river scenes in which the figures dominate the compositions. For his series of riverboat paintings that immediately followed this pivotal work, Bingham abandoned scenes of domestic life and the landscape style. For the riverboat paintings he created a new template, increasing the scale of the figures and portraying their activities within simplified, idyllic river settings.

CASE STUDIES

Fur Traders Descending the Missouri (1845, Pl. 3)

Among the works studied for this essay, *Fur Traders Descending the Missouri* is the earliest dated painting in which the artist based a painted figure directly on a preparatory study. (For a more comprehensive discussion of this painting, see the essay by Elizabeth Kornhauser and Dorothy Mahon.) Bingham created a detailed drawing of the older trader, with graphite and India-ink washes. The study depicts the trader seated in a canoe and holding a paddle, suggesting that Bingham had already conceived the composition before posing the model. He recycled the drawing in altered form for the similar figure in *Trappers' Return* (Pl. 31), and while the artist unquestionably made a drawing for the trapper's young métis (of European and Native American descent) son as well, this drawing is now lost.[44]

The thin paper Bingham used for the figure of the old trader in this painting is singular within his portfolio of drawings. The sheet was particularly vulnerable to mold and moisture and survives today in fragile condition. The artist may have discovered that this paper did not hold up well to the transfer techniques he employed in the creation of *Fur Traders Descending the Missouri*, and this may account for the lost companion drawing of the boy (Fig. 45). Bingham reused these transfer techniques many times over during the preparation of riverboat paintings from 1845 to 1857.

Treating his study of the old trader as a cartoon, Bingham directly transferred the outlines of the figure to the prepared surface of his canvas, presumably with the aid of an interlayer of some type of carbon paper. Indentations in the paper over the ink and pencil lines are visible on the recto and appear as raised, embossed lines on the verso of the paper sheet. The artist carefully incised the outlines of the figure's trousers, shirt, and hand. While incising the study for transfer, the artist corrected the drawing, demonstrating that he continued to rework his drawings throughout the creative process. He made corrections by adding scored lines along the dropped shoulder seam and the folds in the trader's shirt, and he followed these revisions in the final painting (Fig. 46).

The mechanical outlining visible along the left side of the figure's face and hand in the underdrawing for *Fur Traders* is a result of Bingham's direct transfer of the drawing to the prepared canvas; the scale appears to be one to one. Overlays of the study, underdrawing, and painted trader show the slight adjustments Bingham made in completing the painted figure (Fig. 47).

Infrared examination of this painting and others also brought to light a peculiarity of Bingham's underdrawing method. The artist frequently combined different underdrawing techniques within a single painting, and sometimes even within a single figure. Bingham methodically transferred the

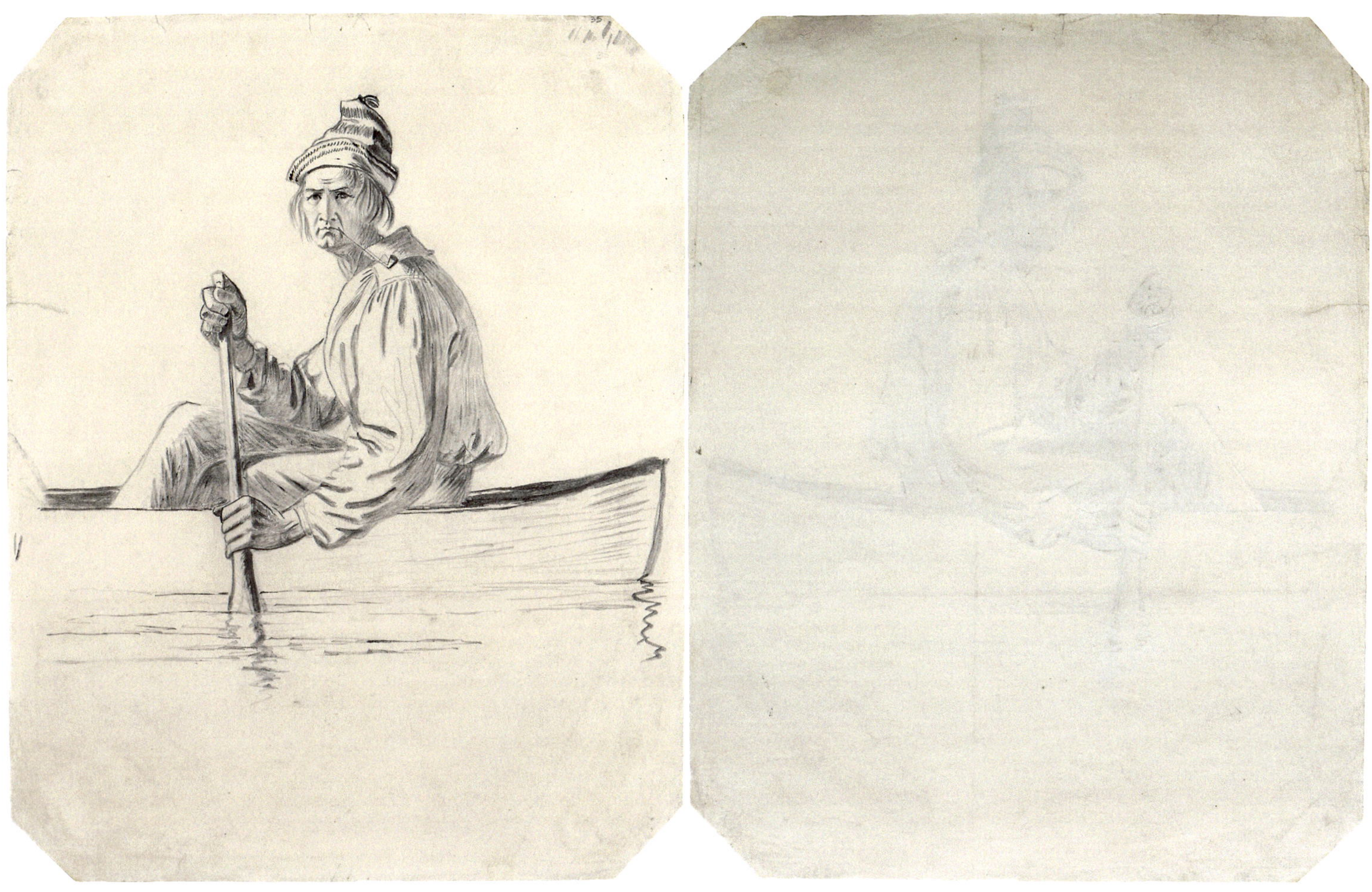

Fig. 45: The recto and verso of the drawing *Fur trader* (Pl. 7), used for *Fur Traders Descending the Missouri* and *Trappers' Return* (Pl. 31), reveal the translucency of the paper and the artist's gray transfer marks. The thin paper that Bingham used for this figure is singular within his portfolio of drawings as the artist typically used a thicker sheet.

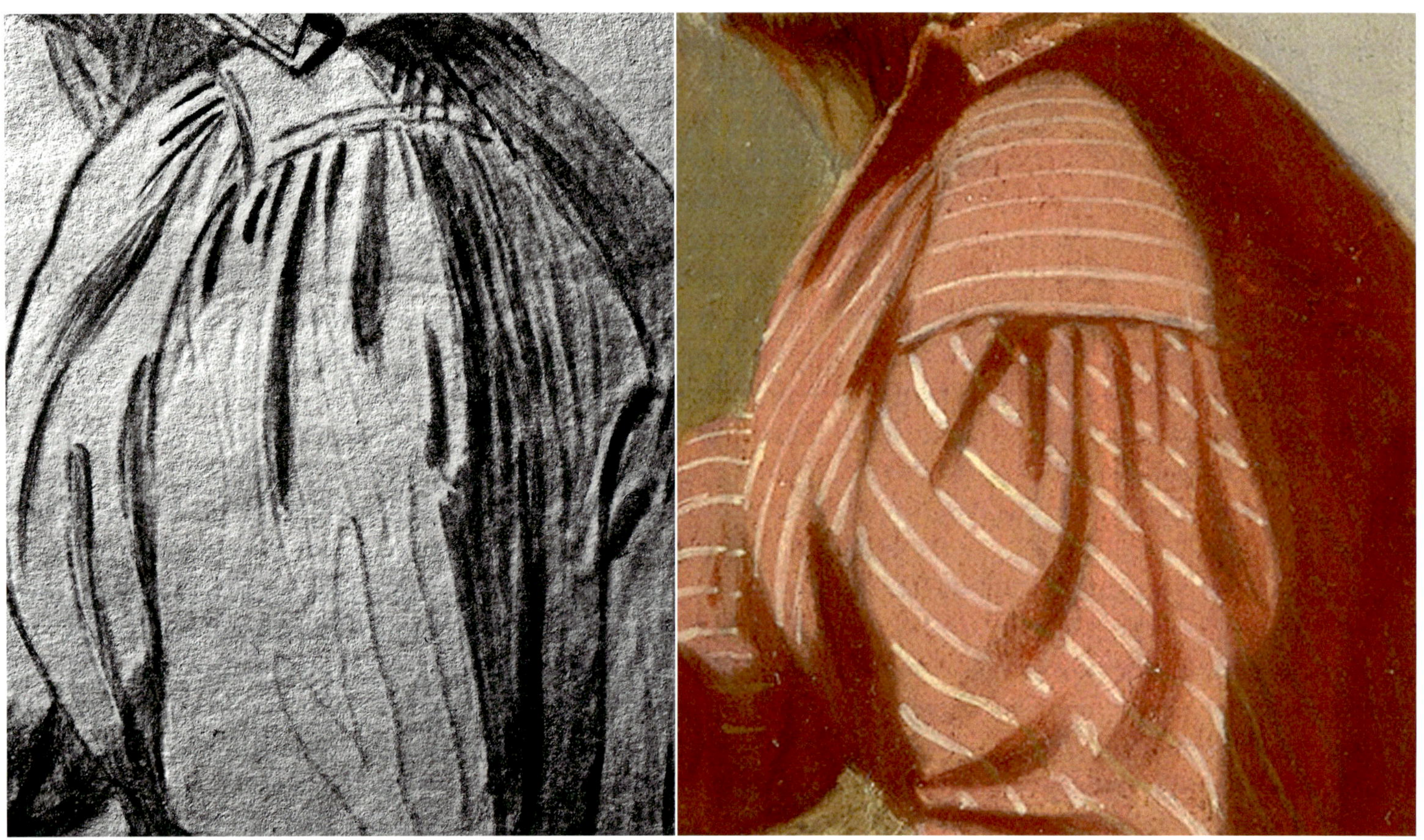

Fig. 46: Details of the drawing *Fur trader* (Pl. 7) and the related figure in *Fur Traders Descending the Missouri* (Pl. 3) show the artist's impressions used to transfer the study to canvas. Bingham used incised lines to correct the study by dropping the shoulder seam during the transfer process, following this revision in the painting.

Fig. 47: Left to right: the study *Fur trader* compared with infrared details of the corresponding figures from *Fur Traders Descending the Missouri* and *Trappers' Return* (Pl. 31). The overlay reveals that the scale of the study to the painted figures is 1:1.

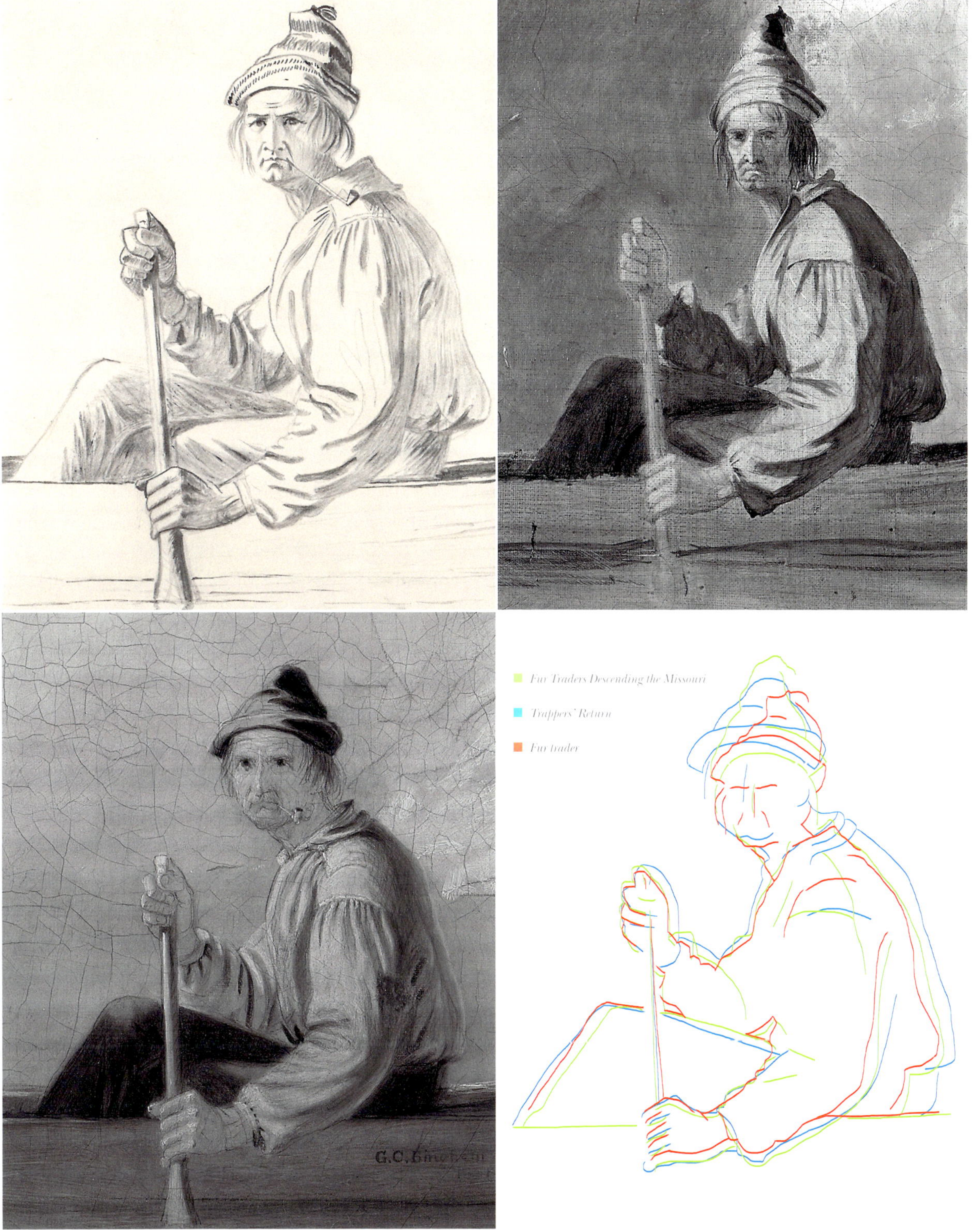
G.C.Bingham
Fur Traders Descending the Missouri
Trappers' Return
Fur trader

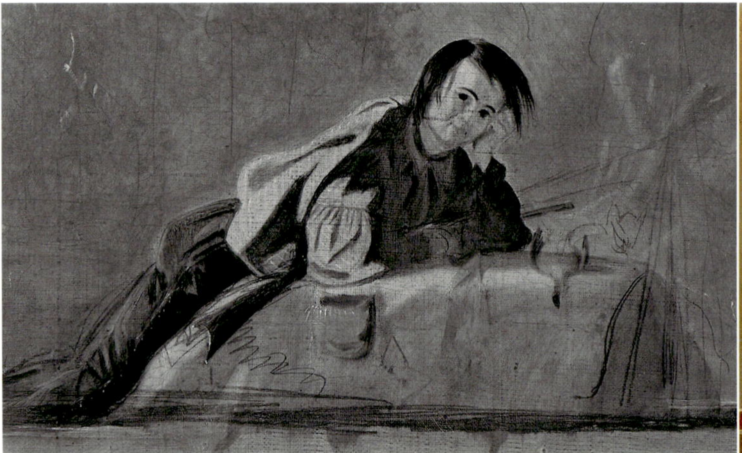

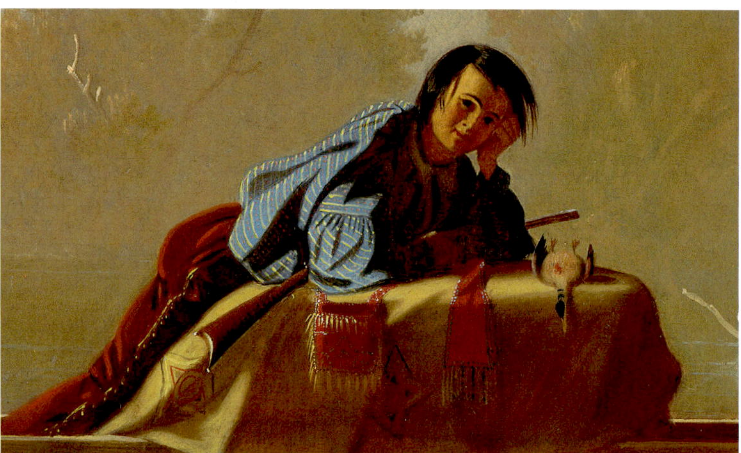

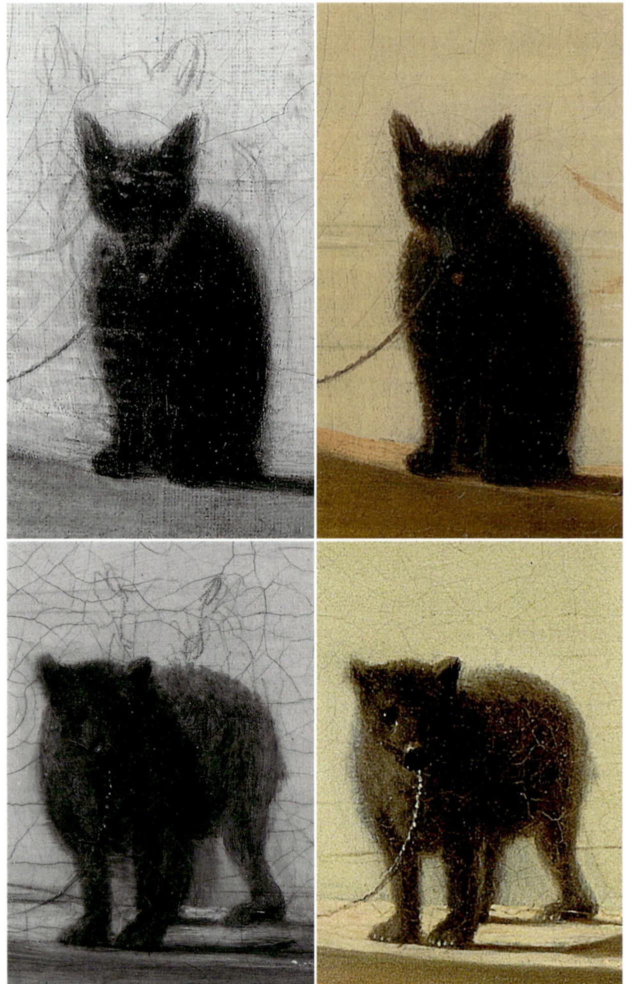

Fig. 48: An infrared detail (left) of the young trader from *Fur Traders Descending the Missouri* (Pl. 3) establishes that Bingham added the young métis son and his rifle after rapidly sketching the outlines of the boat. Note how the lines describing the boy's leg are laid over the summary lines describing the top edge of the vessel.

Fig. 49: Infrared details (left) of the bear cubs in *Fur Traders Descending the Missouri* and *Trappers' Return* (Pl. 31) show the artist's pentimenti in his depictions of the bears, a key narrative detail that he reduced in both paintings.

outlines of the fur trader and his paddle to the primed canvas by directly tracing the study. The artist positioned the reclining youth, freely sketching the legs, only after he established the top and bottom edges of the boat with rapidly applied, coarse outlines using a dry medium (Fig. 48). Infrared examination also showed the artist's quick sketch of the rifle stock.

The loose underdrawing of the bear cub, the legs of the young métis companion, the boat, and the boat's reflection indicate much greater spontaneity than the artist's meticulous handling of the fur trader. Throughout the landscape, Bingham made simple, swift notations, including a few marks

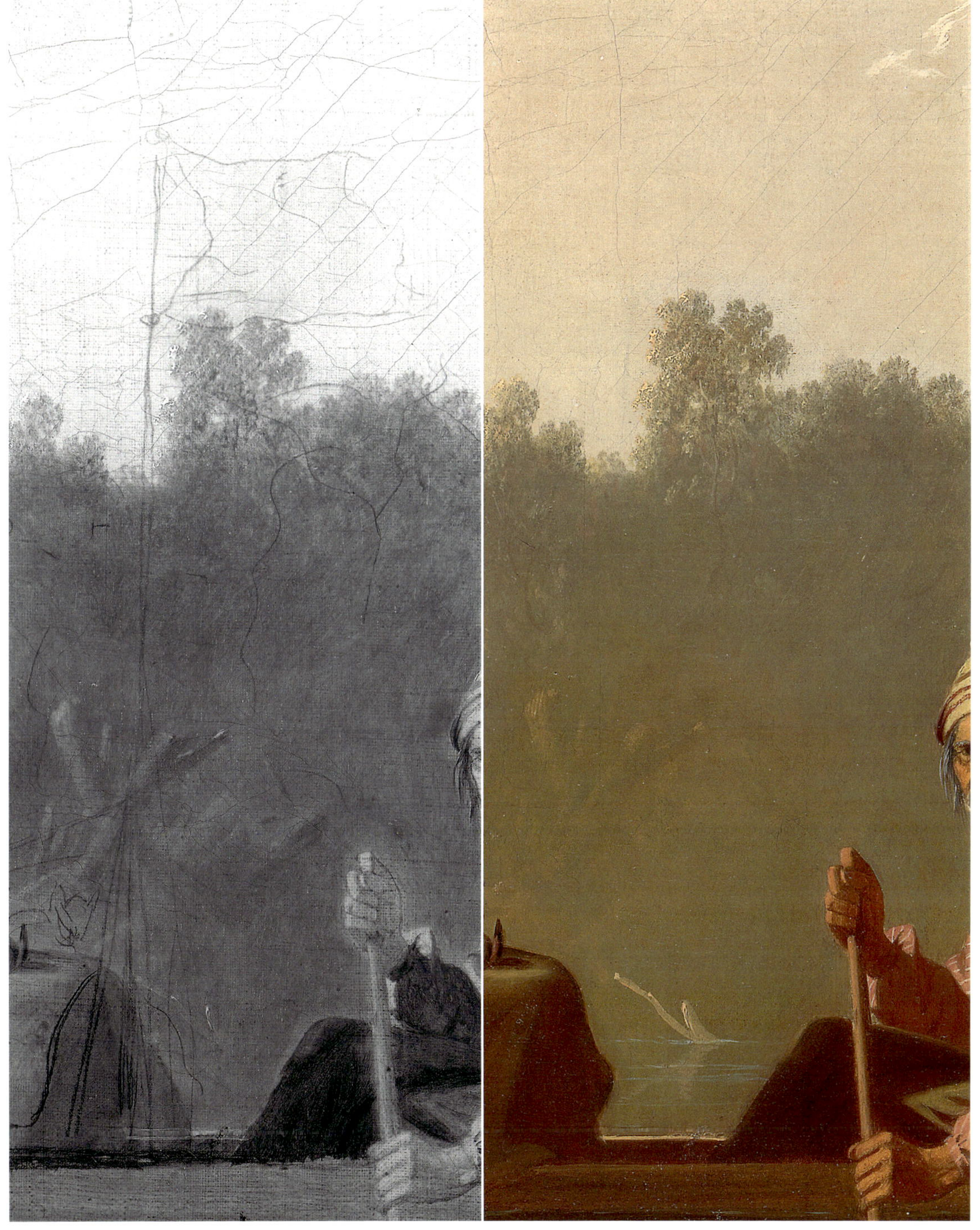

Fig. 50: This infrared detail (left) from *Fur Traders Descending the Missouri* (Pl. 3) shows a billowing flag in the underdrawing that was never realized in the finished composition.

for clouds, a series of parallel lines for tree trunks, and scalloped lines for the foliage behind the boy, perhaps referencing a compositional sketch for *Fur Traders,* now lost, that precluded the need for more detailed underdrawing in these areas. The artist indicated the young trader's reflection in the foreground with summary parallel lines, but he shifted the reflection to the right, corresponding to the position of the youth in the final painting.

Perhaps the most surprising discovery during the infrared examination of *Fur Traders Descending the Missouri* (Pl. 3) were the pentimenti in key narrative details. These revisions from the underdrawing pertain largely to the appearance and location of the bear cub, along with the overall description of the boat and near background. Bingham also reduced the scale of the cub in the painting from the one he first envisioned in his preparatory sketch, and he made similar changes to the animal in *Trappers' Return* (Pl. 31, Fig. 49). He also drew, but never painted, a bear cub to the immediate right of the young fur trader that he later replaced with a dead fowl.

Infrared examination also uncovered Bingham's initial sketch of a vertical mast, secured to the vessel between the two figures, that supports a flag billowing above the background trees (Fig. 50). In eliminating the prominent vertical motifs of the flagpole as well as a large tree first placed to the right of the old fur trader, Bingham emphasized the horizontality of the panoramic river scene. These pentimenti reveal Bingham's efforts to refine the composition and create a more compelling, peaceful image of frontier life that would appeal to eastern viewers. The American Art-Union's acceptance of *Fur Traders Descending the Missouri* invigorated Bingham to expand his output of western genre paintings for a receptive East Coast market.

The Concealed Enemy (1845, Pl. 2)

No drawing by Bingham exists for the Indian he portrayed in *The Concealed Enemy*—one of only two paintings from the artist's riverboat series to feature a Native American. As discussed in the principal essay, the artist likely modeled the pose of the crouching Indian in *The Concealed Enemy* from a print source: the frontispiece for *The Valley of the Mississippi Illustrated,* a periodical that was published monthly beginning in 1841 (Fig. 51).[45] Bingham's appropriation of a figure from a reproduction suggests that the artist may have lacked access to a suitable Native American model. Examination of *The Concealed Enemy* under infrared reflectography revealed little to no underdrawing, implying that—as with his posthumous portrait of Dr. Benoist Troost painted from a photograph—when Bingham modeled his figures after a print source, he dispensed with the need for detailed underdrawing.

Like other Bingham paintings examined for this project, *The Concealed Enemy* contains numerous pentimenti. First, infrared reflectography revealed that Bingham lowered the position of the barrel of the Indian's rifle. Since he presented *The Concealed Enemy* and *Fur Traders Descending the Missouri* together to the American Art-Union, he may have conceived of them as pendants and shifted the rifle in order to point more accurately at the Indian's intended targets: the figures in *Fur Traders.* The artist also eliminated the second figure of a rifle-bearing Indian crouching in the left background (Fig. 52). Perhaps Bingham disliked his unconvincing portrayal of the background Indian, or perhaps he concluded that focusing on a single attacker resulted in a more powerful composition.

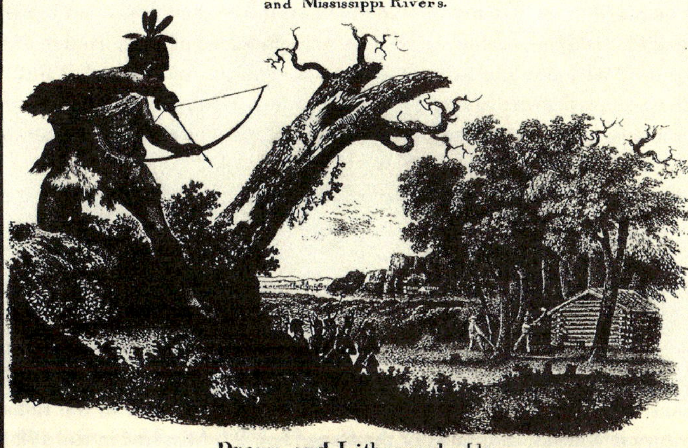

Fig. 51: John Casper Wild (1804–1846), frontispiece for *The Valley of the Mississippi Illustrated*, 1841, lithograph, Library of Congress, Washington, D.C. Bingham modeled the Indian in *The Concealed Enemy* (Pl. 2) after the figure in this print.

Fig. 52: This infrared detail (left) from *The Concealed Enemy* shows a second, crouching figure in the background, later painted over by the artist (see also Fig. 81).

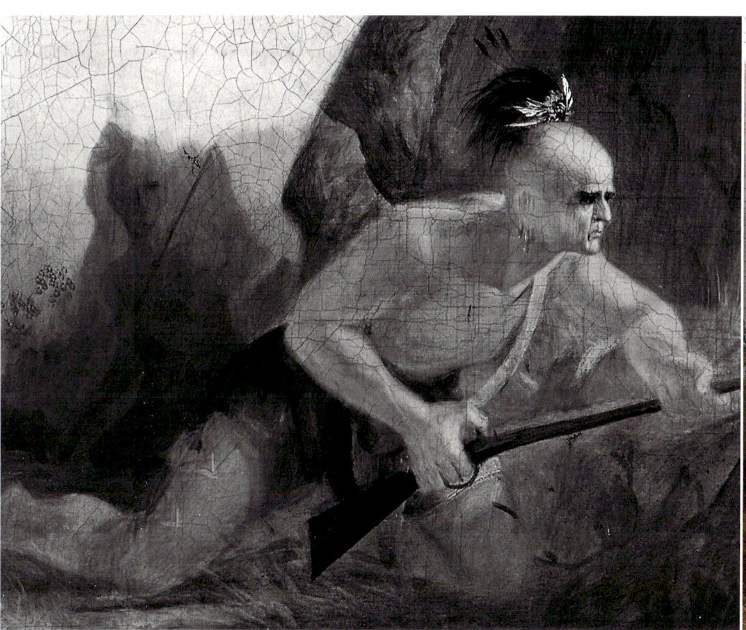

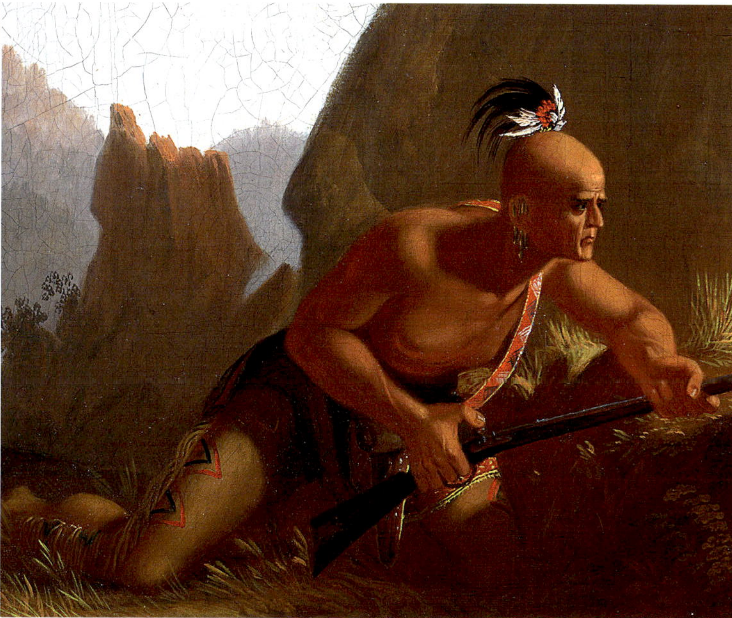

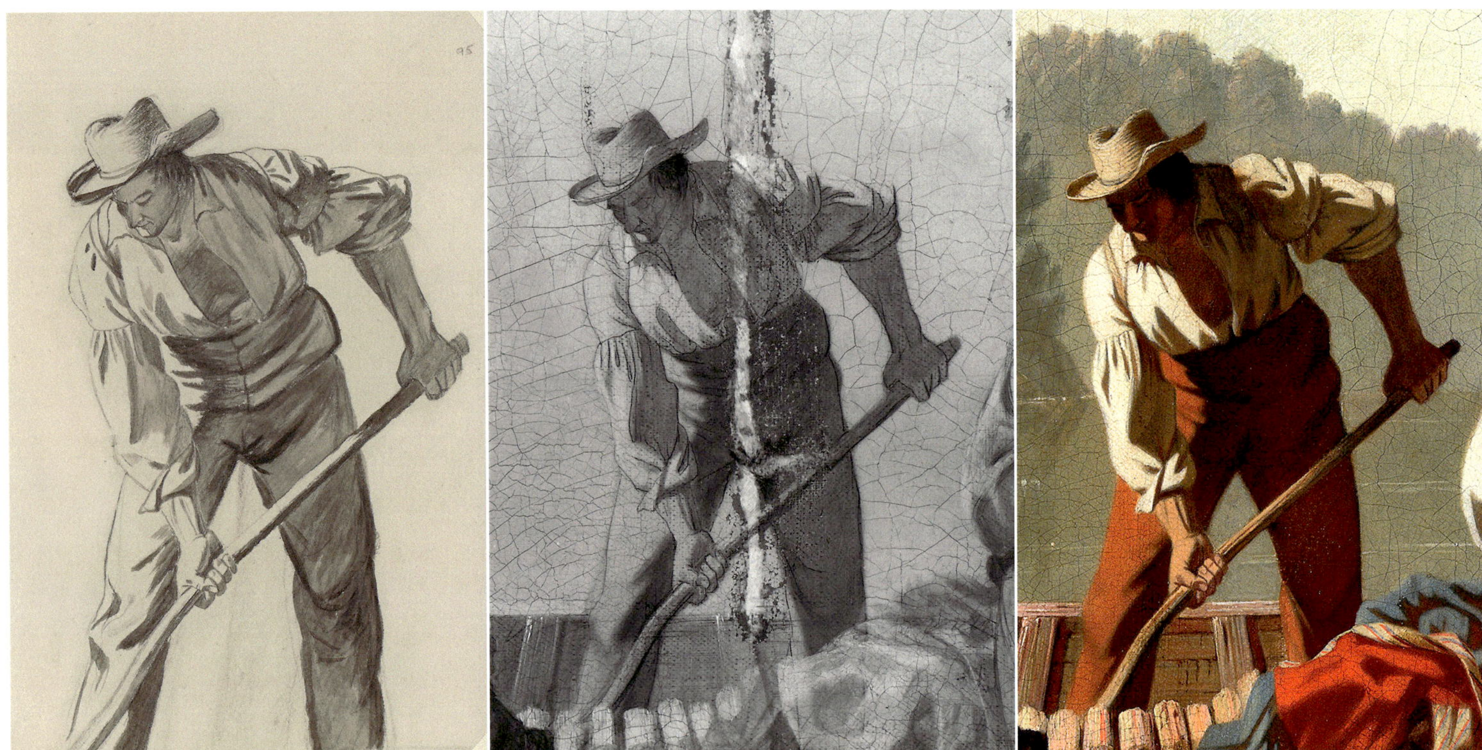

Fig. 53: In infrared light, the underdrawing (center) of the standing figure in *Boatmen on the Missouri* (Pl. 4) shows Bingham's systematic outlining of the figure by tracing the study, *Boatman* (Pl. 9, left). (Infrared light also reveals an old, repaired tear in the canvas.) Bingham likely planned the composition before he posed his model, since like the finished painting (right) the study shows the figure cropped below the knees.

Boatmen on the Missouri (1846, Pl. 4)

Bingham based two of the figures in *Boatmen on the Missouri* directly on two studies titled *Boatman* (Pls. 8 and 9). Infrared examination of the painting shows that the standing boatman has the clearest and most systematic outlining of the three figures; the artist most likely posed the model in the study after he planned the composition, since he cropped the figure below the knees (Fig. 53). In the painting, Bingham placed the figure behind a woodpile and covered the boatman's proper left leg with a blanket. Following his usual approach, Bingham directly transferred the study on paper to canvas by incising the contours of the boatman's hat and facial features from the drawing. He used a system of simple schematic loops for shadows in the shirt folds, a shorthand underdrawing technique that he repeated in many of the later flatboatmen paintings but adopted in *Boatmen on the Missouri* for the first time.

The artist combined different underdrawing techniques in his rendering of the seated boatman wearing a stovepipe hat to the left. He embellished the contours and schematic looping of shadows with freehand shading in the form of parallel hatching in the man's collar, lower back, and along the back of his hand.

Bingham's underdrawing for the third boatman, seated at the right, lacks the clear, mechanical outlines and schematic looping seen in the underdrawing of the other two figures. He probably added this figure last and positioned him on canvas only after outlining the oars and boat, since the figure's leg stops along the top edge of the oar. The boatman's awkward proportions—his head, like that of the man in the middle, is too small for his large body—point to a recurring motif in Bingham's riverboat pictures: the proportions of different body parts within the figures often do not match. This raises the question of whether Bingham might have drawn the figure directly on canvas without the aid of a preparatory drawing. The sketchy character of the underdrawing, with its imprecise contours and parallel hatching and cross-hatching throughout the costume and hat, differs considerably from the more meticulous appearance of the underdrawings traced directly from his studies.

Watching the Cargo (1849, Pl. 27)

The two seated boatmen in *Watching the Cargo* are based on drawings from Bingham's portfolio. A watermarked Whatman paper was used for the study *Boatman* (Pl. 37, Fig. 54), and the drawing was executed on the side of the sheet on which the watermark reads correctly: J. WHATMAN / TURKEY MILL / 1847. Whatman's wove paper, made from high-quality linen fiber, was considered the finest paper available at the time, and the artist used it for several of his studies.

Both of the studies for *Watching the Cargo* contain evidence of several of Bingham's most characteristic techniques for utilizing the studies as cartoons for transferring figures to canvas. The drawings reveal extensive impressions along the contour lines of the figures, the shadows of drapery folds, and the details in the faces and pipe (Pls. 37 and 38). Harsh, raking light on the verso of the drawing of the seated boatman with pipe captures the relief from incising and the distortion of the paper as it stretched from the pressure Bingham applied as he drew and burnished the surface to transfer areas of shading (Fig. 54). Bingham's tracing procedure for creating a reverse pose is demonstrated in the double-sided drawing of the boatman on the left of the painting (Fig. 55). When Bingham placed this drawing facing a light source, perhaps on a window, viewing it in transmitted light, the dark lines and shadow areas of the drawing on the recto would have been easily visible. He was thus able to trace the outline of the figure on the verso of the sheet.

In the underdrawing for the seated boatman on the left, the artist elaborated his customary mechanical outlining of forms with extensive cross-hatching in the shadow areas of the figure's costume, proper right hand, and wrist. These hatch marks are also seen in the impressions on the study, and they demonstrate a more sophisticated, formal approach to shading than seen in the schematic looping of shadows in the underdrawing for *Boatmen on the Missouri* (Pl. 4), executed three years earlier (Fig. 56).

Numerous pentimenti in the underdrawing of the foreground point to the artist's efforts at shifting the wooden poles and tarp and restructuring the overall size and shape of the tented cargo (Fig. 57). Bingham sketched the cargo surrounding the figures in a freehand, summary manner, using cross-hatching in the shadows as he had done for the figures. Although no preliminary sketches for Bingham's riverboat compositions survive, he must have arranged the figures according to a carefully considered, preexisting plan for the overall scene, as E. Maurice Bloch asserted in his catalogue raisonné of Bingham's drawings.[46] In the majority of his preparatory studies, Bingham established the immediate setting of his figure, whether sitting on a box or in a canoe, and the results of close examination of the underdrawings corroborate this process. Infrared examination reveals that while Bingham may have begun his underdrawings with the background, it was most often sketched much more loosely than the figures, and the artist frequently revised the setting as he brought his paintings to completion.

Fig. 54: Raking light on the verso (right) of *Boatman* (Pl. 37) shows the Whatman watermark in reverse and distortion of the stretched paper from Bingham applying pressure and rubbing to transfer areas of shading to the underdrawing on his canvas.

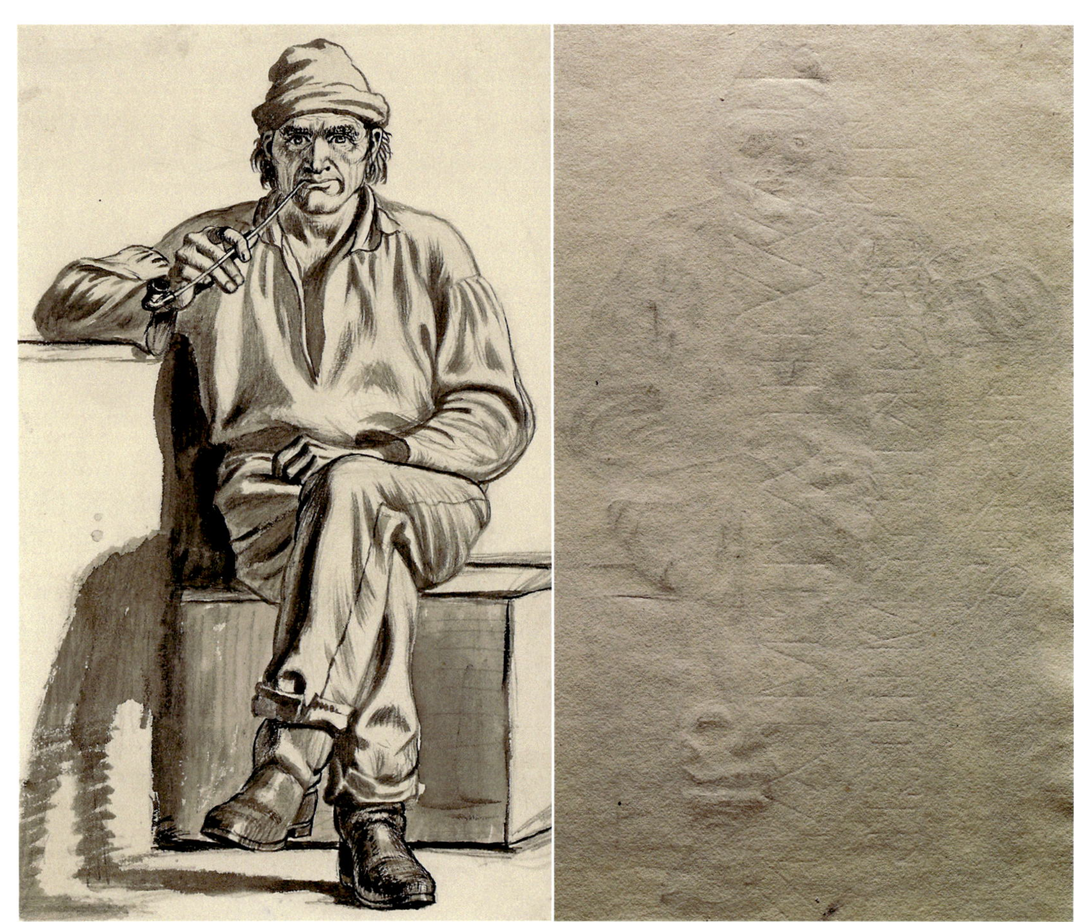

Fig. 55: Bingham's tracing procedure for creating a reverse pose is demonstrated in the double-sided drawing *Boatman* (Pl. 38) in *Watching the Cargo* (Pl. 27).

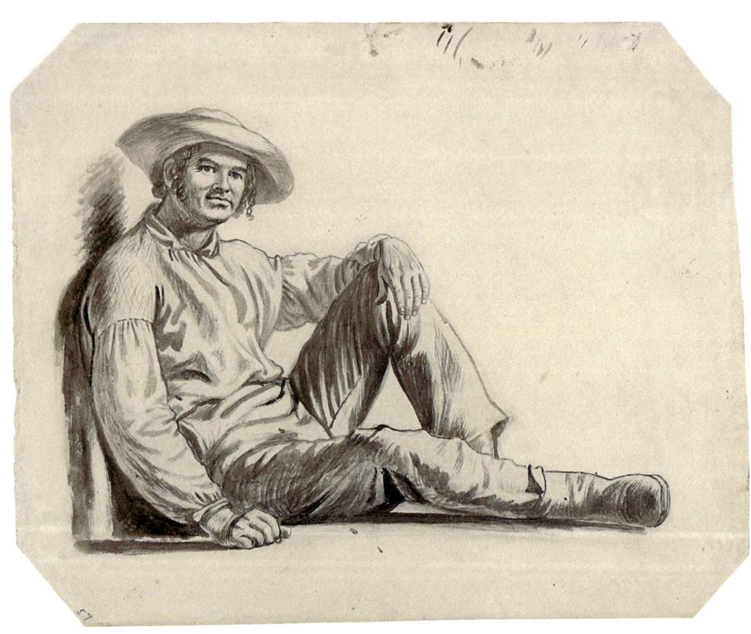

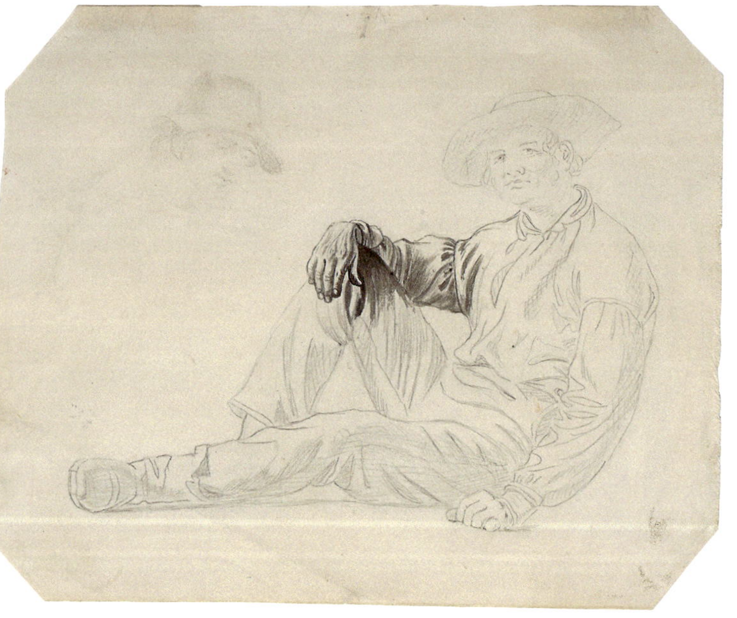

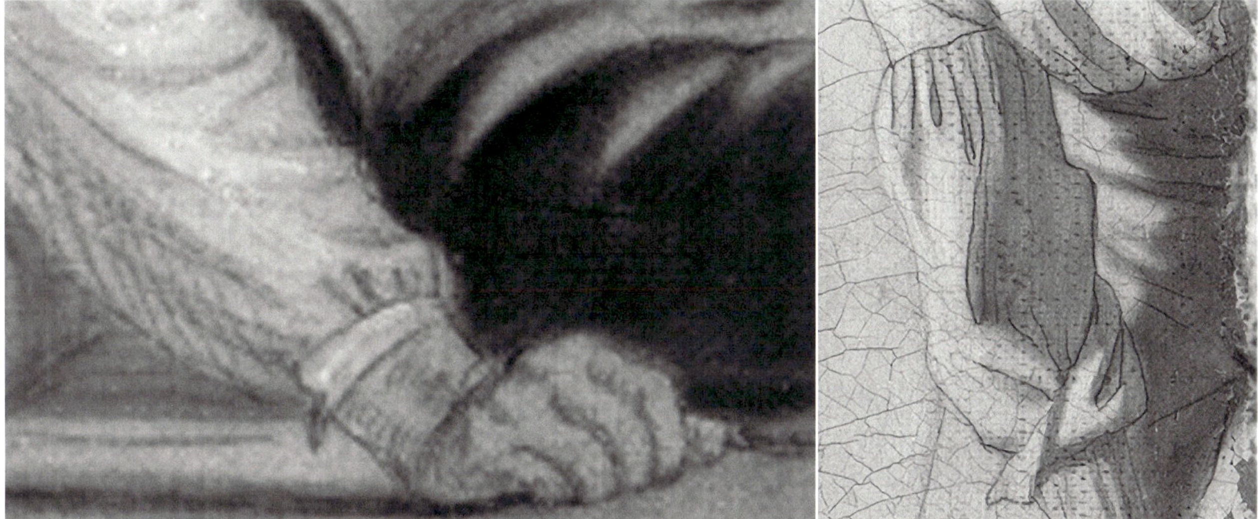

Fig. 56: As seen in infrared light, the cross-hatching that Bingham applied for areas of shading in the figure's hand and wrist (left) in *Watching the Cargo* reflects a more sophisticated drawing approach than the schematic loops he used three years earlier to indicate the shadows in a shirt (right) in *Boatmen on the Missouri* (Pl. 4).

Fig. 57: This infrared detail (left) of the two seated figures in *Watching the Cargo*, when compared to the finished painting, reveals pentimenti in the artist's structuring of the overall size and shape of the tented cargo. Bingham sketched the cargo in a freehand, summary manner but used cross-hatching to indicate shadows in both the figures and background details.

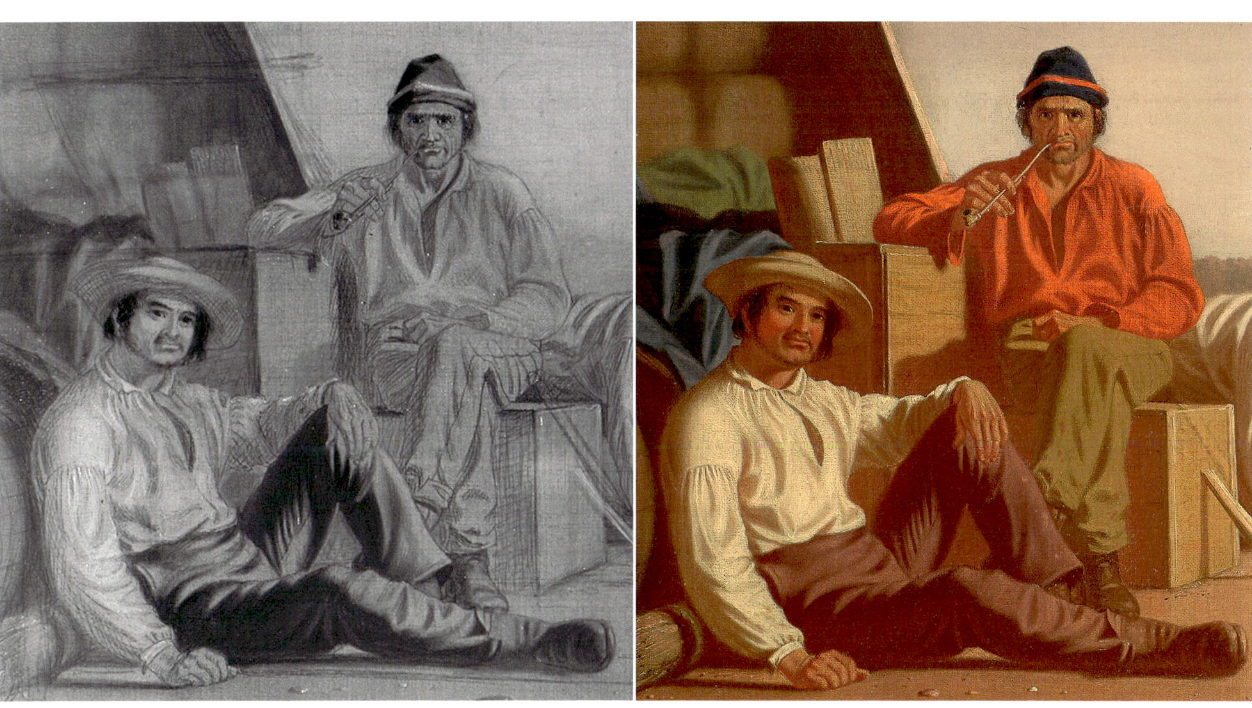

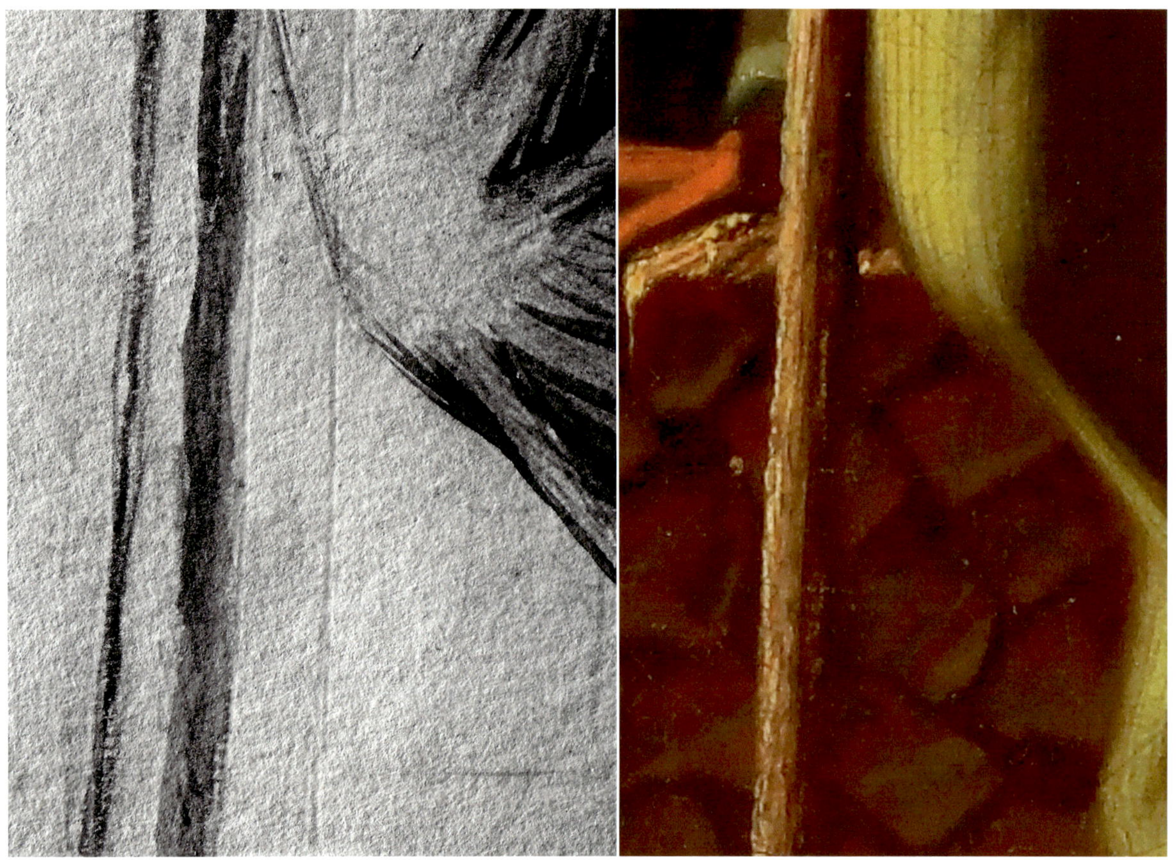

Fig. 58: This detail of the figure's knee in the drawing *Woodboatman* (Pl. 40) alongside its related figure in *The Wood-Boat* shows the artist's impressions used in the transfer process. Bingham incised the vertical pole farther to the right, continuing to refine his composition throughout his creative process.

The Wood-Boat (1850, Pl. 28)

The double-sided drawings for the figures in this painting represent Bingham's draftsmanship at its finest, reflecting the artist's heightened awareness of expression, light, and shadow (Pls. 39, 40, and 41). All three of the drawings show extensive embossed impressions resulting from the artist's direct transfer of the studies to canvas. Examination of the drawing of the standing boatman in raking light shows that Bingham incised the outlines of the vertical pole farther to the right, continuing to refine his drawing throughout his creative process (Fig. 58). He followed the revised outlines of the pole in the completed painting. For the young seated boatman in this painting, Bingham applied extensive underdrawing throughout the figure, treating the shadow areas by combining his simplified looping technique with more detailed parallel hatching and cross-hatching (Fig. 59). The artist lavished the most attention on the wrinkled face of the seated boatman that he meticulously transferred from the study (Fig. 60).

Bingham delineated the contours of the flatboat using a straightedge and made a simple freehand sketch of foreground details, such as the woodpile, using summary outlines. A pentimento exists in the left foreground, where Bingham simplified the composition by eliminating a long pole.

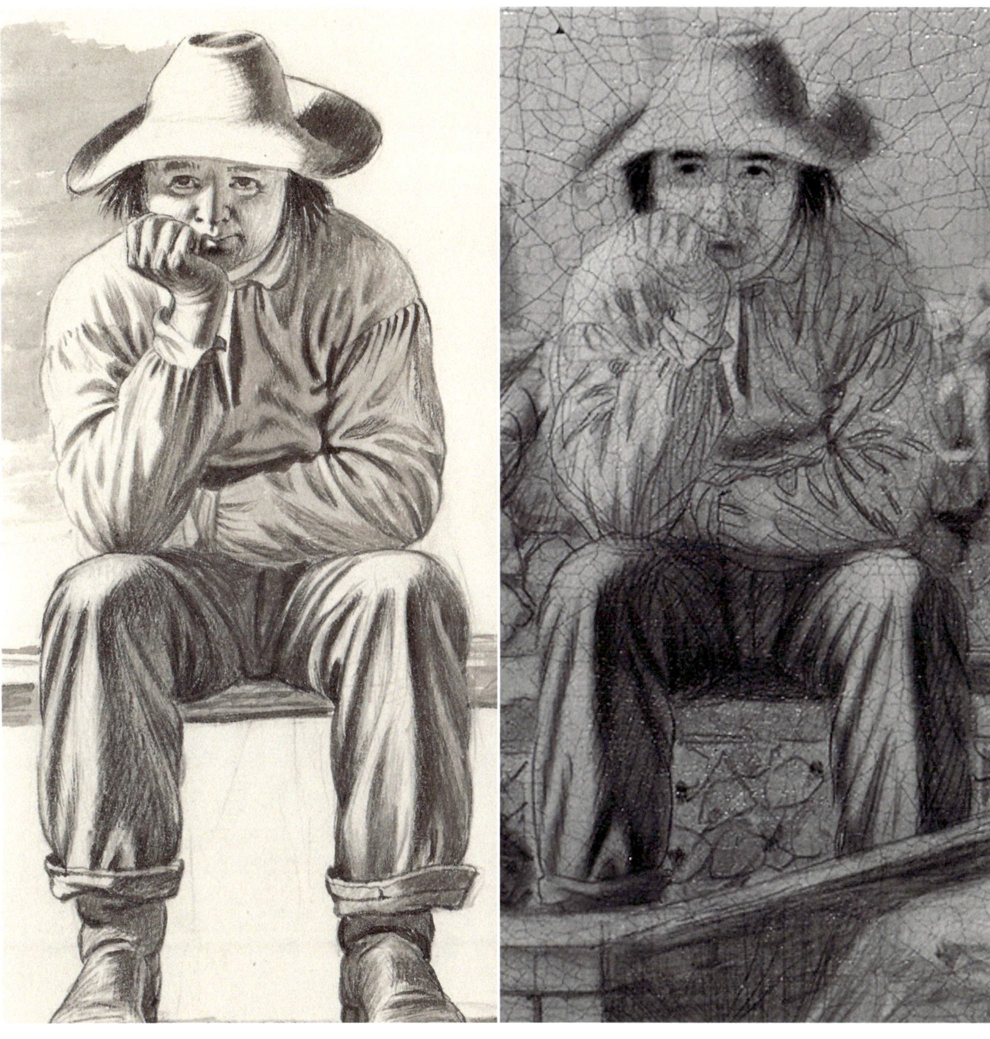

Fig. 59: Details of the drawing *Young woodboatman* (Pl. 41) and the underdrawing of the painted figure (right) in infrared light show that Bingham combined his simplified looping technique with more detailed cross-hatching for the shadows in the underdrawing. This example illustrates the artist's occasional practice of combining different underdrawing techniques within a single figure.

Fig. 60: When an infrared detail (center) of the smoking figure in *The Wood-Boat* (Pl. 28) is seen alongside the related drawing *Woodboatman* (Pl. 39, left), it becomes apparent that the artist lavished attention on the figure's wrinkled face, which he continued to do in the painting (right).

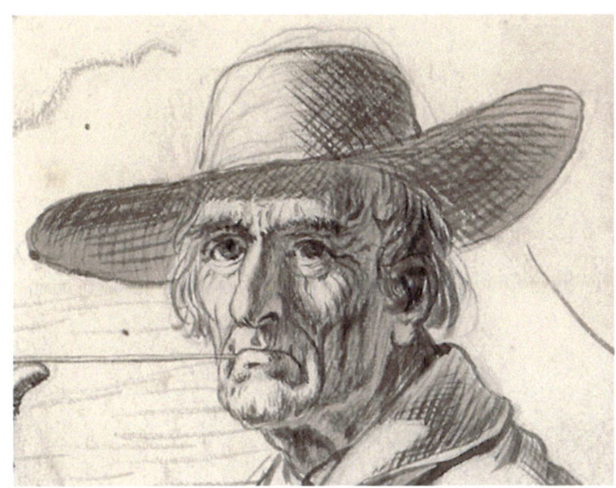

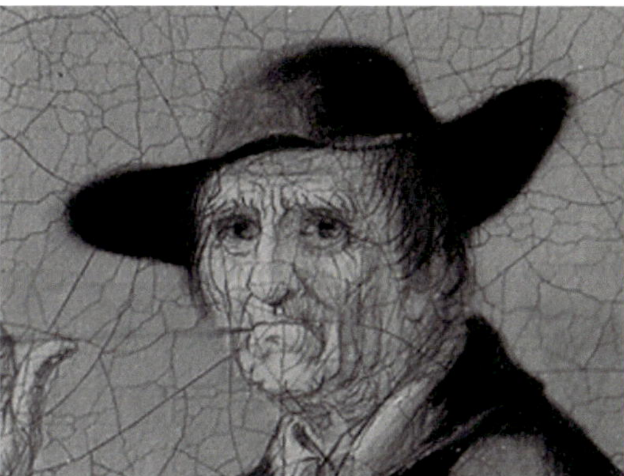

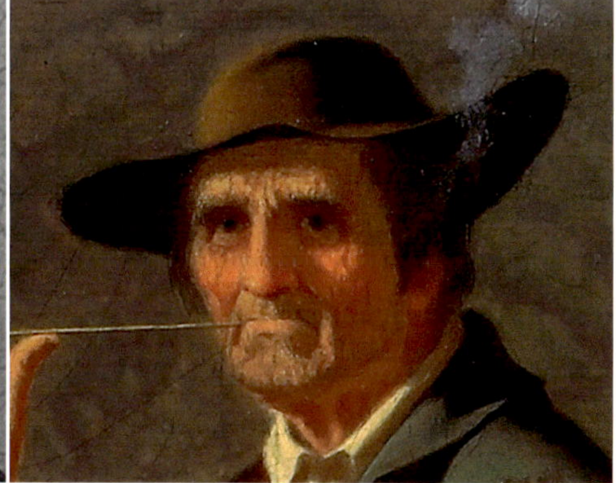

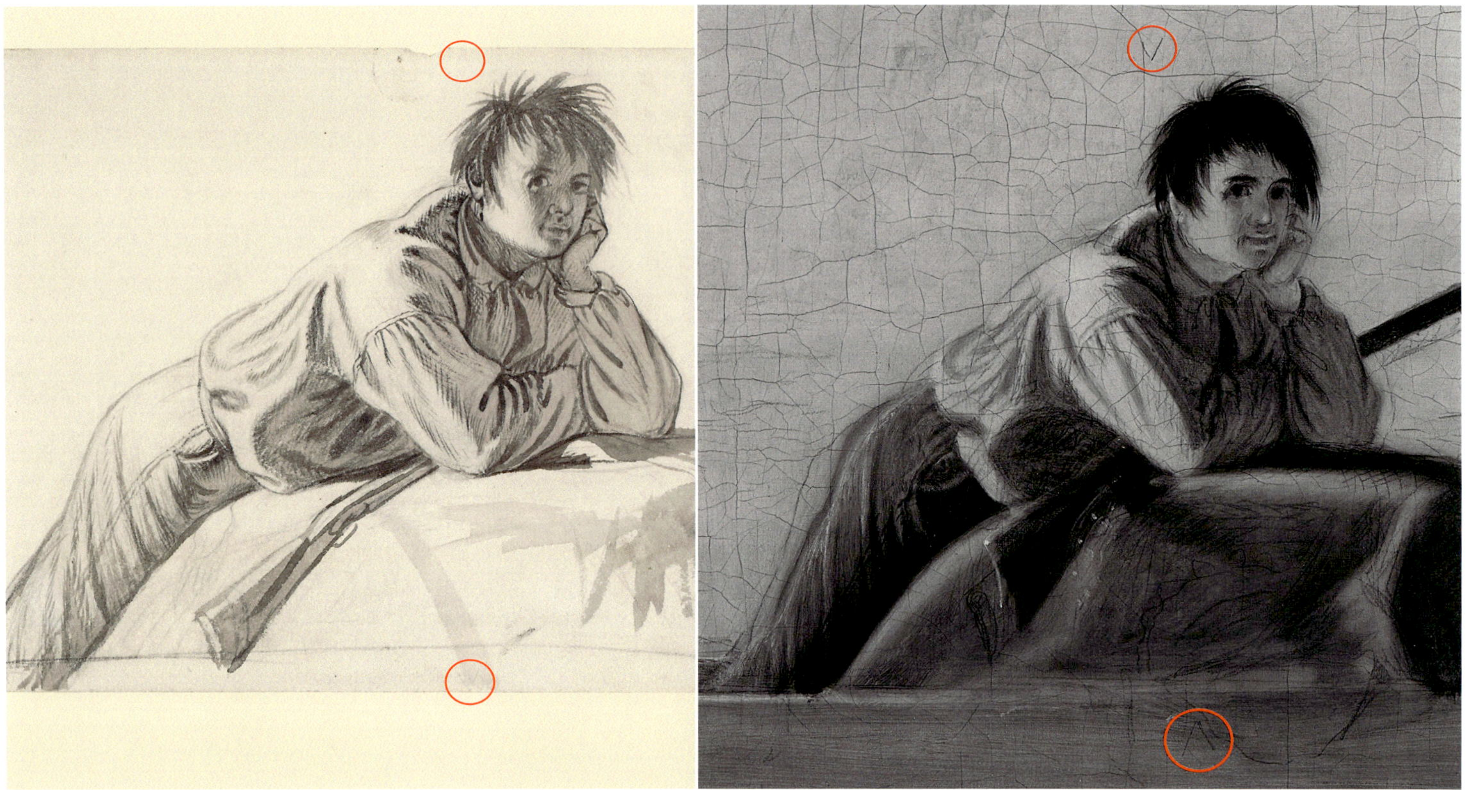

Fig. 61: Details of the young boy from the drawing *Trapper's son* (Pl. 42) alongside the underdrawing of the figure in *Trappers' Return* showing the artist's arrows, or registration marks, circled in red. Bingham aligned corresponding arrows in the study and in the underdrawing, point to point, to carefully position and hold the cartoon still on the canvas during transfer.

Fig. 62: Details (left) of the drawing *Fisherman* (Pl. 50) and an infrared from *Fishing on the Mississippi* (Pl. 43) showing the artist's arrows, or registration marks, circled in red. Bingham used these arrows to align his cartoons on canvas for transfer. Similar registration marks appear on a number of Bingham's studies of flatboatmen and political figures alike.

Trappers' Return (1851, Pl. 31)

Six years after he painted *Fur Traders Descending the Missouri* (Pl. 3), Bingham recycled the drawing of the old boatman for the painting *Trappers' Return* (see Fig. 45). The artist created a new drawing for the boy, selecting a paper that was better suited to his transfer process. The new drawing is executed on a paper support that is heavier and more robust than the thin sheet he had used previously for the study of the old trader. As he had done before, the artist carefully traced the contours of the two figures from his studies and indicated the shadow areas in the shirt folds with parallel hatching and schematic loops. The contour lines visible in the underdrawing for the young boy in *Trapper's Return* correspond to the blind impressions in the paper, indicating direct transfer.

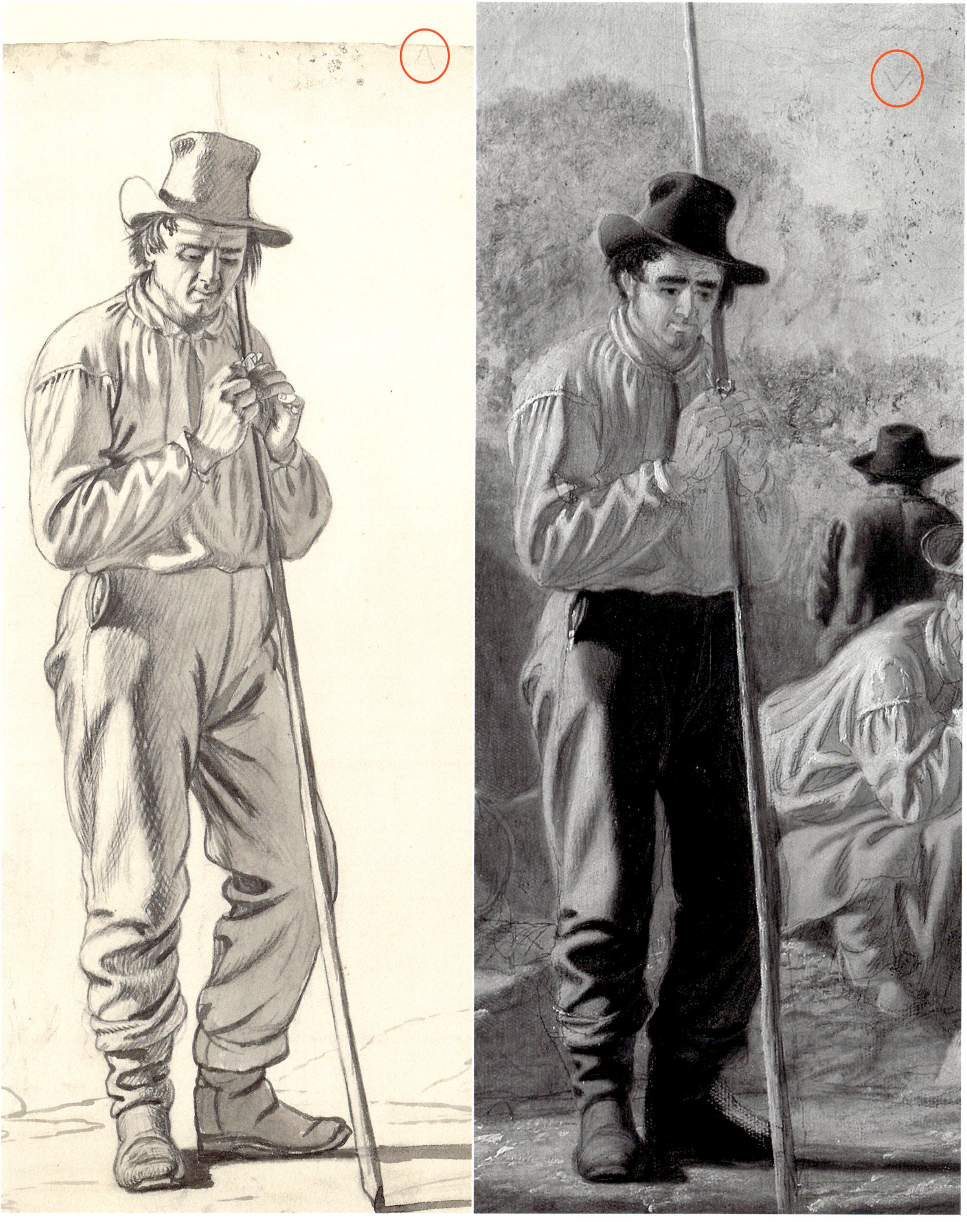

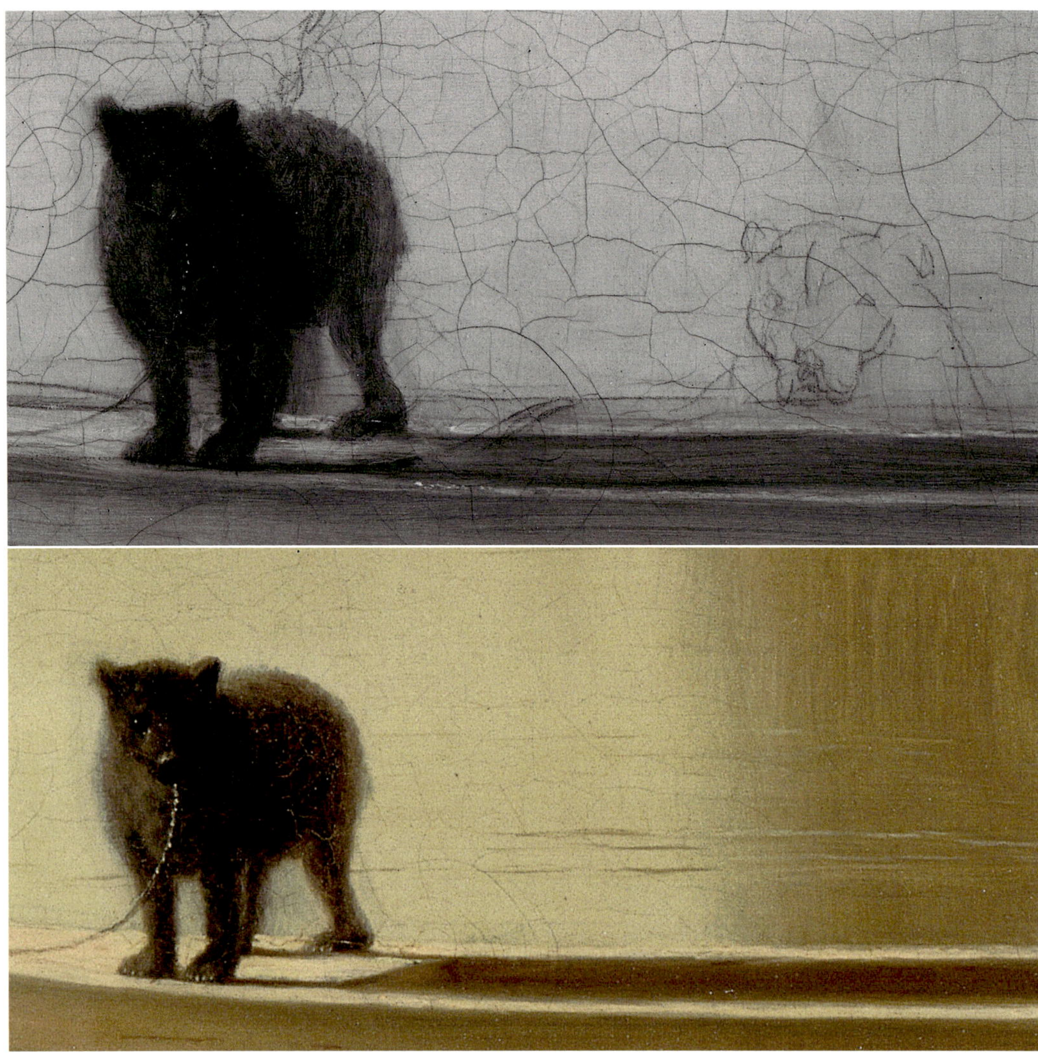

Fig. 63: This infrared detail (top) from *Trappers' Return* (Pl. 31) shows the artist's underdrawing of a larger animal that was never realized in the finished composition (bottom). Bingham also revised the pose of the painted cub to show him standing on all fours, rather than sitting.

Bingham positioned his drawing of the trapper's son on the primed canvas surface by aligning corresponding arrows that he marked on both the drawing and the underdrawing, the arrows matching point to point, where the guide marks appear below the boy's elbow and above his head slightly to the left. While these arrows had been previously noted on this drawing (and several other studies of boatmen and political figures),[47] the discovery for this essay of corresponding marks in the underdrawing confirms that Bingham used these registration marks to position his study on the canvas during the underdrawing stage (Fig. 61). Further evidence of this method was also discovered in the underdrawing of the standing fisherman in *Fishing on the Mississippi* (Pl. 43, Fig. 62).

Following his customary practice, Bingham completed the preparatory drawing of the surrounding landscape, including the boat and background foliage, in *Trappers' Return* with freehand sketching. Once again he struggled with the description, size, and location of the bear cub in this boat—the underdrawing reveals that Bingham abandoned two preliminary sketches for the animal (Fig. 63).

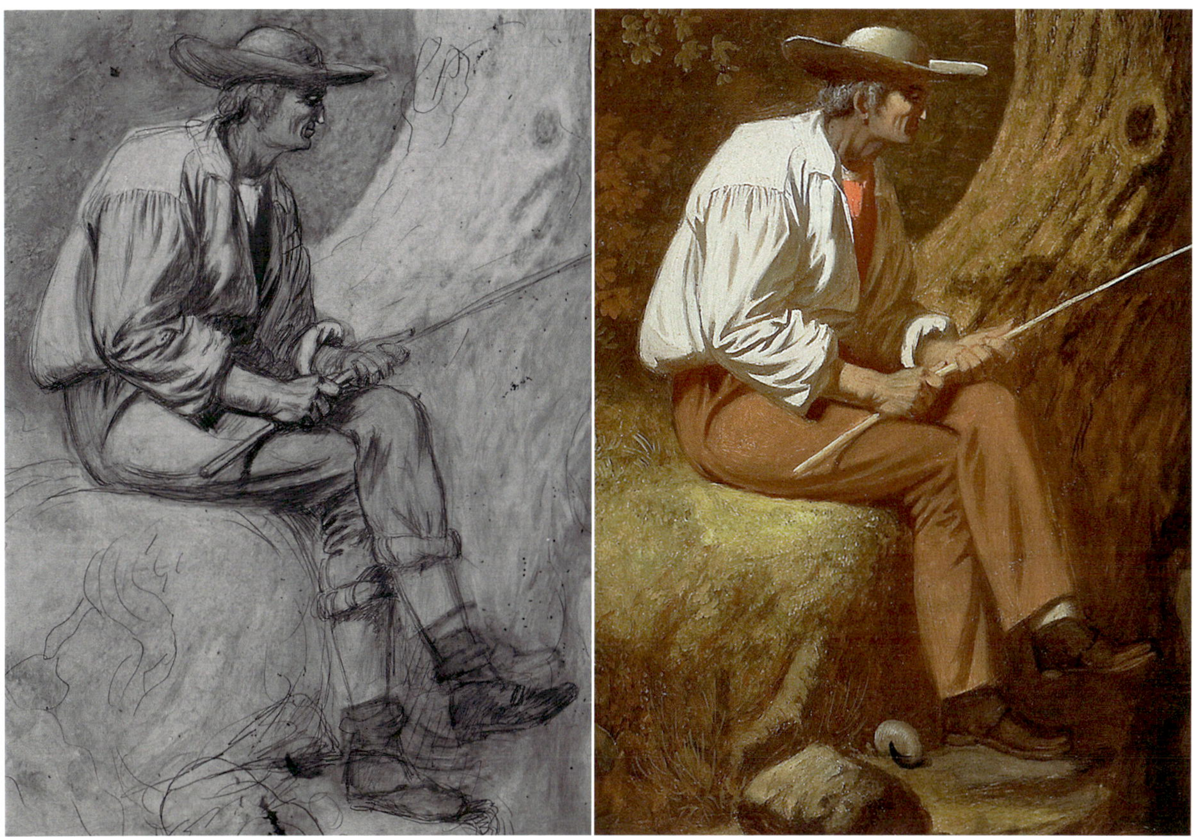

Fig. 64: An infrared detail (left) of the figure in *Mississippi Fisherman* (Pl. 29) shows that Bingham sketched the figure directly on canvas using a dry medium, probably graphite. He heavily worked the shadows with back-and-forth scribbling, and he redrew both of the figure's feet.

Mississippi Boatman (1850, Pl. 30) and *Mississippi Fisherman* (ca. 1850, Pl. 29)

Infrared examination established that Bingham adapted his underdrawing style according to the complexity of his compositions. The underdrawing in the two single-figure paintings examined, *Mississippi Fisherman* and *Mississippi Boatman*, differ from the premeditated approach that the artist generally followed for his multifigure compositions. No study is known to exist for *Mississippi Fisherman*, suggesting Bingham sketched the figure directly on canvas using a dry medium (probably graphite). He defined the outlines of the figure with multiple strokes and heavily worked the shadow areas with parallel hatching and rapid back-and-forth scribbling. Bingham also repositioned the fisherman's feet, partially erasing his earlier attempt (Fig. 64).

As was his usual practice, he summarily sketched the key outlines of the landscape surrounding the figure. His energetic handling of the large rocks and shadows in the foreground presents a striking contrast to the more measured and precise underdrawing seen in most of his complex, multifigure paintings.

By contrast, Bingham modeled the figure in *Mississippi Boatman* after his graphite preparatory study *Boatman* (Pl. 37), which we have seen was likely based on Chapman's illustration for an aged man (see Fig. 42). The painted figure, however, is much larger in scale, and the lack of squaring lines raises the possibility that Bingham may have transferred his boatman drawing to canvas using some means of projection to increase the size of his figure. (This question is addressed further in the following case study of the artist's three versions of the same subject.)

Bingham's underdrawing technique for the figure in *Mississippi Boatman* differs in appearance from his directly traced underdrawings. The artist loosely sketched the outlines of the boatman figure, along with his facial features, but applied only minimal parallel hatching in shadow areas without any evidence of the schematically lassoed shadows usually found in the underdrawings of figures that were directly transferred from paper. Bingham outlined the barrels, crate, and flatboat using cursory lines and shaded the front side of the crate with extensive parallel hatching. Infrared examination also uncovered pentimenti in the size of the crate and flatboat cabin, the latter of which he enlarged in the final painting.[48]

Three Versions of *The Jolly Flatboatmen*

The Jolly Flatboatmen (1846, Pl. 5)

Bingham prepared six known studies for *The Jolly Flatboatmen* of 1846. His most ambitious composition to that time, the painting was reproduced in a mezzotint that was engraved by Thomas Doney, who was active in New York City from 1844 to 1849, and published by the American Art-Union in 1847.[49] All of the existing drawings for the figures are on a similar type of paper, and the support for three of these studies of the river characters has an unidentified watermark, a six-pointed star, that is undocumented in previous Bingham studies. Although slightly thinner, this paper has a cream tone and smooth surface similar to other papers Bingham used in his early drawings.

There are drawings for every major figure in *The Jolly Flatboatmen* with the exception of the central dancer, whose joyous pose is tantalizingly similar to both the bronze Pompeiian *Dancing Faun* from the second century BCE[50] and the ascending figure of Christ in Raphael's *Transfiguration* of 1520 (Fig. 65).[51] These examples illustrate not only Bingham's familiarity with the canon of classical and European Renaissance art but, again, his tendency to borrow key motifs from print sources. Furthermore, as discussed earlier, casts after classical sculpture were certainly part of his workshop inventory.[52] Bingham attracted criticism for borrowing from Renaissance prototypes when he exhibited the first version of his *Flatboatmen* composition in 1847; however, their qualities of stasis probably also made his rough-and-tumble characters accessible to a wider audience.[53]

Although no drawing for the dancing boatman is known to survive, infrared analysis of the underdrawing for the painting reveals that Bingham painstakingly drew the figure's contours and lassoed the shadows of his drapery folds as if the figure had been directly transferred from a study. Pentimenti along the right side of the figure show that Bingham perfected

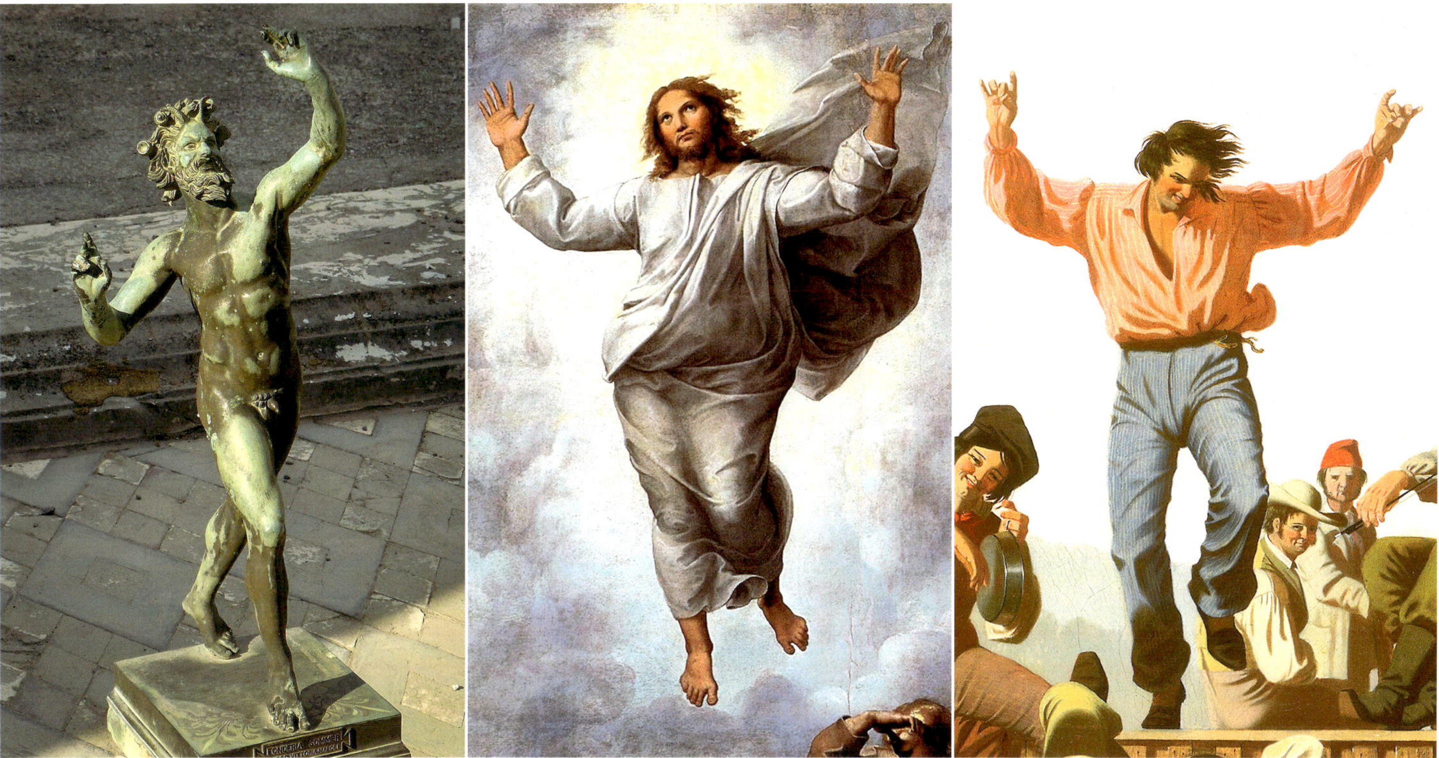

Fig. 65: *Dancing Faun* (second century BCE) from Pompeii and the figure of Christ from Raphael's *The Transfiguration*, 1520, in the Pinacoteca Vatican probably inspired Bingham's pose for the dancing figure in *The Jolly Flatboatmen* of 1846 (Pl. 5). This indicates both the artist's familiarity with the canon of classical and European art and his practice of borrowing key motifs from print sources.

the dancer's pose by repositioning the proper left hand, leg, and foot.

The artist's studies *Fiddler* (Pl. 11), *Flatboatman* (Pl. 12), *Flatboatman* (Pl. 13), and *Skillet-beater* (Pl. 10) all evince a familiar pattern of blind impressions along contours, including indications for the shadows in shirts, from the direct transfer of the drawings to canvas. Hand-drawn overlays confirm all four drawings are exactly to scale, with only minor adjustments in outlines. The figure seated directly behind the dancer's leg appears reduced from the drawing (Pl. 12), but the hand-traced overlay confirms that its scale is one to one, and there are incised contour lines, which indicate direct transfer. A digitally manipulated overlay shows the slight variations from drawing to painting (Fig. 66). Exceptionally, the drawing for the flatboatman at the far right gazing at the viewer shows no incising or evidence of direct transfer, yet the underdrawing reveals the characteristic contours and loops. When the hand-drawn overlay of the drawing was placed over the painted figure, the increase in size again suggested some sort of projection may have been used for transfer (Fig. 67). Bingham may have traced the larger, projected image using contours and loops that were similar in appearance to underdrawings that were directly transferred. Accordingly, the underdrawing for the other four boatmen in the foreground follows Bingham's usual method of transferring figures from studies: carefully outlining the contours of the boatmen and indicating the shadows with schematic loops.

The artist established the outlines of the flatboat and oars with meticulous precision, working with the aid of a straightedge. Changes in angled lines at the bottom left and right corners of the flatboat reflect Bingham's preoccupation with perspective. While some of the objects in the foreground, including the coiled rope and ladder, were planned from the outset, other details, such as the hanging shirt and animal pelt, were added in a later stage of the creative process – the infrared reflectogram mosaic demonstrates that these forms overlap the completed outlines of the flatboat. Bingham made several minor adjustments during the course of painting, such as shifting the position of the dangling rope in the foreground, to achieve a greater sense of balance in the final composition (Fig. 68).

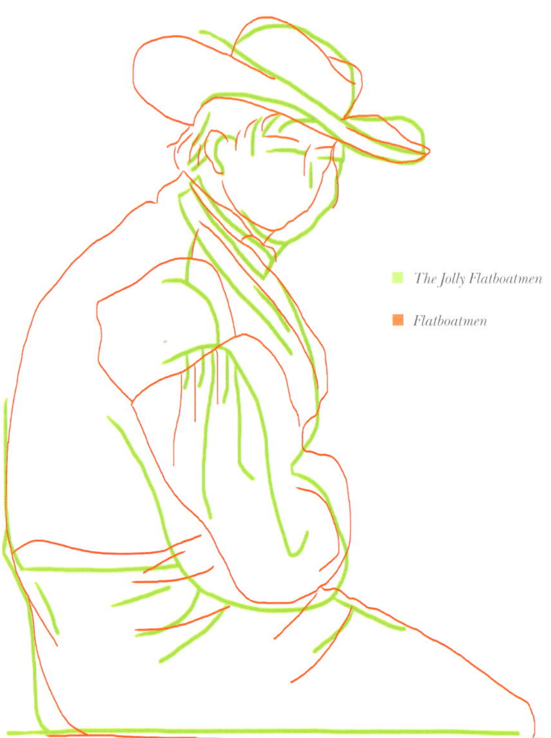

Fig. 66: A digital overlay of the seated boatman directly behind the dancer's leg in *The Jolly Flatboatmen*, 1846 (Pl. 5), when compared to an overlay of the related drawing *Flatboatman* (Pl. 12), shows only slight variations from drawing to painting.

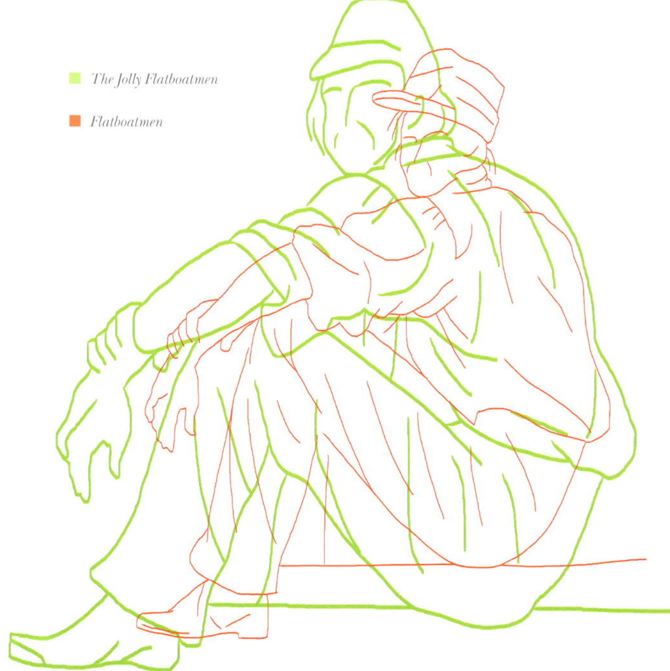

Fig. 67: A digital overlay of the drawing *Flatboatman* (Pl. 13) placed over the painted figure in *The Jolly Flatboatmen*, 1846, reveals an increase in size from drawing to painted figure, suggesting that Bingham employed some method of projection in transferring the drawing to canvas.

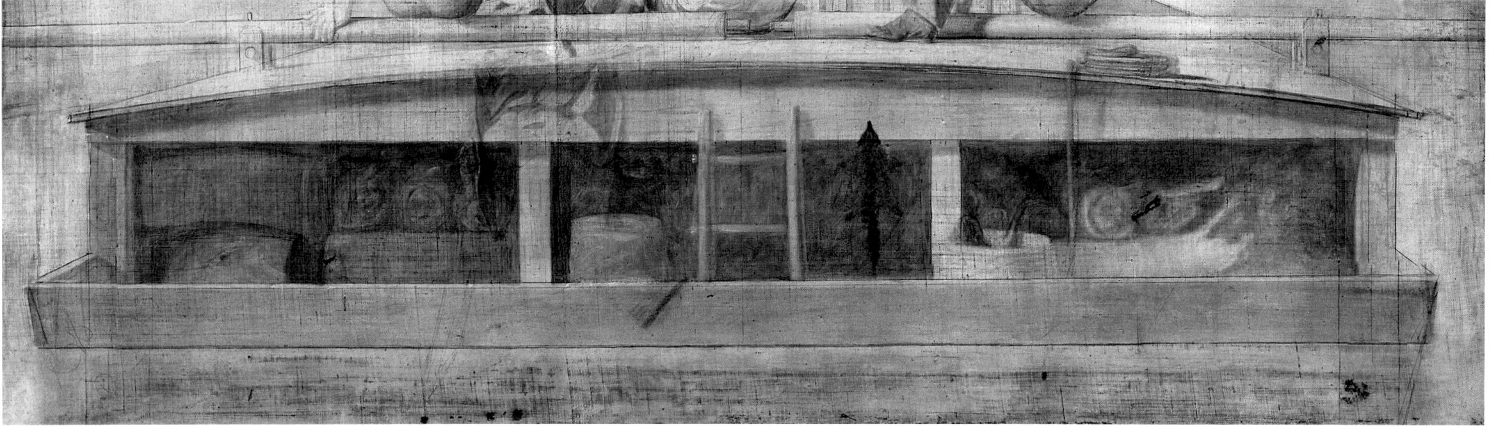

Fig. 68: An infrared mosaic detail of *The Jolly Flatboatmen*, 1846 (Pl. 5), reveals that Bingham established the outlines of the flatboat and oars using a straightedge, then later added the hanging shirt and animal pelt, whose descriptive lines cross over the earlier lines of the boat.

Jolly Flatboatmen in Port (1857, Pl. 47)

In the fall of 1856, Bingham set sail for Europe to continue his artistic education by directly experiencing the great paintings that he had previously known only through prints.[54] He had abandoned the flatboatmen pictures following the closing of the American Art-Union in 1852, which had supported his series of river scenes, and turned his focus toward European-influenced monumental history painting. He spent the early fall of 1856 in Paris accompanied by his daughter, Clara, and his second wife, Eliza Thomas, whom he married following the untimely death of his first wife, Sarah. Bingham found the experience of visiting the galleries of the Musée du Louvre, filled with countless masterpieces of many conflicting schools and artistic styles, almost overwhelming.[55]

After his Paris stay, the artist migrated to the thriving artistic center of Düsseldorf, where he could secure comfortable and reasonable lodging for his family in the smaller and more affordable city. He set up his studio next to that of Emanuel Leutze, joining a group of American artists that included Worthington Whittredge and Eastman Johnson, who were associated with the Düsseldorf Academy.

Teaching at the Düsseldorf Academy emphasized a precise style of history painting that suited Bingham's developing sensibility and artistic goals. The three years he spent there, working and studying, equipped the Missouri painter with a solid European artistic education. Though he temporarily abandoned the river scene pictures for a few years in favor of political paintings and historical portraits, Bingham reprised the jolly flatboatman theme in Germany with the painting *Jolly Flatboatmen in Port.* He now treated the subject as a history painting to record a significant event in the expansion of the American West. Working on an ambitious scale, Bingham greatly expanded the complexity of the earlier composition to emulate the grand traditions of European history painting.[56] In fact, the overall conception of *Jolly Flatboatmen in Port*—from the asymmetric pose of the flag-waving dancer to the crowd of figures on the boat to the distant urban background—

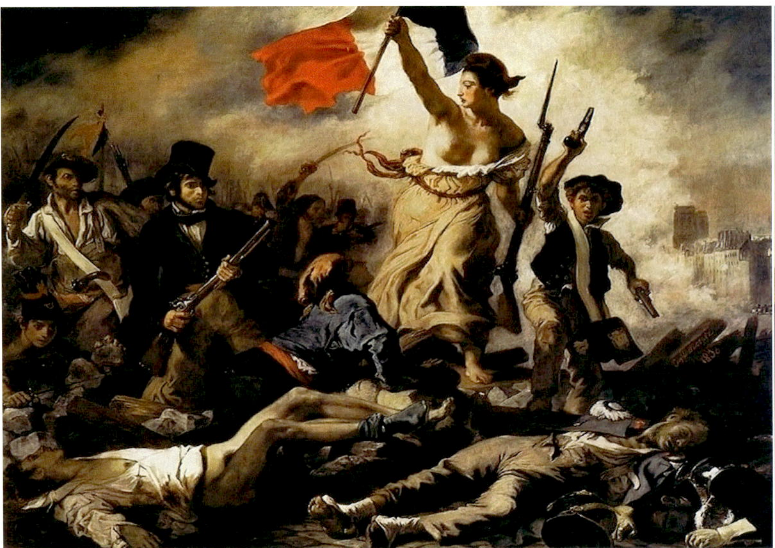 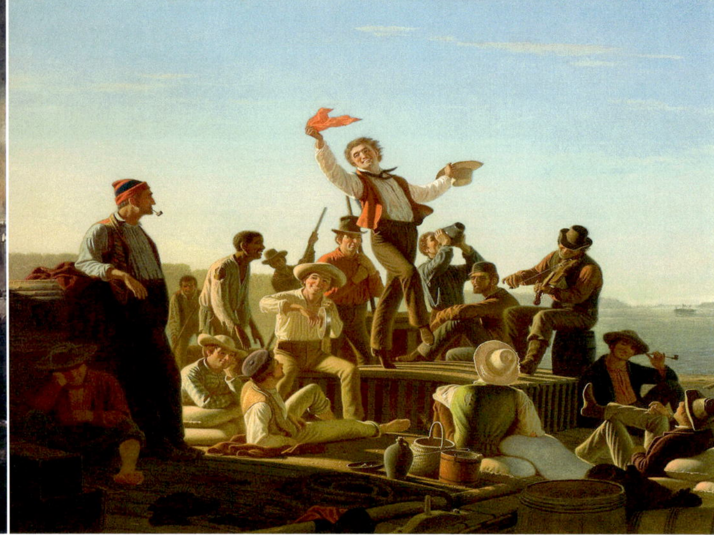

Fig. 69: Eugène Delacroix (1798–1863), *Liberty Leading the People*, 1830, oil on canvas, 102½ × 128 in., Musée du Louvre, Paris. Bingham certainly knew of this masterpiece while he was in Paris, and his *Jolly Flatboatmen in Port* (Pl. 47) bears a striking similarity to Delacroix's work. *Jolly Flatboatmen in Port* is the largest of Bingham's flatboatmen pictures and the only one that he painted in Europe.

recalls Eugène Delacroix's famous composition *Liberty Leading the People* (1830), a print of which Bingham could have seen during his recent sojourn in Paris (Fig. 69).[57] Although it is unlikely that Bingham saw the actual painting, it had been exhibited in Paris the previous year at the popular Exposition Universelle, and he was certainly aware of Delacroix's reputation as one of the most sought-after French painters of the day. Bingham's crowd in *Jolly Flatboatmen in Port* now includes twenty-one figures consisting of urban merchants and rowdy boatmen, a much greater array of cargo, and a view of a steamboat and the port of Saint Louis or perhaps New Orleans in the background.

Bingham expressed the impressive expansion of his hallmark jolly flatboatmen subject in an 1857 letter to Rollins: "I have on hand a large picture of 'life on the Mississippi' . . . which promises to be far ahead of any work of that class which I have yet undertaken."[58] The artist's choice of canvas, an expensive twill weave, and its size (his largest riverboat painting) indicate the importance of this work to the artist and his Missouri roots.

To construct such a complex, multifigure composition, Bingham reprised several of the figure types he had previously employed in his earlier painting of the subject, preparing a new group of larger drawings of these characters for transfer to the canvas. These are *Skillet-beater* (2) (Pl. 60), *Fiddler* (2) (Pl. 58), and *Boatman* (Pl. 59). Considering both the paper type and the scale of these drawings, it is likely that the artist created them in Germany, using his portfolio of river characters for reference and drawing on thick European paper. The stiffness and thickness of the paper of the Düsseldorf drawings did not lend itself to his direct transfer process. The colors of these sheets range from a muddy tan to brown, owing to the varying discoloration of the sheets over time. These are the only drawings in which Bingham employed white chalk or white gouache highlights,

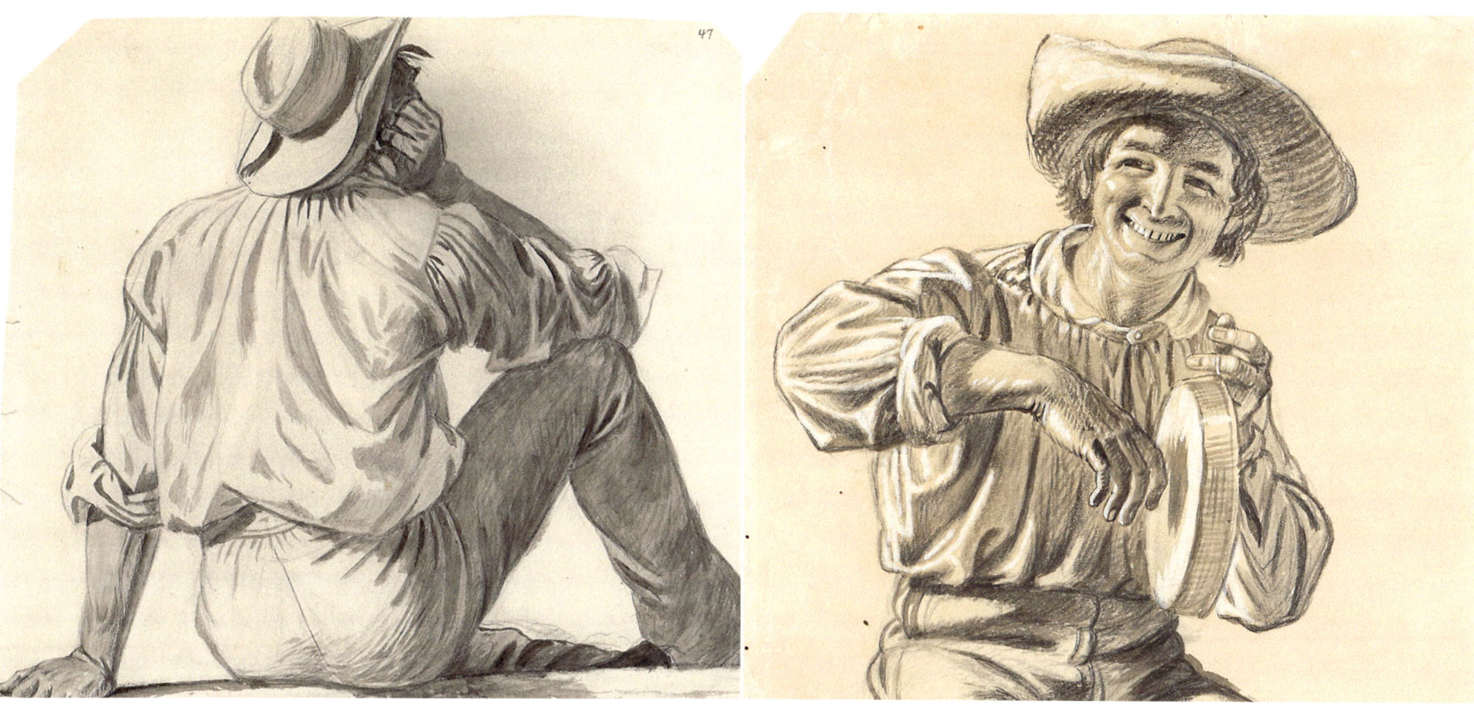

Fig. 70: These details of the drawings *Flatboatman* (Pl. 15) and *Skillet-beater* (2) (Pl. 60) show the artist's white highlights. In the earlier study (left), Bingham created the highlights by showing reserve areas of light paper and by erasing pencil marks in the drawing, while in the later study he rendered the highlights using gouache.

reflecting an evolution in the artist's handling of light in his graphic work. In earlier studies, he followed a more reductive technique by erasing areas or utilizing reserved areas of the support to designate highlights (Fig. 70).

Infrared examination of the underdrawing of *Jolly Flatboatmen in Port*, in conjunction with an examination of the extant drawing papers, suggests that Bingham established the contours of the dancer, skillet beater, and fiddler by tracing the studies. He added the figure of the seated boatman in the foreground on top of the completed boat in a late stage in the working process (Fig. 71). The artist also determined the outlines for the smiling figure of the black man in tattered clothes but shifted the figure slightly to the left in the final painting. This minor but significant adjustment helped to separate the man from the other background figures, drawing greater attention to the contrast of his dark silhouette against the sky.

Bingham's overall system of underdrawing for the numerous figures in *Jolly Flatboatmen in Port* followed a northern European approach in which the primary figures are drawn in greater detail while the less important background figures are indicated with only abbreviated notations. For the dancing figure, Bingham delineated details such as facial features, strands of hair, and drapery folds by summarily indicating the folds and drawing loops around the shadow areas, just as he had done for the other boatmen of this scale. For the pairs of businessmen and children in the lower right, however, the artist reduced his underdrawing to just a few notations in a manner similar to that which he had employed for the boatman behind the dancer.

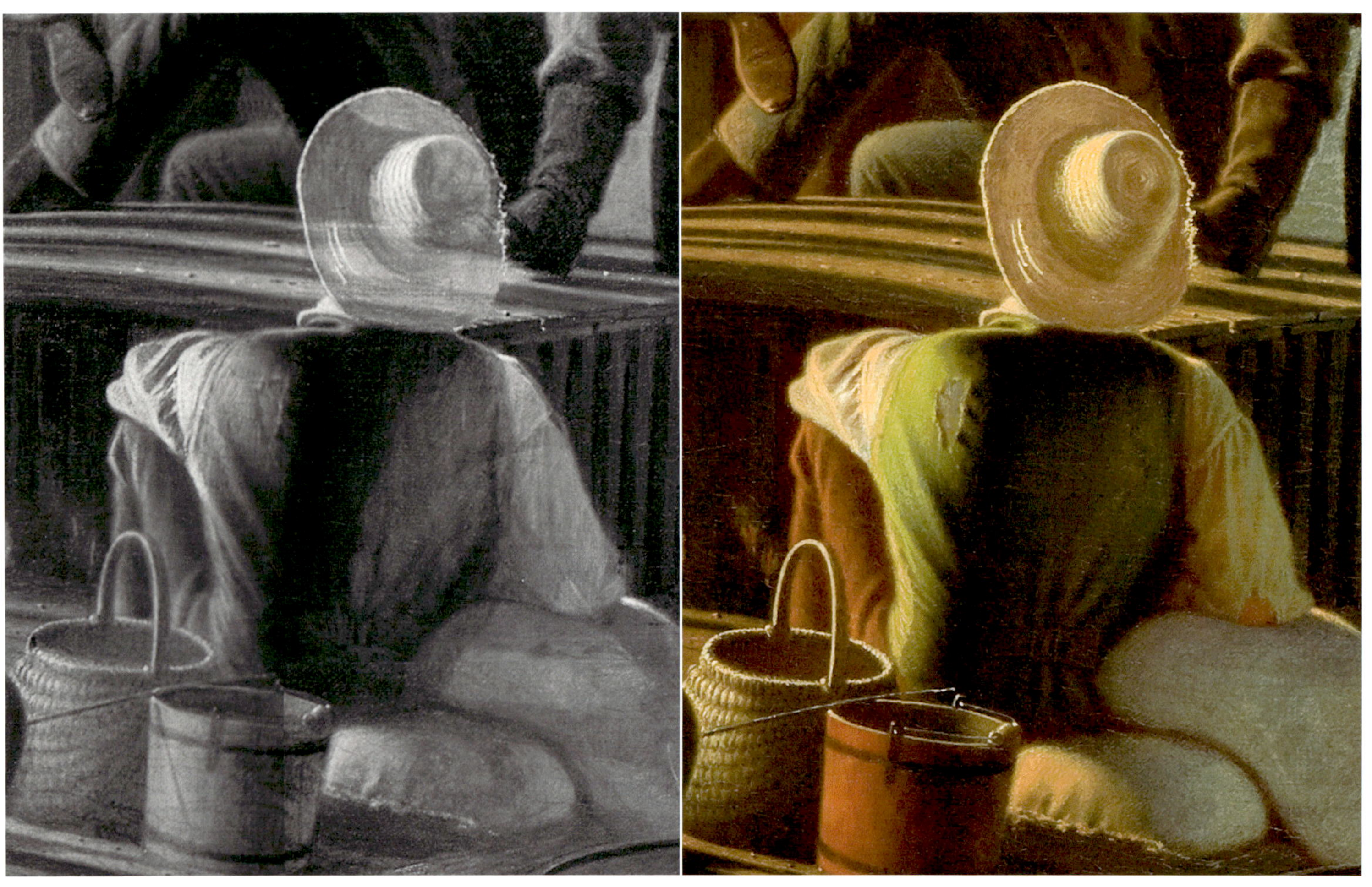

Fig. 71: An infrared detail (left) of *Jolly Flatboatmen in Port* (Pl. 47) shows that Bingham added the figure of the seated boatman in a late stage of the working process.

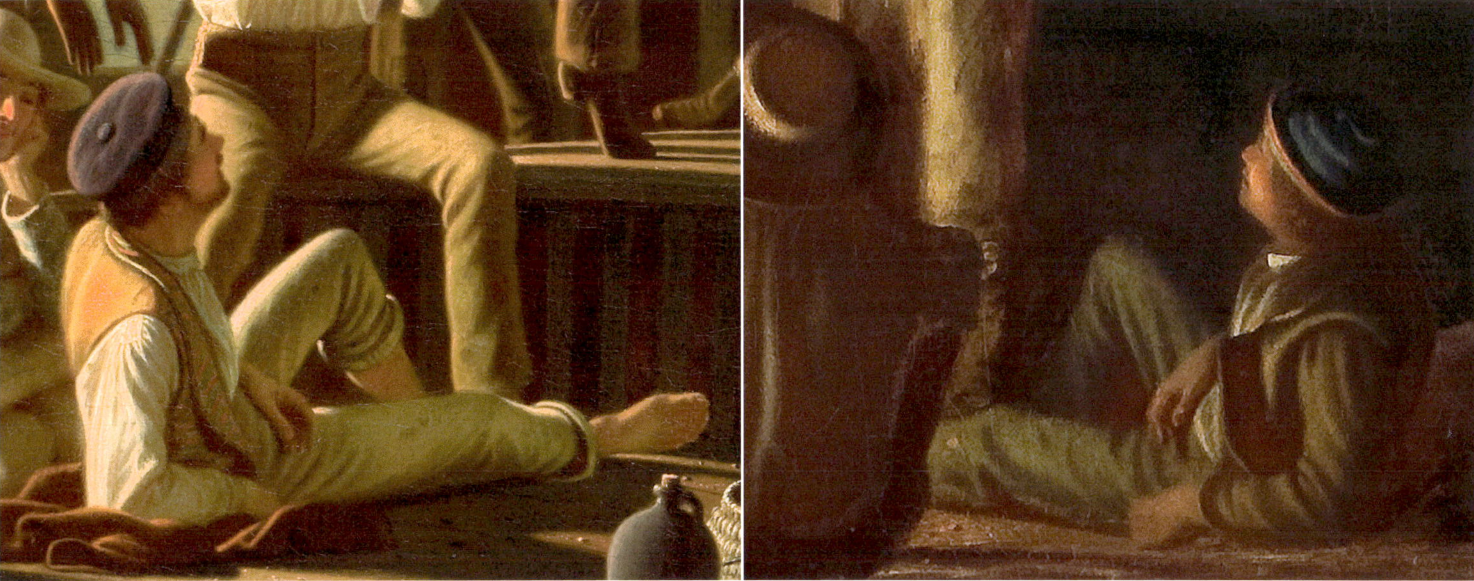

Fig. 72: Bingham recycled the drawing of the reclining boatman (right), first used in *Woodboatmen on a River (Western Boatmen Ashore by Night)*, 1854 (Pl. 45), for *Jolly Flatboatmen in Port*, reversing the pose.

Bingham modeled the pipe-smoking *Dockhand* (Pl. 57), *Raftman dozing* (Pl. 33), and *Raftman* (Pl. 51) on existing drawings in his portfolio. He had used the drawing of the reclining man in an earlier painting, *Woodboatmen on a River (Western Boatmen Ashore by Night)* (Pl. 45), but for this work he reversed the figure (Fig. 72). The close correlation between the larger painted figures and the smaller drawings that inspired them is another indicator that Bingham may have used an optical device to enlarge the scale of these boatmen.

Among the painters Bingham clearly admired, the young Thomas Cole had owned a camera obscura, and Thomas Sully once took notes from a book that recommended the use of the camera obscura and camera lucida.[59] As early as 1816, Rembrandt Peale had introduced his father to an optical device – possibly the camera lucida – and the conservators Lance Mayer and Gay Myers have observed that "cameras, perhaps both lucida and obscura, were perhaps more widely used by American painters in the eighteenth and nineteenth centuries than has been previously thought."[60]

Such optical devices helped both professionally trained and self-taught nineteenth-century artists render likenesses without the need for advanced drawing skills. In 1815 the painter and inventor Bass Otis advertised a tool called the "perspective protractor," which promised that "the outline of any object may be correctly delineated . . . by any person who can draw a line or has the least idea of holding a pencil." A recommendation by Bingham's hero, Thomas Sully, was included in the advertisement, making it likely that Sully at least experimented with the tool.[61] Sully's testimonial, along with his previously documented interest in both the camera obscura and camera lucida, suggests that the artist studied and possibly experimented with a variety of optical devices. This interest could have been transmitted to Bingham when the Missouri artist traveled to Philadelphia in 1838 to study Sully's work.

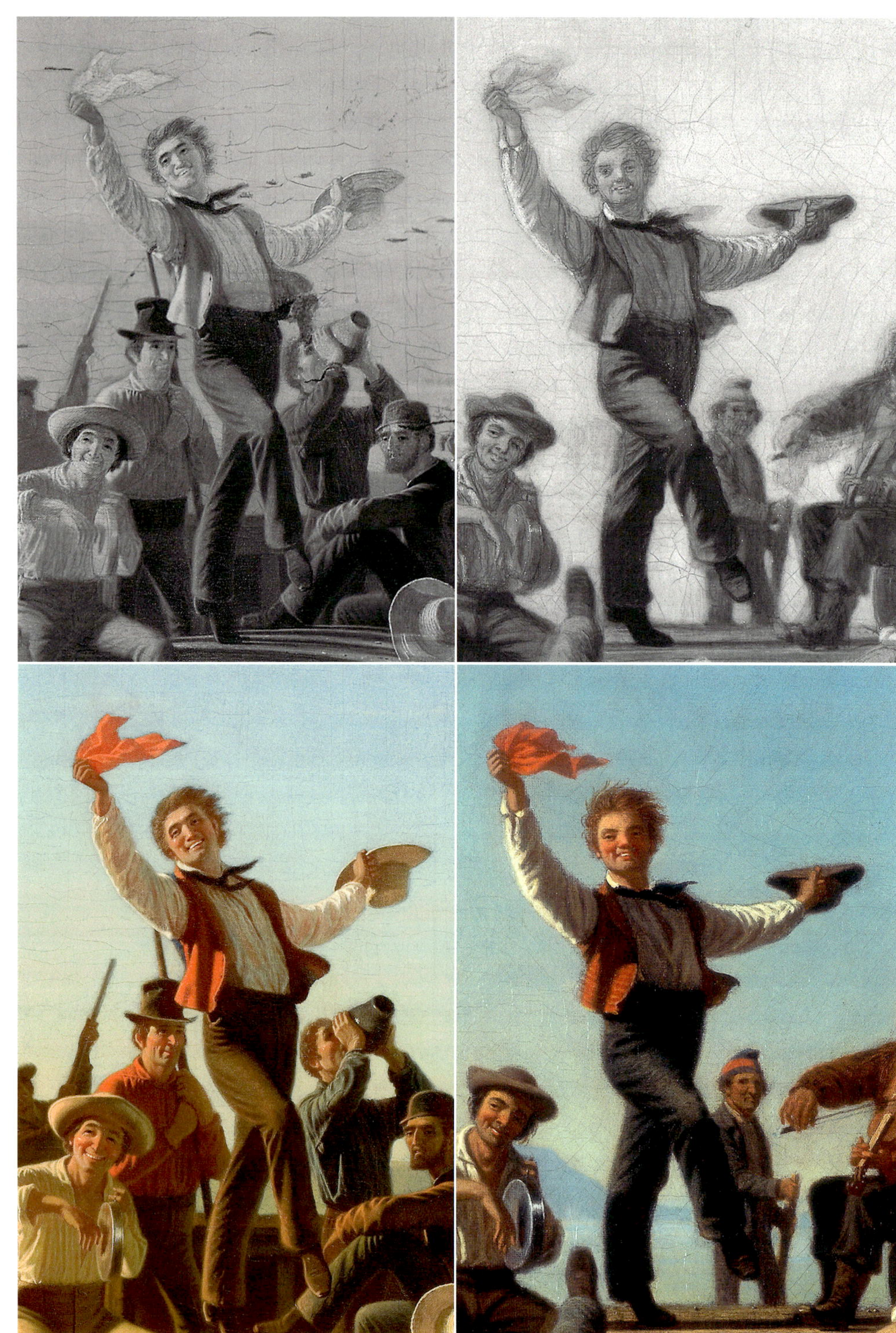

Fig. 73: A comparison of infrared details (top) of the dancing figures in *Jolly Flatboatmen in Port* (left, Pl. 47) and *The Jolly Flatboatmen*, 1877–78 (Pl. 48), reveals that the drawing in the later work is much looser and less deliberate than in the earlier version because Bingham was working without his portfolio of drawings. The later flatboatman also appears shorter and squatter than in the earlier work.

The Jolly Flatboatmen (1877–78, Pl. 48)

Bingham's underdrawing in his last and final version of *The Jolly Flatboatmen* shows that the artist sketched the contours, facial features, and drapery folds of the five leading characters as in the previous versions, but in this case his underdrawing style appears looser and less deliberate than before. Furthermore, the figures appear shorter and squatter than earlier flatboatmen figures. Significantly, Bingham no longer had direct access to the working drawings for these characters; John How, a former mayor of Saint Louis, had bought them from Bingham and in 1868 donated them to the Saint Louis Mercantile Library, where they were bound into an album.[62]

Bingham described the dancing figure in greatest detail, sketching his strands of windblown hair, but the pattern of his drapery folds lacks the precision and methodical, looped outlining of shadows seen in earlier works. Given the inaccessibility of the drawings for direct transfer, it is not surprising that the overall character of this underdrawing resembles a freehand sketch rather than one that was traced from a piece of paper (Fig. 73). Bingham may have sketched the figures from sight using the 1847 mezzotint of *The Jolly Flatboatmen* as a guide. But here again, the absence of squaring lines suggests that he may have transferred the figures to canvas with the aid of a projection tool. Note the apparent distortion of the shorter figures, which may be related to the use of an optical device.

Several pentimenti in Bingham's last flatboatmen painting reflect the artist's usual practice of fine-tuning elements at the time of painting to perfect the balance of the composition. He reduced the size of the dancer's kerchief and hat, and he raised the right arm of the fiddler, increasing his prominence and visibility (Fig. 74). The artist also significantly narrowed the width of the flatboat, combining the use of a straightedge with loose, freehand sketching to describe the outlines of the vessel, its oars, and the water line.

CONCLUSION

George Caleb Bingham combined an innate talent for drawing and portraiture with an original sense of color to create realistic and lasting portraits of Missouri riverboat life. From his earliest childhood years through the European sojourn of his maturity, Bingham continually strived to obtain the type of serious artistic instruction that was inaccessible to him in his rural Missouri home. He honed his drawing skills by drawing from prints, consulting drawing manuals, sketching from casts of antique sculpture, and eventually acquiring some formal training in art academies in Philadelphia in 1838 and Düsseldorf in 1857. A squared pencil sketch found on the reverse of an early portrait reveals that Bingham was already conversant with some academic drawing practices by 1837.[63] He also incorporated academic techniques in his drawings of Missouri flatboatmen that became the starting point for his riverboat paintings. The sophistication of his drawing techniques evolved following his instruction at the Düsseldorf Academy. From his early drawings to later studies, Bingham reserved areas of the cream-colored paper for highlights. By contrast, in the German drawings he extended the tonal range by working on toned papers and adding highlights in white chalk or gouache.

Bingham always carefully planned his riverboat compositions. Using his portfolio of working drawings of models, he produced complex, multifigure compositions by deftly combining, arranging, and directly transferring figures from the paper studies to canvas. Although these drawings appear uncannily realistic, examination confirms that Bingham invented the seemingly authentic frontier characters from costumed models who posed in his studio and that he reused recognizable models for different studies of frontier types. He also borrowed figures from prints and even prototypes from classical and Renaissance art.

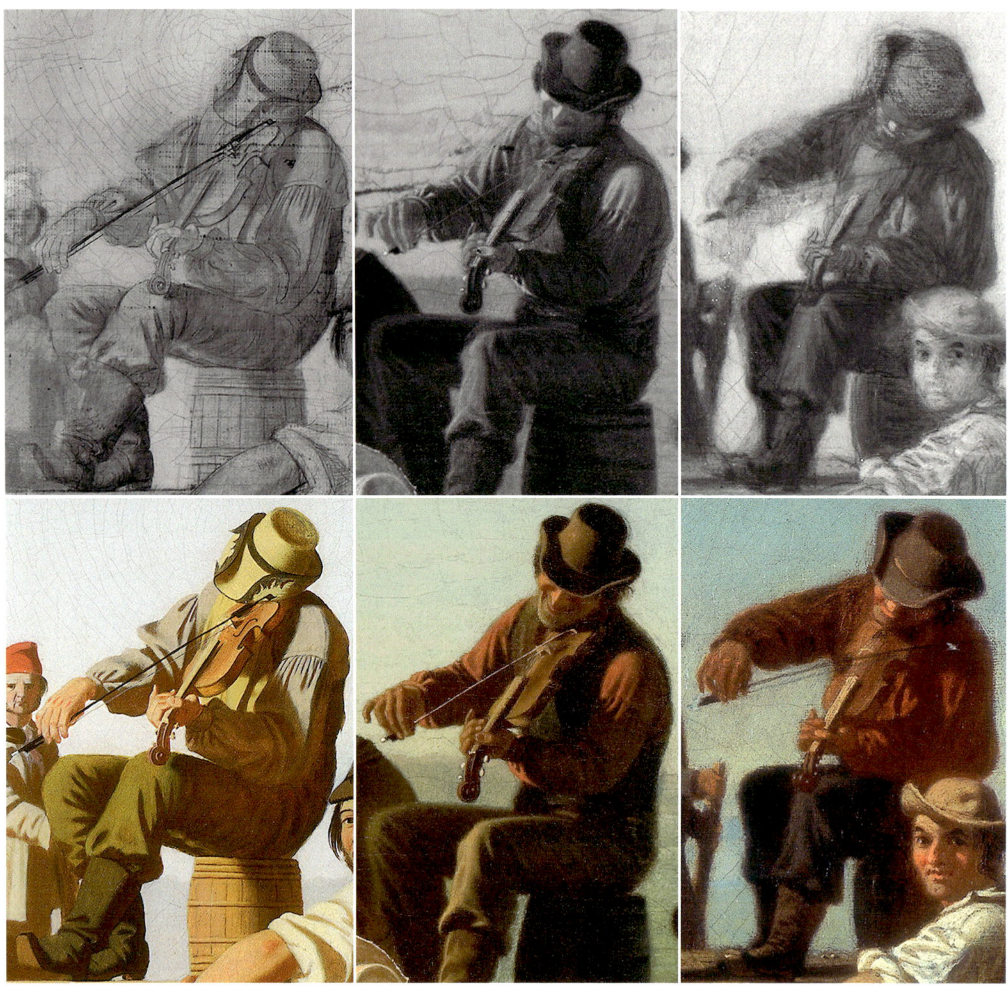

Fig. 74: Three infrared details (top) of the fiddlers in *The Jolly Flatboatmen*, 1846 (left, Pl. 5), *Jolly Flatboatmen in Port*, 1857 (center, Pl. 47), and *The Jolly Flatboatmen*, 1877–78 (Pl. 48), show that Bingham slightly altered the recycled figure as he painted.

Technical examination of Bingham's riverboat paintings under infrared reflectography reveals the artist consistently prepared the canvases with elaborate underdrawings that were generally more comprehensive than those found in his portrait paintings. The artist's preoccupation with rendering convincing representations of river boatmen is reflected in his underdrawing of figures, which is far more detailed than that of their surrounding landscapes. Bingham often drew the landscape freehand, working around the meticulously positioned figures, probably from a preplanned composition.

Many of the drawings are executed on high-quality, cream-colored wove paper, and Bingham worked directly from these sketches in the preparation of his paintings. He typically incised the drawings for transfer to canvas over an interlayer such as carbon paper so that the scale of the figures in the drawings and paintings is usually one to one. The ability of the paper to accept strong impressions from the pressure of the artist's drawing tools made it suitable for Bingham's tracing techniques. The various working marks left on the papers confirm that the artist continued to revise his drawings throughout the creative process, and he also recycled drawings for use in more than one painting. Blind impressions, or incised lines in the paper visible in harsh raking light, usually correspond to the underdrawings seen in the infrared reflectogram mosaics.

Bingham's underdrawing style also changed throughout his career and according to the complexity of the compositions, as well as whether or not he appropriated a print source for his figures. The artist frequently combined different underdrawing techniques within a single painting and sometimes even within a single figure. His underdrawings reflect a variety of techniques, including mechanically traced outlines, hatching, cross-hatching, freehand sketching, and ruled lines, which together demonstrate the flexibility of his creative process. Distinct differences were also found in his underdrawings based on the composition, particularly between the single-figure and multifigure compositions, and whether or not he was modeling his figures after a print source or a preparatory drawing. Although his underdrawings were consistently executed in a dry carbon-based medium, great variety was noted in his manner of application, including the pressure applied and the width of his lines.

Bingham rarely adjusted the scale of the figures from the study to the painting, but in cases where he did, the consistency of overlays between corresponding figures, adjusted for scale, suggests that the artist could have used some form of projection in his working process. Intriguingly, Bingham completed his last flatboatmen canvas without access to his original studies, probably using the mezzotint of the first composition as his model. In this late painting, the overall character of loose, sketchy underdrawing Bingham used for the figures differs dramatically from that of the earlier paintings.

Drawing on a lifelong habit of studying the works of other painters and adapting their techniques to his own creative ends, Bingham employed a red imprimatura for the river landscapes and their figures, a technique that was used by such contemporaries as Thomas Cole and William Sidney Mount. While not unique to Bingham's work, the toned imprimatura so strongly influenced the luminosity and original coloring of these pictures that it became a signature of the artist. The brightly tinted underlayer in the modeling of the half tones infuses Bingham's figures with a physical sense of warmth and life.

Bingham consciously adopted the agenda of the American Art-Union in its advancement of a national art by promoting his identity as a Missouri artist to market his flatboat paintings to a receptive eastern audience. Yet the haunting stillness of his realistic portraits of mid-nineteenth-century Missouri frontier life resulted from the studied, methodical, and original approach to drawing and painting that he achieved through his relentless, lifelong pursuit of an artistic education and exposure to the European schools of painting. His persistent ambition to become a painter of the first rank required that Bingham abandon the frontier lifestyle that he purported to document from firsthand observation. Instead, he navigated lessons learned from master painters in the more developed, industrialized East as well as the art galleries of Europe to create timeless and moving images of unworldly Missouri boatmen whose lifestyle would soon disappear.

NOTES

1. Mark Twain, *Adventures of Huckleberry Finn* (1885; New York: Barnes & Noble Classics, 2003), 109.

2. See E. Maurice Bloch, *The Drawings of George Caleb Bingham with a Catalogue Raisonné* (Columbia: University of Missouri Press, 1975). Although Bloch refers to a pattern book, the drawings probably remained loose sheets in a portfolio format while Bingham used them for reference and for creating his paintings. In 1868, when the Mercantile Library in Saint Louis acquired them, they were mounted into an album. Most of the drawings are owned by The People of Missouri, are managed by the Bingham Trust, and reside in the collections of the Saint Louis Art Museum and the Nelson-Atkins Museum of Art in Kansas City.

3. See ibid., 13. Most probably Bingham's models were found among his friends and casual acquaintances. Bloch quoted Fern Helen Rusk, *George Caleb Bingham: The Missouri Artist* (Jefferson City, Mo.: Hugh Stephens Co., 1917), 35, who claimed that Bingham began with sketches and used the models for the finished studies. Oscar F. Potter, one of Bingham's models, told Rusk (35) of "dressing according to directions and standing in one position without moving for half an hour at a time."

4. *Bulletin of the American Art-Union* 2, no. 5 (August 1849): 12.

5. For the current study, an InGaAS Goodrich camera produced much clearer images of underdrawings than was possible with the Hamamatsu vidicon camera used in the 1990 examination. Access to new cameras and improved technologies has greatly enhanced the current infrared examinations of underdrawings in Bingham's riverboat paintings, providing more information than was available before now. Paul Haner and Nancy Heugh previously examined Bingham's underdrawings in several paintings in preparation for the exhibition *George Caleb Bingham* at the Saint Louis Art Museum in 1990, including *The Wood-Boat, The County Election*, and several portraits, using the Hamamatsu vidicon camera as well as with traditional infrared film. Haner also filmed the infrared examination of Bingham paintings at the Saint Louis Art Museum. Paul Haner, personal communication, May 3, 2012.

6. The following paintings were studied: *Landscape: Rural Scenery* (1845), *Fur Traders Descending the Missouri* (1845), *The Concealed Enemy* (1845), *Boatmen on the Missouri* (1846), the first version of *The Jolly Flatboatmen* (1846), *Lighter Relieving a Steamboat Aground* (1847), *Raftsmen Playing Cards* (1847), *Watching the Cargo* (1849), *Mississippi Boatman* (1850), *Mississippi Fisherman* (ca. 1850), *The Wood-Boat* (1850), *Fishing on the Mississippi* (1851), *In a Quandary* (1851), *Trappers' Return* (1851), *Watching the Cargo by Night* (1854), *Jolly Flatboatmen in Port* (1857), and the second version of *The Jolly Flatboatmen* (1877–78). The following conservators examined the underdrawing on Bingham paintings through infrared reflectography before the current study: the private conservator Barry Bauman examined *Mississippi Fisherman*, and at the National Gallery of Art, Carol Christiansen examined *Mississippi Boatman*. Art Rogers at the Saint Louis Art Museum (SLAM) and Ann Hoenigswald at the National Gallery of Art assisted with measuring and tracing outlines of figures in both the drawings and paintings for comparison. Jean Paul Torno/Photography captured raking-light details in the drawings. At SLAM, Cathryn Gowan, Jon Cournoyer, and Nick Smith provided additional assistance with processing images of drawing details, and Claire Walker completed the XRF analysis of paint samples on several drawings and paintings. We also thank Elizabeth Wyckoff at SLAM and Jodie Utter of the Amon Carter for their support with the ongoing research of watermarks in Bingham's papers. Joan Stack at the State Historical Society of Missouri shared her expertise and arranged for close examination of Bingham's work in that collection.

7. X-radiographs of the following paintings were examined: *Landscape, Rural Scenery* (1845), *Boatmen on the Missouri* (1846), *The Jolly Flatboatmen* (1846), *Mississippi Boatman* (1850), *The Wood-Boat* (1850), and *Jolly Flatboatmen in Port* (1857).

8. Paul C. Nagel, "The Man and His Times," in Michael Shapiro, *George Caleb Bingham* (Saint Louis: Saint Louis Art Museum in association with H. N. Abrams, 1990), 18.

9. Ibid.

10. See Albert Christ-Janer, *George Caleb Bingham of Missouri* (New York: Dodd, Mead & Company, 1940), 12.

11. Leah Lipton, "George Caleb Bingham in the Studio of Chester Harding, Franklin, Missouri, 1820," *American Art Journal* 16, no. 3 (Summer 1984): 90–91. Although Lipton wrote in her 1984 article that Bingham "assisted" Harding in his studio, this is incorrect. Rather, Bingham "visited" Harding in his studio, as transcribed in *"But I Forget That I Am a Painter and Not a Politician": The Letters of George Caleb Bingham*, ed. Lynn Wolf Gentzler (Columbia: State Historical Society of Missouri, 2011), 344–45.

12. James Roth, "A Unique Painting Technique of George Caleb Bingham," *Bulletin of the American Group: International Institute for the Conservation of Historic and Artistic Works* 11, no. 2 (April 1971): 121.

13. Lipton, "George Caleb Bingham in the Studio of Chester Harding," 91.

14. See Nagel, "The Man and His Times," 19.

15. Margaret C. Conrads, "Bingham @ 200: A Bicentennial Celebration," *Antiques & Fine Art*, 2012. This is mentioned earlier in Rusk, *George Caleb Bingham*, 16, where its source is given as Miss May Simonds, *Unpublished Sketch of Bingham's Life.*

16. Roth, "Unique Painting Technique," 121.

17. Lipton, "George Caleb Bingham in the Studio of Chester Harding," 91.

18. In the mid-nineteenth century, the only professional institutions in the United States for aspiring artists were located in the East. Peter C. Marzio, *The Art Crusade: An Analysis of American Drawing Manuals, 1820–1860* (Washington, D.C.: Smithsonian Institution Press, 1976), 69.

19. Lipton, "George Caleb Bingham in the Studio of Chester Harding," 90.

20. E. Maurice Bloch, *The Paintings of George Caleb Bingham: A Catalogue Raisonné* (Columbia: University of Missouri Press, 1986), 9.

21. Margaret C. Conrads, "*Dr. Benoist Troost* and *Mrs. Benoist Troost*," in *The Collections of the Nelson-Atkins Museum of Art: American Paintings to 1945*,

ed. Margaret C. Conrads (Kansas City, Mo.: Nelson-Atkins Museum of Art, 2007), 1:128–30.

22. Gentzler, *Letters of George Caleb Bingham*, 41.

23. Ibid., 43.

24. Bloch, *Paintings of George Caleb Bingham*, 28. William Rudolph, chief curator and curator of American art at the San Antonio Museum of Art, curator of the exhibition *Thomas Sully: Painted Performance* at the Milwaukee Art Museum in 2013, confirmed in an e-mail message to Barry, December 16, 2013, that Sully painted the portrait of Frances Anne Kemble from life, basing her likeness on his memory of her performance as Beatrice in *Much Ado About Nothing*.

25. Bloch, *Paintings of George Caleb Bingham*, 10.

26. Ibid.

27. *Catalogue of the Exhibition of Paintings and Drawings at the Pennsylvania Academy of the Fine Arts and the Artists of Philadelphia at the Artist's Fund Hall* (Philadephia: T. K. and P. G. Collins, Printers, 1843).

28. Shapiro, *George Caleb Bingham*, 27.

29. Marzio, *Art Crusade*, 22.

30. See also John Gadsby Chapman, *The American Drawing Book* (New York: J. S. Redfield, 1847), 52, for instructions on using squared guidelines for the placement of facial features.

31. Unfortunately, the inherent brittleness of the combined layers of ground and paint contributed to the development of mechanical cracks in several of the works, especially in the broad areas of sky in the daylight paintings. Among the paintings exhibiting prominent stress cracks are *Boatmen on the Missouri* (1846), *The Jolly Flatboatmen* (1846), *Lighter Relieving a Steamboat Aground* (1847), *The Wood-Boat* (1850), and *Trappers' Return* (1851).

32. Conrads, "*Fishing on the Mississippi*," in Conrads, *American Paintings to 1945*, 116.

33. Lance Mayer and Gay Myers, *American Painters on Technique: The Colonial Period to 1860* (Los Angeles: J. Paul Getty Museum, 2011), 187.

34. Ibid.

35. Shapiro, *George Caleb Bingham*, 150.

36. Mayer and Myers, *American Painters on Technique*, 198.

37. Technical Notes by Mary Schafer, Catalog 40, Bingham, from conservation files of the Nelson-Atkins Museum of Art.

38. Roth, "Unique Painting Technique," 121.

39. Ibid., 122.

40. See Bloch, *Paintings of George Caleb Bingham*, no. 411, illustrated on 26.

41. Roth, "Unique Painting Technique," 122.

42. Ibid.

43. Shapiro, *George Caleb Bingham*, 97–98.

44. Bloch, *Drawings of George Caleb Bingham*, 176.

45. Nancy Rash, *The Painting and Politics of George Caleb Bingham* (New Haven: Yale University Press, 1991), 4–48.

46. Bloch, *Drawings of George Caleb Bingham*, 12.

47. Nancy Heugh, "Bingham's Drawing and Transfer Techniques and Their Implications" (lecture, Bingham Symposium, Saint Louis Art Museum on February 23, 1990, and National Museum of American Art on June 10, 1990; also conservation records for Bingham Trust, 1982–2013).

48. Carol Christensen, who examined the painting through infrared reflectography, recorded her observations in a memorandum to Sarah Fisher dated July 23, 2003, object conservation file, National Gallery of Art.

49. Katie Steiner, "Seeing Multiples: Paintings as Prints," 4, in *American Stories: Paintings of Everyday Life, 1765–1915* (blog), January 5, 2010, http://blog.metmuseum.org/americanstories/2010/01/05/seeing-multiples-paintings-as-prints.

50. Bloch, *Paintings of George Caleb Bingham*, 94 (Plate 57).

51. Ibid., 85.

52. Bloch, *Drawings of George Caleb Bingham*, 13.

53. Peter John Brownlee, "American Genre Painting: An Art of Encounter," in *American Encounters: Genre Painting and Everyday Life* (Chicago: Terra Foundation of American Art, 2012), 29.

54. Shapiro, *George Caleb Bingham*, 161.

55. John Francis McDermott, *George Caleb Bingham: River Portraitist* (Norman: University of Oklahoma Press, 1959), 122.

56. Shapiro, *George Caleb Bingham*, 168.

57. A lithograph of *La Liberté guidant le peuple* by A. Mouilleron was published by Bertauts in Paris in 1830; see http://gallica.bnf.fr using the keywords Delacroix Liberté. Dr. Eric Lee, director of the Kimbell Art Museum, and Dr. George Shackelford, deputy director of the Kimbell, personal communication, August 2013, Amon Carter Museum of American Art Archives. Thanks are also due to Christophe Leribault, director of the Petit Palais, for confirming the exhibition history of *La Liberté* in Paris in the 1850s.

58. Gentzler, *The Letters of George Caleb Bingham*, 186.

59. Ibid., 130.

60. Mayer and Myers, *American Painters on Technique*, 129–30.

61. Ibid., 130.

62. Bloch, *Drawings of George Caleb Bingham*, cites the accessions entry for the Mercantile Library as December 20, 1868 (No. 17847), p. 9. Either at that time or later, the library mounted the drawings and bound them into an album. Oval Mercantile Library ink stamps are printed on the versos of two drawings that had been mounted in the album.

63. The preliminary sketch, probably for the portrait, is on the recto of *Thomas Miller*, State Historical Society of Missouri, Columbia.

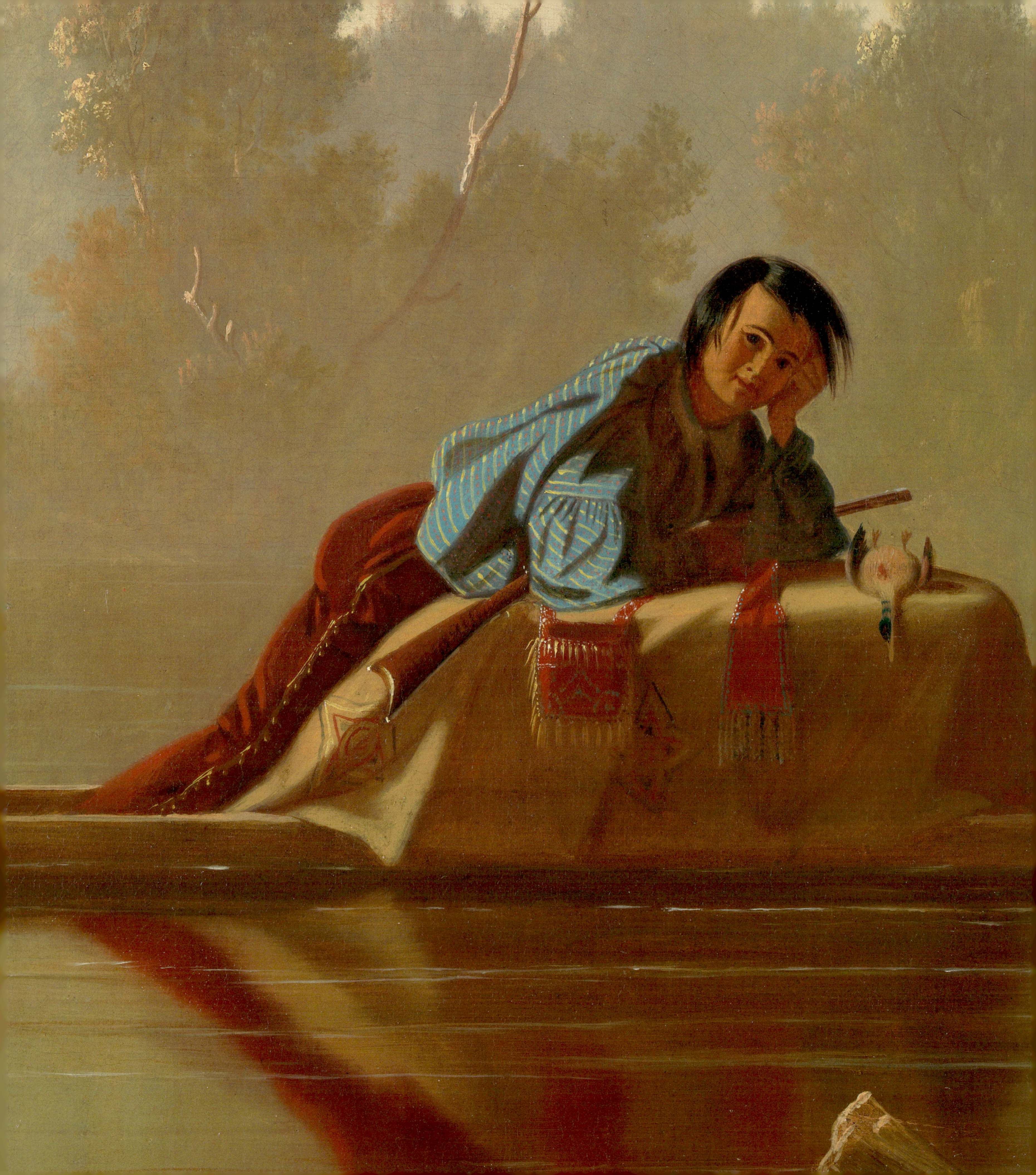

TECHNICAL BRILLIANCE REVEALED

Bingham's *Fur Traders Descending the Missouri*

Elizabeth Mankin Kornhauser and Dorothy Mahon

The year 1845 was an auspicious one for George Caleb Bingham. That December, the American Art-Union in New York City accepted four of his paintings for display in its annual exhibition. The AA-U's purchase of this group—which included two landscape paintings, *Cottage Scenery* (Fig. 75) and *Landscape: Rural Scenery* (Pl. 1), as well as the companion genre scenes *The Concealed Enemy* (Pl. 2) and *Fur Traders Descending the Missouri* (Pl. 3, Fig. 76)—marked the beginning of the artist's long and successful relationship with this pioneering arts organization. Recognizing the quality and appeal of Bingham's work, the AA-U offered this relative newcomer from the western frontier seventy five dollars for *Fur Traders*, the highest price paid for any of the four works, all of which were distributed by lottery.[1]

Painted when Bingham was thirty-four, *Fur Traders Descending the Missouri* is generally considered his finest achievement, an icon of American art. At the same time, it continues to raise questions in the minds of art historians and the public at large, who find themselves both captivated and disarmed by the progressive aspects of the painting but unable to explain the fact that such an advanced work was painted so early in the artist's career. This discrepancy is acknowledged in the Metropolitan Museum of Art's collection catalogue, which states that *Fur Traders* is "one of the masterpieces of American art," and yet "the picture is almost inexplicable in terms of Bingham's previous work."[2] How did this artist, who was largely self-taught and based in the American West, evolve from executing rough, linear journeyman portraits of his fellow Missouri citizens (see Fig. 7) to creating a brilliantly distilled and spectacularly atmospheric composition of life on the Missouri River that appealed to a national audience? Building on previous scholarship, this essay provides a case study of *Fur Traders Descending the Missouri* and presents new information, the gathering of which was inspired by an initial examination of the painting with fellow essayist and conservator Claire Barry for this project. Further exploration of the painting during an intensive technical examination in the Sherman Fairchild Center for Paintings Conservation at the Metropolitan Museum of Art illuminated Bingham's innovative artistic process for this work and for his other river paintings, and it helps explain how he produced this masterful picture. Bingham's careful thought process and use of sophisticated painting techniques are herein revealed by the discovery of his elaborate underdrawing, proof of his direct use of a highly finished study drawing and of his skillful and varied manipulation of the oil medium.

By the mid-1830s, Bingham had achieved some success as an itinerant portrait painter in Missouri. Like many self-taught American artists, he developed his skills as a draftsman in part by copying prints and engravings as well as original artworks. The artist's principal biographer, E. Maurice Bloch, posited

Fur Traders Descending the Missouri (detail), 1845, Plate 3

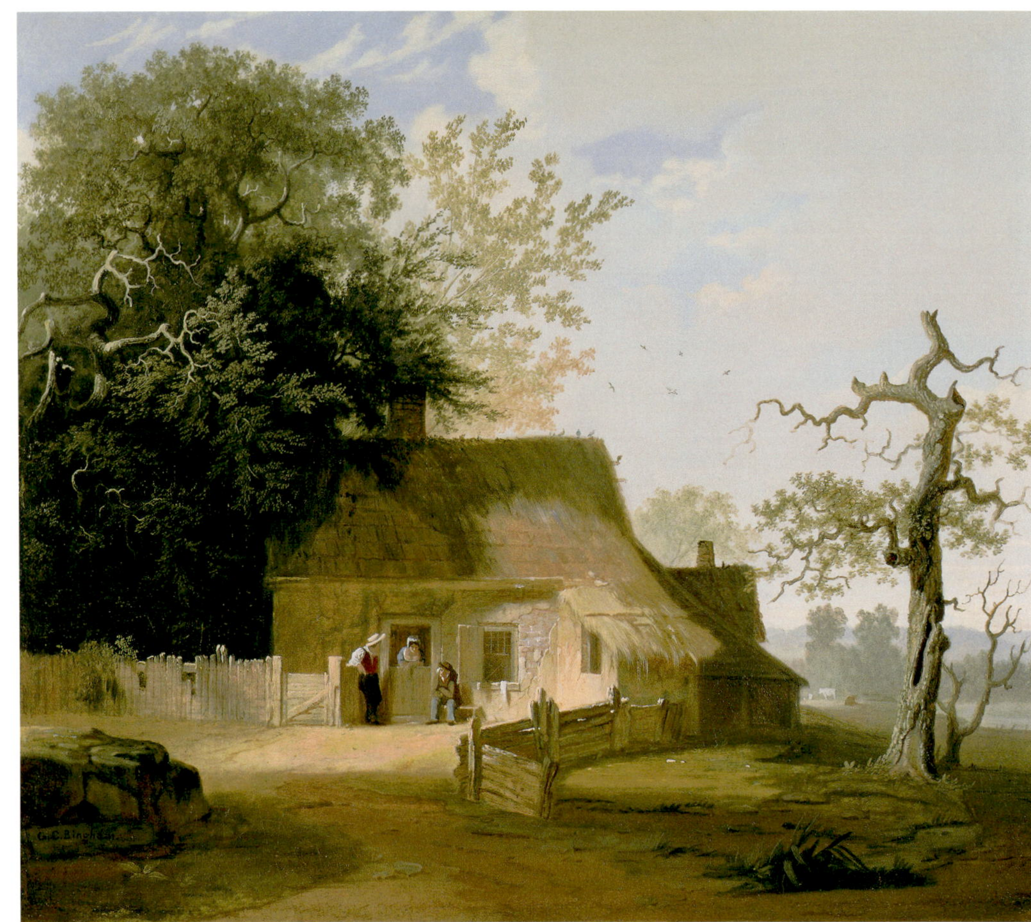

Fig. 75: George Caleb Bingham (1811–1879), *Cottage Scenery*, 1845, oil on canvas, 25½ × 30 in., Corcoran Gallery of Art, Washington, D.C., museum purchase, Gallery Fund and gifts of Charles C. Glover, Jr., Orme Wilson and Mr. and Mrs. Lansdell K. Christie, 61.36

that the artist also likely consulted popular drawing manuals of the time.[3] While a boy living in the Missouri River towns of Franklin and Arrow Rock, Bingham benefited from a number of early encounters with professional artists, particularly the traveling portrait painter Chester Harding, who spent time in Franklin, Missouri, and whose studio Bingham regularly visited as an inquisitive boy.[4] During his travels in the 1830s, Bingham journeyed to Saint Louis, where he was exposed to an emerging art culture, including exhibitions and private collections of art.[5] But Bingham soon developed ambitions beyond portraiture that required him to travel to eastern cities to expand his knowledge. Writing to his friend James Sidney Rollins in 1837, he explained:

I cannot foresee where my destiny will lead me; it may become my interest to settle in some one of the eastern cities. The greater facilities afforded there, for improvement in my profession, would be the principal inducement. There is no honorable sacrifice which I would not make to attain eminence in the art to which I have devoted myself. I am aware of the difficulties in my way, and am cheered by the thought that they are not greater [than] those which impeded the course of Harding, Sully, and many others, it is by combatting that we can overcome them, and by determined perseverance, I expect to be successful.[6]

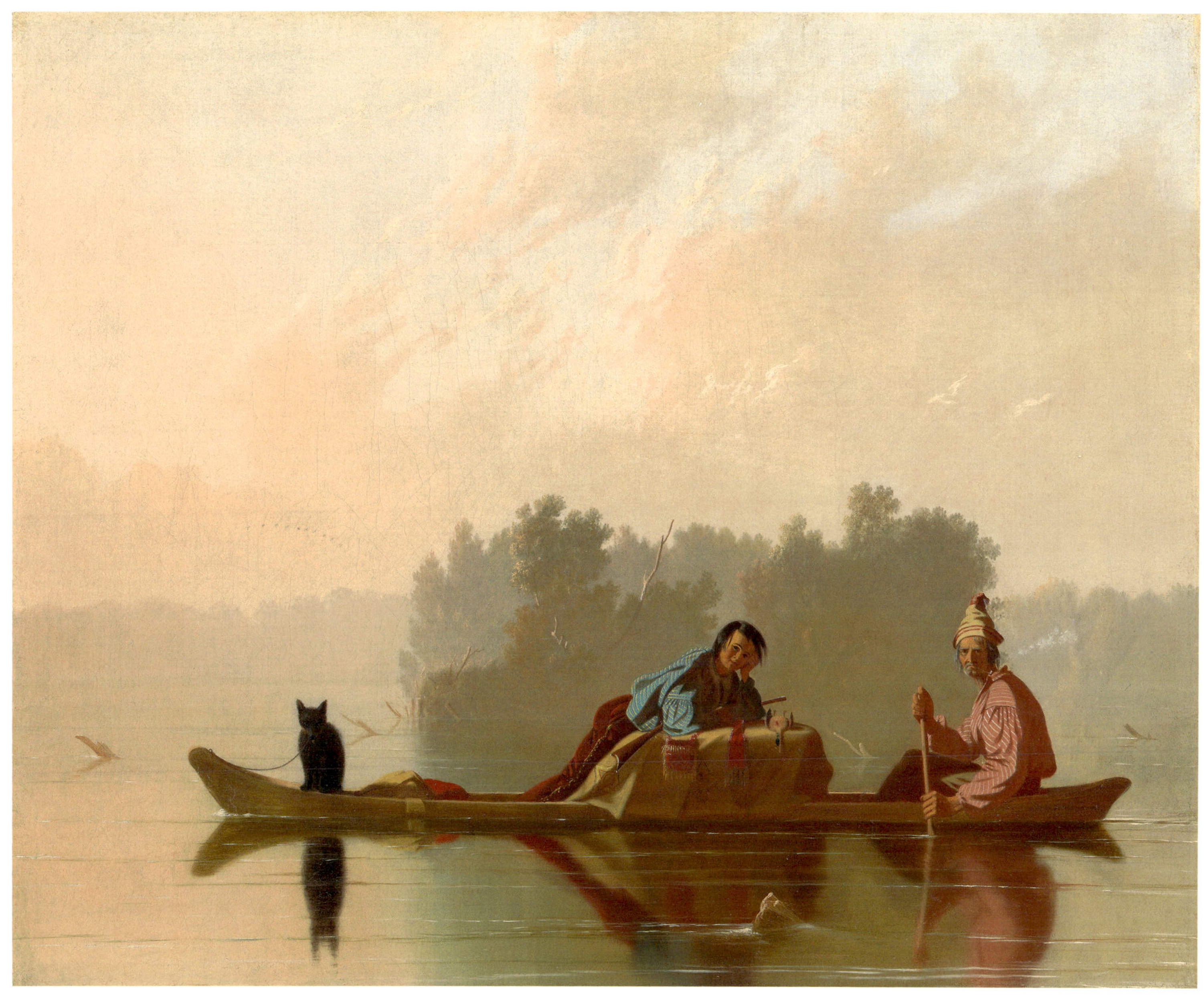

Fig. 76: George Caleb Bingham (1811–1879), *Fur Traders Descending the Missouri*, 1845, oil on canvas, 29¼ × 36¼ in., The Metropolitan Museum of Art, New York, Morris K. Jesup Fund, 1933 (33.61)

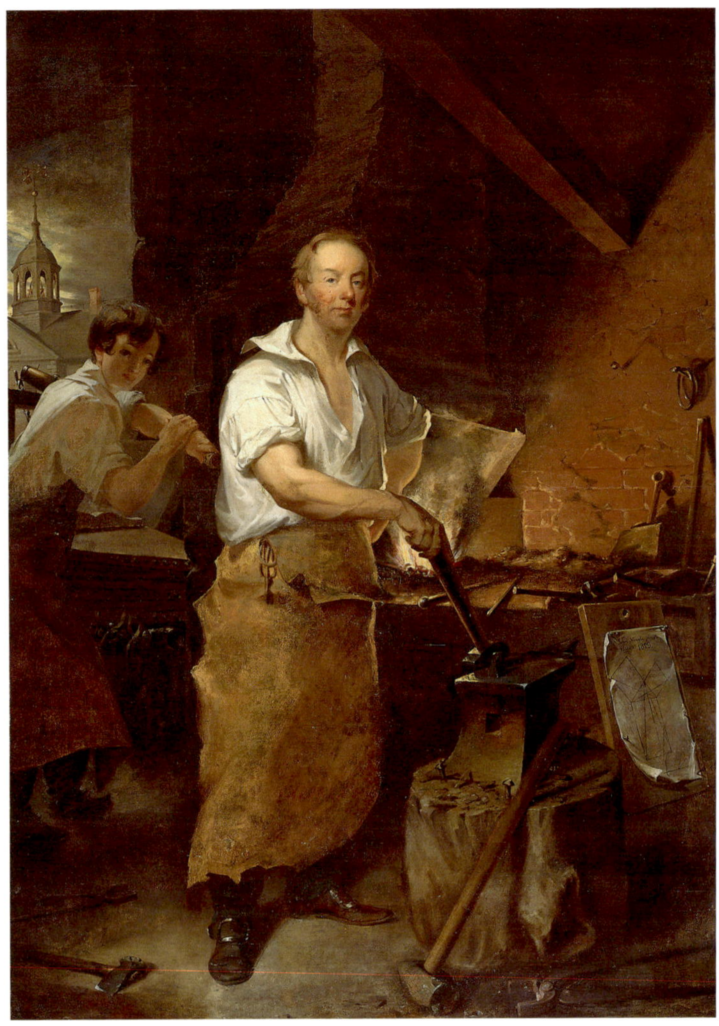

Fig. 77: John Neagle (1796–1865), *Pat Lyon at the Forge*, 1829, oil on canvas, 94½ × 68½ in., courtesy of the Pennsylvania Academy of the Fine Arts, Philadelphia, Gift of the Lyon Family, 1842.1

A year later, in 1838, Bingham traveled to Philadelphia, Baltimore, and New York, and he lived in Washington, D.C., from 1840 to 1844.[7] While in Philadelphia, he was able to study the works on display at the Pennsylvania Academy of the Fine Arts, including paintings by Thomas Cole, Emanuel Leutze, William Sidney Mount, and Thomas Sully. He appears to have absorbed a number of lessons, for example, from John Neagle's portrait *Pat Lyon at the Forge* (Fig. 77). Bingham was impressed by this grand, full-length portrait of an older man and the reclining figure of his young apprentice, documenting an important incident from the sitter's past. Bingham would use this work as a precedent for *Fur Traders*. He also continued his practice of drawing copies of works of art while in Philadelphia, and in preparation for his return home, he wrote to his wife, "I have been purchasing a lot of drawings and engravings, and also a lot of casts from antique sculpture which will give me nearly the same advantages in my drawing studies at home that are present to be enjoyed here."[8] As he continued to hone his skills as a draftsman, Bingham made a careful study of Renaissance and Baroque formulas that he observed in these resources. He later employed these lessons as he developed his symmetrical, classically balanced pyramidal compositions. At the same time, he became aware of the popular success of genre paintings by such artists as Mount and Charles Deas and expanded his repertoire to include subjects from everyday life.

Before his return to Missouri, Bingham made a brief visit to New York City, where he was invited by the artist James Herring to submit a painting to the gallery of the Apollo Association for the Promotion of the Fine Arts in the United States, founded in 1838, which became the American Art-Union four years later. In late 1838 he submitted *Western Boatmen Ashore* (location unknown). This genre painting is among the earliest examples of the artist's ambition to move beyond portraiture, and it was Bingham's first river painting.[9] Following a four-year residence in Washington and a second trip to New York in 1843, Bingham returned to Missouri in 1844 and was elevated in the

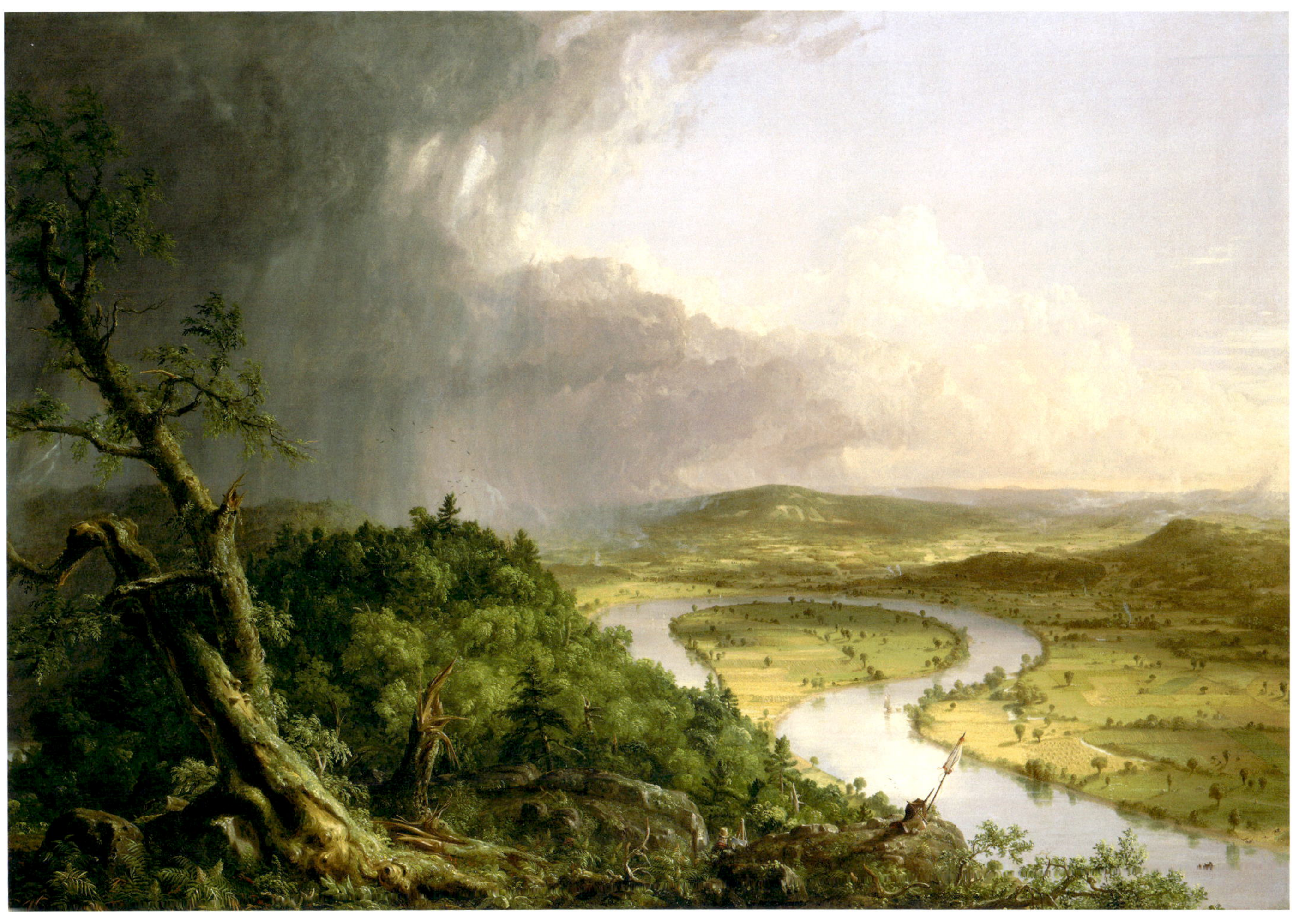

Fig. 78: Thomas Cole (1801–1848), *View from Mount Holyoke, Northampton, Massachusetts, after a Thunderstorm – The Oxbow*, 1836, oil on canvas, 51½ × 76 in., The Metropolitan Museum of Art, Gift of Mrs. Russell Sage, 1908 (08.228)

press from "portrait painter" to "the Missouri Artist."[10] With his artistic experiences broadened during his trips to the East, Bingham extended his subjects to include landscapes as well as genre scenes.

Cole's paintings of wilderness landscape, early settlement, and pastoral scenes constitute a mythic historical narrative of America's origins and development that influenced many American artists of the time, including Bingham, whose conceptual format for his river paintings series bears Cole's influence.[11] In Cole's famous work *View from Mount Holyoke, Northampton, Massachusetts, after a Thunderstorm – the Oxbow* (Fig. 78), for example, the artist employed a bifurcated composition juxtaposing wilderness and settled lands, and he introduced the panoramic format that came to define the Hudson River School. On occasion, Bingham painted pure landscapes in the Romantic style of Cole – *The Storm* is a notable

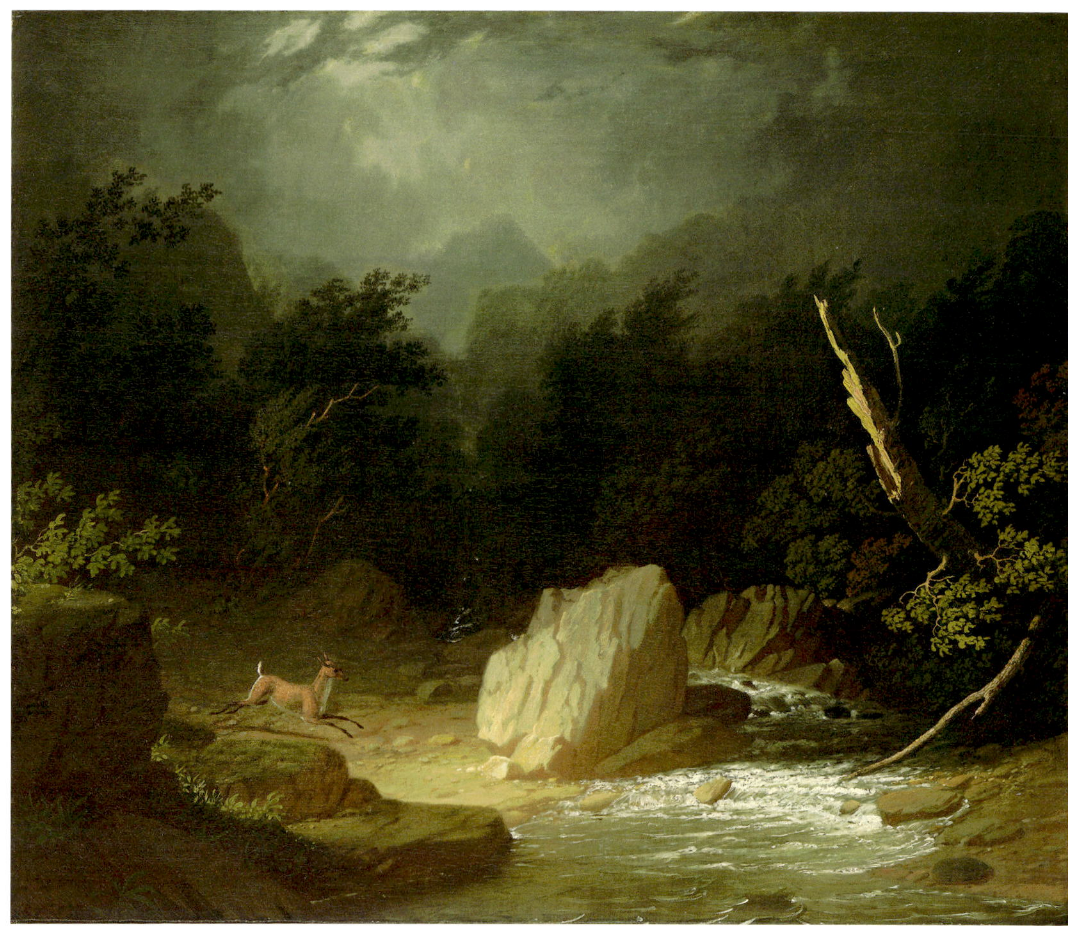

Fig. 79: George Caleb Bingham (1811–1879), *The Storm*, ca. 1852–53, oil on canvas, 25⅛ × 30$^{1}/_{16}$ in., Wadsworth Atheneum Museum of Art, Hartford, Gift of Henry E. Schnakenburg, 1952.74

example (Fig. 79). In addition, Cole's popular four-part allegorical series *The Voyage of Life* (1839–40), which was on view at the Pennsylvania Academy of the Fine Arts during Bingham's presence in the city, provided a resounding precedent for using the river as a metaphor for life. Bingham may also have been influenced by the popularity of Cole's pairs of paintings, such as *The Departure* and *The Return* (both 1837, Corcoran Gallery of Art, Washington, D.C.) and *Past* and *Present* (both 1838, Mead Art Museum, Amherst College, Amherst, Massachusetts), when he envisioned his companion works *The Concealed Enemy* (Pl. 2) and *Fur Traders Descending the Missouri* (Pl. 3). Both pairs of paintings were on view in New York City in 1838 and thus might have been seen by Bingham.[12]

While Cole clearly influenced Bingham's pure landscapes and his river paintings, the latter's unique style and subject matter were far more than a simple continuation of Cole's practice. Bingham was one of the first artists to concentrate on the western territories' great central north–south axis of the Missouri and Mississippi rivers and the first to capture its singular landscape features and atmospheric qualities of light. He focused on the trade and settlement in the West that fueled the nation's economy. He also addressed the issue of race, acknowledging the racially mixed West as seen in the *Fur Traders*' figures of father and son. He chose to focus on imagery that he knew from firsthand experience and that would provide his eastern audience with scenes and characters of the

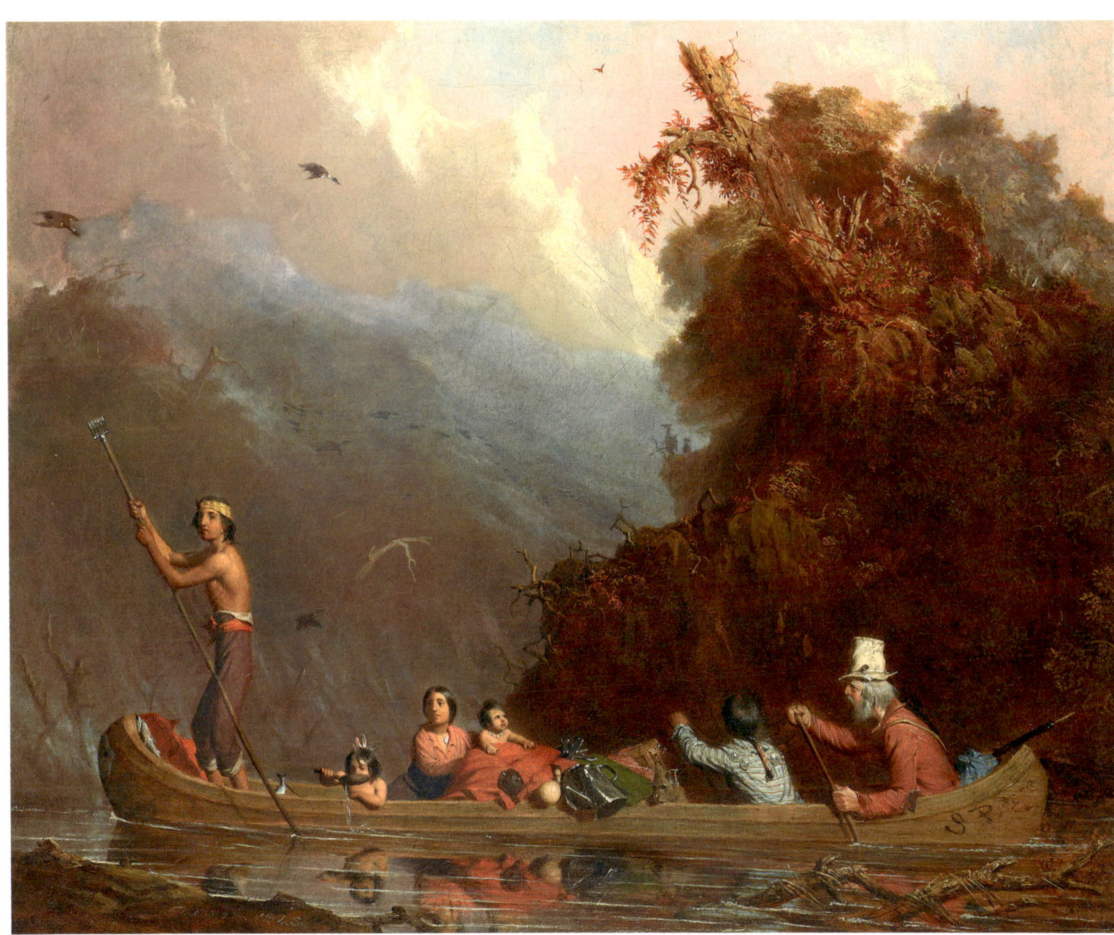

Fig. 80: Charles Deas (1818–1867), *The Voyageurs*, 1845, oil on canvas, 31½ × 36½ in., courtesy of American Museum of Western Art—The Anschutz Collection

western frontier. For *Fur Traders*, Bingham drew on his vivid memories as a boy growing up on the Missouri River. His subjects, which had largely disappeared by the 1830s, had been popularized in the literature of the time. The New York writer Washington Irving's *Astoria* (1836) chronicled the adventures of the French fur trappers and traders, who often intermarried with Native Americans. Bingham's original title for *Fur Traders* was *French Trader & Half Breed Son*, which emphasized the racial exoticism of the inhabitants of the western frontier.[13] Such diversity was rare in the artist's work, and the painting was given a more neutral title by the American Art-Union in order to enhance its appeal to New York audiences and to identify its locale on the Missouri River.[14]

Bingham was undoubtedly aware of the frontier paintings of Indians by George Catlin and Deas, who exhibited their action-filled scenes in Saint Louis during the 1840s.[15] One painting in particular, Deas's *The Voyageurs* (Fig. 80), has been identified as a possible inspiration for Bingham's *Fur Traders*.[16] However, although they were painted in the same year and share a basic organization of figures on a river traveling parallel to the picture plane, the two paintings differ in a number of respects. By portraying a racially mixed family at the center of his work, Deas focused on "the sexually and socially driven alliances between European Americans and Native Americans in the West."[17] Deas also fully embraced the Romantic sublime of Cole's wilderness landscapes in this work, which has the family traveling upstream, back into the wilderness darkened by a storm and accentuated by the inclusion of blasted trees and framed by dramatic, anthropomorphic landscape elements. While Bingham conveyed the mixed-race relationship between father and son in his painting, he concentrated on just two figures in a highly refined composition that increases its dramatic impact. Furthermore, Bingham chose to create a painting nearly devoid of action, seemingly frozen in time.

Fur Traders has a classical balance but at the same time employs a rigorous refinement characteristic of more progressive works painted later in the century. When scholars rediscovered this painting in the mid-twentieth century, they hailed it as a precedent for an American style that they referred to as Luminism and found in it the light-filled, restrained characteristics of works by such artists as Sanford R. Gifford, Fitz Henry Lane, Martin Johnson Heade, and John F. Kensett.[18] As will be demonstrated in this essay, however, Bingham developed an artistic process that was unique to his works. In *Fur Traders*, for example, he added a startling directness to his light-filled composition by placing meticulously rendered figures on the surface who engage the viewer at eye level. A French trapper slowly paddles his canoe down the river; his "half breed" son, as the artist referred to him, leans across the cargo; and a black bear cub is leashed to the bow. A strongly horizontal composition is further emphasized by the lack of framing devices, and the distillation and paring down of the compositional elements create a startling stillness. Bingham wonderfully conveys the early morning atmosphere of calm and stasis; the father and son are in harmony with their wilderness surroundings and are encompassed in a dreamlike morning fog with the sun burning through. The canoe rests low in the water, and the three figures are anchored by their strong reflections on the glassy surface. The wizened father wears a distinctive French voyageur's knitted cap and a brightly colored pink-and-white-striped shirt. A pipe juts from his mouth. His half-Indian son, dressed in an equally bright blue shirt and brown buckskin pants, leans forward on the bale of furs they are taking to market. His bright smiling face, reminiscent of the young apprentice's countenance in Neagle's portrait, conveys his American-European roots, but Bingham identifies the boy's Indian heritage by his straight black hair and the fringed, beaded red bag and sash that he leans on, as well as by the Indian symbols that are painted on the blanket that covers their cargo. He rests casually on his rifle, and placed nearby is a recently shot duck with a blood-stained hole in its breast. The central pyramid is echoed by the shadows of the trapper and son on the surface of the greenish-blue water, but their reflection is partial, while the cub's lean, elongated form is echoed by its full shadow reflected in the pinkish water, creating a proper balance with the two main figures while adding a mysterious element—"a spirit of the wild."[19]

The only indications of motion are the long white lines of paint that signify ripples on the water and around the snags in the river and the white smoke emerging from the trapper's pipe. The background, seen through the atmospheric haze, becomes simplified and condensed as it progresses from the central foliage through the layers of landscape that recede into the distance. Bingham's ability to capture the mysterious, mist-infused effects of the Missouri River at dawn is an extraordinary artistic achievement. The artist heightened the impact of *Fur Traders* by submitting to the American Art-Union a companion work, *The Concealed Enemy* (Pl. 2), a painting of an American Indian warrior positioned high above the river, poised with a rifle and hidden behind a boulder. The dark foreground, sharply juxtaposed with the light of the setting sun, adds to the drama of the scene. In contrast with the stillness of dawn in *Fur Traders*, this painting presents an image of the savagery and danger to be found on the river. As Henry Adams suggested, when the two works are hung side by side, they form, from left to right, the progression from savagery to civilization.[20] Like *Fur Traders*, this scene refers to a time twenty years earlier, before the Indians were forced to relocate farther west and disappeared from the Missouri landscape. Unlike *Fur Traders*, this work shows no evidence of underdrawing. The only evidence of Bingham's rethinking of the composition is the presence of the painted figure of a second Indian emerging from behind the boulder, which the artist eliminated in the final composition (Fig. 81).[21]

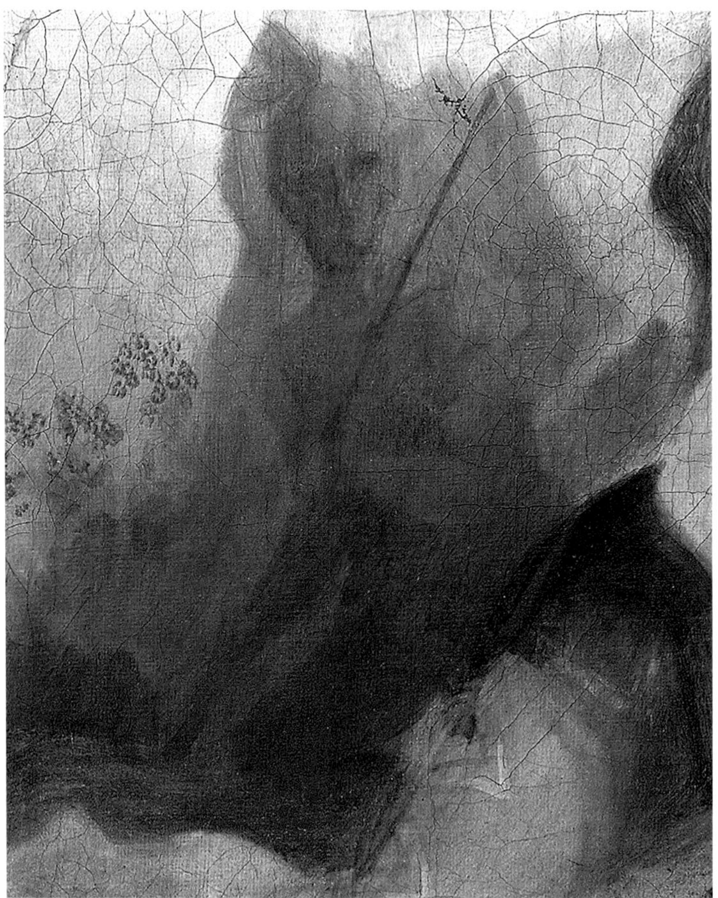

Fig. 81: This infrared reflectogram detail of *The Concealed Enemy* (Pl. 2) reveals the figure of a second Indian that was not included in the final composition.

ARTIST'S TECHNIQUE

Bingham's success with *Fur Traders Descending the Missouri*, including his artistry and the clarity of his message, is better understood through an examination of his process, one that he developed and employed for the first time with this painting. His underdrawing provides a look over the artist's shoulder as he envisioned his finished canvas—in other words, a look into the artist's creative mind.

Bingham gave careful thought to his composition beforehand and began his process with elaborate underdrawing on the canvas, most of which is very freely executed. The older man in the painting, however, is precisely underdrawn and is based on the carefully drawn character study *Fur trader* (Pl. 7), whose placement, when transferred to the canvas, established the compositional perspective. There is also evidence of underpainting in the form of elaborate landscape details. Bingham rethought the composition and carefully altered and pared down the initial underdrawn and painted elements, many of which were eliminated, so that the finished scene shows just the bare essentials. In addition, an examination of his painting technique reveals a highly sophisticated use of the best materials available, including a limited number of high-quality pigments. Finally, Bingham employed an extraordinary range of brushwork and paint application to achieve the qualities of sunrise on the river. His elaborate and thoughtful process resulted in a beautifully balanced, spare composition that is devoid of superfluous or narrative details.

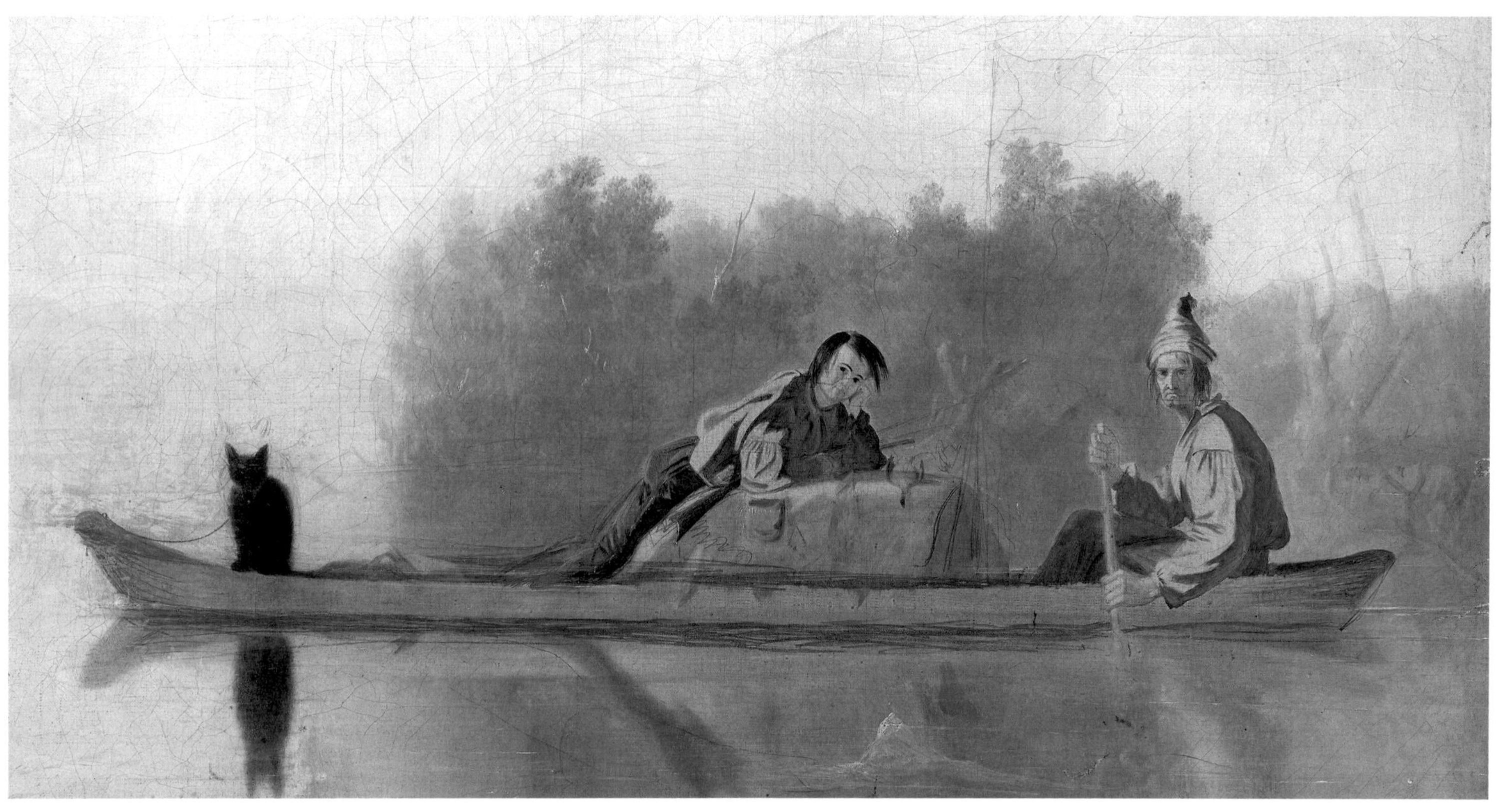

Fig. 82: Using infrared imaging, extensive underdrawing can be seen beneath the layers of paint in this detail of *Fur Traders*.

Technical investigation has provided insight into the planning and execution of the earliest of Bingham's surviving river paintings. Infrared reflectography reveals that, unlike his habit with previous paintings,[22] the artist began *Fur Traders* with extensive underdrawing using a dry carbonaceous drawing material, probably graphite pencil, and that the composition underwent many changes before the painting process began (Fig. 82). A one-to-one comparison of the painted surface with the drawing of the fur trader demonstrates that the sizes correspond exactly, confirming that the extant study was created specifically for transfer into the composition (Fig. 83). Although there is no firm evidence as to how Bingham made the transfer, for centuries artists have employed various methods to accomplish this task. For example, artist's treatises available during this period describe a process called "calking," in which an intermediate piece of paper was rubbed on one

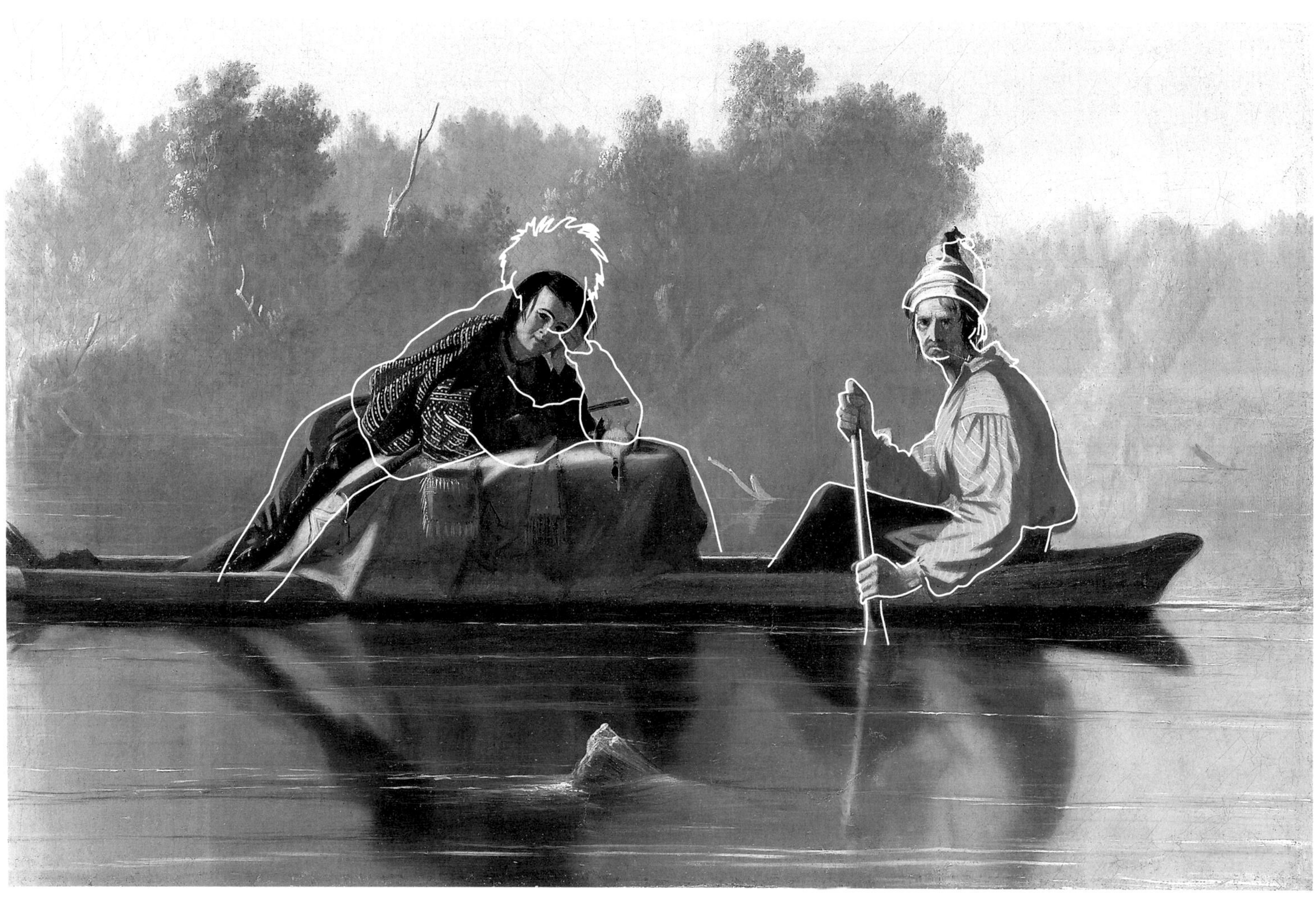

Fig. 83: This black-and-white detail of *Fur Traders* is overlaid with outlines of two of the artist's preparatory drawings. The drawing of the boy (Pl. 42) was used for the later painting *Trappers' Return* (Pl. 31) and, when compared with the similar subject in *Fur Traders*, shows a marked difference in scale. The drawing of the old trader (Pl. 7), however, corresponds exactly to the painted figure.

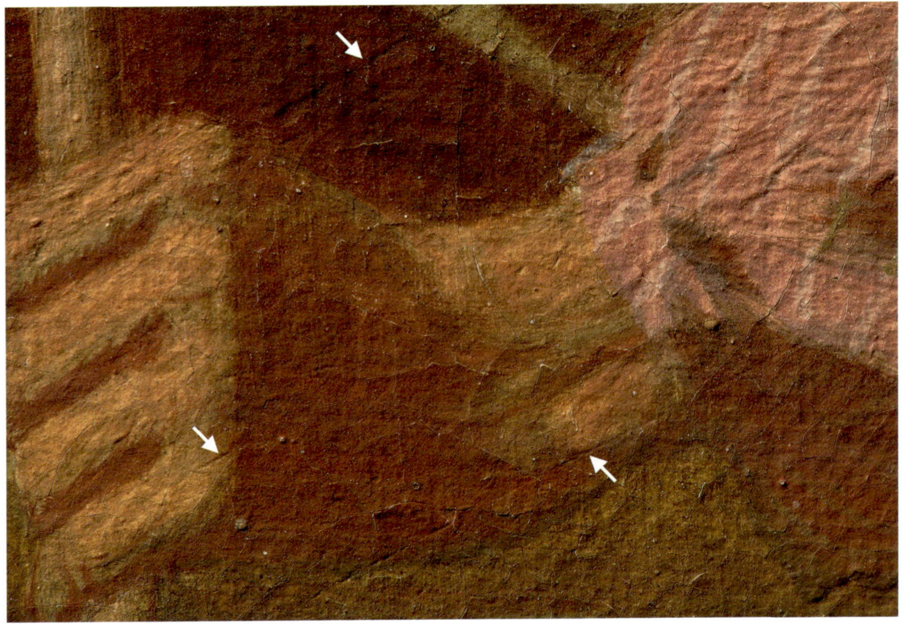

Fig. 84: The arrows in this detail of the old trader's left hand point to scored lines that might have served as registration marks for transferring the drawing.

Fig. 85: In this detail of the old trader's right hand, arrows point to locations where the artist's underdrawing is visible to the naked eye.

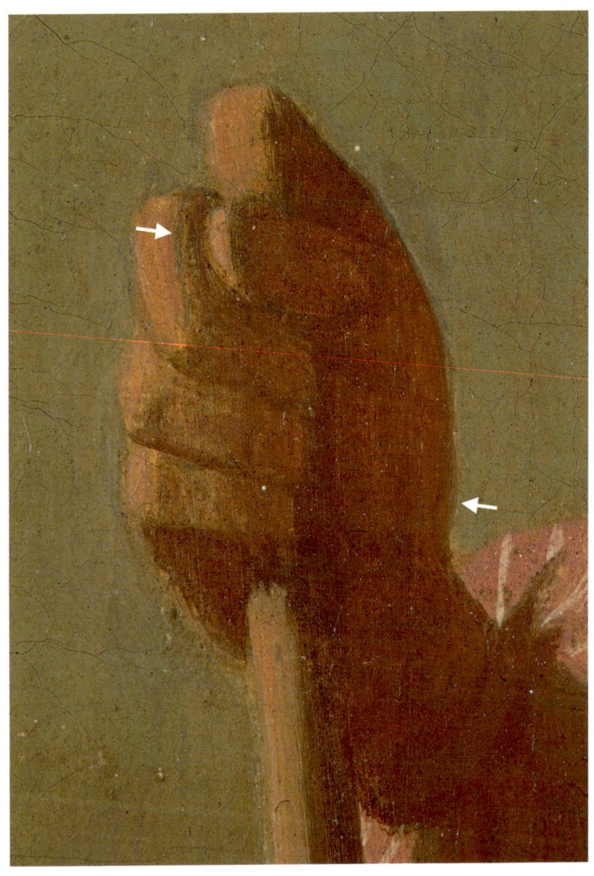

side with white or red chalk or charcoal and placed between the original drawing and painting support.[23] By applying pressure with a stylus to the outlines, the drawing was effectively transferred without soiling the original. On the surface of the painting there is a vertical score mark in the background to the left of the fur trader that corresponds to the left edge of the drawing when it is aligned with the painting; there are also several short, straight score marks in and around the figure of the fur trader (Fig. 84). These marks may be evidence of a system used to register the study drawing during the transfer process. The precise, controlled, and delicate underdrawing of the fur trader was followed so exactly during the painting of this figure that it can be observed only when the infrared reflectogram is magnified. For the most part, the drawing is concealed, but

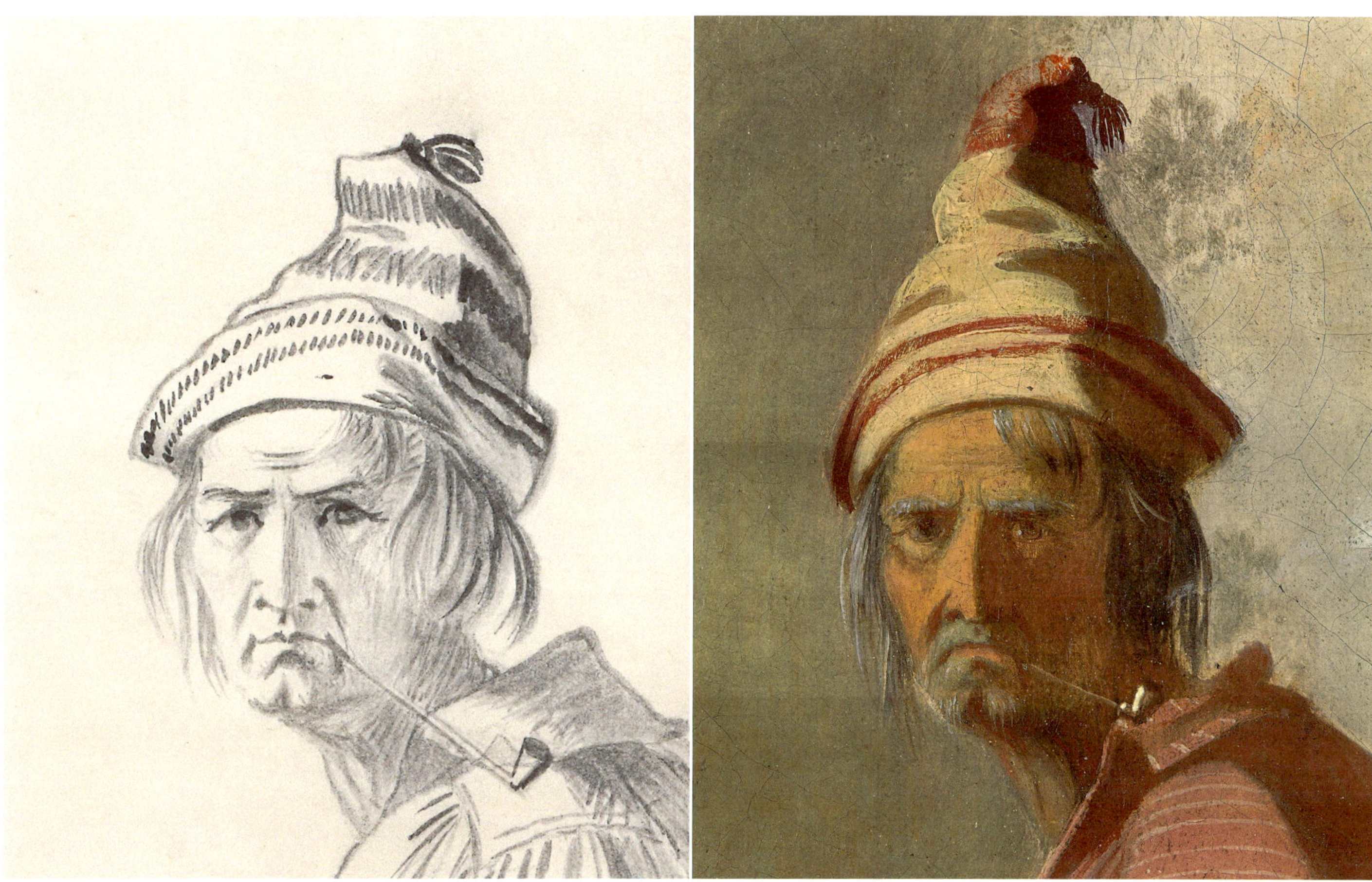

Fig. 86: A detail of the drawing *Fur trader* (Pl. 7) beside a detail of the painting reveals the artist's modifications to the figure in the final composition.

when the surface is examined with the stereomicroscope, it is visible in a few places beneath thinly applied paint and along the contours (Fig. 85).

After Bingham transferred his drawing of the fur trader to the canvas, he continued to refine the figure. A comparison of the drawing with the painted figure reveals that Bingham decided to give his fur trader an older, more wizened and weathered face by adding wrinkles to the forehead and around the eyes, which now have a more penetrating gaze than in the drawing; he also painted in heavy eyebrows, a beard and mustache, and longer grayish-white hair (Fig. 86). He also made the hat taller and painted it with more flair, using bright colors of red and creamy white. The fur trader's shirt is painted in pink with white stripes and is given lively shading and shadows. Bingham elevated the pipe in the fur trader's mouth slightly so that it is above his collar line, and he added a bright glint on the bowl and a small cloud of white smoke drifting away. Collectively, such beautifully rendered details add much to the power of the finished work.

The portions of the composition that were freely sketched in the underdrawing include the canoe, the bear depicted in the bow, and the boy and cargo mound on which he rests

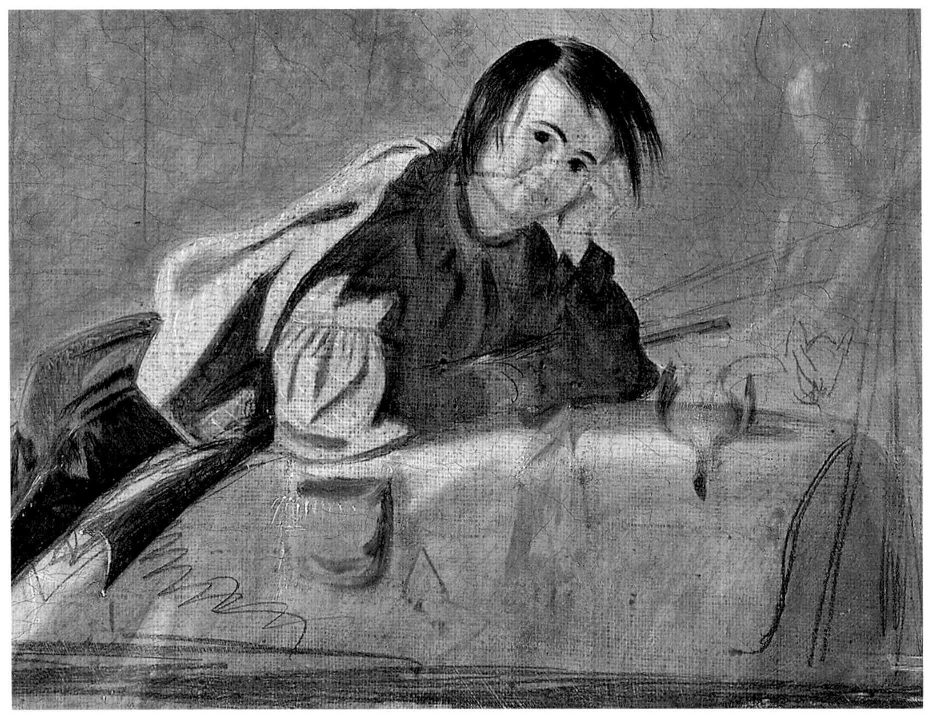

Fig. 87: This infrared reflectogram detail reveals the artist's freely sketched underdrawing of the trader's son, the position of the rifle and cargo mound, and a small animal lying on top of the mound that was not included in the final composition.

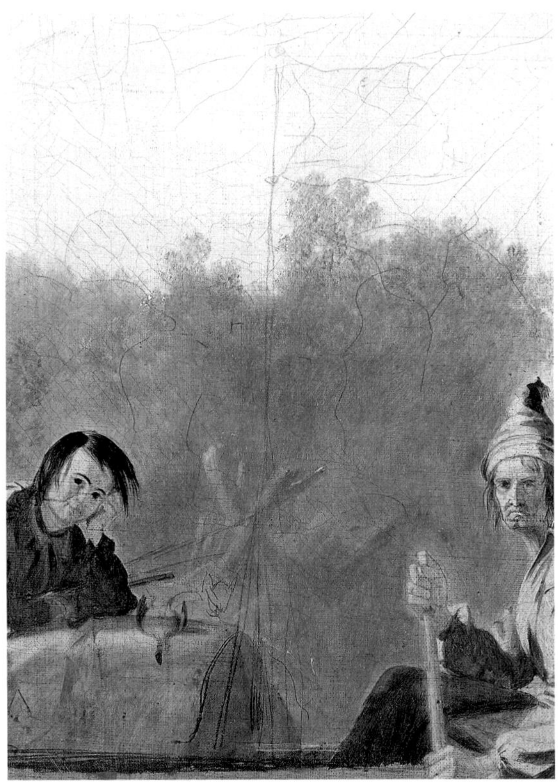

Fig. 88: This infrared reflectogram detail reveals an underdrawn mast and flag that were not included in the final painting.

(Fig. 87). The reflections in the water are loosely indicated, as are the sweeping cloud formations and massing of trees in the background. Features that were loosely sketched but do not appear in the final composition include a very small bear sitting on top of the cargo mound and a mast and flag placed between the boy and his father (Fig. 88).

Particular aspects of the underdrawing confirm that Bingham had a fairly clear idea of the overall composition before he started. He began with a loose sketch placing the features as described above. The figure of the fur trader was then transferred into the composition, very precisely, employing the study drawing, which surely had been drawn using a posed model. At this stage, the artist realized that he needed to correct the perspective of the compositional sketch, which he had drawn from a higher viewpoint than the eye-level orientation of the figure study. The distant gunwale was lowered, the

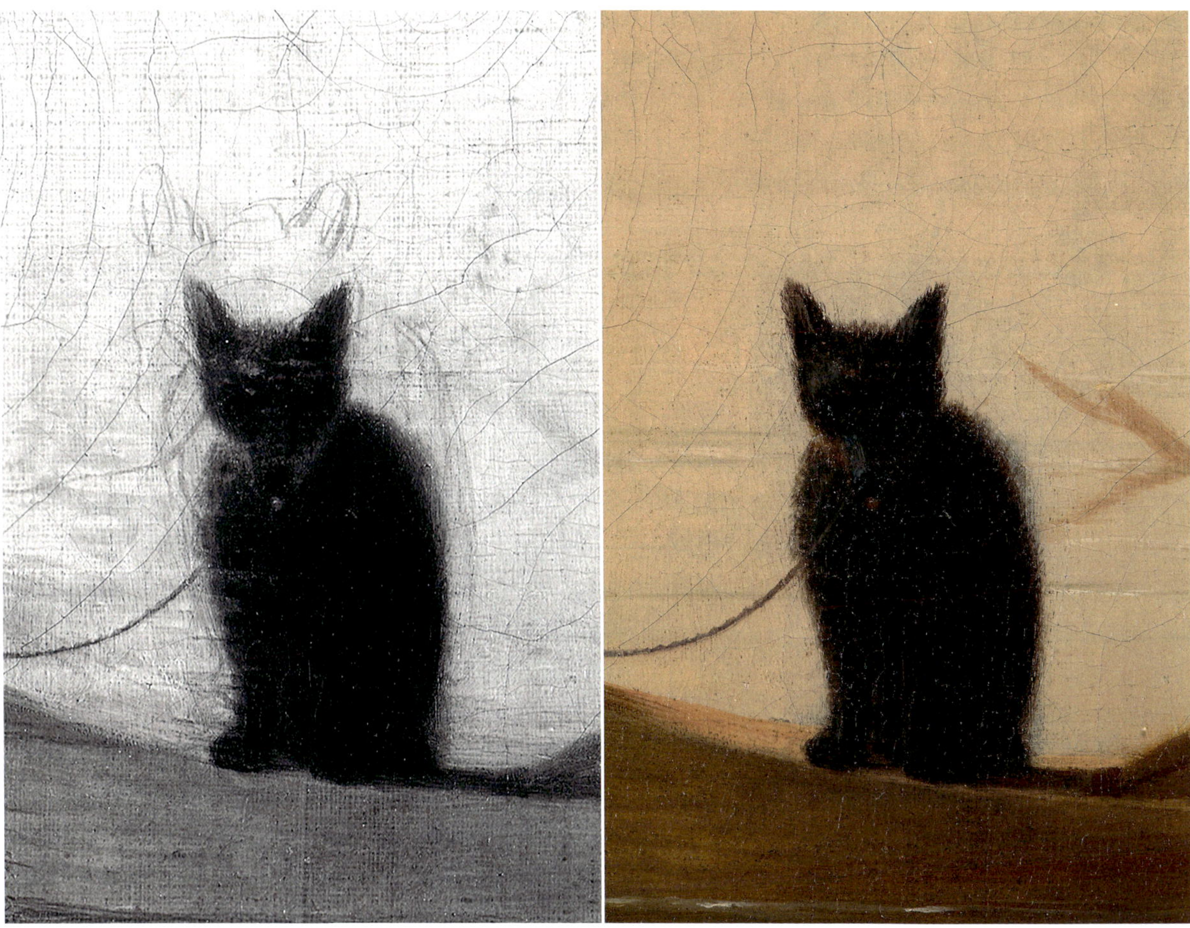

Fig. 89: The bear's ears in the underdrawing, seen in the infrared reflectogram detail at left, are rounded and more bear-like than those in the finished painting.

bow was made smaller, the bear was repositioned lower and reduced in size with his head facing forward, and the cargo mound was shifted left to create more space between the figures. It was likely at this point, too, that the artist decided to eliminate the tiny bear on the cargo mound, as well as the mast and the flag. With regard to Bingham's working methods, it is of particular interest that these compositional adjustments stemmed from the direct use of the highly finished drawing of the fur trader. This is the first indication of how crucially important this working method would become for Bingham as he developed the increasingly complex figural groupings in his later river paintings.

The underdrawing of the bear in the bow puts to rest any remaining confusion regarding the identification of the animal. The ears are drawn with rounded tops, which is the typical shape for bears' ears. Misidentification may have ensued because the fine strokes of paint describing the tufts of hair projecting from the top of the ears make them appear somewhat pointed (Fig. 89). The animal's face, when photographed in strong light, confirms the bearlike features (Fig. 90).

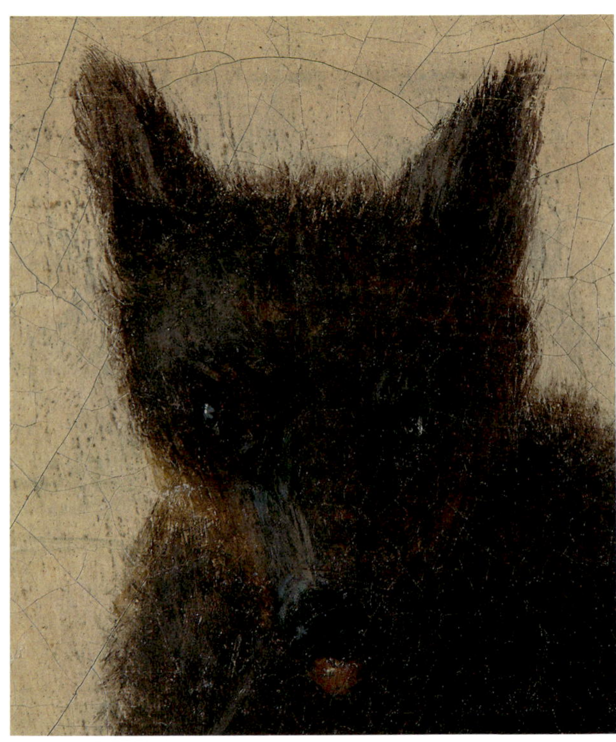

Fig. 90: Though there has been much debate as to what type of animal is in the traders' bow, the underdrawing, strong light, and a close-up detail confirm the animal's ursine features.

Infrared reflectography also reveals that the artist made changes during the painting process. Initially, the riverbank extended to the right edge of the composition and included a dead tree stump that projected to the sky above the distant treetops. Beneath the surface there is also a fully painted grouping of dead tree stumps in the background between the two figures and river debris along the bank (Fig. 91). Eliminating these features simplified and enhanced the serenity of this beautifully classical grouping.

When the surface of *Fur Traders* is examined with a stereomicroscope, which provides a relatively low level of magnification, the subtle hues and transition of tones in the landscape, water, and sky that appear so colorful and luminous in normal viewing become elusive. There is little pigmentation, and the paint layer overall appears extremely thin, except in the few areas where the artist applied delicate, crisp highlights and final details (Fig. 92). Along the perimeter of the painting, minute paint samples were removed from eight areas and mounted in cross section to analyze the pigments and more precisely understand the paint structure and technique the artist used to achieve the atmospheric and subtle effects.[24] The samples revealed that the particle size in all of the paint layers is divided to a remarkably fine degree. *Fur Traders* was painted at a time when it was necessary for an artist either to prepare his own oil colors or to purchase hand-ground paints from a commercial colorman. The preparation of oil paint is an extremely laborious process that involves grinding pigment into a drying oil, such as linseed oil.[25] Bingham may have prepared his own colors, but judging from the apparent quality used in *Fur Traders*, it is more likely that he purchased commercially prepared oil paint and prestretched and primed canvas while he was still in the East.[26] The colorman Edward Dechaux maintained an establishment at No. 328½ and 325 Broadway in New York City and issued a catalogue dating from 1836–40 that offered "Oil Colors prepared (dry) either in Tubes or Bladders."[27] The dimensions of *Fur Traders* match one of the many standard sizes of stretched and primed canvas that were offered for sale in this catalogue.[28] Regardless of the specific source, the high quality of the materials Bingham used is an indication of the sophistication and ambitions of an artist who was anticipating establishing a successful studio practice in a provincial location.

The layers revealed in a cross section of a sample removed from the lower left of the work, where the water passes from light to shadow, demonstrate the masterful way in which Bingham manipulated the optical qualities of oil paint. The shimmering pinkish hue of the water shifts to a subtle greenish hue where it is shaded by the trees. Bingham's effects of light and color are achieved with thin paint layers containing a sparse distribution of colored pigments in pure, finely ground

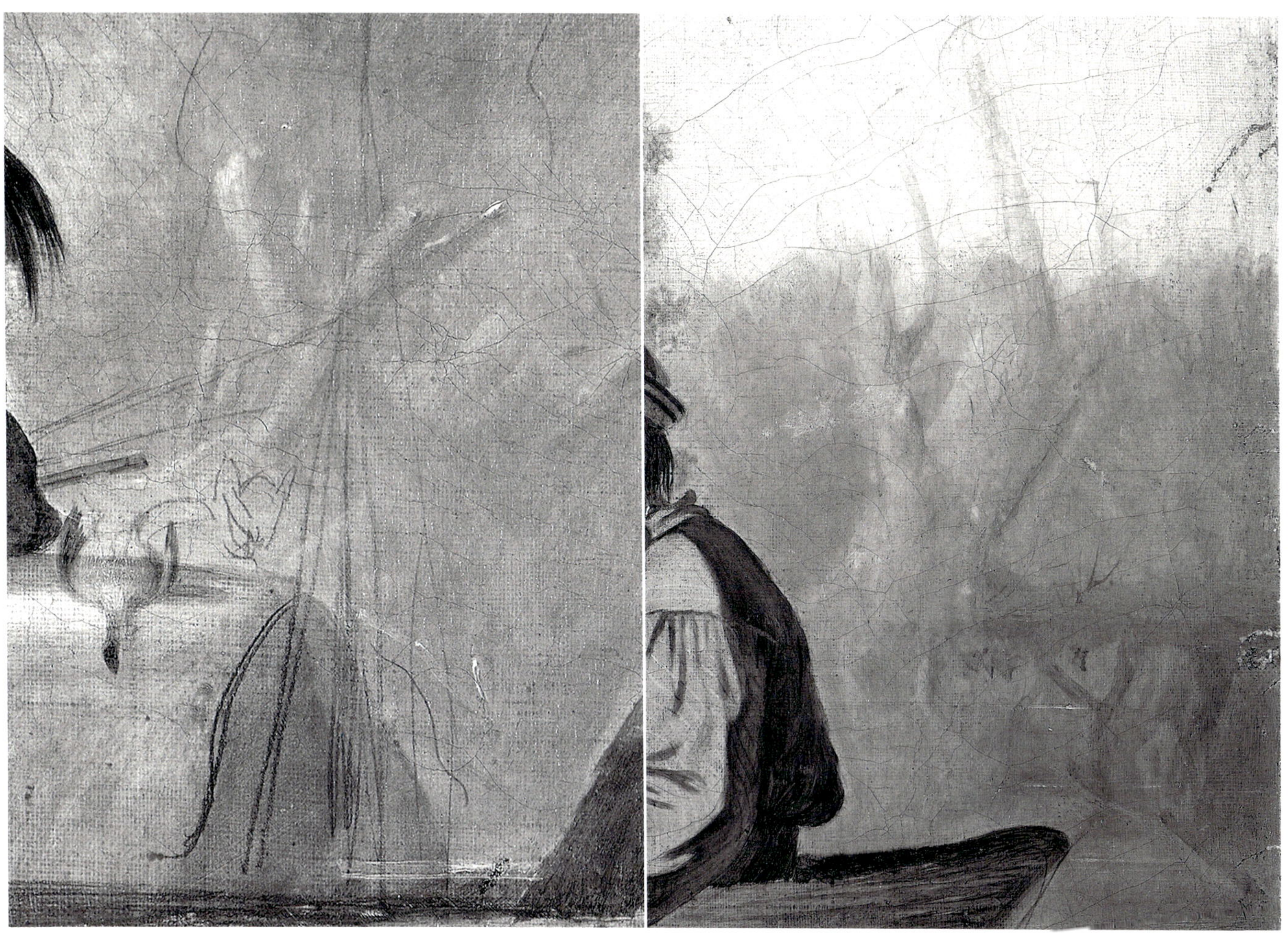

Fig. 91: Infrared reflectogram details reveal painted features that were not included in the final composition, including tree stumps and river debris in the background between the figures and, at right, a dead tree that rises above the horizon.

Fig. 92: This detail of the river snag at left shows the generally thin paint application and delicate, low-relief texture of the highlights.

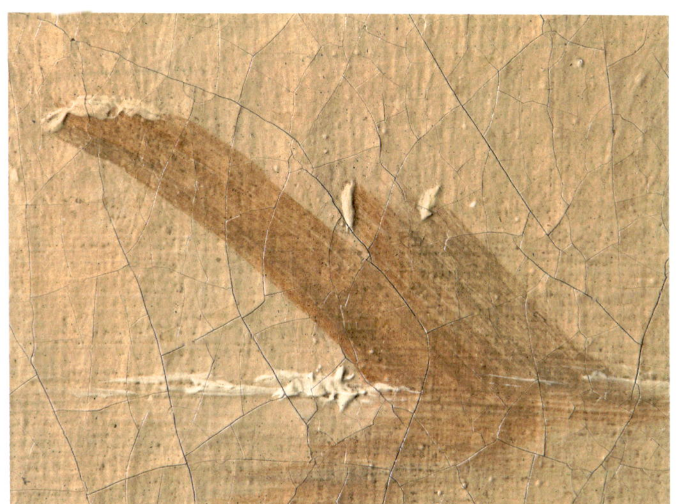

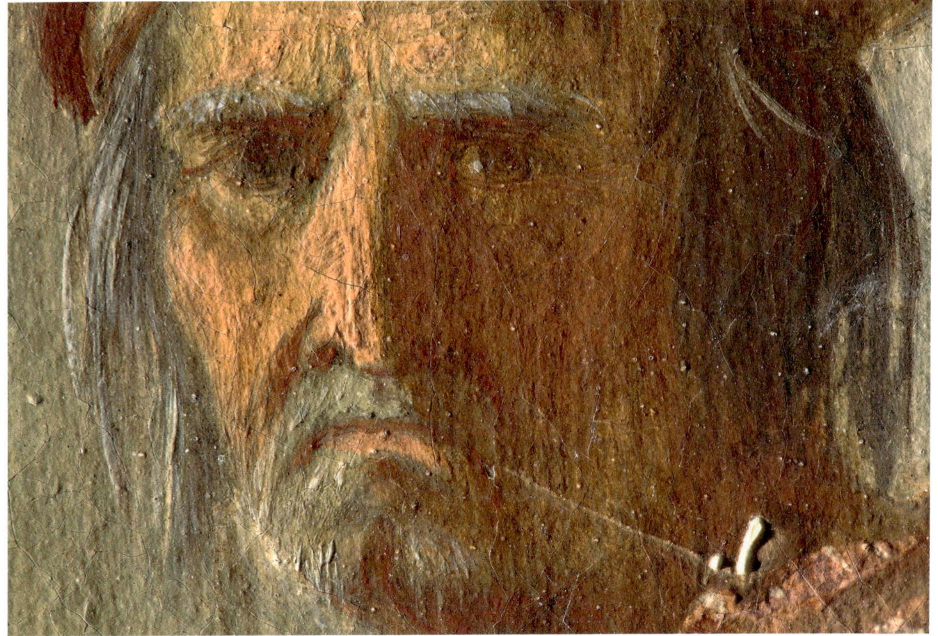

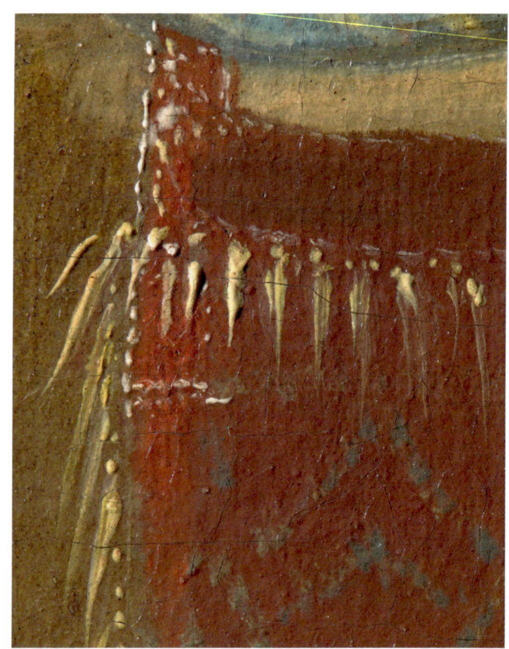

Fig. 93: Detail of the fur trader's face.

Fig. 94: The yellow fringe on the son's beaded bag is painted with a chrome containing yellow pigment, demonstrating Bingham's preference for using colors that had only recently been introduced to the artistic palette.

lead white. The paint mixture for the shaded greenish water contains a few particles of carbon black and a yellow earth pigment. The pinkish water to the left, which reflects the sky, is a delicate application of lead white with a few particles of vermilion and red iron earth. A thin veil of this semiopaque tincture is used to soften the transition where the water shifts from light to shade. Bingham skillfully exploited the semitransparency of very thinly applied paint layers containing finely ground lead white with only a little colored pigment to achieve the effect of deep, translucent water.

All of the eight paint samples mounted in cross section consistently demonstrate the artist's skillful manipulation of the optical properties inherent in a masterful use of the oil technique. From passage to passage, the tinctures are adjusted with great sensitivity as the landscape shifts from foreground to middle and far distance. The recession into the distance is handled in a classic way by using four distinct gradations in tone. The deepest tones appear in the vegetation, which is closest to and directly behind the figural group, lightening in gradual stages and culminating in the lightest passage in the most distant landscape along the horizon. This aspect of the technique is most clearly demonstrated by the adjustments the artist made when painting out the portion of the landscape that originally extended all the way to the right. A very thin layer consisting of lead white with a few particles of ultramarine blue and vermilion was painted over the trees to open up the view to a distant riverbank.[29] The cool, hazy, purplish appearance of this passage was achieved by employing a technique known as scumbling, in which a light, semiopaque translucent mixture is applied over a dark underlayer to create an optical blue or a cooler tone. The paint application is so thin that the underlying tree was always visible to a degree. And because the final paint layer has become more transparent with age, this underlying feature has grown more visible. The hazy appearance of the land in the far distance at left was achieved in a similar way by scumbling a mixture of lead white containing very few particles of ultramarine and vermilion over a dark, warm-toned underlayer, which is a mixture of carbon black, ultramarine, a red iron earth, and finely ground lead white. The pale pinks, creams, and barely blue hues that color the windswept sky are equally subtle. These were also achieved by thin layers containing primarily lead white with a few particles of color. The pale pink coloration throughout the sky was surely intended, and there is no evidence of fading, as the spare distribution of the opaque red pigments vermilion and hematite (a red iron earth) are what colors this paint. Finally, it is important to appreciate how richly and delicately colored this painting appears despite the fact that the artist employed so few pigments. In addition to black and white, the paint layers contain only red, blue, yellow, and brownish earth pigments.

Bingham used two distinctly different techniques to paint the figures and the landscape. For the latter, he exploited the superb optical qualities inherent in the oil medium, applying his paint in delicately thin, translucent layers. The shimmering effects achieved in the painting of the landscape, water, and sky are so atmospheric that these passages envelop and enhance the figural grouping. By contrast, the figures are executed in a tactile and more highly finished manner with opaque applications of color. Painted in a haptical way, with paint layers that emphasize a sense of surface reality, they directly contrast with the optically painted landscape and water surroundings (Figs. 93–96). This juxtaposition of haptical and optical techniques is magical and significantly enhances the painting's overall aura, beauty, and atmosphere. No doubt the brilliant and skillful use of these contrasting techniques has contributed to this painting's universal appeal.

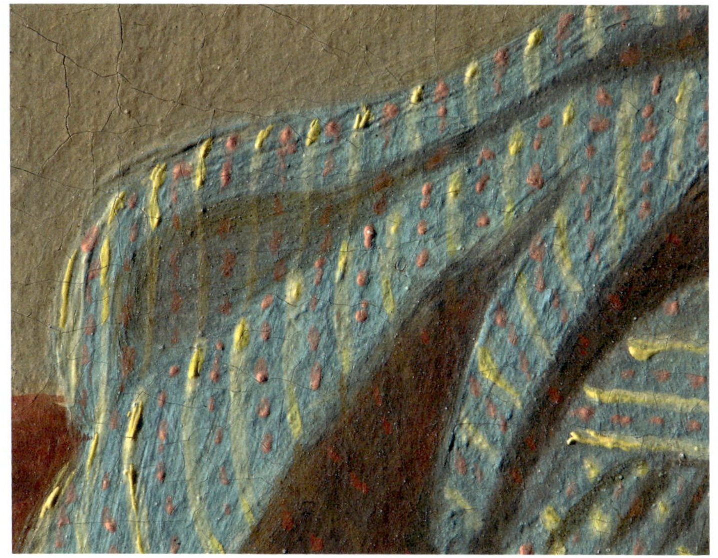

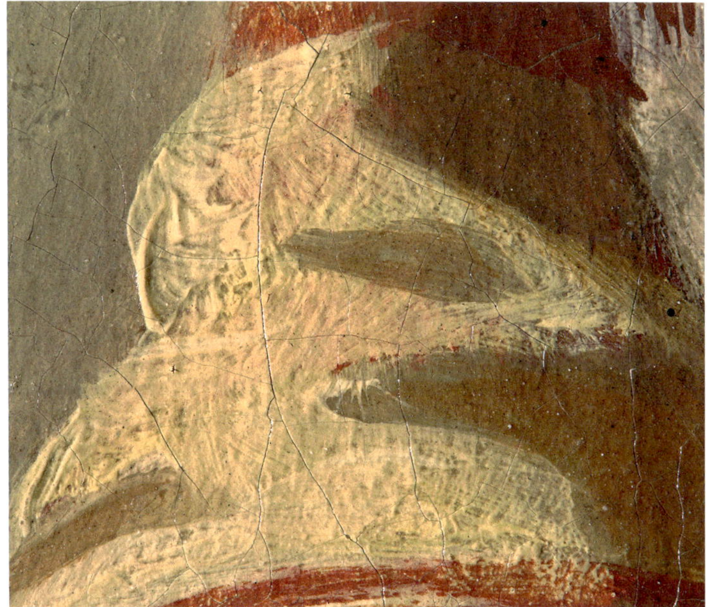

Fig. 95: The boy's shirt is painted with ultramarine, and the pattern was made with vermilion and a chrome containing yellow pigment.

Fig. 96: The original red color of the trader's hat is visible through the freely brushed creamy white that Bingham used to change the striped pattern.

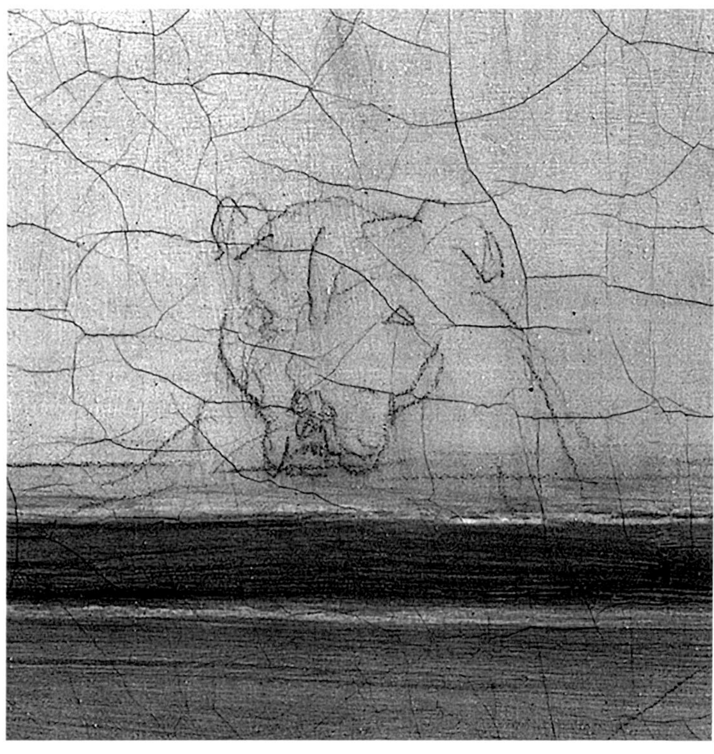

Fig. 97: This infrared reflectogram detail of *Trappers' Return* (Pl. 31), in which Bingham revisited his earlier theme of father-and-son trappers, shows little evidence of major change in the underdrawing—with the exception of the head of a large dog placed between the bear and boy.

CONCLUSION

Bingham is known to have revisited a number of his compositions, and among them is *Trappers' Return* (Pl. 31), which is a slightly smaller variant of *Fur Traders Descending the Missouri.* Painted six years later, this work shows little evidence of major change in the underdrawing, with the exception of the head of a large dog placed between the bear and the boy, which is not seen in the final composition, and there is no evidence of pentimenti (Fig. 97).[30] In many ways, this second version helps position the 1845 example in sharper focus as an early masterwork created in a moment of artistic inspiration.

Following its public presentation at the American Art-Union in New York in 1845, *Fur Traders Descending the Missouri* was won in the lottery by Robert S. Bunker of Mobile, Alabama. It descended in Bunker's family until 1933, when it was offered for sale in New York City. Although unaware of the artist but recognizing the innate quality of the painting, Harry B. Wehle, a curator at the Metropolitan Museum of Art, New York, quickly purchased it for the museum. Having been out of public view for nearly ninety years, *Fur Traders* helped revive Bingham's reputation and led to an exhibition of the artist's work at the Museum of Modern Art, New York, in 1935. Since that time, *Fur Traders* has continued to captivate audiences and engage scholars' attention as they contemplate the trader and his son, who together appear in tune with wild nature as they glide down the river toward civilization. By conducting a careful technical study of Bingham's artistic process in making this work, it is now possible to appreciate the painting as a product of its own time, but one that is in many ways exceptional in Bingham's career as an early, inspired burst of artistic and largely untutored brilliance.

NOTES

We would like to thank Carol Troyen, Curator Emerita of American Paintings at the Museum of Fine Arts, Boston, for her insightful comments on an early draft.

1. *The Concealed Enemy* achieved $40 and *Cottage Scenery*, $35; see E. Maurice Bloch, *The Paintings of George Caleb Bingham: A Catalogue Raisonné* (Columbia: University of Missouri Press, 1986), 172–73.

2. John Caldwell and Oswaldo Rodriguez Roque, with Dale T. Johnson, *American Paintings in the Metropolitan Museum of Art*, vol. 1, *A Catalogue of Works by Artists Born by 1815* (New York: Metropolitan Museum of Art in association with Princeton University Press, 1994), 540.

3. E. Maurice Bloch, *George Caleb Bingham: The Evolution of an Artist* (Berkeley: University of California Press, 1967), 88–90.

4. Leah Lipton, "George Caleb Bingham in the Studio of Chester Harding, Franklin, Missouri, 1820," *American Art Journal* 16, no. 3 (Summer 1984): 90–91.

5. Margaret C. Conrads, "*Fishing on the Mississippi*, 1851," in *The Collections of the Nelson-Atkins Museum of Art: American Paintings to 1945*, ed. Margaret C. Conrads (Kansas City, Mo.: Nelson-Atkins Museum of Art, 2007), 1:114, 118n8.

6. Bingham to James S. Rollins, May 6, 1837, in *"But I Forget That I Am a Painter and Not a Politician": The Letters of George Caleb Bingham*, ed. Lynn Wolf Gentzler (Columbia: State Historical Society of Missouri, 2011), 43.

7. Bloch, *George Caleb Bingham*, 49–68.

8. Bingham to his wife, June 3, 1838, quoted in ibid., 37–38.

9. Bloch, *George Caleb Bingham*, 48.

10. Quoted in Conrads, "*Fishing on the Mississippi*, 1851," 114, 118n3 citing "The Festival at Rocheport," *Boone's Lick Times* (Fayette, Mo.), July 4, 1840, 2.

11. William H. Truettner and Alan Wallach, *Thomas Cole: Landscape into History* (New Haven: Yale University Press; Washington, D.C.: National Museum of American Art, 1994), 77, 79.

12. Cole's *The Departure* and *The Return* were acquired by William P. Van Rensselaer, who placed them on view in the parlor of his New York City house for art enthusiasts and the media to see, beginning in December 1837; see Ellwood C. Parry III, *The Art of Thomas Cole: Ambition and Imagination* (Newark: University of Delaware Press, 1988), 198–99. Cole's *Past* and *Present* were exhibited to the public in New York City in 1838 at the *William Dunlap Benefit Exhibition*, at Stuyvesant Institute; see ibid., 214–15.

13. See American Art-Union, American Art-Union Records, Reel 1, Minutes of Annual Meetings, 1839–1850, Management Committee Minutes, vol. 1, December 8, 1845.

14. *Proceedings of the American Art-Union Annual Meeting*. December 19, 1845, 29.

15. Bloch, *George Caleb Bingham*, 80, 110.

16. Charles D. Collins, who was unaware of Deas's 1845 oil *The Voyageurs*, suggested that a related, but undated, watercolor by Deas, *The Trapper and His Family* (Museum of Fine Arts, Boston), was a source for Bingham's painting. See Collins, "A Source for Bingham's *Fur Traders Descending the Missouri*," *Art Bulletin* 6, no. 4 (December 1984): 678–81.

17. Carol Clark et al., *Charles Deas and 1840s America* (Norman: University of Oklahoma Press in cooperation with the Denver Art Museum, 2009), 106–10.

18. Barbara Novak, *American Painting of the Nineteenth Century* (New York: Praeger, 1969), 158–59, characterizes *Fur Traders* as demonstrating "the unique polarity of luminist vision"; *Fur Traders* was described as a "proto-luminist work . . . an archetypical example not only of luminist light but of luminist structure," in John Wilmerding et al., *American Light: The Luminist Movement, 1850–1875* (Washington, D.C.: National Gallery of Art, 1980), 28. For a later reassessment of Luminism, see Alan Wallach, "Rethinking 'Luminism': Taste, Class, and Aestheticizing Tendencies in Mid-Nineteenth-Century American Landscape Painting," in *The Cultured Canvas: New Perspectives on American Landscape Painting*, ed. Nancy Siegel (Durham: University of New Hampshire Press, 2011), 115–48.

19. Robert Hughes, *American Visions: The Epic History of Art in America* (New York: Alfred A. Knopf, 1997), 175. The bear cub has long been a source of controversy, described variously as a bear, fox, and cat. Over time, however, scholars have come to accept the animal as a black bear cub, a fact verified by the technical analysis in this essay. See Albert Christ-Janer, *George Caleb Bingham* (New York: Dodd, Mead & Company, 1984), 38; John Francis McDermott, *Bingham: River Portraitist* (Norman: University of Oklahoma Press, 1959), 51; John Demos, "George Caleb Bingham: The Artist as Social Historian," *American Quarterly* 17 (1965): 288; Henry Adams, "A New Interpretation of *Fur Traders Descending the Missouri*," *Art Bulletin* 65, no. 4 (December 1983): 675–80; and Christopher Kent Wilson, "Bingham's Bear Cub," *Art Bulletin* 67, no. 1 (March 1985): 154.

20. Adams, "New Interpretation of *Fur Traders Descending the Missouri*," 676.

21. Our thanks to Claire Barry, Director of Conservation, Kimbell Art Museum, for providing this IRR image.

22. Our thanks to Evan Read, Associate Manager of Technical Documentation, Department of Paintings Conservation, The Metropolitan Museum of Art, who documented the infrared images with an Indigo Systems Merlin Near Infrared camera (InGaAs sensor range: 900–1,700 nanometers [nm]) with a StingRay Optics macro lens optimized for this range, in conjunction with a National Instruments IMAQ PCI-1422 frame grabber card and IRvista 2.51 software).

23. Laughton Osborn, *Handbook of Young Artists and Amateurs in Oilpainting* (New York: Wiley and Putnam, Broadway, 1846), 170.

24. Our thanks to Silvia A. Centeno, Research Scientist, and Mark T. Wypyski, Research Scientist, Department of Scientific Research, The Metropolitan Museum of Art, for providing pigment analysis. Raman spectra were recorded with a Renishaw Raman system 1000, configured with a Leica DM LM microscope and equipped with 785 nm and 514 nm lasers. With the aid of the attached microscope, the beam was focused on layers of sample cross sections. A 50x objective lens attached to the microscope allowed special resolution in the order of 3 microns. Integration times were set between 10 and 120 seconds. To avoid changes in the sample materials, neutral density filters were used to set the laser power at the sample to values between 0.2 and 4 mW. The Raman analyses were conducted by Silvia A. Centeno. Scanning electron microscopy-energy dispersive X-ray spectrometry (SEM-EDS) analyses were performed using an Oxford Instruments AZtec Energy Advanced Microanalysis system with an X-MaxN 80 silicon drift detector, attached to a Zeiss sigma HD variable pressure field emission scanning electron microscope. The analyses were done on uncoated samples with SEM operated in low pressure mode, at an accelerating voltage of 20kV. The SEM-EDS analyses were carried out by Mark T. Wypyski. Qualitative noninvasive X-ray fluorescence spectroscopy (XRF) analyses were performed using an Artax 400 unit equipped with a rhodium (Rh) target and a 650 µm collimator. All locations were analyzed for equal live-times of 200 seconds at 40kV and 500 µA. The XRF analyses were conducted by Silvia A. Centeno.

25. Drying oils harden by a chemical process that requires oxygen, so it has always been necessary for artists to prepare and use the colors immediately or store any unused oil paint protected from exposure to air. Artist treatises and correspondence describe various imperfect methods employed to preserve oil paint from drying before use, but one of the most common methods was to store it in small animal-skin bladders. Also, by the early nineteenth century, various types of metal or glass tubes are mentioned for this purpose. See Lance Mayer and Gay Myers, *American Painters on Technique: The Colonial Period to 1860* (Los Angeles: J. Paul Getty Museum, 2011), chap. 11, "Store Bought Supplies and New Materials in the 1830s, 1840s, and 1850s."

26. Ibid., 143–46.

27. Alexander W. Katlan, *American Artists' Materials: A Guide to Stretchers, Panels, Millboards, and Stencil Marks*, vol. 2 (Madison, Conn.: Sound View Press, 1992), 318.

28. The support is a plain-weave fabric with 14/15 (horizontal) and 13/14 (vertical) threads per square inch. Although the tacking margins were removed when the painting was relined before it entered the collection of the Metropolitan Museum of Art in 1933, cusping visible along the perimeter in the X-radiograph confirms that it retains the original dimensions. Also visible in the X-radiograph along the perimeter are markings about one inch wide that indicate the thickness of the original stretcher members. The presence of these markings also indicates that the fabric was attached to the stretcher before the application of the ground preparation, which is white and composed of lead white bound in oil. Pressure imposed by stretcher bars during application of a lead-containing ground results in a slightly thinner layer along the perimeter, which is recorded in an X-radiograph.

29. The analytical techniques used for this study do not distinguish between natural ultramarine and artificial ultramarine. However, judging from the particle size and facture when examined with polarizing light microscopy, the ultramarine blue appears to be natural ultramarine.

30. Our thanks to Alfred Ackerman, Chief Conservator, Detroit Institute of Arts, for supplying this IRR image.

PLATES 43–60

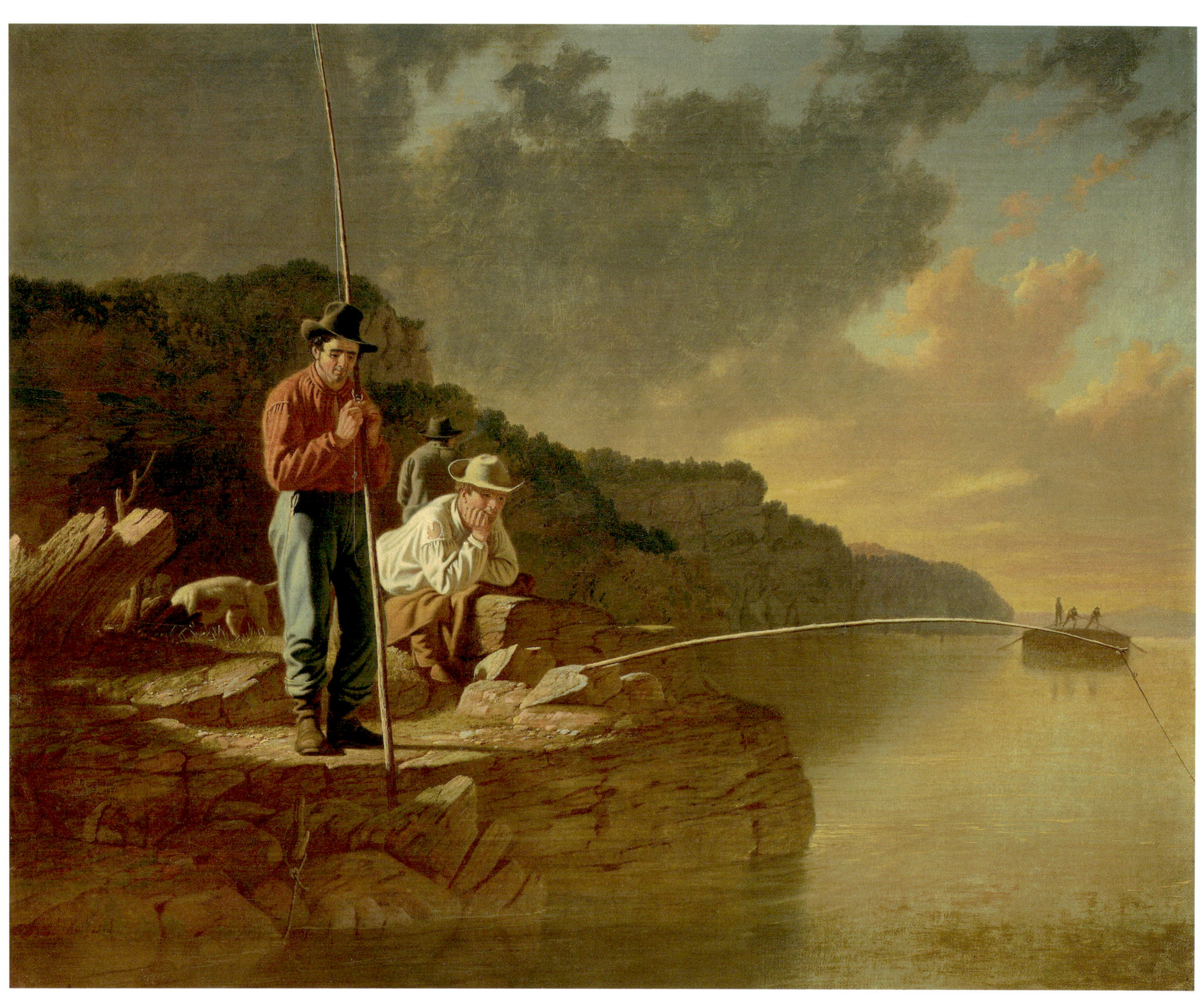

Plate 43: *Fishing on the Mississippi*, 1851

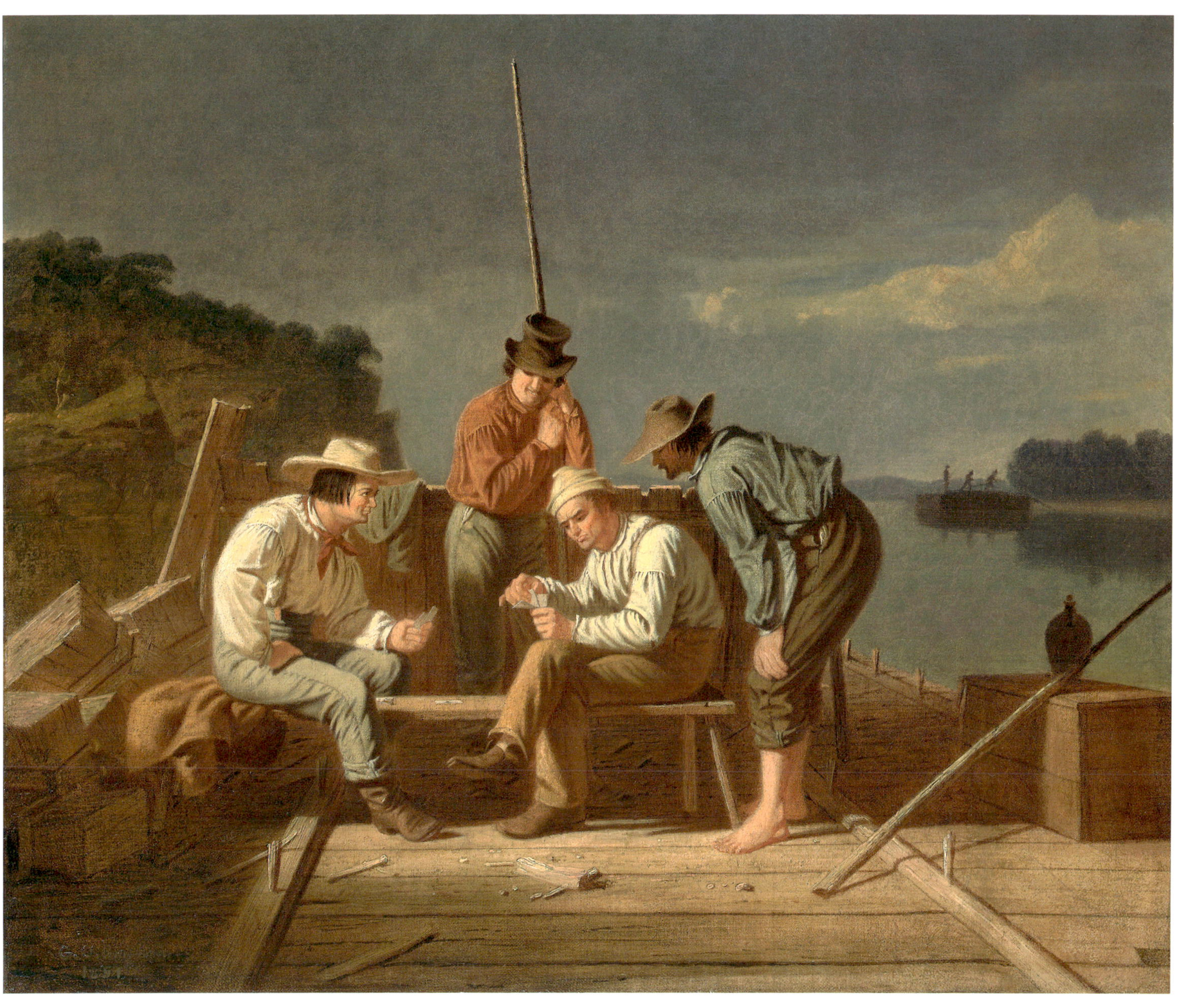

Plate 44: *In a Quandary* or *Mississippi Raftmen at Cards*, 1851

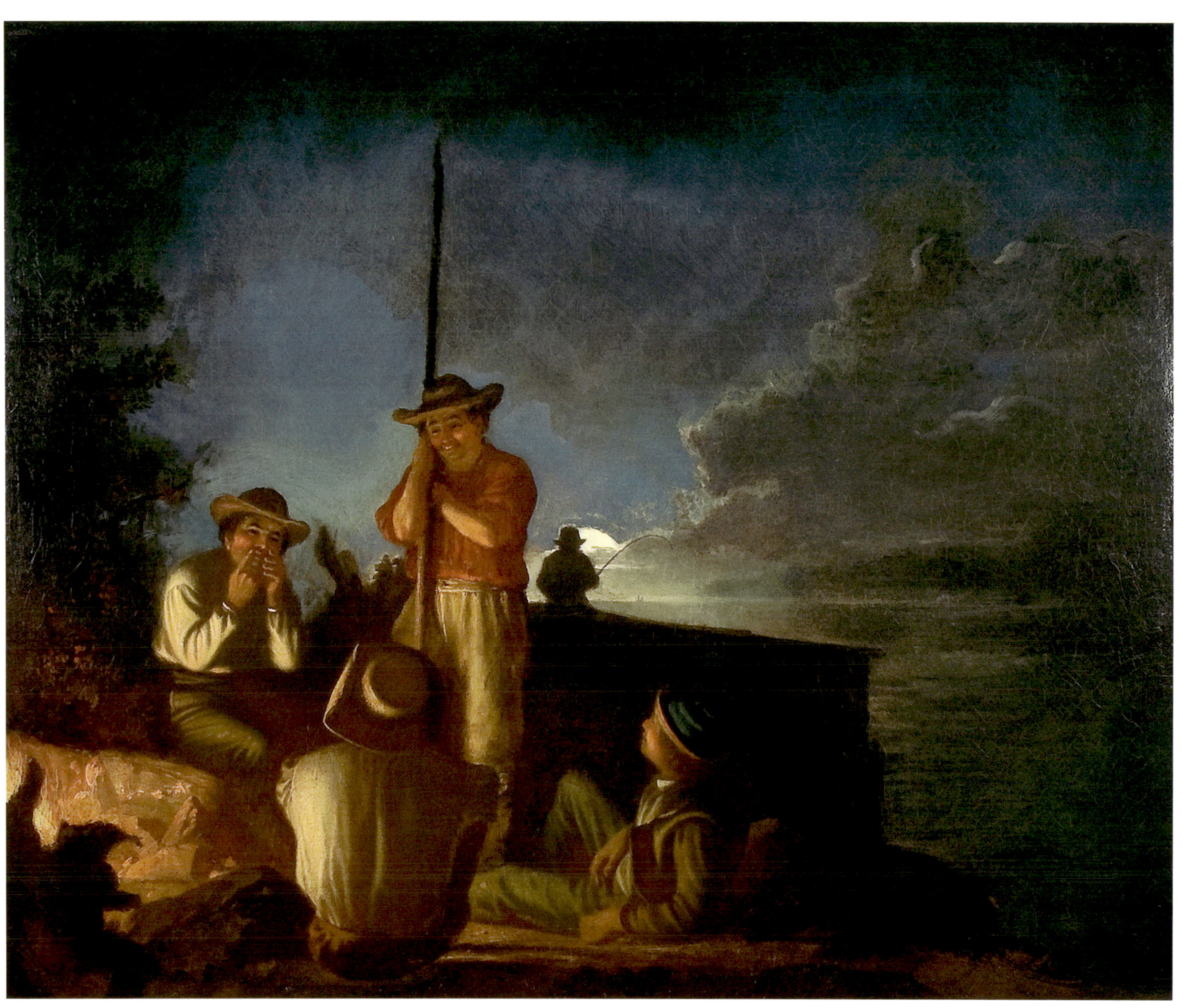

Plate 45: *Woodboatmen on a River (Western Boatmen Ashore by Night)*, 1854

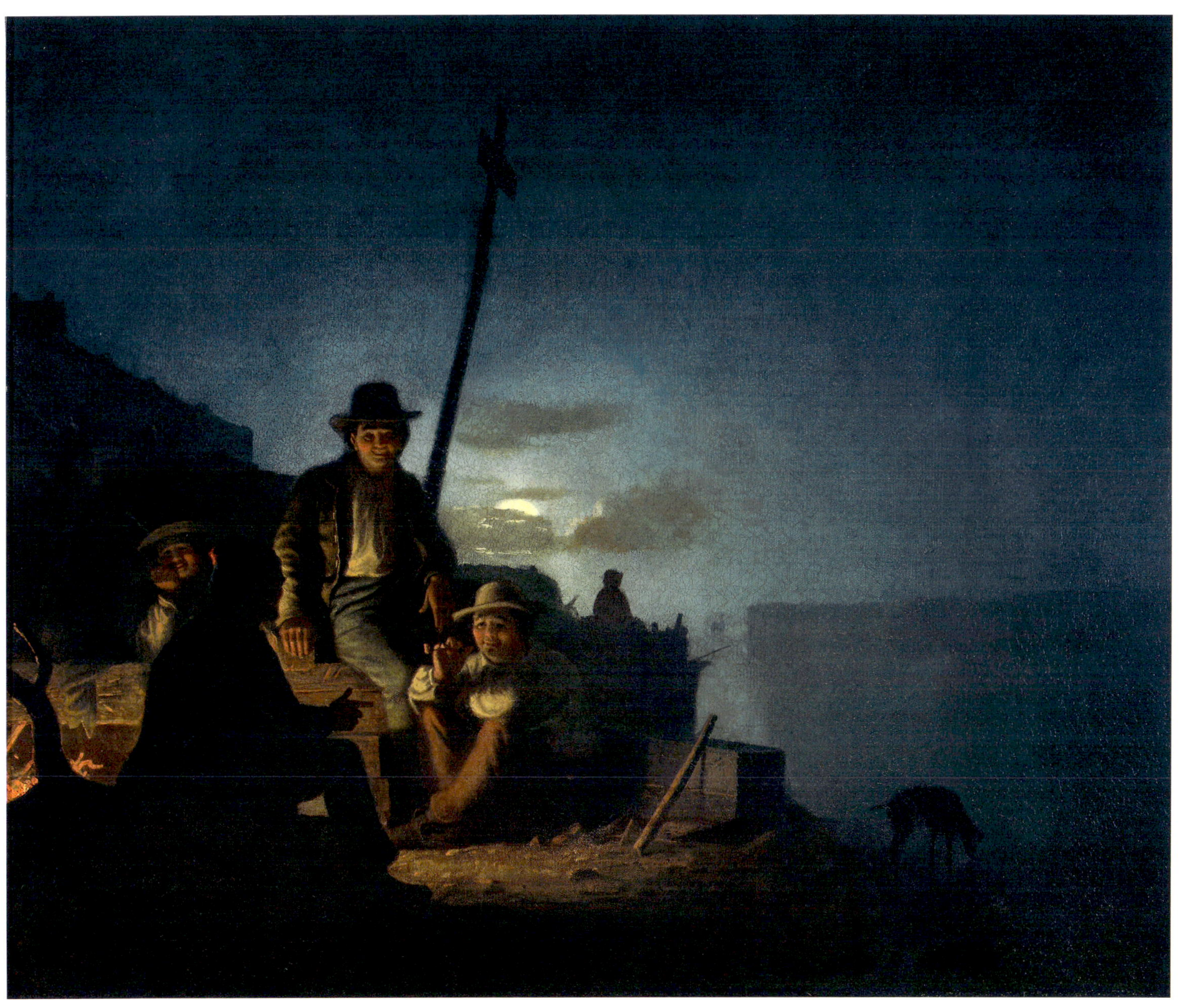

Plate 46: *Watching the Cargo by Night*, 1854

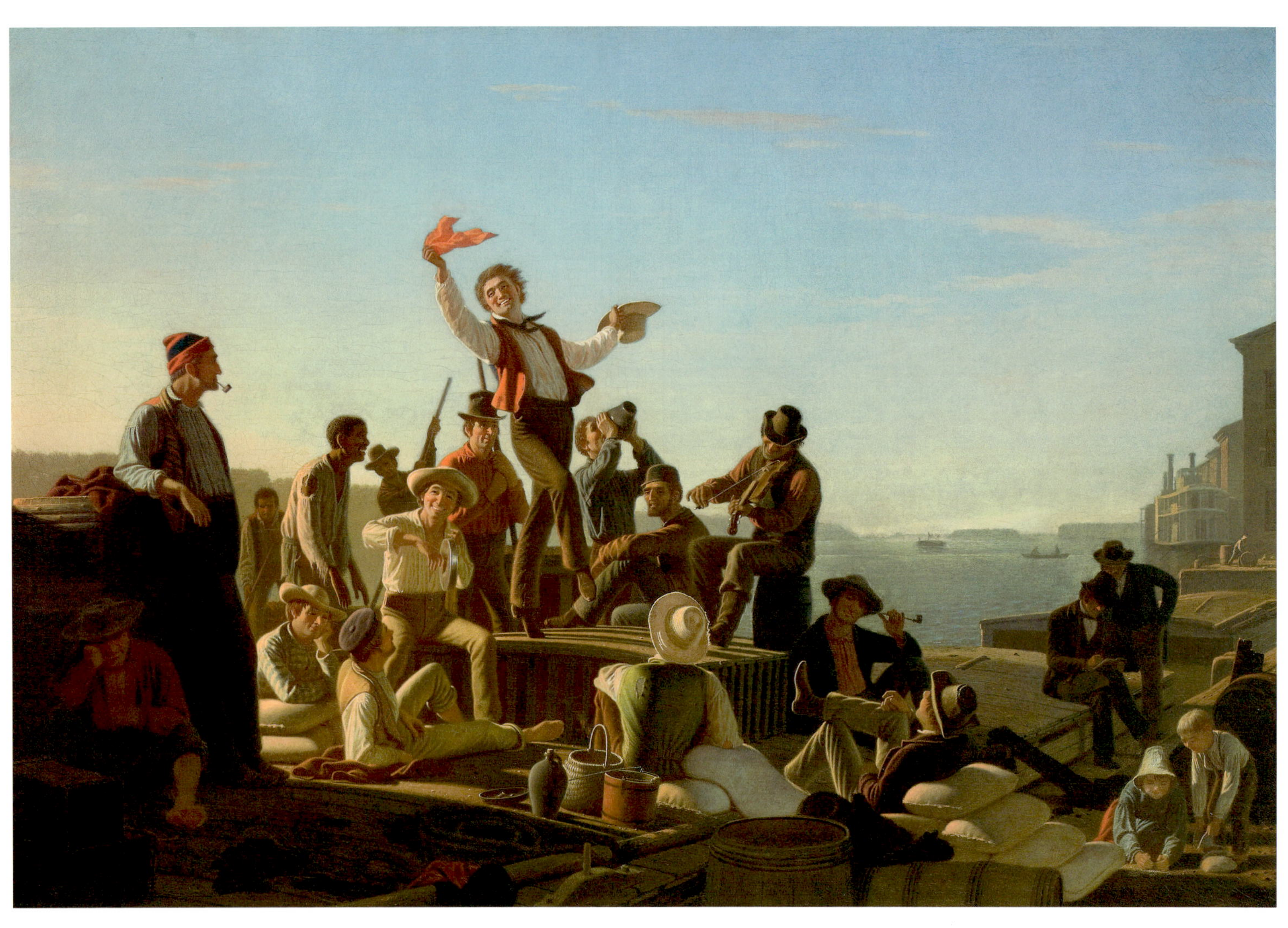

Plate 47: *Jolly Flatboatmen in Port*, 1857

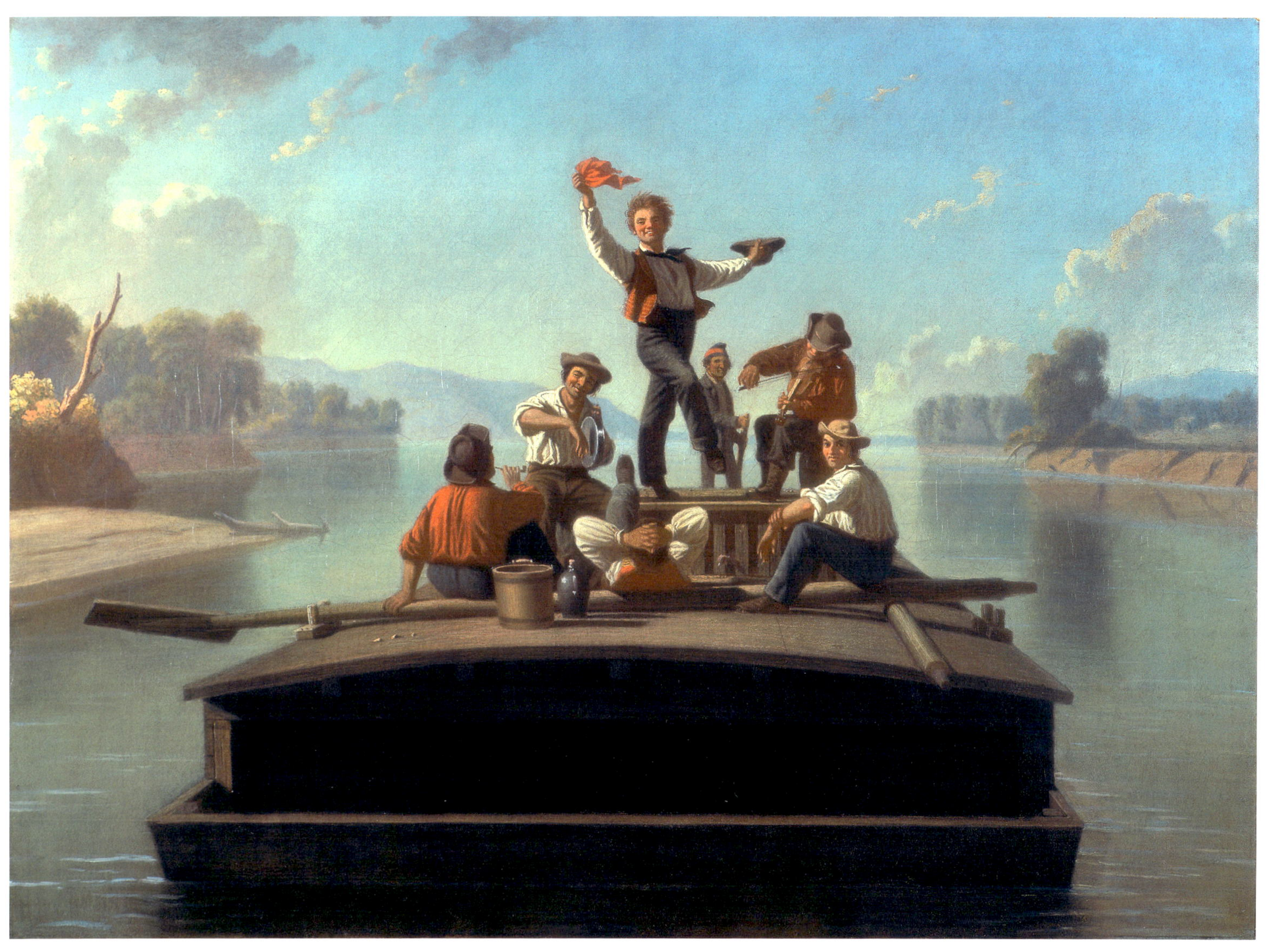

Plate 48: *The Jolly Flatboatmen*, 1877–78

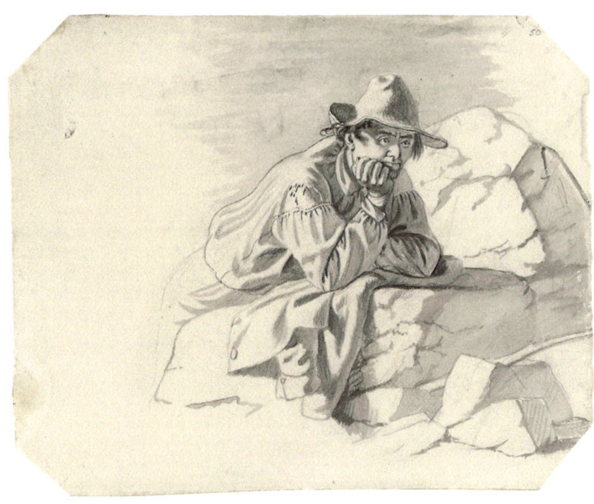

Plate 49: *Fisherman waiting for a bite*, for *Fishing on the Mississippi* (1851)

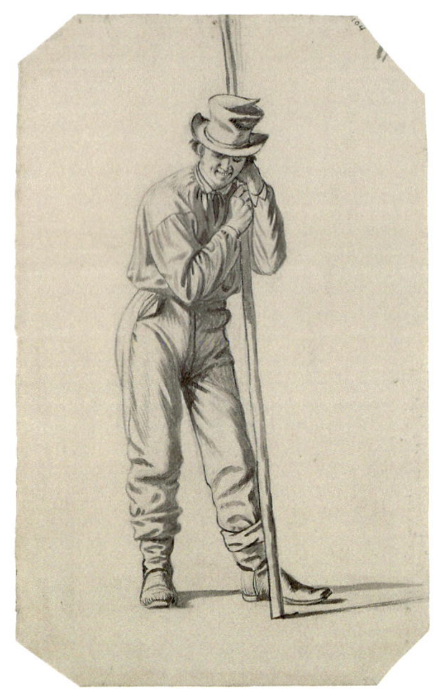

Plate 51: *Raftman*, for *In a Quandary* or *Mississippi Raftmen at Cards* (1851) and possible alternate study for *Jolly Flatboatmen in Port* (1857)

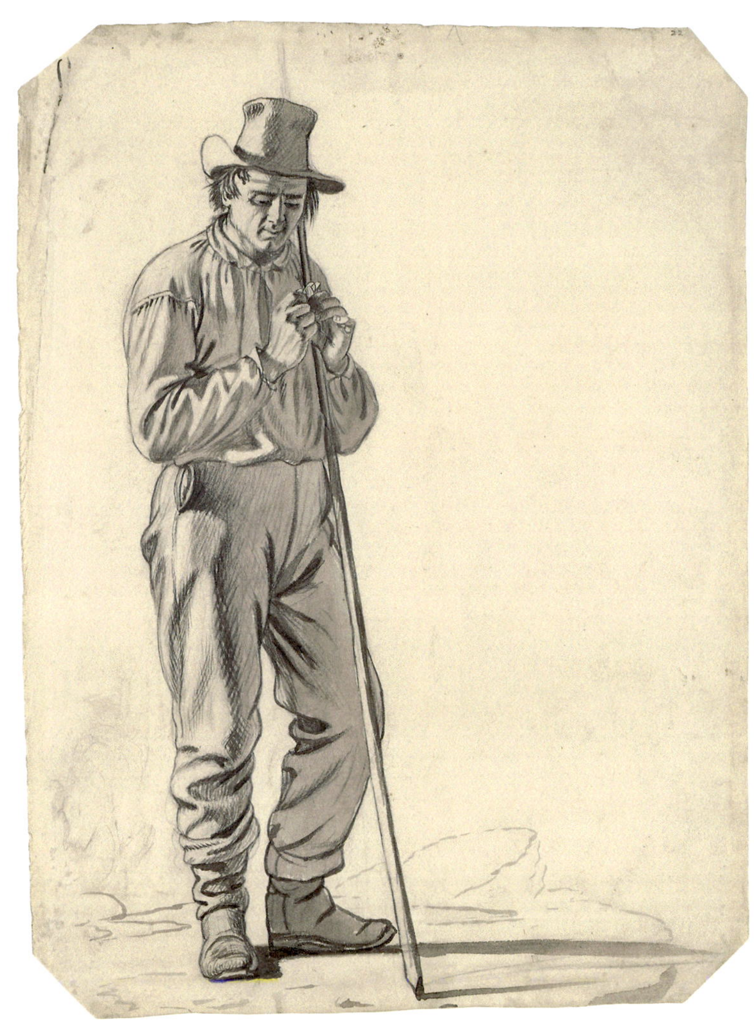

Plate 50: *Fisherman*, for *Fishing on the Mississippi* (1851)

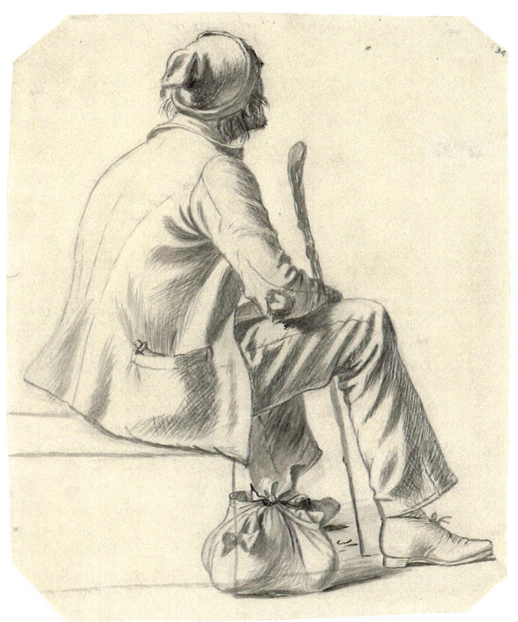

Plate 52: *Wayfarer*, for *Watching the Cargo by Night* (1854) with alterations and possible study for *St. Louis Wharf* (1849; lost)

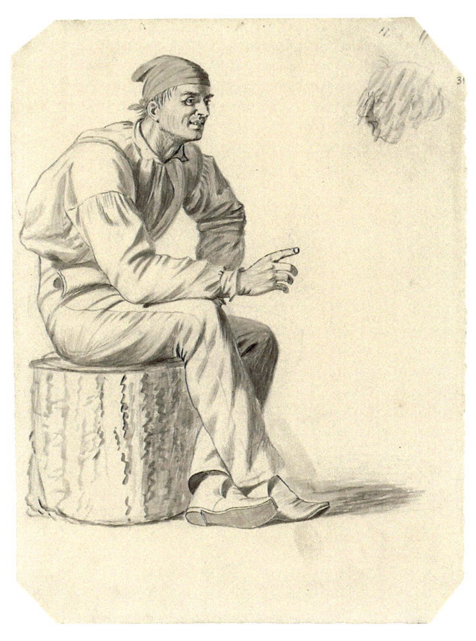

Plate 53: *Story-teller*, possible study for *Watching the Cargo by Night* (1854) with alterations and possible study for *Raftmen on the Ohio* (1849; lost)

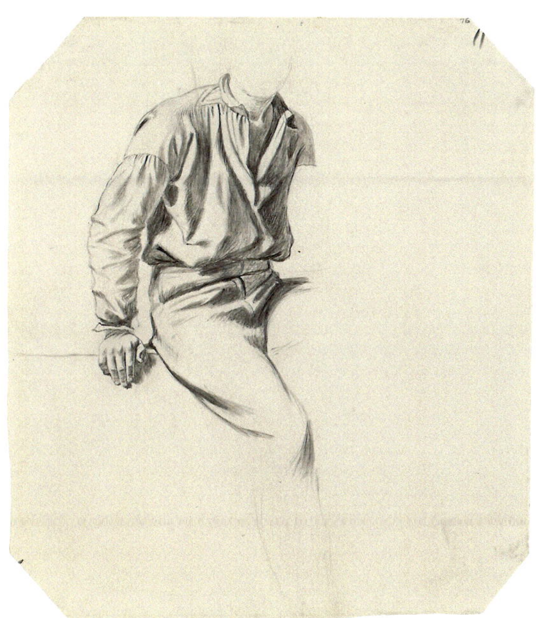

Plate 54: *Raftman*, for *Watching the Cargo by Night* (1854) with alterations

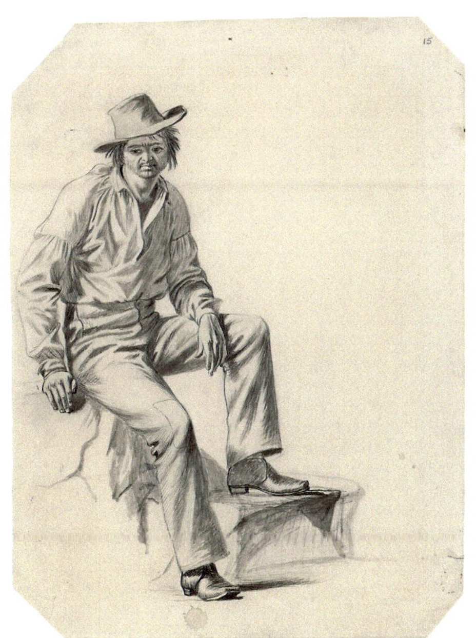

Plate 55: *Raftman*, for *Watching the Cargo by Night* (1854) with alterations and a possible study for *St. Louis Wharf* (1849; lost)

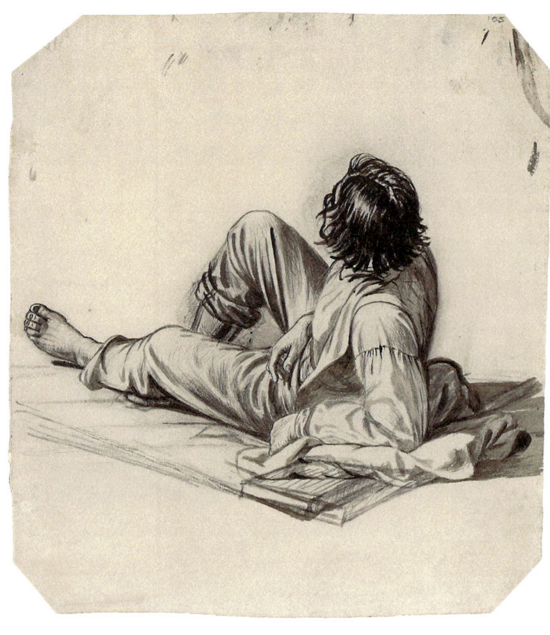

Plate 56: *Raftman*, (recto) for *Woodboatmen on a River (Western Boatmen Ashore by Night)* (1854) with alterations and possible study for *Raftmen on the Ohio* (1849; lost); (verso) for *Jolly Flatboatmen in Port* (1857) with alterations

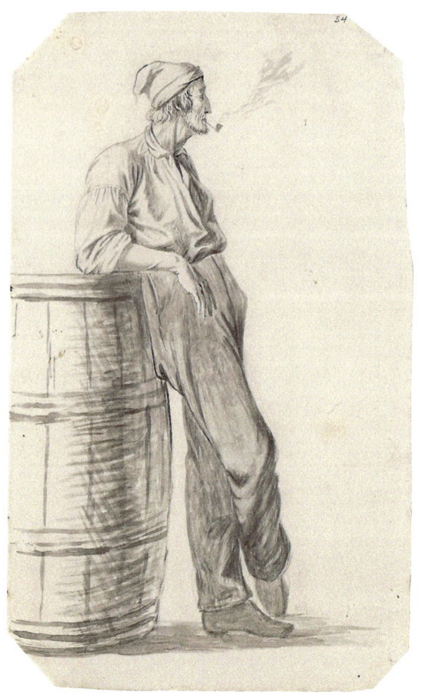

Plate 57: *Dockhand*, for *Jolly Flatboatmen in Port* (1857)

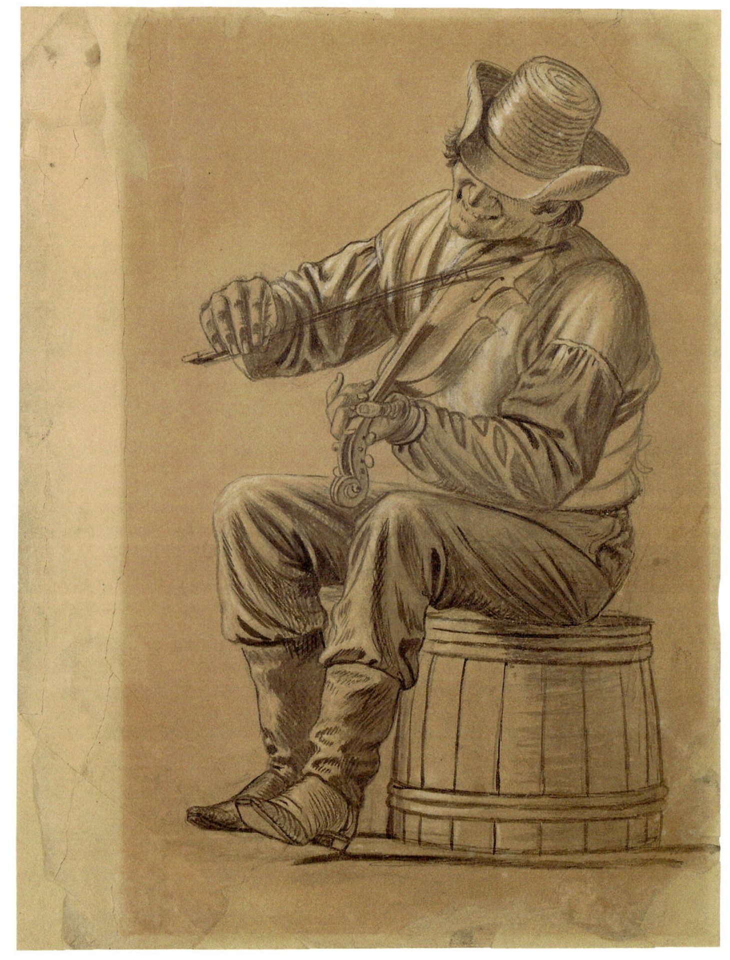

Plate 58: *Fiddler* (2), for *Jolly Flatboatmen in Port* (1857) and *The Jolly Flatboatmen* (1877–78) with alterations

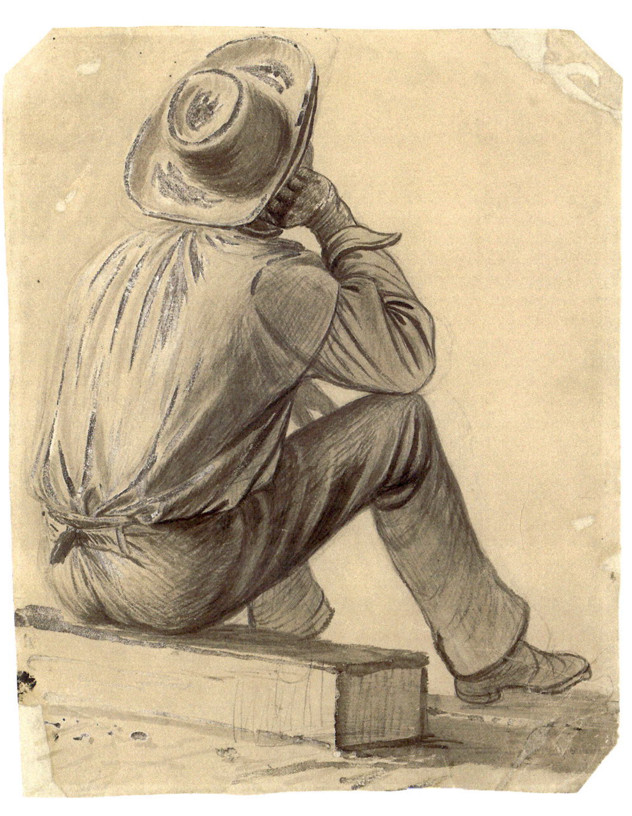

Plate 59: *Boatman*, for *Jolly Flatboatmen in Port* (1857)

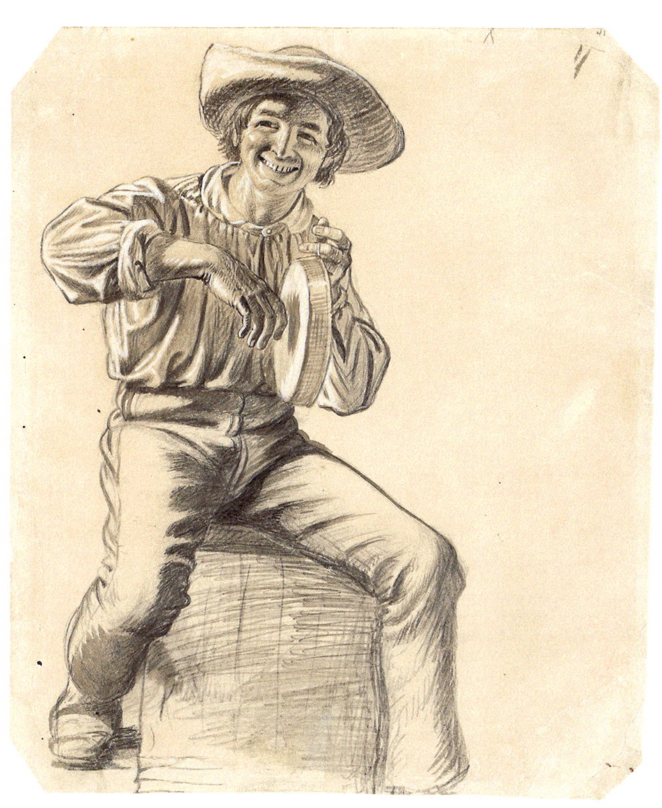

Plate 60: *Skillet-beater* (2), for *Jolly Flatboatmen in Port* (1857) and *The Jolly Flatboatmen* (1877–78) with alterations

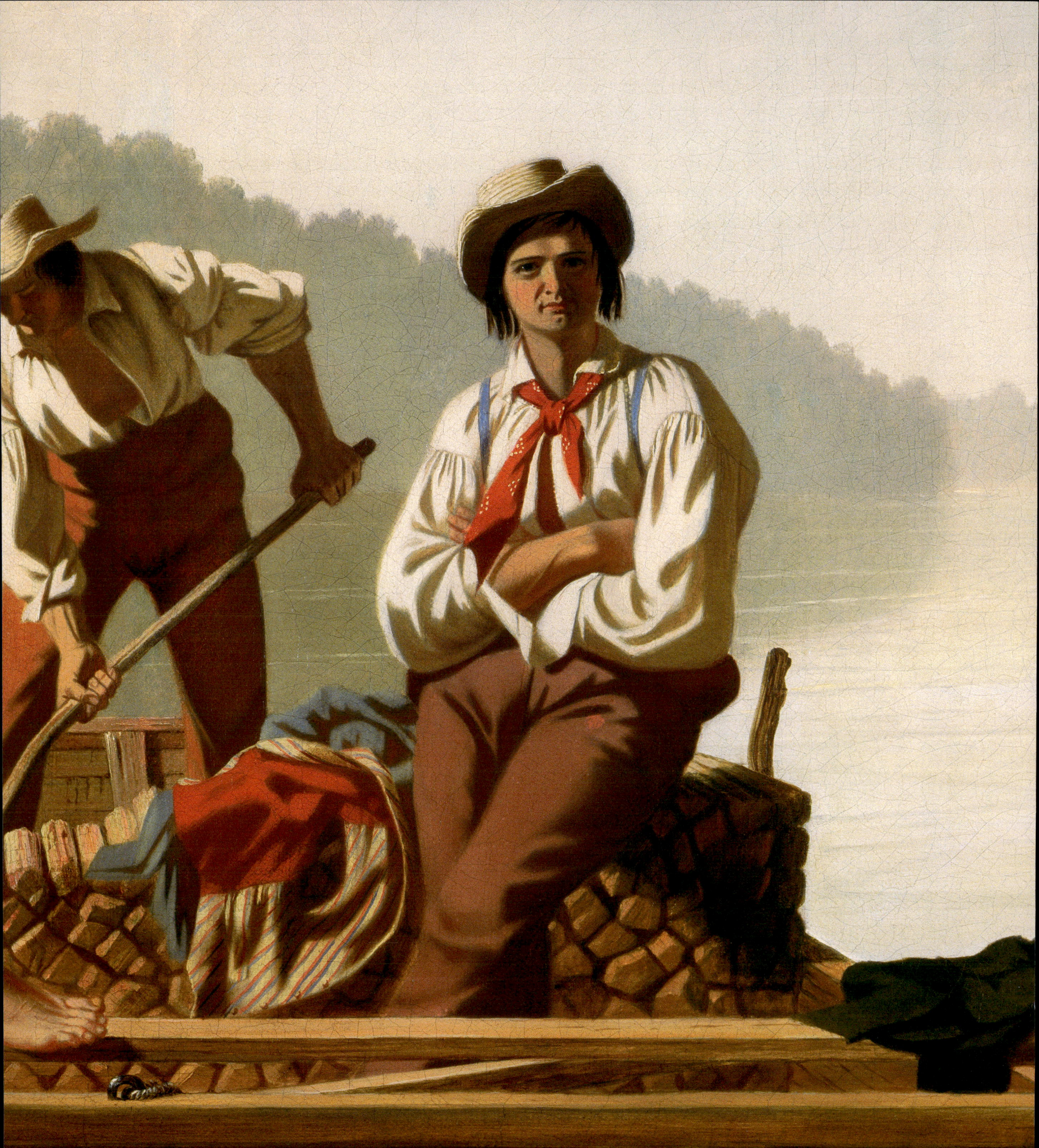

GEORGE CALEB BINGHAM

A Twentieth-Century Revival

ANDREW J. WALKER AND JANEEN TURK

It says much about George Caleb Bingham's legacy that in 1967—nearly ninety years after the artist's death—the Amon Carter Museum of American Art determined that it needed a Bingham river painting in its collection. Ruth Carter Stevenson, then the museum's board president, rued that by that time the museum "couldn't acquire anything like *The Jolly Flatboatmen*"[1] because Bingham's twentieth-century resurgence and acceptance into the canon of American art had long been under way. His river paintings, considered his masterpieces, had all found other homes.

Still, it was essential to have his work in the collection. Stevenson and her colleagues understood the larger picture—that the Missouri artist's creative output embodies "part of American history and the movement west"[2] and that a painting by Bingham, a regional artist whose work had become engrained in the nation's visual narrative, was a requisite touchstone of American collections. When the opportunity arose, the Amon Carter acquired Bingham's 1872 *View of Pike's Peak* (Fig. 98), one of his last paintings. It is not a river picture per se, but as Michael Shapiro has noted, "Although nearly a quarter-century had passed since Bingham painted his series of views of life along the Missouri and Mississippi rivers, even in this mountain scene he placed his lone hunter on the banks of a river."[3]

Boatmen on the Missouri (detail), 1846, Plate 4

1933: EARLY INSTITUTIONAL ACQUISITIONS

In the twentieth century, the meanings assigned to Bingham's river paintings were fluid and changeable, just as they had been in the nineteenth century, as Nenette Luarca-Shoaf has articulated earlier in these pages. As his river work was rediscovered and presented to new audiences, it was perceived differently and deployed to serve different agendas in Missouri and in New York. The artist's revival began in earnest in 1933, when Missouri became the site of a reintroduction of his work to a twentieth-century audience. In March of that year, it was announced that "one of the finest of Bingham's river scenes" had been purchased for the William Rockhill Nelson Gallery of Art (today the Nelson-Atkins Museum of Art) in Kansas City.[4] The painting, *Fishing on the Mississippi* (Pl. 43), had been in the eastern United States since at least 1851, when it was sold to the American Art-Union, an organization formed a decade earlier to patronize a wide range of art from across the country.[5] The Nelson Gallery brought the painting west to serve as part of its foundational collection, assembled in preparation for the institution's grand opening.

The following spring, the Metropolitan Museum of Art purchased another of Bingham's river paintings, *Fur Traders*

A version of this essay was originally given as a paper titled "'Engaging Specimens of Provincial Genre': George Caleb Bingham's River Paintings in Historical Perspective," by Andrew J. Walker in 2006, as the Harry and Doris Rubin Lecture in American Art at the Metropolitan Museum of Art, New York.

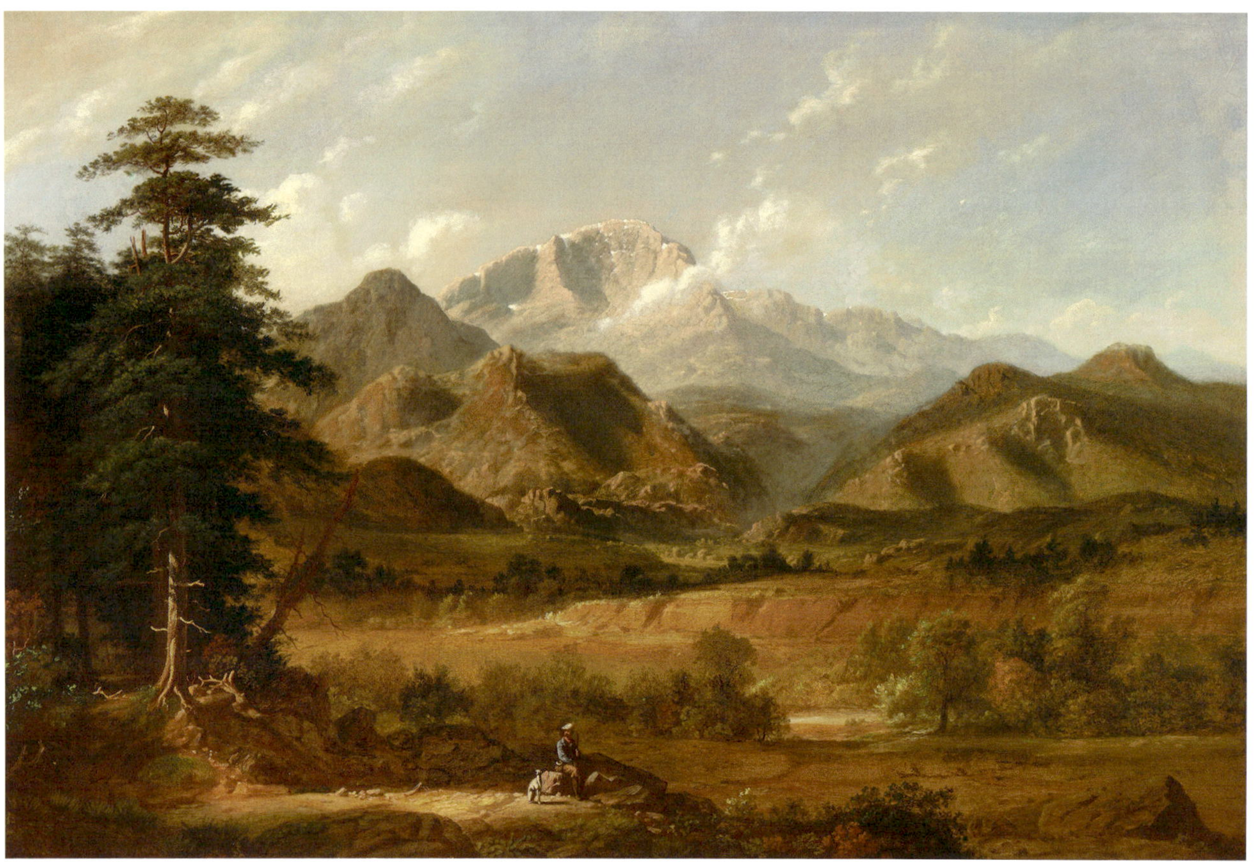

Fig. 98: George Caleb Bingham (1811–1879), *View of Pike's Peak*, 1872, oil on canvas, 28 × 42⅛ in., Amon Carter Museum of American Art, Fort Worth, Texas, 1967.27

Descending the Missouri (Pl. 3). Met curator Harry B. Wehle found the oil in a Madison Avenue antique shop. As he stated in his proposal to the acquisition committee, "Bingham's paintings of this type are rare, and present the clearest picture obtainable of Western frontier life prior to the Civil War."[6] The painting's value hinged not just on its technical accomplishment but on its documentary value. The article Wehle published in the museum's bulletin in 1933 clearly indicates that he regarded the painting as an authentic record by an artist who had lived among those "restless spirits" for whom "the wilderness with its dangers and its freedom became an incurable habit."[7] As further evidence of this authentic vision, Wehle tracked down and published Bingham's related drawing, *Fur trader* (Pl. 7), then in the collection of the Mercantile Library in Saint Louis.

Fur Traders Descending the Missouri filled a critical gap in the history of American painting then under construction at the Met. As one of the earliest paintings that Bingham sent to New York City for display, the work seemed especially appropriate for the nation's great museum as it built a representative collection of American art. The painting was one of Bingham's first submissions to the AA-U, and Wehle remarked on this in his article about the acquisition.[8] Wehle associated *Fur Traders Descending the Missouri* with contemporary American Scene painting and fit the work into the Met's narrative of American art history. He accomplished both of these ends by comparing the painting's visual qualities with the style of another, more widely known nineteenth-century artist considered to be a forerunner of the American Scene movement:[9]

> *Relieved against the hazy trees and the smooth surface of the river these personalities are sharply vitalized, and the artist's means prove adequate to make refreshing and worth while his simple endeavor to show his spectator what he saw before him. For instinctive sense of form and vivid naturalism the nearest parallel to this work is seen perhaps in the early paintings of Winslow Homer.*[10]

According to a piece in the *Art Digest*, the Met's purchase brought Bingham's work "considerable attention nationally,"[11] proving to be both a watershed moment for Bingham's revival and the momentous event that ushered him into the canon.[12] Of course, the import of the Met's purchase did not go unnoticed in Missouri, where it was rather snidely presented as proof of the good judgment of a Kansas City institution. "The belated action of the Metropolitan Museum in acquiring one of the few Bingham paintings of this period," gallerist J. H. Bender observed, "justifies the purchase made by the Trustees of the Nelson Gallery nearly a year ago."[13] Indeed, while the Met initiated a national renewal of interest in Bingham, the more sustained advancement of his work would take place in his home state of Missouri, where the artist's regional origins and subjects had greatest importance.

1934–35: ANCESTOR OF THE AMERICAN SCENE

Mirroring the pattern of his lifetime reputation, in the twentieth century Bingham's work was first appreciated in Missouri, then publicized through the Met's acquisition in the East. This geographic circulation continued with the first major show of Bingham's work in decades, held in Saint Louis in 1934. There, viewers followed the eastern pattern of connecting the artist's work to that of contemporary American Scene painters. But for Saint Louisans, the exhibition and appreciation of Bingham's art were also inflected by their city's location at the confluence of the rivers that had served as the settings for some of the artist's most successful work.

Bingham's first major retrospective, *Paintings and Color Prints by George Caleb Bingham* (March 15–April 15, 1934), was held at the City Art Museum of Saint Louis (today the Saint Louis Art Museum) and coincided with an ambitious riverfront development. Like many cities at this time, Saint Louis was enmeshed in elaborate programs for urban renewal. Planners feared that the flight of industries and population away from cities to their suburbs would cause the death of urban centers. They also increasingly perceived that as economies changed, a vital downtown could provide a center for cultural and community activities. In Saint Louis, these concerns influenced major land redevelopment initiatives that attempted to balance the city's future prospects—as a national leader in commerce and industry—with its historical identity.[14] The most important of these efforts centered on the city's waterfront, bringing pride of place to the Mississippi River. In 1934, the same year as the exhibition, the city set upon a plan to clear thirty-seven blocks of Saint Louis's waterfront district. This clearance was intended to make land available to build a major federal monument: the Jefferson National Expansion Memorial (Fig. 99). The monument would commemorate the nation's westward development since the Louisiana Purchase, Thomas Jefferson's great real-estate deal of 1803, and, the planners hoped, reimagine the Mississippi waterfront as a site of cultural heritage. Amid this broad-ranging marriage of past and future along the river in Saint Louis, Bingham received his most forceful study to that date.[15]

For City Art Museum director Meyric Rogers, the river paintings were indispensable to the validation of the artist's

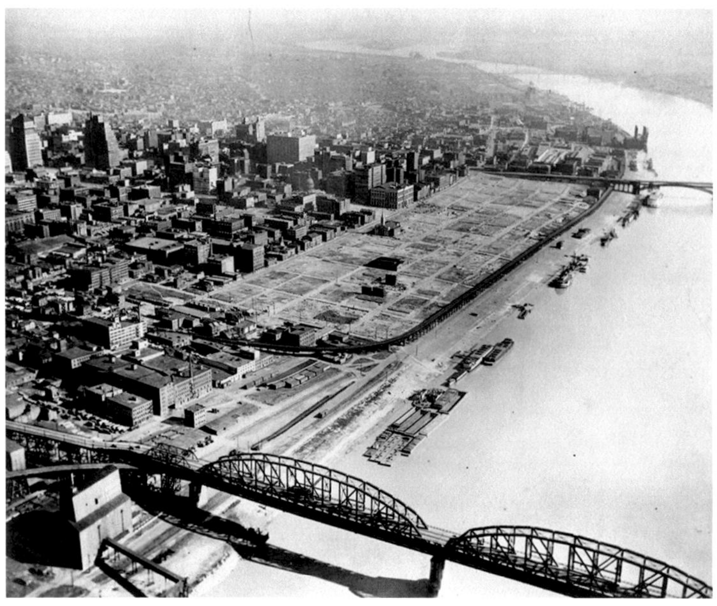

Fig. 99: The Saint Louis riverfront after demolition of warehouses, ca. 1942, Jefferson National Expansion Memorial Archives, V106-4838

merit. As he planned his exhibition checklist, Rogers focused not on Bingham's numerous portraits of local notables but rather on his genre subjects, rehabilitating the aspect of Bingham's oeuvre that had attracted particular recognition in his lifetime.[16] In the museum bulletin that doubled as the exhibition catalogue, Rogers categorized the genre paintings as the artist's "most important contributions sociologically and also artistically."[17] The river paintings made up more than half the number of genre paintings exhibited in the show. A later newspaper article followed Rogers's lead, valuing one of the river scenes as "typical of many of Bingham's best pictures."[18]

For Rogers, a concentration on life along the Mississippi would show Bingham at his artistic epitome and promote the state's contribution to the art history of the nation.[19] Even as Rogers pursued loans for the show, he explained his plan as decisively regional and of national importance. He wrote to the owner of *The Jolly Flatboatmen* (1877–78; Pl. 48), "We feel [the exhibition] will be very significant for a general revival of interest in Bingham's work and an emphasis on one of Missouri's significant contributions to the artistic history of the country."[20] The press took note of this boosterism for a local artist, and the *Art Digest* declared, "Missouri is proud of her American 'old master.'"[21]

The exhibition was a resounding success. Attendance was high, and the response was positive.[22] Marquis Childs, art critic for the *Saint Louis Post-Dispatch*, wrote a review that announced the return of Bingham in exactly the terms Rogers had hoped for. "Bingham, a Missouri painter with an unfailing eye for the teeming life around him," Childs wrote, "has at last won unqualified recognition."[23] Childs also wrote about Bingham's oeuvre in terms of its relevance to contemporary art, an approach that would further establish the artist's legacy. "The revival of interest in Bingham is in part evidence of what many critics regard as a radical shift in style and taste back in the direction of representation and narrative values," the critic noted.[24] Childs referred in his review to American Scene painting, a then-contemporary movement distinguished by realism and narrative as values of a strongly felt, if debated, American tradition. In Saint Louis, discussing Bingham's work from this perspective was a hopeful step toward confirming the artist's status in the broader history of American art.

Much to Rogers's satisfaction, Childs's prescient review was circulated to a wider audience when the *American Magazine of Art* picked it up as part of a series intended to chart the progress of American art.[25] Childs's article was not the only example of the Saint Louis press casting Bingham as a precursor of American Scene painting. A later column in the *Post-Dispatch* declared,

> *Bingham painted the Western American scene. . . . As a pioneer in the pictorial recording of our social history, he plowed virgin soil now being tilled scientifically by such well-known moderns as Grant Wood of Iowa and John Steuart Curry of Kansas.*[26]

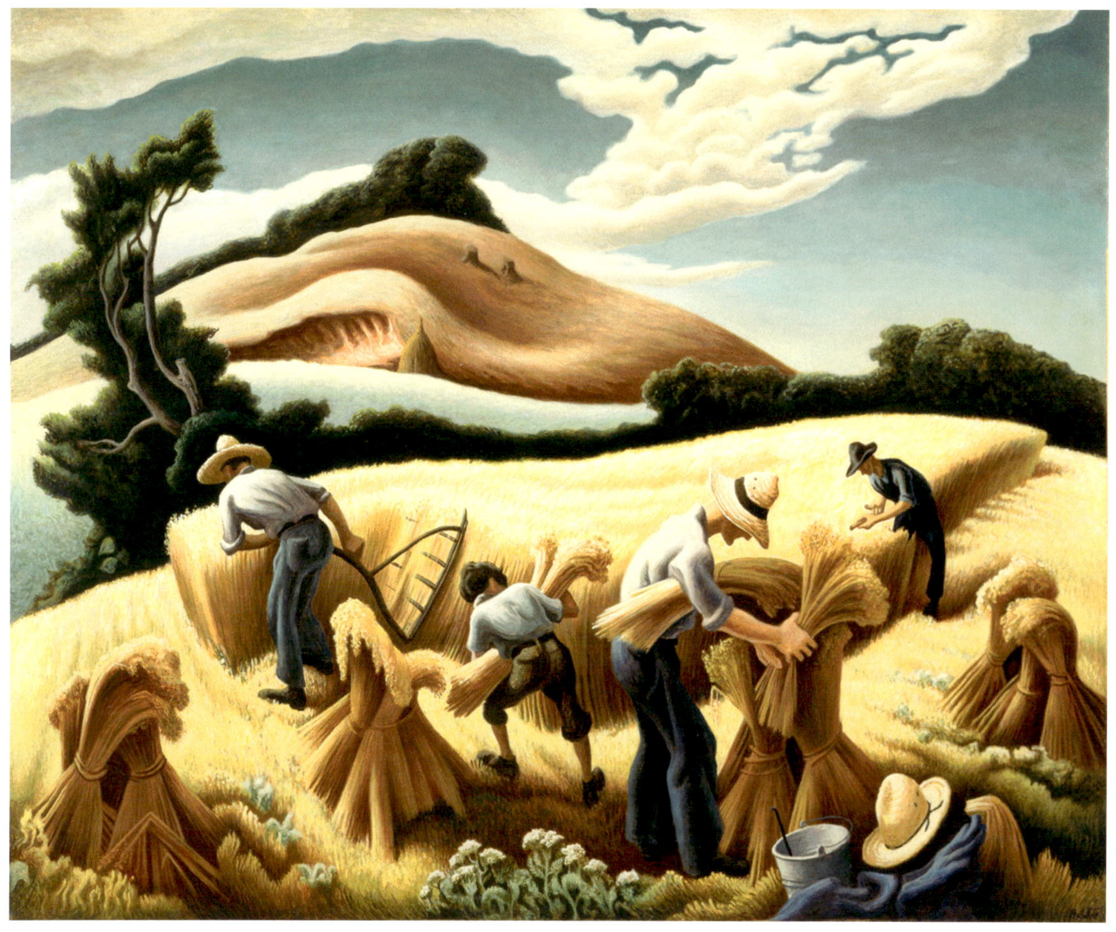

Fig. 100: Thomas Hart Benton (1889–1975), *Cradling Wheat*, 1938, tempera and oil on board, 31¼ × 39¼ in., Saint Louis Art Museum, Museum Purchase, 8:1939, © T. H. Benton and R. P. Benton Testamentary Trusts / UMB Bank Trustee / Licensed by VAGA, New York, NY

An article in the *Saint Louis Star* articulated more plainly the potential of such associations to propel Bingham to greater celebrity: "Bingham's fate as a great figure depends upon the heights to which the painters of the 'American scene' soar. . . . It will only be as a forerunner that he can arrive at a high station. . . . [The 'American scene' movement] may make George Caleb Bingham a great Missourian and a great American."[27]

The City Art Museum's acquisition strategies reflected this same link between Bingham's work and twentieth-century American Scene painting. Over the next few years, while curators at the Saint Louis museum were purchasing paintings like *Cradling Wheat* (Fig. 100) by Thomas Hart Benton (1889–1975) and *The Mississippi* (1935) by John Steuart Curry (1897–1946), they were also acquiring Bingham river scenes such as *Raftsmen Playing Cards* (Pl. 26) and *Jolly Flatboatmen in Port* (Pl. 47). Like *Raftsmen Playing Cards*, Benton's *Cradling Wheat* features a small group of regional laborers, individuals at work in the environment in which they live. With the acquisition of *Raftsmen*, Meyric Rogers cemented the City Art Museum's commitment to Bingham. During the loan negotiations for the work with the Berkshire Museum in Pittsfield, Massachusetts, he had discovered that the Berkshire might be willing to part with the painting. Laura Bragg, the museum's director, believed that the work was better suited for the Saint Louis institution and agreed to a sale for $1,500.[28] This acquisition of a major painting by the artist—the first for the Saint Louis collection—built

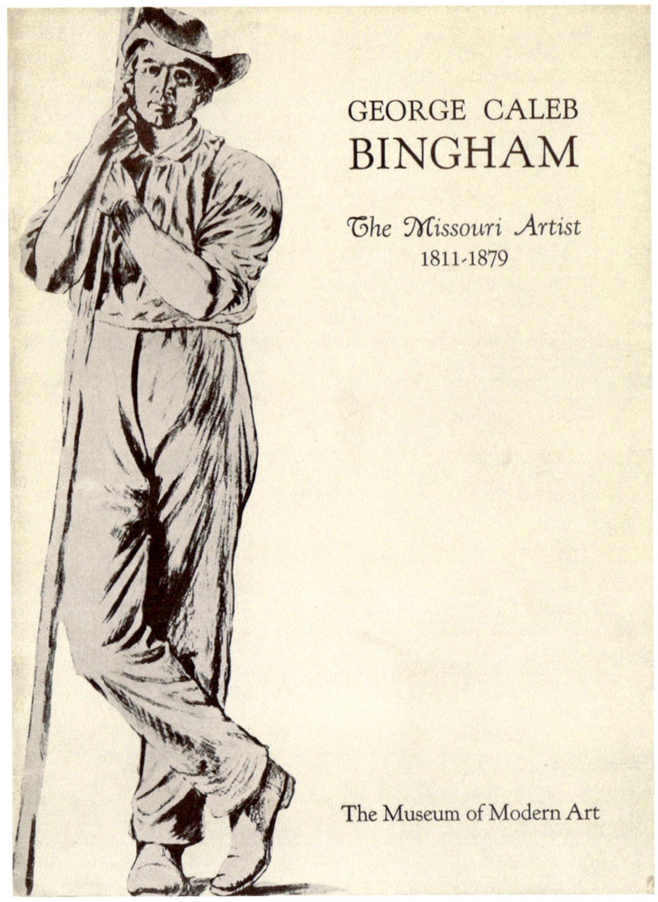

Fig. 101: Catalogue cover: *George Caleb Bingham: The Missouri Artist, 1811–1879*, New York: The Museum of Modern Art, 1935 (New York: W. E. Rudge's Sons)

on enthusiasm for the Bingham exhibition.[29] Thus, a painting portraying western river life, one that Bingham had sent east in 1847, circled back to the artist's home state in 1934.

Shortly before the opening of the Bingham exhibition in Saint Louis, Alfred H. Barr Jr., director of the Museum of Modern Art in New York City, wrote Rogers to congratulate him on the project.[30] Rogers replied, "My own enthusiasm for Bingham has much increased as a result of the work on the show and I feel very decidedly that he deserves much more recognition than has heretofore been accorded him. He is really a very important figure in the history of American painting."[31] Barr was willing to assist in garnering further acclaim for Bingham, and when the Met declined to serve as a New York venue, he volunteered MoMA as an alternative, pending the endorsement of his trustees. While Barr indicated that the show would be an unusual one for them, saying, "It is rather too near the middle of the nineteenth century for our Museum,"[32] the trustees must have been supportive. MoMA took the show, *George Caleb Bingham: The Missouri Artist, 1811–1879* (January 30–March 7, 1935), and published a catalogue featuring one of the artist's preparatory drawings on the cover (Pl. 40; Fig. 101).

It is both ironic and prophetic that Bingham's work would appeal to the arbiters of one of the most progressive art institutions in the country.[33] As Rogers set to work securing the extension of the loans, he highlighted the additional venue as an opportunity to bring more attention to Bingham, drawing a comparison to the artist's nineteenth-century New York exhibitions. "Mr. Barr," he explained to one lender, "has been fired with enthusiasm for Bingham and is planning to stage an exhibition of his works in New York next October. . . . This looks as though our efforts with the Saint Louis exhibition have met with the publicity success desired. . . . It would certainly put Bingham on the Eastern map as he has not been since the days of the American Art Association [*sic*]."[34] As in 1845, so in 1934: reputation building flowed east. Rogers's comment also credited the persistent influence of New York's cultural infrastructure in validating, even defining, the contours of a national art history.[35]

Barr was at this time in the midst of developing a complex schematic of the evolution of abstract art that would define for at least a generation the ascendancy of a formal modernism. Showing Bingham in the galleries of MoMA stretched the mission of the institution, but it also tidily achieved two institutional ends. It allowed Barr to address the current interest in American Scene painting and to integrate historical American painting into his construction of an account of the development of western art.[36]

Like Marquis Childs's review of the Saint Louis venue, the foreword in MoMA's catalogue connects Bingham to the growing American Scene movement, recognizing him as a forerunner of that trend: "A full generation before Homer and Eakins, [Bingham] painted the 'American Scene,' making a vivid record of life in the Mississippi Valley."[37] The museum's press release includes the same theme: "[Bingham's] pictures of life on the Mississippi . . . anticipate the present-day interest in the American scene as a subject for art."[38] Reviewers also responded to this take on Bingham's revival. "The Bingham exhibition belongs to the series which illustrates the influences upon or the ancestors of significant movements in contemporary art,"[39] one explained. "[It] is appropriate at this moment because of the present preoccupation on the part of a large group of American painters with the 'American scene.'"[40]

1949: BINGHAM'S RIVER PICTURES IN CONTEXT

Although postwar abstraction was ascending to a place of dominance on the American art scene in the late 1940s, Bingham's river works were again placed at the center of a national narrative in 1949 when the City Art Museum organized a massive exhibition of visual culture surrounding the Mississippi River. The prevailing aesthetic national debate may have been about abstraction, but the legacy and celebration of the regional were still strong.

The brainchild of dynamic and industrious director Perry Rathbone, *Mississippi Panorama* (October 10–November 27, 1949) encompassed nineteenth-century depictions of life in the Mississippi River Valley, a rubric that included the Missouri and the Mississippi rivers, just as it had in the previous century. The exhibition and its attendant catalogue addressed the centrality of the rivers to the history of both the region and the nation, and Bingham's river paintings were crucial to conveying that context. In Rathbone's view, "the idea of the exhibition . . . was suggested, almost inevitably, by the paintings of river boat life by George Caleb Bingham."[41] He went so far as to identify Bingham as "the central artistic personality of the show."[42] Perhaps most important, Bingham's work in the exhibition presented the historical commercial significance of the region; his river paintings were part of a medley of visual culture that promoted the material success enjoyed by the city and region in the past. Twentieth-century urban development once again supplied a context for his pictures, coupling the artist's representations of a lively and profitably engaged river with the present and future of the city's waterfront.

Unsurprisingly, associations with regional boosterism emerged when Bingham's work was shown as part of *Mississippi Panorama*.[43] Literature surrounding the exhibition addressed the role of the Mississippi and Missouri rivers in nineteenth-century trade and the related prominence of Saint Louis in this context. Rathbone characterized the Mississippi as a "teeming avenue of commerce and travel" and attributed the "pre-eminence of the city . . . to its advantageous location at the confluence of the two great streams."[44] A brochure commemorating the exhibition labels Saint Louis "The Hub of River Trade."[45] Bingham's work furthered this perception of the region. The nineteenth-century relationship of his pictures to a regional context, to commerce, and to trade between the eastern and the western United States has been well established in recent scholarship, and this would have been appreciated in 1940s Saint Louis.[46]

Although many aspects of river life were represented in the exhibition, an ample contingent of images provided a context of economic energy and viability for Bingham's scenes of river life. The arts writer for the *Saint Louis Post-Dispatch* observed that some might even see the rest of the exhibition checklist as merely "a setting for the consummate artistry of the genre pictures of Bingham."[47] Works such as Hippolyte Sebron's *Giant*

Steamboats at New Orleans (Fig. 102) and William Aiken Walker's *The Levee—New Orleans* (1883) show steamboats at dock with a wealth of goods on shore ready for transport or delivery—barrels, lumber, cotton bales, furs, and sundry sacks and bundles aptly convey the flourishing trade along the Mississippi. The nineteenth-century texts paired with the catalogue illustrations furthered this concept. A quote accompanying a rafting scene describes "the moving picture of life on board the boats . . . the numerous animals, large and small, which they carry, their different loads, the evidence of the increasing agriculture of the country above, and more than all, the immense distances which they . . . will have to go," underscoring the idea that the goods the riverboats carried were a sign of the abundance of the region and that a national market awaited.[48] Together, images and historical quotes place Bingham's scenes of river workers in a setting that captures the excitement and economic vibrancy of years gone by.

The implications of a celebration of the region's nineteenth-century importance for its rank in the twentieth century and beyond were also evident in the audience response to the show. A writer for the *Saint Louis Globe-Democrat* argued that the exhibit "goes to the roots of what we are by showing what we have been. And if it looks behind, it points ahead."[49] The conjoining of the high standing of the region in the past and in the present was also marked by additional developments with the plans for the riverfront.

Ultimately, over the course of the 1940s, business leaders and city planners expanded their objective for the riverfront development to encompass a modernist cultural project to boost metropolitan growth and attract new business to the city. In 1948, during the planning of the exhibition, the Jefferson National Expansion Memorial committee selected Eero Saarinen's design for the memorial's major monument. An enthusiastic reader of the exhibition catalogue recognized the relationship between the efforts to reshape the riverfront and the City Art Museum's project, writing, "I believe the results of this Exhibit of River paintings, drawings, prints . . . and steamboat appurtenances will go a long ways in stimulating interest in the proposed Jefferson National Museum on the Mississippi River Water Front."[50] The City Art Museum was well aware of the plans for the riverfront and had demonstrated support for the project by exhibiting a large model of the Saint Louis Gateway Arch and "the entire riverfront memorial site" the previous year.[51] Thus, a vision of the river's glorious past, embodied in the works of Bingham and his contemporaries, followed a display devoted to its promising future.

1954: BINGHAM AND MANIFEST DESTINY

In 1954, Bingham's river works were displayed at the City Art Museum in another innovative show. While the exhibition furthered the theme of regional boosterism envisioned in the 1949 show, it shifted the meaning of Bingham's work to more directly support the celebration of a distinctly national ethos: Manifest Destiny.

Westward the Way (October 23–December 6, 1954) marked the sesquicentennial of the Louisiana Purchase through more than 350 works of art across a broad spectrum of media: paintings, lithographs, watercolors, and ephemera, all dating from about 1803 to 1903. In this exhibition, Bingham's work was deployed to advance the notion of Saint Louis as a gateway from the East to the West and as a critical locale in the narrative of postwar national growth. The *Saint Louis Globe-Democrat* praised the show and referenced the Louisiana Purchase as an enterprise in which "Saint Louis had so proud a part," and another article reiterated the city's identity as "gateway to the new country."[52] While the Mississippi had been the focus of the 1949 exhibition, in 1954 the river's liminal position as the border of the Louisiana Purchase, boundary between East and West, was emphasized.[53] With *Westward the Way*, examples of Bingham's river scenes were integrated into an exhibition that promoted not only the commercial success and importance of

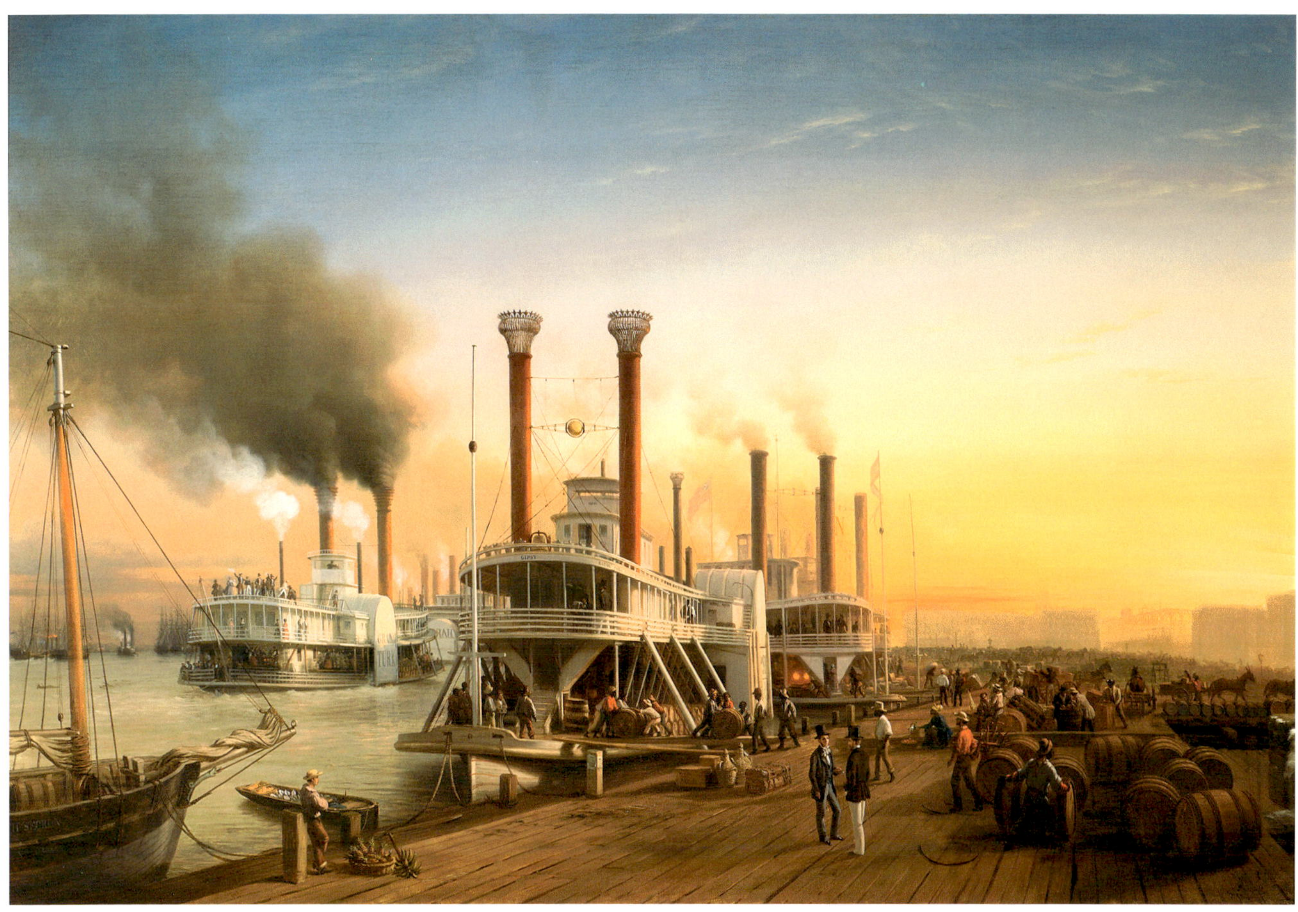

Fig. 102: Hippolyte Sebron (1801–1879), *Giant Steamboats at New Orleans*, 1853, oil on canvas, 48 × 72 in., Newcomb Art Gallery, Tulane University, New Orleans, Gift of D. H. Holmes Company, New Orleans. Photograph by Owen Murphy

the Mississippi River and the city of Saint Louis but also their national role in westward settlement and expansion.

Bingham was again understood as "technically and esthetically, a leading figure in the show."[54] The power of his river work to signify Saint Louis's historical success had been evidenced in 1933, when *Fur Traders Descending the Missouri* (Pl. 3) evoked for an East Coast audience not only the Louisiana Purchase and commerce but also the significance of Saint Louis in America's nationhood. When the painting was acquired, Harry Wehle wrote that "when . . . the Louisiana Purchase had been consummated, Saint Louis was becoming a large and prosperous town, the center of the vast fur trade."[55] But beyond advertising the prosperity of Saint Louis and the river region, *Westward the Way* sought to present an unambiguously laudatory retelling of Manifest Destiny that underscored the role of the city.

Saint Louis also intended to celebrate the sesquicentennial of the Louisiana Purchase and the region's future with a lavish Festival of Progress. The cover for the festival's promotional brochure combined the nineteenth and twentieth centuries in a logo design pairing a watercraft of Bingham's era with the atom, perhaps the most potent symbol of modern life

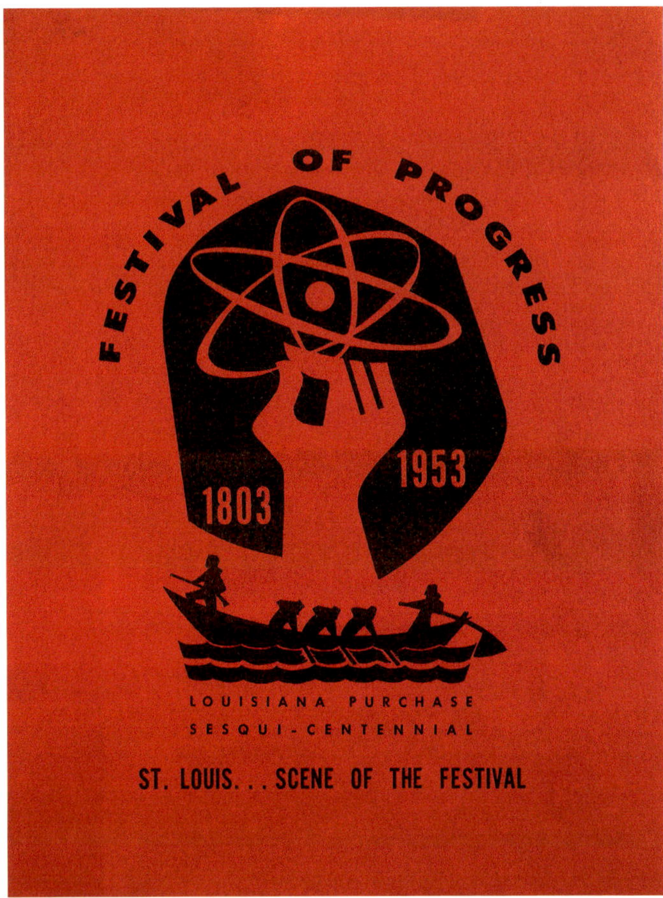

Fig. 103: Festival of Progress brochure, cover and page 1; Director's Office, Special Exhibition Correspondence, box 45, file 13, Saint Louis Art Museum Archives, Saint Louis, Missouri

(Fig. 103). The importance of Saint Louis for the Louisiana Purchase, and therefore westward expansion, allowed for the imagining of the city's bright prospects.

The Jefferson National Expansion Memorial neatly complemented both the planned festival and the exhibition. In his 1953 article "Celebrating 150 Years of the Louisiana Purchase," historian Bernard De Voto referenced the Gateway Arch and waxed poetic about Saint Louis, the city through which "the American people streamed westward to occupy, settle and develop the vastness that had been called Louisiana," and emphasized the importance of its location near "the meeting of the Missouri and Mississippi."[56] He credited the Louisiana Purchase with having "created Manifest Destiny," and he saw the arch as the result of a search for "a monument . . . that would best symbolize [Saint Louis's] past, present, and future."[57] Indeed, as Joseph Heathcott and Márie Agnes Murphy have written, the building of Saarinen's Arch offered "local leaders" and city planners an opportunity "to link the ideals embedded in the city's romanticized American past with the preeminent symbol of its imagined future"[58] (Fig. 104). Like *Westward the Way*, the Arch celebrated the function of Saint Louis in Bingham's day as Gateway to the West, even as its sleek form advertised the forward-looking modernity of the city.

Rathbone underlined the national import of Manifest Destiny in the catalogue for *Westward the Way*, declaring that "the history of the United States has been in large part the history of the westward migration of the American people from the Atlantic to the Pacific," adding that "the annexation of Louisiana gave the drive to the West by far its greatest impulse."[59] He characterized this process as "the subjugation of the West."[60] A commitment to Manifest Destiny as an organizing principle was reflected in the arrangement of the exhibition and the catalogue into sections—the Land, the Indian, the Birds and Animals, the White Man, the Settlements, and Westward by Land and by Water—that together constituted the elements of the story of westward expansion. Bingham's works cut across the exhibition, represented in the Land, the Indian, and the White Man sections.

The Indian section included Bingham's *The Concealed Enemy* (Pl. 2). The painting had never before been reproduced, and it was highlighted both in the press and in the exhibition catalogue, where it served as the lead image for the section. Rathbone described the painting as the only known instance of "Bingham [relaxing] his interest in landscape, Missouri politics and the life of the boatmen to paint a purely Indian subject . . . representing an Osage brave in ambush."[61] As in 1949, excerpts from nineteenth-century texts accompanied each checklist illustration. A number of these passages detailed the perceived desirability of the demise of Native American cultures and the spread of white civilization. For example, in the Indian section, a telling quote from George Frederick Ruxton read "The savage Indian skulked through the woods and prairies, lord of the unappreciated soil which now yields its prolific treasures to the spade and plough of civilised man."[62]

In the White Man section, the most widely publicized of the eight Bingham paintings displayed was the newly discovered *The Jolly Flatboatmen* (1846; Pl. 5). The picture embodied what Rathbone referred to as "the boatmen's harum-scarum life on the rivers of the West" and the experience "of the white men in . . . the great new world of the Louisiana Territory."[63] In the accompanying catalogue, Rathbone credited *The Jolly Flatboatmen* for making Bingham famous and granting him a "sudden reputation."[64] Although the painting was lost for many years, the composition was well known because of the thousands of prints published by the American Art-Union. Rathbone himself had encountered the image many times in his grandmother's home in Greene, New York. His great-grandfather had been an honorary secretary of the AA-U, one of the network of regional ambassadors (described by Luarca-Shoaf) who effected the circulation of Bingham's work throughout the country; he had apparently acquired the print as a benefit of his own membership.[65] After 1954, the painting was lost no longer. Rathbone located it in a Washington, D.C., collection and heralded its discovery as a special offering of the exhibition.[66]

The exhibition organizers had hoped to borrow another painting for the White Man section from a private collection in Texas, a work that only recently had left the holdings of Washington University in Saint Louis. For them, Frederic Remington's *A Dash for the Timber* (Fig. 105) captured the drama of the frontier and perfectly rendered an encounter of eight white men in the West "struggling against huge odds,"[67] in this case a larger group of Native Americans. Rathbone's

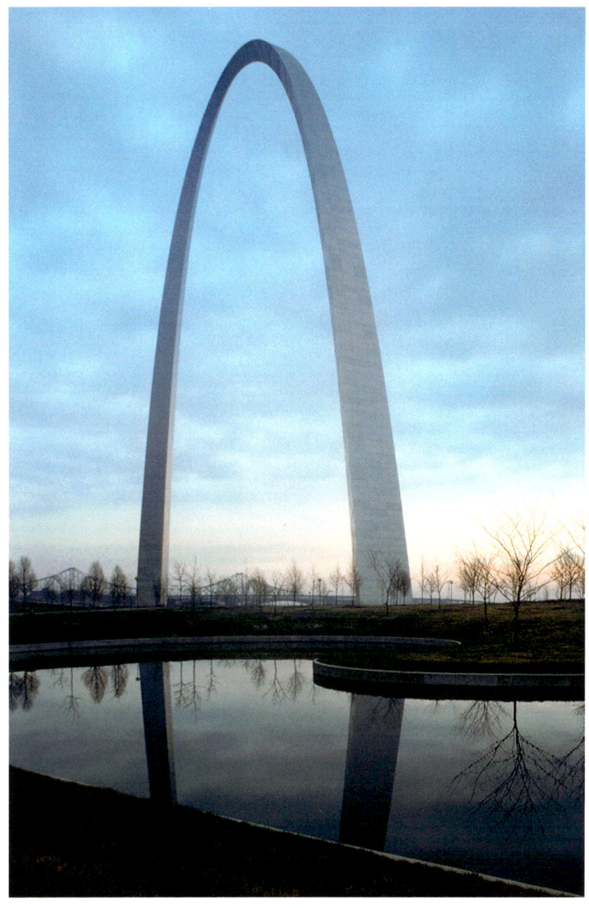

Fig. 104: Saint Louis Gateway Arch (originally Jefferson National Expansion Memorial), Saint Louis, Missouri, 1947–65, dedicated 1968. Photograph by Balthazar Korab. The Balthazar Korab Archive, Library of Congress Prints and Photographs Division, Washington, D.C.

assistant, William N. Eisendrath Jr., learned that the work belonged to Amon G. Carter (1879–1955). Eisendrath wrote repeatedly asking to borrow the work, even enlisting a contact at another museum to assist him in putting forward the request. He could receive no satisfaction on this account, however, other than a letter from the collector's secretary informing him that it was "Mr. Carter's purpose to construct a museum to house his Western art items and until such time he

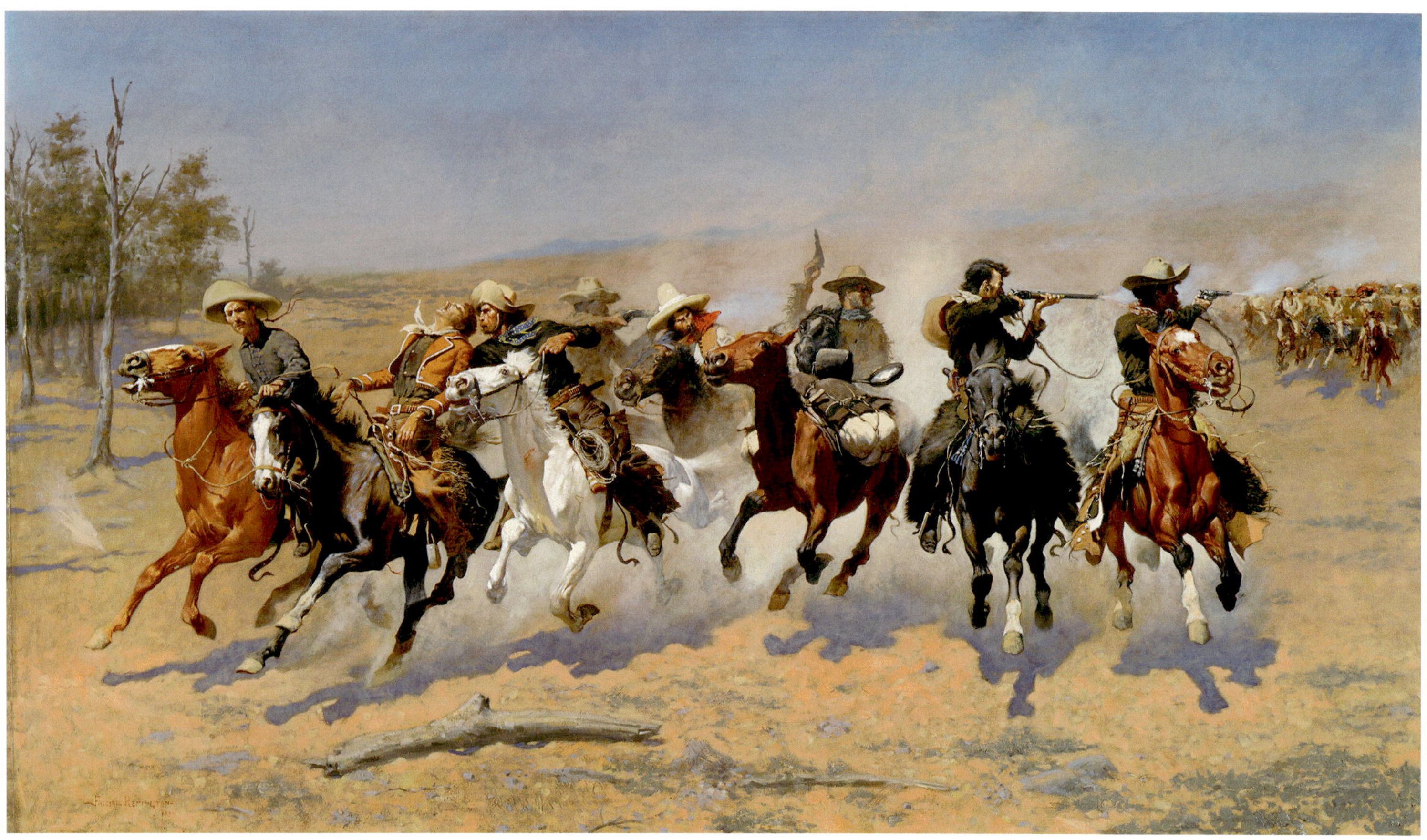

Fig. 105: Frederic S. Remington (1861–1909), *A Dash for the Timber,* 1889, oil on canvas, 48¼ × 84⅛ in., Amon Carter Museum of American Art, Fort Worth, Texas, 1961.381

. . . does not wish to have them exhibited."[68] Of course, Carter's museum would be realized in 1961 and thrive over the following decades to one day partner on Bingham's work with the very institution that Rathbone had once directed.

CONCLUSION

Bingham's twentieth-century revival alternated between West and East. In 1933, the Nelson Gallery in Kansas City initiated his home-state resurgence by announcing the acquisition of *Fishing on the Mississippi* (Pl. 43), which had been back East for more than eighty years. Later that year, the Metropolitan Museum of Art purchased the artist's masterpiece *Fur Traders Descending the Missouri* (Pl. 3). The following year, the City Art Museum in Saint Louis mounted the first major retrospective of Bingham's work. That exhibition then traveled to New York City, where it dazzled audiences at the Museum of Modern Art and earned the artist the distinction of being a key predecessor of the American Scene "a full generation before Homer and Eakins."[69]

In those early years of rediscovery, Bingham's interest in Missouri—and the raftsmen, farmers, and politicians who lived there—certainly made him the forerunner to such artists as Thomas Hart Benton, Joe Jones (1909–1963), Grant Wood (1891–1942), and others whose identities are inextricably linked to a particular place and its people. At a time of complex conversations about modernism, Bingham brought historic legitimacy to these artists attempting to establish a distinctive American pictorial language that was patriotic, social, and often political. Civic engagement flowed beneath Bingham's subjects, as it did with the subjects of his contemporaries.

In the 1930s and the decades that followed, Bingham's paintings of western river life would reclaim the flexibility of meaning that had distinguished them during his lifetime. Missouri had a history of being on the line between the American East and West, and cultural leaders there recognized Bingham's value to the history of the region in a manner that stretched beyond current aesthetic debate. While never losing their significance as accomplished works of art, Bingham's depictions of the river were engaged to advance a shifting sequence of narratives about the magnitude of the region in a national context, so that it emerged as a key player in various aspects of the nation's past and, by implication, its future.

The single venue projects in both 1949 and 1954 at the City Art Museum presented Bingham as a central figure in the nation's irresistible ethos of Manifest Destiny. Against a panorama of material culture, George Caleb Bingham may have been the "central artistic personality," to echo Rathbone, in this story of the region's impact on the nation's history, but his singular artistic achievement took a backseat to the larger historical narrative. Such a shift, as with any revival, responds to the pressures of the historical moment. Bingham's rediscovery turned not only on an artistic achievement that was seen as authentically rooted in a distinct place but also on an approach that served the goals of his twentieth-century advocates: a reverence for that place and the people who lived there.

NOTES

1. Ruth Carter Stevenson, "Oral History, Addenda 4, Acquisitions," Amon Carter Museum of American Art Archives, 199.

2. Ibid.

3. Michael Edward Shapiro, "The River Paintings," in *George Caleb Bingham* (New York: Henry N. Abrams in association with the National Museum of American Art, Smithsonian Institution, 1993), 135.

4. "In Gallery and Studio," *Kansas City Star*, March 18, 1933, 4.

5. For the work's provenance, see Margaret C. Conrads, *The Collections of the Nelson-Atkins Museum of Art: American Paintings to 1945*, ed. Margaret C. Conrads (Kansas City, Missouri: Nelson-Atkins Museum of Art, 2007), 2:50.

6. Acquisition proposal, April 11, 1933, Metropolitan Museum of Art Archives, New York, New York.

7. Harry B. Wehle, "An American Frontier Scene by George Caleb Bingham," *Bulletin of the Metropolitan Museum of Art* 28, no. 7 (July 1933): 120.

8. Ibid., 122.

9. For a consideration of the Met's acquisition and the response to this event in the context of the revival of nineteenth-century genre painting and the growing interest in American Scene painting as well as a discussion of Winslow Homer as a recognized forerunner of 1930s American Scene painting, see John Fagg, "'That Abused Word: Genre': The 1930s Genre Painting Revival," *The Space Between* 7, no. 1 (2011): 55–79. For another discussion of the twentieth-century interest in Bingham, including the 1935 monographic exhibition at the Museum of Modern Art, as well as other nineteenth-century American artists and contemporary American art, see Elizabeth Johns, "Histories of American Art: The Changing Quest," *Art Journal* 44, no. 4 (Winter 1984): 338–344.

10. Wehle, "An American Frontier Scene by George Caleb Bingham," 121.

11. "Bingham Exhibit Reflects Pioneer Days," *Art Digest* 8, no. 1 (April 1934): 19.

12. For an exploration of canon building, museum collections, and the importance of the Met's purchase of its first major Bingham, see Bruce Robertson, "The Tipping Point: Museum Collecting and the Canon," *American Art* 17, no. 3 (2003): 2.

13. J. H. Bender, "George C. Bingham, Esq.," *Fine Prints* (Kansas City, MO) 2, no. 7 (September 1933): 164–166, Director's Special Exhibition Correspondence, box 9, file 5, Saint Louis Art Museum Archives, Saint Louis, Missouri.

14. For remarks about nineteenth-century perspectives on rivers as a means of addressing both past and future, see Angela Miller, "The Mechanisms of the Market and the Invention of Western Regionalism: The Example of George Caleb Bingham," *Oxford Art Journal* 15, no. 1 (1992): 10. For a meditation on the place of rivers in twentieth-century regionalist concerns related to the past,

modernity, national destiny, commerce, and connectedness, see Leo G. Mazow, *Shallow Creek: Thomas Hart Benton and American Waterways* (State College: Pennsylvania State University Press, 2007), 8–17.

15. For a discussion of the importance of marrying past and future in Saint Louis in later years, see Joseph Heathcott and Márie Agnes Murphy, "Corridors of Flight, Zones of Renewal: Industry, Planning, and Policy in the Making of Metropolitan St. Louis, 1940–1980," *Journal of Urban History* 31 (January 2005): 176.

16. Meyric Rogers to C. B. Rollins, January 26, 1934, Director's Special Exhibition Correspondence, box 9, file 4, Saint Louis Art Museum Archives, Saint Louis, Missouri.

17. Meyric Rogers, "An Exhibition of the Work of George Caleb Bingham, 1811–79: 'The Missouri Artist,'" *Bulletin of the City Art Museum of Saint Louis* 19, no. 2 (April 1934): 18.

18. "Art Museum Buys Bingham Paintings," *Saint Louis Post-Dispatch*, January 15, 1935.

19. Miller makes note of nineteenth-century commentary that casts the artist in a similar light. See Miller, "The Mechanisms of the Market," 11.

20. Meyric Rogers to T. C. Mastin, January 22, 1934, Director's Special Exhibition Correspondence, box 9, file 4, Saint Louis Art Museum Archives, Saint Louis, Missouri.

21. "Bingham Exhibit Reflects Pioneer Days," 19.

22. Homer Bassford, "Special Exhibit of Bingham Pictures Now at Museum," *Saint Louis Times*, Publicity Scrapbook no. 9, 1934, Saint Louis Art Museum Archives, Saint Louis, Missouri.

23. Marquis W. Childs, "Rediscovering a Forgotten Missouri Painter," *Saint Louis Post-Dispatch*, March 11, 1934.

24. Ibid.

25. F. A. Whiting to Meyric Rogers, March 26, 1934, Director's Special Exhibition Correspondence, box 9, file 4, Saint Louis Art Museum Archives, Saint Louis, Missouri. For the *American Magazine of Art* reprint, see Marquis Childs, "George Caleb Bingham," *American Magazine of Art* 27 (November 1934): 594–599.

26. "George Caleb Bingham in New York," *Saint Louis Post-Dispatch*, February 11, 1935.

27. "Artist Bingham's Works Continue to Grow Popular," *Saint Louis Star*, July 8, 1935.

28. Laura Bragg to Meyric Rogers, May 23, 1934, and Bragg to Rogers, October 10, 1934, Director's Office Special Exhibition Correspondence, box 9, file 5, Saint Louis Art Museum Archives, Saint Louis, Missouri.

29. The Museum had already received as gifts a small portrait, two prints, and a landscape by Bingham.

30. Alfred H. Barr Jr. to Meyric Rogers, April 3, 1934, Director's Office Special Exhibition Correspondence, box 9, file 4, Saint Louis Art Museum Archives, Saint Louis, Missouri.

31. Meyric Rogers to Alfred H. Barr Jr., April 6, 1934, Director's Office Special Exhibition Correspondence, box 9, file 4, Saint Louis Art Museum Archives, Saint Louis, Missouri.

32. Alfred H. Barr Jr. to Meyric Rogers, April 10, 1934, Director's Office Special Exhibition Correspondence, box 9, file 4, Saint Louis Art Museum Archives, Saint Louis, Missouri.

33. Alan Wallach, "Regionalism Redux," *American Quarterly* 43, no. 2 (1991): 260.

34. Meyric Rogers to C. B. Rollins, May 25, 1934, Director's Office Special Exhibition Correspondence, box 9, file 4, Saint Louis Art Museum Archives, Saint Louis, Missouri.

35. See also Robertson, "The Tipping Point," 2–11.

36. For an overview of developments in twentieth-century American art history, including the interest in nineteenth-century artists as predecessors of "new developments," as well as the 1949 *Mississippi Panorama* and 1954 *Westward the Way* exhibitions, see Elizabeth Johns, "Scholarship in American Art: Its History and Recent Developments," *American Studies International* 22, no. 2 (October 1984): 3–40. Fagg also considers the MoMA exhibition and attendant critical response in the context of the twentieth-century revival of nineteenth-century genre painting and twentieth-century American Scene painting. See Fagg, "'That Abused Word,'" 55–79.

37. Alfred H. Barr Jr., "Foreword and Acknowledgement," in *George Caleb Bingham: The Missouri Artist, 1811–1879* (New York: Museum of Modern Art, 1935), 5. The MoMA exhibition and catalogue foreword, along with the the context of American Scene painting, are also discussed in Wallach, "Regionalism Redux," 260–263.

38. "New Publications of the Museum of Modern Art," Museum of Modern Art press release, January 28, 1935, Museum of Modern Art Archives, New York, New York.

39. H.A.R. "George C. Bingham, Pioneer of the American Scene," *Brooklyn Eagle*, February 3, 1935.

40. Ibid.

41. Perry Rathbone, *Mississippi Panorama* (Saint Louis: City Art Museum of Saint Louis, 1950), 7.

42. Perry Rathbone to Floyd C. Shoemaker, January 24, 1946, Director's Special Exhibition Correspondence, box 37, file 1, Saint Louis Art Museum Archives, Saint Louis, Missouri.

43. For a discussion of local boosterism and *Mississippi Panorama*, see Andrew J. Walker, "Introduction: Art, Memory, and Community: John Caspar Wild and

Urban Development in Historical Perspective," in *John Caspar Wild: Painter and Printmaker of Nineteenth-Century Urban America*, by John W. Reps (Saint Louis: Missouri Historical Society Press, 2006), xii–xvii.

44. Rathbone, *Mississippi Panorama*, 28, 7.

45. "The Mississippi: Saint Louis Shows Art of the River's Great Past," n.d., Publicity Scrapbook no. 28, Saint Louis Art Museum Archives, Saint Louis, Missouri.

46. See, for example, Elizabeth Johns, "Settlement and Development: Claiming the West," in *The West as America: Reinterpreting Images of the Frontier, 1820–1920*, ed. William H. Truettner (Washington, D.C.: Smithsonian Institution Press, 1991), 214–215; Elizabeth Johns, *American Genre Painting: The Politics of Everyday Life* (New Haven: Yale University Press, 1991), 82–83; Nancy Rash, *The Painting and Politics of George Caleb Bingham* (New Haven: Yale University Press, 1991), 40–90. For a more extensive discussion, see Miller, "The Mechanisms of the Market," 3–20. Additionally these publications provide useful overviews of Bingham's work and career as well as its nineteenth-century context. Many of the themes highlighted in these publications–such as the significance and resonance of regional associations and subjects, issues of authenticity, varying reception in the East and West, and the river as a site of connection between past, present, and future as well as a setting for the celebration and promotion of trade, westward expansion, the region, and its economic success–emerge again in our consideration of the artist's twentieth-century revival.

47. Howard Derrickson, "Art and Artists: Voyage into Yesterday," *Saint Louis Post-Dispatch*, October 16, 1949.

48. Timothy Flint, *Recollections of the Last Ten Years* (1826), quoted in Rathbone, *Mississippi Panorama*, 157.

49. "History Made Visible," *Saint Louis Globe-Democrat*, October 12, 1949.

50. Leroy Cook to *Waterways Journal*, December 2, 1949, Director's Office Special Exhibition Correspondence, box 38, file 16, Saint Louis Art Museum Archives, Saint Louis, Missouri.

51. "Riverfront Memorial Model, with Arch, at Art Museum," *Saint Louis Post-Dispatch*, May 6, 1948; "Art Museum Displays Model of Saarinen's Prize-Winning Arch," *Saint Louis Star*, May 6, 1948; "Saint Louis–Gateway to the West," *Newcomers' News*, October 8, 1948.

52. Francis A. Klein, "Louisiana Purchase Art Collection Is Masterpiece," *Saint Louis Globe Democrat*, October 22, 1954; George McCue, "History in Pictures," *Saint Louis Post-Dispatch Pictures*, October 31, 1954.

53. This role had, however, been referenced in the 1949 catalogue; see Charles van Ravenswaay, "Character and History of the Mississippi," *Mississippi Panorama*, 18. For a consideration of Bingham's position in the context of this liminality, see Johns, *American Genre Painting*, 83.

54. Howard Derrickson, "Unfamiliar Painting by Bingham to Be in Art Museum Exhibition," *Saint Louis Post-Dispatch*, October 20, 1954.

55. Wehle, "An American Frontier Scene by George Caleb Bingham," 120. Fagg has also noted Wehle's consideration of *Fur Traders Descending the Missouri* in light of a celebration of Manifest Destiny. See Fagg, "'That Abused Word,'" 57.

56. Bernard De Voto, "Celebrating 150 Years of the Louisiana Purchase," *Collier's*, March 21, 1953, 52.

57. Ibid., 56, 52.

58. Heathcott and Murphy, "Corridors of Flight," 176.

59. Perry Rathbone, *Westward the Way* (Saint Louis: City Art Museum of Saint Louis, 1954), 7–8.

60. Ibid., 167.

61. Ibid., 73.

62. George Frederick Ruxton, *Life in the Far West* (1849), quoted in Rathbone, *Westward the Way*, 177.

63. Rathbone, *Westward the Way*, 167, 165.

64. Ibid., 167.

65. We assume that the Rathbone print was one of those circulated by the American Art-Union. Howard Derrickson, "Art Museum to Exhibit Famous Long-Lost Painting by Bingham," *Saint Louis Post-Dispatch*, October 15, 1954.

66. Ibid.; Rathbone, *Westward the Way*, 167; Catherine Filsinger and William N. Eisendrath Jr., *Westward the Way*, 187.

67. Ibid.

68. William N. Eisendrath Jr. to Kay Deakins, February 2, 1954, Director's Office Special Exhibition Correspondence, box 44, file 7; William N. Eisendrath Jr. to Eugene Kingman, February 22, 1954, Director's Office Special Exhibition Correspondence, box 44, file 9; Kay Deakins to William N. Eisendrath Jr., February 25, 1954, Director's Office Special Exhibition Correspondence, box 44, file 10, Saint Louis Art Museum Archives, Saint Louis, Missouri.

69. Barr, "Foreword and Acknowledgement," 5.

EXHIBITION CHECKLIST

All works in the exhibition are by George Caleb Bingham (1811–1879) with the exception of the panorama by John J. Egan (active mid-nineteenth century). The drawings are unsigned and undated, with the exception of two that are believed to be inscribed by another hand. Drawings related to paintings appear in the plate sections of this volume; drawings unrelated to known paintings appear only below.

Landscape: Rural Scenery, 1845
Oil on canvas; 29⅜ × 36⅜ in.
Godel & Co. Fine Art, Inc., New York
PLATE 1

The Concealed Enemy, 1845
Oil on canvas; 29¼ × 36½ in.
Stark Museum of Art, Orange, Texas, 31.221.1
PLATE 2

Fur Traders Descending the Missouri, 1845
Oil on canvas; 29¼ × 36¼ in.
The Metropolitan Museum of Art, New York, Morris K. Jesup Fund, 1933 (33.61)
PLATE 3

Boatmen on the Missouri, 1846
Oil on canvas; 25⅛ × 30¼ in.
Fine Arts Museums of San Francisco, Gift of Mr. and Mrs. John D. Rockefeller III, 1979.7.15
PLATE 4

The Jolly Flatboatmen, 1846
Oil on canvas; 38 × 48½ in.
Manoogian Collection
PLATE 5

Lighter Relieving a Steamboat Aground, 1847
Oil on canvas; 30¼ × 36 in.
White House Historical Association (White House Collection), 492
PLATE 6 (not in the exhibition)

Fur trader, for *Fur Traders Descending the Missouri* (1845) and *Trappers' Return* (1851) with alterations
Brush, black ink, and wash over pencil on off-white wove paper; 11⅞ × 9⁹⁄₁₆ in.
Lent by The People of Missouri
Acquired through the generosity of Allen P. and Josephine B. Green Foundation
PLATE 7

Boatman, for *Boatmen on the Missouri* (1846)
Brush, black ink, and wash over paper; 9½ × 8 in.
Lent by Mr. and Mrs. Stuart P. Feld
PLATE 8

Boatman, for *Boatmen on the Missouri* (1846)
Brush, black ink, and wash over pencil on cream wove paper; 8¹⁄₁₆ × 8¹³⁄₁₆ in.
Lent by The People of Missouri
In memory of Gloria M. Goldstein
PLATE 9

Skillet-beater, for *The Jolly Flatboatmen* (1846)
Brush, black ink, and wash over pencil on cream wove paper; 10¼ × 9⅜ in.
Lent by The People of Missouri
In memory of Charles Valier (1841–1913)
PLATE 10

Fiddler, for *The Jolly Flatboatmen* (1846)
Brush, black ink, and wash over pencil on cream wove paper; 9¹⁵⁄₁₆ × 8⅛ in.
Lent by The People of Missouri
Acquired through the generosity of The Louis D. Beaumont Foundation
PLATE 11

Flatboatman, for *The Jolly Flatboatmen* (1846)
Brush, black ink, and wash over pencil on cream wove paper; 10 × 8 in.
Lent by The People of Missouri
PLATE 12

Flatboatman, for *The Jolly Flatboatmen* (1846) and *The Jolly Flatboatmen* (1877–78) with alterations
Brush, black ink, and wash over pencil on cream wove paper; 9⅝ × 7 9/16 in.
Lent by The People of Missouri
Acquired through the generosity of Governor and Mrs. Christopher S. Bond
PLATE 13

Flatboatman, for *The Jolly Flatboatmen* (1846) and *The Jolly Flatboatmen* (1877–78) with alterations
Brush, black ink, and wash over pencil on cream wove paper; 9⅝ × 9⅛ in.
Lent by The People of Missouri
PLATE 14

Flatboatman, for *The Jolly Flatboatmen* (1846) and *The Jolly Flatboatmen* (1877–78) with alterations
Brush, black ink, and wash over pencil on cream wove paper; 9⅛ × 9⅝ in.
Lent by The People of Missouri
PLATE 15

Seated man in a broad-brimmed hat, possible alternate study for *Lighter Relieving a Steamboat Aground* (1847)
Graphite, brush, and gray wash on paper; 7 7/16 × 9 5/16 in.
Museum of Fine Arts, Boston
Gift of Maxim Karolik for the M. and K. Karolik Collection of American Watercolors and Drawings, 1800–1875
PLATE 16

Boatman, for *Lighter Relieving a Steamboat Aground* (1847) and possible study for *Watching the Cargo by Night* (1854) with alterations
Brush, black ink, and wash over pencil on cream wove paper; 10 3/16 × 8½ in.
Lent by The People of Missouri
PLATE 17

Study of legs, for *Lighter Relieving a Steamboat Aground* (1847)
Brush, black ink, and wash over pencil on cream wove paper; 5 × 8½ in.
Lent by The People of Missouri
Acquired through the generosity of E. A. Martin Machinery Company
PLATE 18

Boatman, (recto) for *Lighter Relieving a Steamboat Aground* (1847) and (verso) possible study for *Watching the Cargo by Night* (1854) with alterations
Brush, black ink, and wash over pencil on cream wove paper; 6⅛ × 7⅜ in.
Lent by The People of Missouri
Acquired through the generosity of Seven-Up Company
PLATE 19

Boatman drinking, for *Lighter Relieving a Steamboat Aground* (1847)
Brush, black ink, and wash over pencil on cream wove paper; 14⅜ × 9¾ in.
Lent by The People of Missouri
Acquired through the generosity of Union Electric Company
PLATE 20

Sceptic, possible alternate study for *Lighter Relieving a Steamboat Aground* (1847)
Brush, black ink, and wash over pencil on cream wove paper; 11 × 6 15/16 in.
Lent by The People of Missouri
PLATE 21

Rapt listener, for *Lighter Relieving a Steamboat Aground* (1847)
Brush, black ink, and wash over pencil on cream wove paper; 10 11/16 × 8⅜ in.
Lent by The People of Missouri
Acquired through the generosity of Anheuser-Busch Foundation
PLATE 22

Boatman, for *Lighter Relieving a Steamboat Aground* (1847) with alterations
Brush, black ink, and wash over pencil on cream wove paper; 10 9/16 × 8⅜ in.
Lent by The People of Missouri
PLATE 23

Young boatman, possible alternate study for *Lighter Relieving a Steamboat Aground* (1847)
Brush, black ink, and wash over pencil on cream wove paper; 10¾ × 8½ in.
Lent by The People of Missouri
In memory of Benton Roblee Duhme
PLATE 24

Boatman, possible alternate study for *Lighter Relieving a Steamboat Aground* (1847)
Brush, black ink, and wash over pencil on cream wove paper; 8⅞ × 11 in.
Lent by The People of Missouri
PLATE 25

Raftsmen Playing Cards, 1847
Oil on canvas; 28 1/16 × 38 1/16 in.
Saint Louis Art Museum, Bequest of Ezra H. Linley by exchange, 50:1934
PLATE 26

Watching the Cargo, 1849
Oil on canvas; 26 × 36 in.
On loan for the State Historical Society of Missouri Columbia Research Center and Gallery, Columbia, Missouri
PLATE 27

The Wood-Boat, 1850
Oil on canvas mounted on board; 25 1/8 × 30 in.
Saint Louis Art Museum, museum purchase, 14:1951
PLATE 28

Mississippi Fisherman, ca. 1850
Oil on canvas; 29½ × 24½ in.
Jamee and Marshall Field
PLATE 29

Mississippi Boatman, 1850
Oil on canvas; 24 3/8 × 17½ in.
National Gallery of Art, Washington, D.C., John Wilmerding Collection, 2004.66.1
PLATE 30

Trappers' Return, 1851
Oil on canvas; 26¼ × 36¼ in.
Detroit Institute of Arts, Gift of Dexter M. Ferry Jr., The Bridgeman Art Library
PLATE 31

Cardplayer, for *Raftsmen Playing Cards* (1847) with alterations and for *In a Quandary* (1851) with alterations
Brush, black ink, and wash over pencil on cream wove paper; 11 × 8 7/16 in.
Lent by The People of Missouri
Acquired through the generosity of the Friends of Southeast Missouri State University and the Citizens of Southeast Missouri
PLATE 32

Raftman dozing, for *Raftsmen Playing Cards* (1847) and *Jolly Flatboatmen in Port* (1857)
Brush, black ink, and wash over pencil on cream wove paper; 9½ × 8½ in.
Lent by The People of Missouri
Acquired through the generosity of Schoenberg Foundation, Inc.
PLATE 33

Raftman, for *Raftsmen Playing Cards* (1847) and *In a Quandary* (1851)
Brush, black ink, and wash over pencil on cream wove paper; 10¾ × 8 3/8 in.
Lent by The People of Missouri
PLATE 34

Raftman, for *Raftsmen Playing Cards* (1847) and *Jolly Flatboatmen in Port* (1857)
Brush, black ink, and wash over pencil on cream wove paper; 10 13/16 × 8 3/8 in.
Lent by The People of Missouri
PLATE 35

Cardplayer, for *Raftsmen Playing Cards* (1847) and *In a Quandary* (1851)
Brush, black ink, and wash over pencil on cream wove paper; 10 11/16 × 8 3/8 in.
Lent by The People of Missouri
PLATE 36

Boatman, for *Watching the Cargo* (1849) and *Mississippi Boatman* (1850)
Brush, black ink, and wash over pencil on cream wove paper; 11 × 8½ in.
Lent by The People of Missouri
Acquired through the generosity of Mercantile Trust Company, N.A.
PLATE 37

Boatman, for *Watching the Cargo* (1849)
Brush, black ink, and wash over pencil on cream wove paper; 9 × 11½ in.
Lent by The People of Missouri
Acquired through the generosity of The Louis D. Beaumont Foundation
PLATE 38

Woodboatman, for *The Wood-Boat* (1850)
Brush, black ink, and wash over pencil on off-white wove paper; 11¾ × 9 in.
Lent by The People of Missouri
Acquired through the generosity of The Ralston Purina Trust Fund
PLATE 39

Woodboatman, for *The Wood-Boat* (1850)
Brush, black ink, and wash over pencil on off-white wove paper; 15 1/8 × 9 5/8 in.
Lent by The People of Missouri
Acquired through the generosity of Monsanto Fund
PLATE 40

Young woodboatman, for *The Wood-Boat* (1850)
Brush, black ink, and wash over pencil on off-white wove paper; 11¾ × 8 7/8 in.
Lent by The People of Missouri
PLATE 41

Trapper's son, for *Trappers' Return* (1851)
Brush, black ink, and wash over pencil on cream wove paper; 6⅞ × 9⅞ in.
Lent by The People of Missouri
Acquired through the generosity of Interco Incorporated Charitable Trust
PLATE 42

Fishing on the Mississippi, 1851
Oil on canvas; 28¾ × 36 in.
Nelson-Atkins Museum of Art, Kansas City, Missouri, William Rockhill Nelson Trust
PLATE 43

In a Quandary or *Mississippi Raftmen at Cards*, 1851
Oil on canvas; 17¼ × 21 in.
© Courtesy of the Huntington Library, Art Collections, and Botanical Gardens, Gift of the Virginia Steele Scott Foundation
PLATE 44

Woodboatmen on a River (Western Boatmen Ashore by Night), 1854
Oil on canvas; 29 × 36¼ in.
Lent by Hirschl & Adler Galleries, New York
PLATE 45

Watching the Cargo by Night, 1854
Oil on canvas; 24 × 29 in.
Joslyn Art Museum, Omaha, Nebraska, Gift of Foxley & Co., 1997.33
PLATE 46

Jolly Flatboatmen in Port, 1857
Oil on canvas; 47¼ × 69⅝ in.
Saint Louis Art Museum, museum purchase, 123:1944
PLATE 47

The Jolly Flatboatmen, 1877–78
Oil on canvas; 26¹⁄₁₆ × 36⅜
Terra Foundation for American Art, Chicago, Daniel J. Terra Collection, 1992.15, photography © Terra Foundation for American Art
PLATE 48

Fisherman waiting for a bite, for *Fishing on the Mississippi* (1851)
Brush, black ink, and wash over pencil on cream wove paper; 8⅞ × 11³⁄₁₆ in.
Lent by The People of Missouri
PLATE 49

Fisherman, for *Fishing on the Mississippi* (1851)
Brush, black ink, and wash over pencil on cream wove paper; 14¹¹⁄₁₆ × 11⅛ in.
Lent by The People of Missouri
Acquired through the generosity of Mr. and Mrs. Herman Robert Sutherland
PLATE 50

Raftman, for *In a Quandary* or *Mississippi Raftmen at Cards* (1851) and possible alternate study for *Jolly Flatboatmen in Port* (1857)
Brush, black ink, and wash over pencil on cream wove paper; 10⅞ × 6¹⁵⁄₁₆ in.
Lent by The People of Missouri
PLATE 51

Wayfarer, for *Watching the Cargo by Night* (1854) with alterations and possible study for *St. Louis Wharf* (1849; lost)
Brush, black ink, and wash over pencil on cream wove paper; 9¾ × 8⅜ in.
Lent by The People of Missouri
Acquired through the generosity of The Hallmark Education Foundation
PLATE 52

Story-teller, possible study for *Watching the Cargo by Night* (1854) with alterations and possible study for *Raftmen on the Ohio* (1849; lost)
Brush, black ink, and wash over pencil on cream wove paper; 10⅞ × 8½ in.
Lent by The People of Missouri
PLATE 53

Raftman, for *Watching the Cargo by Night* (1854) with alterations
Brush, black ink, and wash over pencil on off-white wove paper; 9¾ × 8¾ in.
Lent by The People of Missouri
PLATE 54

Raftman, for *Watching the Cargo by Night* (1854) with alterations and a possible study for *St. Louis Wharf* (1849; lost)
Brush, black ink, and wash over pencil on off-white wove paper; 12¾ × 9⅝ in.
Lent by The People of Missouri
Acquired through the generosity of the Missouri Women's Bingham Shirt Project
PLATE 55

Raftman, (recto) for *Woodboatmen on a River (Western Boatmen Ashore by Night)* (1854) with alterations and possible study for *Raftmen on the Ohio* (1849; lost); (verso) for *Jolly Flatboatmen in Port* (1857) with alterations
Brush, black ink, and wash over pencil on cream wove paper; 10¼ × 9½ in.
Lent by The People of Missouri
Acquired through the generosity of Mr. and Mrs. L. Max Lippman Jr. in memory of Arthur C. Hoskins
PLATE 56

Dockhand, for *Jolly Flatboatmen in Port* (1857)
Brush, black ink, and wash over pencil on cream wove paper; 10⅝ × 6½ in.
Lent by The People of Missouri
Acquired through the generosity of Edward K. Love Realty Company
PLATE 57

Fiddler (2), for *Jolly Flatboatmen in Port* (1857) and *The Jolly Flatboatmen* (1877–78) with alterations
Brush, black ink, and wash over pencil heightened with white chalk on brown wove paper; 15⅛ × 11¾ in.
Lent by The People of Missouri
Acquired through the generosity of The Arts and Education Council of Greater Saint Louis
PLATE 58

Boatman, for *Jolly Flatboatmen in Port* (1857)
Brush, black ink, and wash over pencil heightened with white gouache (oxidized) on tan wove paper; 14⅜ × 11¾ in.
Lent by The People of Missouri
Acquired through the generosity of ITT Blackburn Company
PLATE 59

Skillet-beater (2), for *Jolly Flatboatmen in Port* (1857) and *The Jolly Flatboatmen* (1877–78) with alterations
Brush, black ink, and wash over pencil heightened with white gouache on tan wove paper; 13⅝ × 11¾ in.
Lent by The People of Missouri
Acquired through the generosity of The Kansas City Star
PLATE 60

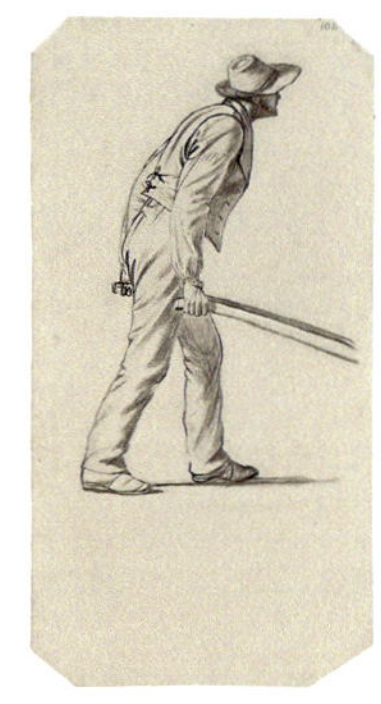

Dockhand, possible study for *St. Louis Wharf* (1849; lost)
Brush, black ink, and wash over pencil on off-white wove paper; 9 × 4¾ in.
Lent by The People of Missouri

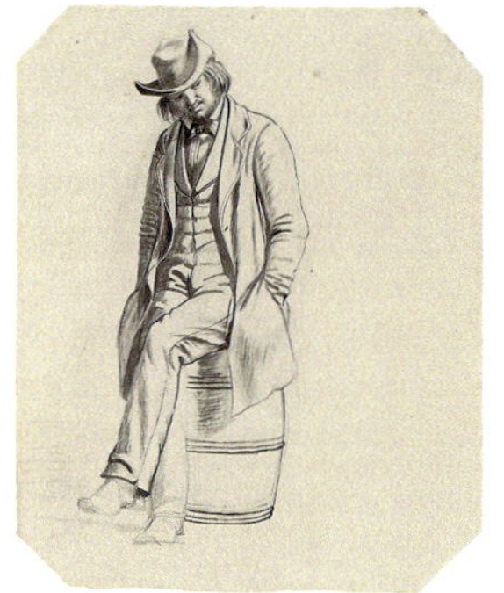

Slick character, possible study for *St. Louis Wharf* (1849; lost)
Brush, black ink, and wash over pencil on off-white wove paper; 11¾ × 9⅝ in.
Lent by The People of Missouri

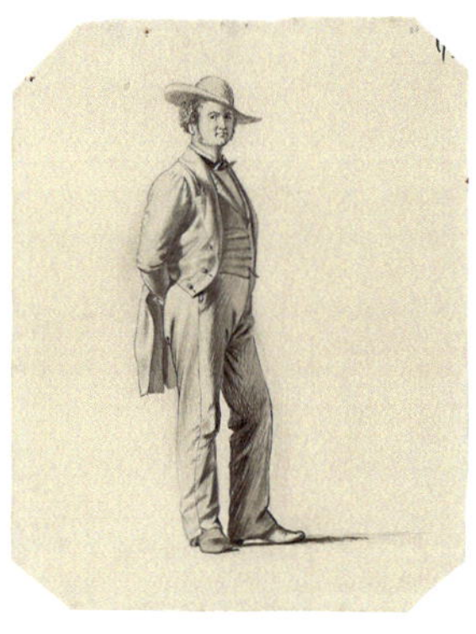

Dandy, possible study for *St. Louis Wharf* (1849; lost)
Brush, black ink, and wash over pencil on cream wove paper; 12 × 9⅝ in.
Lent by The People of Missouri

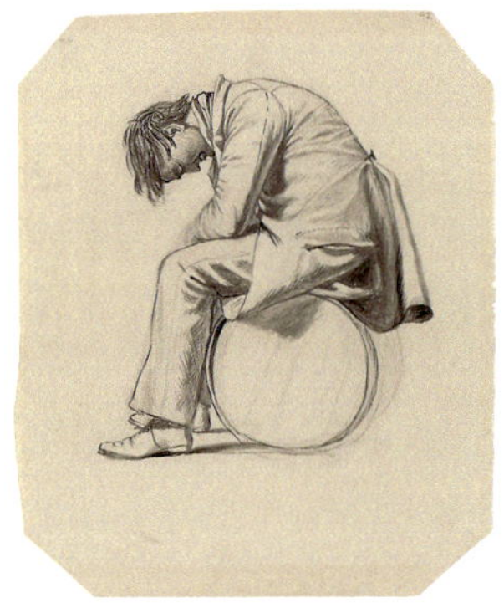

Weary traveler, possible study for *St. Louis Wharf* (1849; lost)
Brush, black ink, and wash over pencil on cream wove paper; 10 × 8⅜ in.
Lent by The People of Missouri
Acquired through the Generosity of Members of the Missouri Society of Association Executives

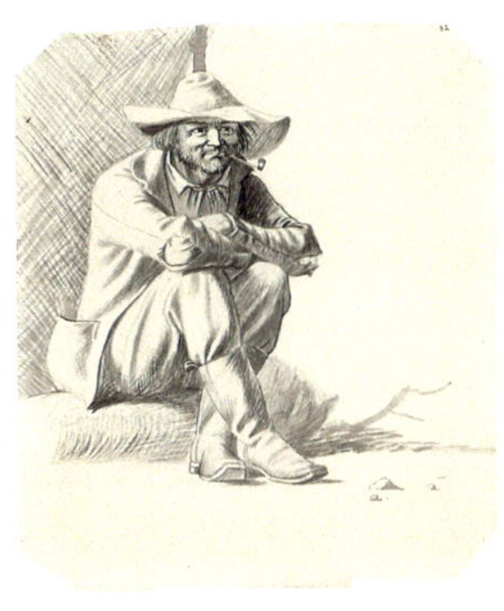

Woodboatman, possible study for *The Woodyard* (1849; lost)
Brush, black ink, and wash over pencil on off-white wove paper; 10¾ × 9½ in.
Lent by The People of Missouri

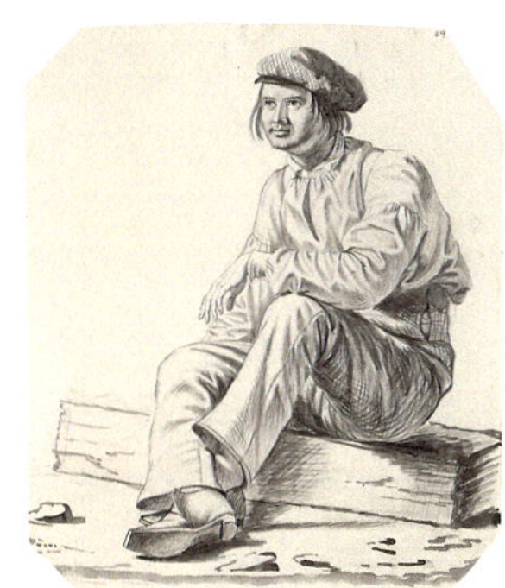

Young boatman, possible study for *Raftmen on the Ohio* (1849; lost)
Brush, black ink, and wash over pencil on off-white wove paper; 8⅛ × $6\frac{15}{16}$ in.
Lent by The People of Missouri

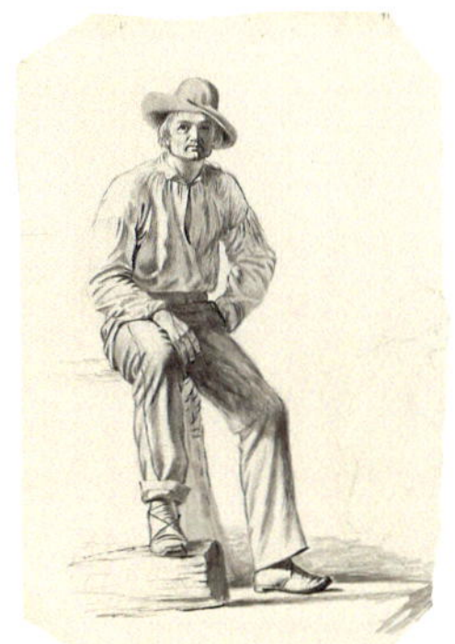

Good listener, possible study for *Raftmen on the Ohio* (1849; lost)
Brush, black ink, and wash over pencil on off-white wove paper; 12¾ × 8¾ in.
Lent by The People of Missouri

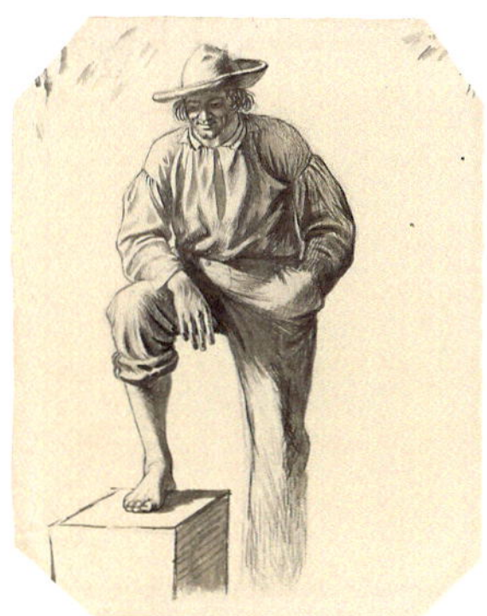

Interested onlooker, possible study for *Raftmen on the Ohio* (1849; lost)
Brush, black ink, and wash over pencil on cream wove paper; $11\frac{11}{16}$ × 9½ in.
Lent by The People of Missouri
Acquired through the generosity of The Missouri Federation of Women's Clubs

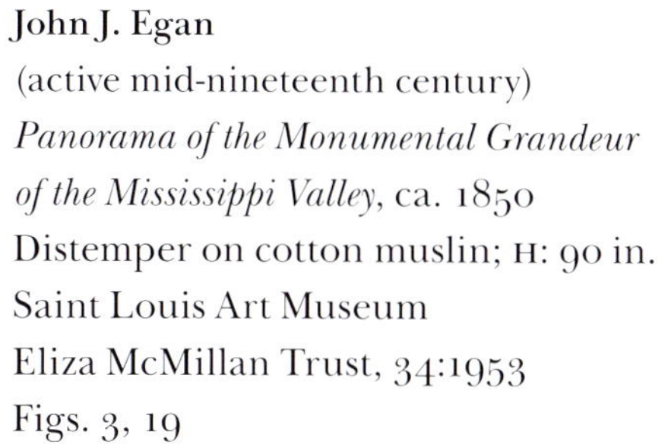

John J. Egan
(active mid-nineteenth century)
Panorama of the Monumental Grandeur of the Mississippi Valley, ca. 1850
Distemper on cotton muslin; H: 90 in.
Saint Louis Art Museum
Eliza McMillan Trust, 34:1953
Figs. 3, 19

ACKNOWLEDGMENTS

Many people were instrumental in bringing this exhibition and publication to fruition, including numerous colleagues and associates who graciously shared their knowledge or otherwise facilitated the project. The two organizing institutions and contributing essayists to the catalogue wish to recognize these individuals in the published record of this endeavor.

At our sister institutions and galleries across the country, and for their professional services: We thank Patrick Albano, Aaron Galleries; Kenneth J. Myers, Detroit Institute of Arts; Emma Acker and Timothy Anglin Burgard, Fine Arts Museums of San Francisco; Thomas B. Hall III, Friends of Arrow Rock, Inc.; Katherine Baumgartner, Godel & Company Fine Art; John Murdoch and Jessica Todd Smith, Huntington Library, Art Collections, and Botanical Gardens; Cheryl Robledo, Manoogian Collections; Christine Svec, Marshall A. Field Collection; Patrick Murphy, Morse Study Room; Nancy Anderson and Franklin Kelly, National Gallery of Art; Stephanie Knappe and Julie Mattsson, Nelson-Atkins Museum of Art; Scott Erbes, Speed Art Museum; Joan Stack, State Historical Society of Missouri; Peter John Brownlee and Cathy Ricciardelli, Terra Foundation for American Art; and William Allman and Lydia S. Tederick, White House. We are grateful as well to the Kimbell Art Museum, whose long-standing paintings-conservation program shared with the Amon Carter Museum of American Art was indispensable to this project. For their work on the catalogue, we are grateful to Mary Jane Crook, editor; Patrick Dooley, catalogue designer; Patricia Fidler, Yale University Press; Laura Iwasaki, proofreader; Fronia Simpson, editor; Marie Weiler, catalogue typesetting and layout assistance; and the exceptionally able staff at Marquand Books, Inc.

At the Amon Carter Museum of American Art: We are grateful to Margaret C. Conrads, Deputy Director of Art and Research; Lori Eklund, Senior Deputy Director; Pamela Graham, former Executive Assistant to the Director and the Board of Trustees; Lauren Lively, Department Assistant to Administration; Carol Noel, Director of Development; Randy S. Ray, Chief Financial Officer; and Andrew J. Walker, Director. Claire Barry, Director of Conservation at the neighboring Kimbell Art Museum, oversees the joint paintings-conservation program with the Amon Carter, and with early assistance from Bart Devolder, former Associate Paintings Conservator, she played a pivotal role in the technical study of Bingham's paintings for this project. In the Amon Carter's conservation lab, Jodie Utter served as a key sounding board for the study of the artist's drawings. For their critical role in handling and displaying the exhibition objects, we thank Ross Auerbach, Jim Belknap and his team, Marci Driggers, and Jacqueline Stevens. In the research library, thanks are due to Sam Duncan, Jonathan Frembling, and Mary Jane Harbison. Shirley Reece-Hughes, Assistant Curator of Paintings and Sculpture, and Alessandra Guzman, Exhibition Manager, oversaw the project with the assistance of their curatorial colleague Claudia Sanchez, along with Luce Fellow Laura Patrizi and intern Gibson Banta. We are indebted to our development colleague Judy Ivey for her productive efforts, and in the education and public relations departments we thank Stacy Fuller, Tracy Greene, Jessica Poole, and Peggy Sell. For their expert work on the catalogue we are grateful to Stefanie Ball Piwetz, Will Gillham, and Steven Watson, and we thank Roger Westerman for the splendid design of the Fort Worth exhibition.

At the Saint Louis Art Museum: We thank Brent R. Benjamin, Director; Jason T. Busch, Deputy Director for Curatorial Affairs and Museum Programs; Carl Hamm, Deputy Director for Development and External Affairs; Carolyn J. Schmidt, Deputy Director; Linda Thomas, former Assistant Director for Exhibitions and Collections; and Deborah Zumwalt, Special Projects Manager, Director's Office. Our understanding of many of the works in the exhibition benefited from the skills and insight of the museum's conservation department members, especially Paul Haner, Nancy Heugh, Brian Koelz, Art Rogers, and Claire Walker, supported by Elaine Harris. We are particularly grateful to Jeanette Fausz and her dedicated staff in the registrar's office, including Diane Mallow, Courtney McCarty, Ella Rothgangel, Shannon Sweeney, and Rachel Shoup Swiston, as well as the installation crew. The design for the exhibition is a credit to our design department, headed by Philip Atkinson and including Fontella Bradford, Jon Cournoyer, Lauri Kramer, Jessi Mueller, and Nick Smith. In the Richardson Memorial Library, great thanks are due to Marianne Cavanaugh, Christopher Handy, Norma Sindelar, Clare Vasquez, and Bryan Young. The interpretation and educational programs surrounding the exhibition were brilliantly managed by a team including Cheryl Benjamin, Ann Burroughs, Narni Cahill, Jennifer Doyle, Renee Franklin, Sabrena Nelson, Anne Perry, Lindsey Schifko, Sherri Williams, and Danielle Zeis. Special thanks also to Brigid Flynn, for her tireless and successful pursuit of grants and sponsorships for the project, and to Matthew Hathaway and his media-relations team.

Nenette Luarca-Shoaf: For their comments on early drafts and ideas, I wish to thank Wendy Bellion, Leah Bowe, Marie-Stephanie Delmaire, and Camara Dia Holloway. I am also particularly grateful to the following people for their research assistance: Gigi Barnhill, Paul Erickson, and Elizabeth Pope at the American Antiquarian Society; Jonathan Frembling and Jodie Utter at the Amon Carter Museum of American Art; Joan Stack at the State Historical Society of Missouri; Alex Pezzatti at the University of Pennsylvania Museum of Archaeology and Anthropology; and the staff of the print study rooms at the Museum of Fine Arts, Boston, and the Philadelphia Museum of Art. For their editorial input, I thank Will Gillham and Fronia Simpson.

For the exhibition at the Amon Carter, I am grateful to Andrew J. Walker for his faith in me, Margaret C. Conrads for her stewardship of this project, and Stacy Fuller and Peggy Sell for their expertise on interpretive strategies. Finally, I owe special thanks to Shirley Reece-Hughes at the Amon Carter and Janeen Turk in Saint Louis for their support and collegiality throughout the planning process.

Claire Barry and Nancy Heugh: We are indebted to numerous colleagues and lenders for providing invaluable assistance in examining the river paintings included in this study and capturing the underdrawings through infrared reflectography. We are grateful to John Delaney at the

National Gallery of Art for advising on the setup of the Goodrich InGaAs camera at the Kimbell Art Museum, where Bart Devolder helped initiate the technical study. Katie Dillow Cooper at the Kimbell completed the infrared reflectogram mosaics for all these paintings, along with several others in the study, and expertly assembled the overlays and illustrations for our essay. We especially thank Ann Hoenigswald and Douglas Lachance at the National Gallery for carrying out the infrared reflectography examination of *Mississippi Boatman*, *The Jolly Flatboatmen* of 1846, and *Lighter Relieving a Steamboat Aground*; we also thank Carol Christiansen at the National Gallery for sharing results from her previous technical examination of *Mississippi Boatman*.

Thanks are also due to the following colleagues: Kelly J. Keegan and Frank Zuccari, Art Institute of Chicago; Alfred Ackerman, Detroit Institute of Arts; Elise Effmann Clifford, Fine Arts Museums of San Francisco; Jenine Culligan, John Farley, and Margaret Mary Layne of the Huntington Library, Art Collection, and Botanical Gardens; Yvonne Szafran, J. Paul Getty Museum; Eric Lee and George Shackelford, Kimbell Art Museum; Cheryl Robledo, Manoogian Collection; Michael Gallagher, Elizabeth Kornhauser, and Dorothy Mahon, Metropolitan Museum of Art; Jay Krueger, National Gallery of Art; Elisabeth Batchelor, Scott A. Heffley, and Mary Schafer, Nelson-Atkins Museum of Art; Christophe Leribault, Petit Palais, Musée des Beaux-Arts de la Ville de Paris; Paul Haner and Claire Walker, Saint Louis Art Museum; Sarah E. Boehme, Stark Museum of Art; Peter John Brownlee, Cathy Ricciardelli, and Bonnie Rimer, Terra Foundation for American Art; and William Allman and Lydia S. Tederick, White House.

Elizabeth Kornhauser and Dorothy Mahon: We thank the many scholars who helped in shaping the ideas for this essay, in particular Margaret C. Conrads at the Amon Carter Museum of American Art; Christopher C. Oliver at the Virginia Museum of Fine Arts; and Carol Troyen, Curator Emerita of American paintings at the Museum of Fine Arts, Boston.

The following painting conservators supplied critical infrared reflectography images for this essay: Alfred Ackerman, Detroit Institute of Arts, and Claire Barry, Kimbell Art Museum. We also thank our colleagues at the Metropolitan Museum of Art, Sean Digney-Peer and Evan Reed, for their invaluable assistance with infrared and computer imaging, and Silvia A. Centeno and Mark T. Wypyski for providing pigment analysis.

Andrew J. Walker and Janeen Turk: At the Saint Louis Art Museum, we thank David Conradsen, Ann-Maree Walker, and Elizabeth Wyckoff for their assistance with research and planning for the exhibition. Emily Allred and Beth Rubin also provided stellar research assistance, and Zoey Hasselbring and Jeanne Rosen provided critical administrative support. Numerous staff in Fort Worth contributed to this project, but for our essay we especially thank Will Gillham, Pamela Graham, and Shirley Reece-Hughes. Stefanie Ball Piwetz, Jonathan Frembling, and Steve Watson are also due a special note of gratitude.

Beyond our two institutions, we deeply appreciate the assistance offered by Cara Cooper, Stephanie Knappe, Brittany Lockard, and Holly Wright, all at the Nelson-Atkins Museum of Art. We also thank Maria R. Ketcham and Virginia Reynolds, Detroit Institute of Art; Jessica Todd Smith, Huntington Library, Art Collections, and Botanical Gardens; and Jim Moske and Lauren Ritz, Metropolitan Museum of Art. Special thanks are due as well to Eric P. Newman for assisting with research regarding the publications of Montroville Wilson Dickeson.

ABOUT THE AUTHORS

Claire Barry is the director of conservation at the Kimbell Art Museum in Fort Worth, Texas. She holds an MA and a certificate of advanced study in paintings conservation from the Cooperstown Graduate Program, State University of New York, Oneonta, and an AB from Oberlin College, Oberlin, Ohio. Since 1992 she has directed a joint paintings conservation program for the Kimbell and the neighboring Amon Carter Museum of American Art. She has lectured and published on a broad range of conservation topics, and she has authored technical studies on American artists Thomas Cole, Charles Demuth, Thomas Eakins, and Martin Johnson Heade in addition to a number of technical studies on European artists.

Margaret C. Conrads is deputy director of art and research at the Amon Carter Museum of American Art. For eighteen years, she served as the Samuel Sosland Senior Curator of American Art at the Nelson-Atkins Museum of Art in Kansas City. She was the editor of and a contributor to *American Paintings to 1945: The Collections of the Nelson-Atkins Museum of Art* (2007), and she was the curator and author of the landmark exhibition and publication *Winslow Homer and the Critics: Forging a National Art in the 1870s* (2001). Conrads received her PhD in art history from the Graduate Center, City University of New York.

Nancy Heugh is the paper conservator at the Saint Louis Art Museum. She served previously as associate conservator at the Nelson-Atkins Museum of Art; senior conservator of art on paper at the Harry Ransom Center, University of Texas, Austin; and head paper conservator at the laboratory of the Intermuseum Conservation Association, Oberlin, Ohio. After founding Heugh-Edmondson Conservation Services, LLC, and working independently as an art-on-paper conservator, she joined the staff at the Saint Louis Art Museum in 2008. She continues as the paper conservator for the Bingham Trust. Heugh's degrees include a BA in art history from Boston University and an MA in art conservation with a certificate of advanced study from Cooperstown Graduate Program, State University of New York, Oneonta.

Elizabeth Mankin Kornhauser is the Alice Pratt Brown Curator of American Paintings and Sculpture at the Metropolitan Museum of Art. In 2012 she completed the installation of the new American Painting Galleries in the American Wing; she is currently at work on *Rediscovering Thomas Hart Benton's "America Today" Murals* (2014) and *John Singer Sargent's Portraits of the Arts: Artists, Writers, Actors, and Musicians* (2015). From 1997 to 2010, she served as chief curator and Krieble Curator of American Painting and Sculpture at the Wadsworth Atheneum Museum of Art, Hartford, Connecticut, where she organized and authored catalogues for major exhibitions on Ralph Earl, the Hudson River School, and Marsden Hartley.

Nenette Luarca-Shoaf holds a PhD in art history from the University of Delaware, Newark, and an MA in the humanities from the University of Chicago. Her research has been supported by the Smithsonian Institution, Terra Foundation for American Art, American Antiquarian Society, and the McNeil Center for Early American Studies. From 2010 to 2011, she was the Barra Foundation Curatorial Fellow at the Philadelphia Museum of Art, and she has worked in the education departments of the Art Institute of Chicago, the Saint Louis Art Museum, and the Smart Museum of Art, Chicago.

Dorothy Mahon received her MA in the history of art and a certificate of advanced study in conservation from the Institute of Fine Arts, New York University. In 1981, she joined the staff of the department of paintings conservation at the Metropolitan Museum of Art, where she has worked on paintings spanning the collection, with a particular emphasis on the technical examination and treatment of American paintings and European paintings of the fifteenth and nineteenth centuries.

Janeen Turk is the assistant curator of American art at the Saint Louis Art Museum, where she has worked for the past decade. She was a contributing author to the catalogue *Joe Jones: Radical Painter of the American Scene* (2010) and contributor to the National Gallery of Australia publication *Turner to Monet: The Triumph of Landscape Painting*. Her most recent project was the 2013 reinstallation of the Saint Louis Museum's American collection. She holds an MA in art history from Northwestern University.

Andrew J. Walker is the director of the Amon Carter Museum of American Art. He was previously the assistant director for curatorial affairs and curator of American art at the Saint Louis Art Museum, a position he held for six years. During his tenure there, he oversaw eight curatorial departments and organized five special exhibitions, including major examinations of American artists George Caleb Bingham and Joe Jones. He has also held curatorial positions at the Missouri History Museum, Saint Louis, and the Art Institute of Chicago. Walker received his BA from Bowdoin College in Brunswick, Maine, and his PhD in the history of art from the University of Pennsylvania, supported by the Henry Luce Foundation, American Council of Learned Societies Dissertation Fellowship for the Study of American Art, and the Jacob Javits Fellowship with the United States Department of Education. He serves on the board of directors of the World Chess Hall of Fame, Saint Louis; has delivered numerous articles for publication in scholarly journals; and has lectured widely on American art.

INDEX

Navigating the West: George Caleb Bingham and the River has been organized by the Amon Carter Museum of American Art, Fort Worth, Texas, and the Saint Louis Art Museum, Saint Louis, Missouri. This publication was supported in part by generous grants from the Henry Luce Foundation and the National Endowment for the Arts.

Amon Carter Museum of American Art
Fort Worth, Texas
October 2, 2014, through January 18, 2015

Saint Louis Art Museum
Saint Louis, Missouri
February 22 through May 17, 2015

The Metropolitan Museum of Art
New York, New York
June 16 through September 20, 2015

© 2014 Amon Carter Museum of American Art
and the Saint Louis Art Museum.
All rights reserved. This book may not be reproduced, in whole or in part, including illustrations, in any form (beyond that copying permitted by Sections 107 and 108 of the U.S. Copyright Law and except by reviewers for the public press), without written permission from the publishers.

Amon Carter Museum of American Art
3501 Camp Bowie Boulevard
Fort Worth, Texas 76107
cartermuseum.org

Saint Louis Art Museum
One Fine Arts Drive
Forest Park
Saint Louis, Missouri 63110
slam.org

Distributed by
Yale University Press
302 Temple Street
PO Box 209040
New Haven, Connecticut 06520-9040
yalebooks.com/art

Library of Congress Cataloging-in-Publication Data
Navigating the West : George Caleb Bingham and the river / Nenette Luarca-Shoaf, Claire Barry, Nancy Heugh, Elizabeth Mankin Kornhauser, Dorothy Mahon, Andrew J. Walker, and Janeen Turk ; with contributions by Margaret C. Conrads, Brent R. Benjamin, and Andrew J. Walker.
pages cm
Includes bibliographical references and index.
ISBN 978-0-300-20670-8 (alk. paper)
1. Bingham, George Caleb, 1811–1879–Exhibitions. 2. Rivers in art–Exhibitions. 3. West (U.S.)–In art–Exhibitions. I. Luarca-Shoaf, Nenette. II. Amon Carter Museum of American Art. III. St. Louis Art Museum. IV. Metropolitan Museum of Art (New York, N.Y.)
N6537.B53A4 2014
759.13–dc23 2014009532

The Board of Trustees of the Amon Carter Museum of American Art

Karen J. Hixon
President

Robert M. Bass
Bradford R. Breuer
Michael Conforti
Walker C. Friedman
John P. Hickey Jr.
Mark L. Johnson
J. Luther King Jr.
Carter Johnson Martin
Richard W. Moncrief
Stephen P. Smiley
Benjamin F. Stapleton III
Nenetta Carter Tatum
Alice L. Walton

Andrew J. Walker
Director

For the Amon Carter Museum of American Art

Stefanie Ball Piwetz
Publications Manager

Will Gillham
Director of Publications

Shirley Reece-Hughes
Assistant Curator of Paintings and Sculpture

Steve Watson
Senior Photographer

Board of Commissioners of the Saint Louis Art Museum

Barbara B. Taylor, *President*
John R. Musgrave, *Vice President*
Freida L. Wheaton, *Secretary*
W. Randolph Baker, *Treasurer*
Jeffrey T. Fort
Charles A. Lowenhaupt
Linda M. Martinez
Rex A. Sinquefield
Mark S. Weil
Gary Wolff

For the Saint Louis Art Museum

Brent R. Benjamin
Director

Jason T. Busch
Deputy Director for Curatorial Affairs and Museum Programs

Nancy Heugh
Paper Conservator

Linda Thomas
Former *Assistant Director for Exhibitions and Collections*

Janeen Turk
Assistant Curator of American Art

Frontispiece: *Self-Portrait* (detail), ca. 1877, Fig. 37
Page 4: *Watching the Cargo* (detail), 1849, Pl. 27

Produced by Marquand Books, Inc., Seattle
www.marquand.com

Edited by Will Gillham and Fronia Simpson
Proofread by Stefanie Ball Piwetz and Laura Iwasaki
Designed by Patrick Dooley with layout by Marie Weiler
Typeset in ITC New Baskerville and Belizio by Marie Weiler
Indexed by Elizabeth Chapple
Principal photography by Steve Watson
Image management by iocolor, Seattle
Printed and bound in China by Artron Color Printing Co., Ltd.